INCONVENIENT FICTIONS

INCONVENIENT FICTIONS

Literature and the Limits of Theory

BERNARD HARRISON

YALE UNIVERSITY PRESS ·
NEW HAVEN AND LONDON

For Gabriel Josipovici

Set in Sabon by Excel Typesetters Co., Hong Kong
Printed and bound in Great Britain by The Bath Press, Avon

Library of Congress Cataloging-in-Publication Data

Harrison, Bernard
    Inconvenient Fictions: literature and the limits of theory /
Bernard Harrison.
        p.   cm.
    Includes bibliographical references and index.
    ISBN 0–300–05057–7
            1. Literature—History and criticism—Theory,
etc.   I. Title.
    PN5.H384 1991
    801′.95—dc20   90–25697
                                                        CIP

Contents

Preface

The ideas which this book now brings together have developed piecemeal over the past ten years, by way of a good deal of discussion with many friends and colleagues. In this respect I owe a particular debt of gratitude to my friends Gabriel Josipovici and A. D. Nuttall, both of whom have read and commented on virtually the entire book at one stage or another, and both of whom have shown endless, patient willingness to argue the issues. The book in its present form arose out of a discussion between Nuttall and myself about Derrida, which in turn arose out of my comments on a draft of his *A New Mimesis*. My debt to this and other work of his is particularly apparent in Chapters 1 and 9. Others to whom debts of a like kind are owed include Stephen Medcalf, A. A. H. Inglis, with whom for a number of years I have had the pleasure of teaching a course on philosophy and the novel at the University of Sussex, Jeremy Tambling, with whom all too briefly I helped teach a similar course on the Romantics, Virgil Aldrich, Martin Battestin, Rickie Dammann, Terry Diffey, Bob Firmage, Ben Gibbs, Fred Hagen, Patricia Hanna, J. Paul Hunter, Yukio Kachi, Michael Krausz, George Watson, Laurence Lerner, John Llewellyn, David Novitz, Stephen Prickett, Elinor Shaffer, Henry Staten, A. K. Thorlby, Leona Toker, Martin Warner, Barry Weller and Fay Zwicky. I am particularly obliged to Henry Staten and John Llewellyn, both far better Derrida scholars than I can claim to be, for confirming my halting sense of what is central to Derrida's position; and to P. N. Furbank for calming, out of his far greater knowledge of E. M. Forster, my initial fear that Chapter 3 might just be wildly astray in its estimate of Forster's intentions. None of these people are to be held responsible for such of my errors as, being ineradicable by reason, remain.

I am grateful, too, to the University of Sussex for granting me a term of unpaid leave to work on the book in the autumn of 1987, and to the University of Utah Department of Philosophy for appointing me to visiting posts in 1983–4 and in 1989. The peace and the convivially stimulating atmosphere which marked those visits enabled me to make a solid start on the book during the first visit and to finish it during the second. Elizabeth Hanna made the work go much faster on the second of these occasions by kindly affording me the use of her word-processor.

Thanks and gratitude are also due to the Centre for Literary Studies at the Hebrew University of Jerusalem, for inviting me, in the spring of 1990, to present some of the material which now forms part of the book to some very productively critical audiences, as part of their research project on 'Literature and Moral Philosophy'; and to Catharine Carver for her skilled and immensely helpful editing.

B. H.

Lewes, East Sussex
December 1990

Acknowledgements

The following studies included in this book have previously appeared in journals or anthologies: 'Deconstructing Derrida' in *Comparative Criticism*, ed. E. S. Shaffer, vol. 7 (1985), and 'The Defence of Wit: Sterne, Locke and the Particular' in vol. 10 (1988) of the same journal, published from Cambridge by Cambridge University Press; 'Forster and Moore' in *Philosophy and Literature*, Spring 1988, and 'The Truth about Metaphor' in *Philosophy and Literature* for Spring 1986; 'Muriel Spark and Jane Austen' in *The Modern English Novel*, ed. Gabriel Josipovici (London: Open Books, 1976); 'The Text as Interrogator: Muriel Spark and Job' in *Critical Philosophy*, vol. 4 (1988); 'Parable and Transcendence' in *Ways of Reading the Bible*, ed. Michael Wadsworth (Brighton: Harvester Press, 1981). 'Secrets and Surfaces', written for a conference on the work of Frank Kermode at the University of Warwick, March 1989, is to appear in a forthcoming *festschrift, Addressing Frank Kermode: Essays in Criticism and Interpretation*, ed. Martin Warner (London: Macmillan, 1991). I am grateful to the editors and publishers concerned for granting permission for all this work to reappear in the present volume.

B. H.

What shocks the virtuous philosopher delights the camelion Poet.

Keats, letter to Richard Woodhouse, 27 October 1818

Besides, there is nothing so plain boring as the constant repetition of assertions that are not true, and sometimes not even faintly sensible; if we can reduce this a bit, it will be all to the good.

J. L. Austin, *Sense and Sensibilia*, Lecture I

Introduction

It is a widespread belief among us that serious narrative fiction and its study are essential to the intellectual life of a civilized society. A separate but equally widespread belief has it that the goal of serious intellectual life is the acquisition of knowledge. One would expect a culture committed to such a combination of beliefs to have elaborated some rather ingenious philosophical story about why the study of fictions might, however improbably, be expected to yield knowledge. And so indeed ours has. The trouble at present is not that we lack such a story, but that we are saddled with two seemingly incompatible ones. The thesis of this book is that both of them, in most of their current versions, are badly misconceived.

One such story, of comparatively recent provenance, goes like this. Informative discourse rests upon the twin pillars of reference and truth. Its terms pick out real, actually existing individuals and features and its sentences formulate true statements about them. Narrative fiction neither makes nor can plausibly sustain any such claim to extra-textual reference and truth. Like the poet, in Sidney's phrase, it nothing affirmeth. Its function in our lives cannot thus be to enlarge our knowledge or understanding of the world, and must therefore be something else. The stage is now set for an investigation of what that other function might be. Such investigations take many forms, but their common object is to deconstruct the claim of the text to extra-textual reference in the interests of making it the raw material of one or another style of "theory": structuralist, Derridean, Barthesian, Foucaultian, Marxist, feminist, and so on. The "theorizing" of the text *is*, of course, reckoned to be a procedure which produces knowledge, and the fact that the knowledge in question is *theoretical* in character can only count in favour of the

1

seriousness of the enterprise of producing it, at least within the academy.

The other, older and still powerful view has it that the discourse of narrative fiction *is* extra-textually referential, notwithstanding all that deconstructionists and others allege to the contrary, and hence does convey, at least to the competent or instructed reader, knowledge in the shape of 'insights' about life which exercise, as Leavis put it, 'the kinds of profound concern – having the urgency of personal problems, and felt as moral problems, more than personal – that lie beneath Jane Austen's art, and enable her to assimilate varied influences and heterogeneous material and make great novels out of them.'[1]* (My intention here is by no means to guy Leavis: indeed my hope is that by the end of the book I shall have demonstrated the possibility of plucking just such a position virtually unscathed from between the jaws of deconstruction.) These insights are not, however, necessarily evident to the casual reader. Their recovery from the text, by the provision of a "reading" in the shape of a paraphrase or *explication de texte*, is the business of the professional critic.

In arguing that both these positions, as usually developed, are misconceived, it is not my intention to suggest that either is intellectually negligible. Far from it: what each says is, in certain respects and under the saving *caveat* 'in one way', perfectly correct, and each has produced, as it seems to one who, as a philosopher, has no professional or financial stake whatsoever in defending any of it, a large body of interesting and valuable work. It is just that the two are not nearly as incompatible as they are commonly supposed to be. The central tenets of each are richly susceptible of alternative interpretations, and under certain of these interpretations (the most plausible and / or sustainable ones, as it happens) large parts of each can be made entirely consistent with large parts of the other to yield a composite view more powerful than either and critically fruitful in its own right. My object, in other words, is to bring not a sword but peace, partly out of a rooted conviction that the intellectual gains of controversy for controversy's sake are less than the controversially inclined imagine, and partly because, as the British press teaches us afresh each morning, there are few things more tedious than acrimony sustained more or less solely by intellectual confusion.

It is noticeable, to begin with, that both views, despite their rooted and vehement opposition to one another in certain respects, are in

---

* Superior figures refer to the Notes at p. 279.

certain other respects collusive. Both hold, for instance, that the task of processing imaginative literature into knowledge requires the services of the professional critic. It follows that if there is to be any intellectually and morally serious outcome of the business of producing and consuming narrative fiction, it can come about only through the intervention of the academy. For both views, that is, the possibility of serious interchange between writer and reader proceeding without the intervention of the professional critic or theorist is implicitly discounted. Indeed in the work of some recent critics – J. Hillis Miller offers some striking instances of the tendency – it begins to look as if the text considered as an object worthy of serious attention is more or less the free creation of the critic.

Both views, on a deeper level, share a certain conception of what it is to possess knowledge. There is a distinction, real though perhaps not immediately obvious, to be drawn between knowledge whose acquisition does not require personal change as a condition of coming to possess it, and knowledge which does. The information that the temperature outside is 88°F is a piece of knowledge of the former kind. I do not have to reassess my outlook, character or assumptions about life in order to come to possess it; all I need do is listen to the radio or consult the thermometer outside my window. That done, the information, for whatever it is worth, is available to me as a passive amenity, ready to be deployed in the service of whatever ends and strategies happen at the moment to be mine. Knowledge of why, and in just what way, *as seen from her point of view*, certain habits of mine have caused my wife to suffer since our marriage, offers an example of knowledge of the second kind. It is important to see that such knowledge may be just as *factual*, just as much knowledge of *how things stand in the world*, as knowledge of the temperature outside. Because its content can only be formulated in terms of the structure of an alien point of view, however, I cannot come to possess it without at least admitting the possibility that some truths about how things stand in the world may just not be accessible from the standpoint of a person with my present tastes, habits and assumptions; and may be accessible from the standpoint of a person differently constituted in those respects.[7] The acquisition of such knowledge may not in the event change me fundamentally, since many things may intervene to neutralize its effect, including reinterpretation, self-deception, poverty of desire or simple forgetfulness and failure to focus. But such knowledge, unlike knowledge of some bit of scientific information, has the potentiality to set the established structures of my self in motion towards change: it is, in short, *dangerous* knowledge.

In Western societies, and increasingly since the seventeenth century and the inception of the scientific revolution, the dominant paradigm of knowledge has equated it with knowledge of the first kind; knowledge of impersonal fact; knowledge as amenity. We take it for granted that the function of knowledge in general is not to change us but to enable us to master and change the world. We acquiesce in Hume's vision of knowledge and reason in general as passive servants of our passions and of the Will, considered as a unitary point-source of goals and strategies, which reasons and knows, indeed, but which cannot be changed in its function as Will, as originary giver of value and meaning, by reason or by the acquisition of knowledge.

This Humean vision of knowledge as an amenity, entirely subservient to an unchanging meaning-bestowing Will, is implicit in both our present accounts of the relationship between narrative fiction and the cognitive and sociological structures of knowledge. Both critical theory and interpretative paraphrase subject literary texts to a detached and academic contemplation which is generally very far from threatening the self-image or the fundamental perspectives of those who engage in either. Both theory and interpretation, indeed, serve as the intellectual cement of professional groups within each of which a comfortable unanimity of thought and feeling generally prevails, and dissent and disconfirmation, while remaining real possibilities in certain areas, are for the most part rendered marginal.

My claim in this book is that our dominant paradigm of knowledge is misapplied to the concerns of literature. What literature in general, and narrative fiction in particular deals in is not knowledge as an amenity of the Will, but dangerous knowledge: knowledge the price of whose acquisition is the risk the reader runs of being changed in his or her self by what he or she reads. My suggestion, indeed, is that the peculiar value of literature in a culture such as ours, the thing which really does make it essential to a civilized society, is its power to act as a standing rebuke and irritant to the dominant paradigm of knowledge. To the extent that both our current conceptions of criticism obscure and deflect that power, both are to be resisted.

My suggestion amounts, perhaps, to this: Plato was right about poetry in one way; wrong in another. He was right to regard poetry as intrinsically *anti-theoretical*: intrinsically out to break the hold exercised upon us by theoretical knowledge. He was wrong, however, to imagine that theoretical knowledge is the only kind of knowledge there is. Knowledge for Plato was the product of rational argument and dialectic. A distantly related view constitutes a third area of agreement between the radical and conservative wings of the current critical debate. Both sides tacitly assume that the relation between texts and extra-textual reality, if there is such a thing, must run by way of reference and truth.

The argument here seems simple and conclusive. What a text offers us is meaning. That can only be taken as offering knowledge of the extra-textual if meaning is fixed externally to the text in a way which excludes the generation of meanings purely internal to the text by shifts in the relationships in which the signs which compose the text stand to one another. A further claim of this book is that this seemingly transparent and watertight argument can quite simply be stood on its head. To see how, it is not necessary to invoke arguments which attempt to weaken the force of our ordinary (that is, broadly speaking, Realistic) conceptions of reference and truth; or to accept parallel kinds of relativism which make simple facts about how things stand in the world (say, the fact that it is 88° F outdoors this morning), facts only relative to the language in which they are expressed. All that is needed is to recognize the vacuity of the notion (first questioned by Nietzsche, repeatedly attacked by philosophers of the most diverse intellectual persuasions this century, but still exercising a profound sway over our minds)[3] that there is, or could be, a single standpoint, a single intellectual perspective, from which all that is the case about how things stand in the world might in principle be made simultaneously available to the mind. The opposite view, alien and painful though it still seems to many minds accustomed to envisage Reason as a unified specular faculty giving access to an equally unified Truth, can be illustrated by evident truisms. It is hard for instance to see how, without the invention of the theoretical and conceptual structures of Newtonian mechanics, we could have gained access to the facts about, say, the flight of projectiles, which Newtonian mechanics makes available to us.

To take an earlier example, a necessary condition of my coming to grasp the facts about the nature of the distress my wife feels at the way I carry on is that I come to see matters from her point of view. To grasp another point of view, now, is to see how signs, meaning what they mean, can combine in configurations other than those which I take for granted. The disseminative potency of language, I shall argue, does not result simply in an idle play of signs, but constitutes the agency by which, for the most part, we are enabled to transcend limitations of perspective. That, rather than the kind of transcendence *of textuality* mediated by truth, reference and factuality as those are commonly understood, is the kind of transcendence that can be contrived within a text. To such transcendence it is precisely necessary that signs should *not* stand still, fixed in their possibilities of recombination by considerations external to the text, but that they should remain free to be shaken in their courses, to move against one another.

The main theoretical claim to be defended here is that the possibilities revealed by such movements are more than merely formal or syntactic ones: that their implications sometimes overflow the limits of the text and affect, rightly, our assessments of the range of natural possibility. As the signs which compose the text shift in their relationships to one another, not the world but our perception of the possibilities of the world changes: curtains rise, veils thin; we begin to see, not how it is with the world (we could see *that* anyway and it wearied us) but how, in ways we should not naturally or immediately have envisaged before beginning to read, it *might be*. That is why literature has the dangerous power to move and change us. It is an art of limits: the knowledge it offers is knowledge of limits and of limitations: ours.

But such knowledge of that sort as it offers, it can only actually bestow upon those who are prepared to give up the fiction of the single epistemically guaranteed standpoint from which all that is the case about the world stands ready to be perceived; who are prepared, in short, setting aside what Paul Ricoeur has called the 'hermeneutics of suspicion', to trust and move with the text. One can come to perceive the limits of one's own standpoint only by crossing them. It is because literature possesses this power over frontiers and limits that Plato and the long train of his disciples who wish, invariably ultimately for moral reasons, to show the poets politely to the gate of the City should be resisted. Theoretical knowledge, admirable and useful possession though it is, does not steadfastly or even very often call upon its possessors to question their own limitations as knowers. And without not only the possibility but the regular practice of transcendence of viewpoint morality itself withers.

To mate Derridean dissemination with self-transcendence in this way is clearly in turn to transcend the terms of many of the current disputes between "humanist" and "post-structuralist" critics. It becomes possible to envisage a critical outlook which, while in a broad sense humanistic in character, could quite happily take on board the central insights of deconstruction. The task of defining such a position, along the lines so far sketched, is one that clearly needs to proceed on two levels simultaneously. On the one hand a good deal of theoretical argument is going to be needed to fill out the numerous blank cheques I have just presented. On the other, theoretical discussion alone will not suffice. For one thing, once one jettisons the notion that reference and truth are what connect narrative fiction with reality, the notion that there is *one general kind* of connection between the two goes with them. The kinds of textual mechanism which yield such a connection in the various cases of metaphor (Chapter 10), biblical parable (Chapters 6 and 8), Forsterian irony (Chapter 3) or Sterne's stylistic innovations (Chapter 2) turn out to have as little functionally in common as the tools in Wittgenstein's toolbox at *Investigations* I.11. In short, the ways in which purely intra-textual considerations and mechanisms can serve to put pressure on the perspectives from which we view the world exhibit an irreducible diversity which can only be got at through detailed analysis. For another thing, part of my object in this book is to explore the resources of a certain critical point of view: a point of view from which what is of interest is certainly the *textuality* of the text, but from which textuality appears not as something isolating the text from any power to influence our relationship to the extra-textual, but as something which gives it that power.

Some of the time, therefore, I write as a principled turncoat in the long war between the poets and the philosophers. A good deal of what I have to say in this vein concerns specific interactions between literature and ideas, but on the whole in this book the writers have the best of it in these tussles. I am arguing, in short, for the existence of a genuine power on the part of literature to rebuke and discipline the products of our purely theoretical intelligence. This too, by its nature, is not a case which can be made out on a purely theoretical level: it requires close and detailed attention to actual texts, which must in the process be rescued from their imposed status as sources or illustrations of theoretical knowledge, in order that they may regain their power to shift the familiar relationships of signs and categories which sustain our ordinary conviction that the possibilities inherent in things themselves are coextensive with those inherent in our habitual way of looking at things, and tumble the reader unawares into a new perspective.

The modest role I have assigned to myself in these chapters is closer to that of the Socratic midwife than to those of either the *hermeneus* or the deconstructor. I am not out, that is, to uncover the "true meaning" of the text, but neither am I out to dissolve it into a mere play of disseminating signs. My object is rather to restore the power of its textual mechanisms to contest the presuppositions with which one or another reader might approach it and to produce *bouleversements* of a more than merely formal or textual nature. These demonstrations are simply exemplary, however: they do not, and cannot, short of a closure in which I no more than Derrida believe, exhaust the power of the text to irritate or astound in other ways. They are meant only to get a certain kind of reading going: to suggest what can be got out of a text when we follow Sterne's advice and, instead of attempting either to fix its true meaning or to subject it to some theoretical reduction, allow our imaginations to be led by it.

The book thus contains studies of two kinds, "theoretical" and "critical", at least to the extent that, though both these modes figure to some extent in every chapter, one or the other may over-whelmingly predominate in a given chapter. The main spine of theoretical argument is carried by Chapters 1, 4, 9, 7 and 10. The remaining five, predominantly "critical", chapters are to be read sometimes as amplifying and developing specific passages and aspects of the argument (there is a close connection of this kind between Chapters 9 and 6, for instance), but more often as supplying the supplement of detailed textual analysis which the argument needs if it is to do more than sketch a set of abstract and thus rather imponderable possibilities. Each of the chapters, at the same time, stands on its own feet and can be read as an independent essay. But something is lost in the process: both the theoretical underpinnings of the criticism and the critical implications of the theory become harder to grasp when the book is read in that way than when it is read as what I hope it is: a variegated but coherent whole.

The nature of the book as a series of separate but connected explorations has produced, inevitably, occasional overlappings and repetitions. I considered attempting to remove these, but decided against it: there are not all that many, and the reinsertion of a point into a new context generally brings with it some corresponding gain in clarity or insight.

One thing which has been lost by adopting this structure for the book is any systematic attempt at "placing" the views it defends with respect to other current ones. This is not in itself a very terrible loss. In this respect there are two ways of writing a book of this kind. One can proceed, as I have done here, to elaborate, defend and illustrate an argument with no more than passing or tactical reference to other views. Or one can proceed by way of a survey of 'the literature', passing in review all the stalls recently opened in this corner of the intellectual market-place, and defining one's own wares by comparison and contrast with theirs. There is much to be said for this second way of proceeding; it may be more scholarly, and it certainly leaves one in no doubt where one's author stands; but that did not seem to be the kind of book that wanted to get itself written. On the other hand, something of the sort, preferably brief, needs to be said. There has been quite a lot of excellent recent discussion of the issues I raise here, and many of the things I say will raise echoes of other writers and other views in the reader's mind. Experience has persuaded me that, unless I provide some explicit indication of where I take myself to be in agreement, and where in disagreement, with other views which resonate or clash in some respect or other with mine, there is a danger either that important differences may be missed and hasty assimilations prevail, or that minor disagreements may be misconstrued as root-and-branch opposition. What needs to be said, however, can probably be said most conveniently in an introductory note, where it will interfere least with the progress of the argument in the body of the book.

One of the thoughts which dominate this book is that Locke, and other founders of the seventeenth-century paradigm of knowledge which includes the ideal of a unified science whose basic deliverances would be expressed in an austere, pre-theoretical language of bare empirical description, were mistaken in thinking this ideal attainable. They were wrong to think that everything deserving the name of knowledge is either accessible from a single standpoint or expressible in a single language with a unified and coherent conceptual vocabulary. This thought has become in our time a philosophical commonplace, and one which has been repeatedly used lately as a basis for elaborating what used to be called an apology for poetry but is nowadays more likely to be called an investigation of the nature and functions of literary language. There are (at least) two reasonably well-explored paths which are taken to lead from it towards this goal, neither of which I wish to go down.

The first, represented, for instance, by Nelson Goodman (*Ways of Worldmaking; Languages of Art*),[4] Paul Ricoeur (*Temps et Récit*; 'The Function of Fiction in Shaping Reality')[5] or Peter J. McCormick's recent *Fictions, Philosophies and the Problems of Poetics*,[6] transforms the anti-Lockeian thought that the world may not be cognitively capturable by a single language or a unitary system of concepts into the thought that different languages, with different conceptual schemes, give access to different worlds. One way of envisaging this possibility is to think of the worlds in question as refractions, or versions, of the one, actual World: another, associated with Goodman, leans towards treating the actual world as, at best, some sort of logical construction out of world-versions. Either way it looks as if this approach might succeed in making some sense of the idea of "literary truth": truth of the kind possessed by those Great Truths – 'the best that has been known and thought in the world' –

often supposed to constitute the reward of the serious study of literature. One leading, and deeply Romantic, thought here is that the world we call The Real World is a world that, in some yet to be specified way and to some yet to be specified extent, we make for ourselves; so that our fictions, in so far as they help to compose that world about us, and us in that world, necessarily formulate truths about us and our world.[7]

The other way of extracting an apology for poetry from our current disenchantment with Locke's ideal of a plain language serving an equally plain metaphysic of scientific Realism is the one represented, say, by Richard Rorty and by the nominalist strain in Goodman. For Rorty there is simply no need to defend literature against the charge that, unlike Locke's plain discourse of empirical matter-of-fact, it does not tell the truth, since (i) truth itself, as pragmatists have always claimed, is a notion we could and should dispense with, and (ii) from the point of view of any plausible truth-substitute, literature and science are on all fours with one another. What Derrida has shown us is the truth of Textualism, 'the claim that there are only texts'. Weak textualists according to Rorty are simply people who cannot bear this much reality.

> ... such critics have not grasped that, from a full-fledged pragmatist point of view, there is no interesting difference between tables and texts, between protons and poems. To a pragmatist these are *all* just permanent possibilities for use, and thus for redescription, reinterpretation, manipulation. But the weak textualist thinks, with Dilthey and Gadamer, that there is a great difference between what scientists do and what critics do. . . . The strong textualist simply asks himself the same question about a text which the engineer or physicist asks himself about a puzzling physical object: how shall I describe this in order to get it to do what I want?[8]

Similar implications are supported by the more nominalist, radically relativist developments of Goodman's ideas about Worldmaking, and are common enough in the literature of Critical Theory.

Neither of these enterprises is mine, though mine has points of contact with each of them. So far as I am concerned language does not constitute 'worlds' or 'world-versions', unless that is no more than a high-flown way of saying either that we do not possess, and most likely never will possess, any exhaustive or complete description or explanation of the one, actual world we all inhabit; and that most often, grasping some new feature or aspect of the world goes hand-in-hand with the elaboration of some new way of talking and (what comes in the end to the same thing) thinking about that (*the*) world;

or that verisimilitude and the systematic coherence which sustains it are familiar literary devices. Again, so far as I am concerned, there is no such thing as "literary truth". Literature is just a collection of old and new stories about people who never existed and things that never happened. The place to look for Great Truths is not in a novel but in a physics text.

My claim is that literature addresses not our (rather frantic and obsessive, as it seemed to Keats) desire for Truth, but our need to be (endlessly and repeatedly) delivered from the damaging delusions into which we are betrayed by our persistent urge to persuade ourselves that we have achieved that desire. Pursuing the Lockeian phantom of the language which tells it all just as it is, we cast our own imperfect and partial languages, outlooks, habitual ways of looking at things, in that august but chimerical role, conferring upon them an exhaustiveness and an absolute power to penetrate the mystery of things comically at variance with their actual limitations (virtues, even) of modest and local insight. Literature inhabits the gap between the majestic but to us altogether inaccessible Unity of Absolute Truth and the actual plurality of tongues and visions; each a more or less cunning blend of limited insight and overweening self-aggrandizement. Its mission is not to impart Great Truths but to unhinge and destabilize them. What it has to say is never 'this is how it is', but always, rather, 'might it not be otherwise than an unwise and hasty epistemic confidence leads you to think? Might it not be . . . like *this*?'

It will be evident from this why I concur with Rorty's admirable rephrasing of what I, also, take to be the central insight to be gained from reading Derrida: that there neither is nor could be a point of vision or absolute epistemic grasp ('a view of all possible views') such that one 'who *had* levitated to such a point would have the right to look down on writing, to view it as a second-best (like Plato) or as an abnormal activity to which sin has condemned him (like Rousseau), or as something which a discipline can dispense with on reaching the secure path of a science'.[9]

But, equally evidently, the position I outlined a moment ago commits me to denying the connection which Rorty endeavours to forge between that Derridean insight and 'strong textualism', the thesis that 'there are only texts'.[10] If literary texts possess the power to administer shocks to the systems of categories and assumptions which we inhabit, they must put us in contact with something harder and more authoritative than other texts: with reality, in fact. I thus face an obvious question. If literature offers us nothing in the way of truths, even homely and provisional ones, let alone the finality of vision offered, however delusively, by metaphysics or the more metaphysically triumphalist versions of naturalism and scientism, how can it be said in any way at all to put us in contact with reality?

The answer I defend in Chapter 1 is that language is shot through with reference to reality not only at the level of the relationship between a sentence and the considerations which make it true, but also at the deeper level at which the terms and the conceptual contrasts in which the language we possess allows us to formulate a sententially expressible set of beliefs are constituted. The limits of sense are set by the involvement of words, via the practices in terms of which their meanings and relationships to one another are established, with the common conditions of human existence. There is, as Wittgenstein says, something deeper than truth and falsity, and that deeper something is the possibility, granted by the common reality we inhabit, of *acting* in certain ways.[11]

As not every reader of Wittgenstein has noticed, that way of looking at the relationship between language and reality, although it belongs to Wittgenstein's later work, is faithful to a feature of language which the earlier Wittgenstein of the *Tractatus* emphasized: the fact that, once we know the meanings of words, we can use them to sketch 'pictures' of how things *might* stand in reality as well as pictures of how they *do* stand; such that we do not need to verify the actual existence of such a state of affairs to know that it *is* possible, that things *might* stand in the world like that; the mere fact that the words make sense when arranged in such an order being sufficient to establish *that*. So much, after all, is implicit in Wittgenstein's remark at *Tractatus* 4.027: 'It belongs to the essence of a proposition that it should be able to communicate a *new* sense to us.' The thought which I explore in this book is that the communication of a new sense, though enacted merely through the demonstration of a new way of ordering words so that they compose such a meaning, has (because words are not, *pace* Hobbes, merely counters, but, given the genesis of meaning in action, reflect natural possibility in their possibilities of relationship to one another) the power to disturb our customary sense of what meaning / meanings are possible, and with it our sense of the limits of natural possibility: of how things in the world can stand to one another.

This way of going about things has a number of affinities with the work of Stanley Cavell. Among other things I find congenial in his writing is the conception of the interaction between meaning, practice and people's estimates of the possibilities of life which Cavell formulates in passages like the following one from *The Claim of Reason*:

And we can also say: When you say 'I love my love' the child learns the meaning of the word 'love' and what love is. *That* (*what you do*) will *be* love in the child's world; and if it is mixed with resentment and intimidation, then love is a mixture of resentment and intimidation, and when love is sought *that* will be sought. When you say 'I'll take you tomorrow, I promise', the child begins to learn what temporal durations are, and what *trust* is, and what you do will show what trust is worth. When you say 'Put on your sweater', the child learns what commands are and what *authority* is, and if giving orders is something that creates anxiety for you, then authorities are anxious, authority itself uncertain.[12]

Another conviction which I share with Cavell, and also with Martha Nussbaum, is that the most fruitful stance to adopt towards a work of literature is not necessarily the armed, mistrustful and impersonal stance of a theorist towards the objects of his theoretical enquiry. Cavell and Nussbaum both have the merit of taking seriously the question, What is the *point* of reading novels, or poems, or going to plays?, and of trying seriously to answer it. Both think – and I agree with them – that any serious answer must pay attention to the personal involvement of the reader in what he reads, the playgoer in the spectacle unfolding before him: an involvement which in many ways resembles and overlaps with the kinds of personal involvement which link us to others in real life.

One burden of Cavell's excellent essay on *King Lear*, 'The Avoidance of Love', is that there is a distinction to be drawn between acquiring some piece of information about another and *acknowledging* that other; a distinction further developed in the essay on 'Knowing and Acknowledging' in the same volume. Cavell's reading of the play makes it *inter alia* a play about readiness and failure to accept and acknowledge love; but he also thinks that the effect of the play upon an audience depends not just upon its grasping intellectually the general adequacy of some such 'reading', but on its abandoning the distance created by intellectual analysis sufficiently to be drawn into the 'present' of the characters – so that, after a fashion, the audience acknowledges the characters as real persons whose actions and predicaments can have some emotional bearing upon its own.

In the nature of the situation as a piece of theatre the acknowledgement can never be a complete one, such as might take place between actual persons. But its incompleteness, the nature of which Cavell explores in some detail, is part of its effect. As witness to the events on the stage I remain inviolable and in darkness: about me personally nothing is revealed: 'Who my Gloucester is, and where my Dover is, what my shame attaches to, and what love I have exiled in order to remain in control of my shrinking kingdom – these are still my secrets.'[13] But these aspects of me are engaged and addressed, all the same; and my very impotence to change or intervene in what is going forward upon the stage perhaps brings me nearer to acknowledging them.

> *Macbeth* closes not with promises of further words, but just with promises, a hurried string of them, as if to get out of the range of Macbeth's eyes, there in his head; as if those present know, but do not care now to linger over the knowledge, that there are still witches unaccounted for. It is at such inopportune moments that we are cast into the arena of action again, crossroads again beneath our feet. Because the actors have stopped, we are free to act again; but also compelled to. Our hiddenness, our silence, and our placement are now our choices.[14]

Martha Nussbaum in 'Fictions of the Soul' suggests a related distinction between the calm, unified knowledge of the Platonic philosopher who has risen above the body and its passions, and the anguished self-knowledge born of the emotional upheavals of art and life, using as one of her examples of the latter Marcel's sudden discovery, through the anguish he suffers at the revelation of her interest in Vinteuil's daughter, that he is not, after all, bored with Albertine, but both loves and needs her. Love cannot be observed and anatomized by the philosopher or the scientist, that is; it can only be lived, either in actuality or through the medium of a fiction.

> But there is another possibility [distinct from that of treating love as a possible object of dispassionate theoretical investigation]. Here we would see the knowing of love, for example, as very different from a grasping of some independent fact about the world; as something that is in part constituted by the experience of responding to a loss with need and pain. . . . Love is not a thing in the heart to be observed, the way God can see the blemishes upon Gertrude's soul; it is embodied in, constituted by, experiences of loving which prominently include experiences of suffering. . . .
>
> What we are saying, then, and finding in Proust, is that suffering is not just one route to the same kind of knowing that Plato talks about. It is part and parcel of, constitutive of, completely intrinsic to, a different sort of knowing and self-knowing. A god who lacked our impediments and also lacked our emotional responses could not, in this view, know some parts of our souls. What happens to Marcel when his rationalization is disrupted by the shock of Albertine's departure is not that some set of curtains are drawn back and he sees clearly, with the same scientific sort

of vision, what he had been trying to see in this way before without success. It is that for the scientist's knowing is substituted something quite other, something deeper.[15]

This admirable piece of analysis recalls Cavell's reflections, which I quoted a moment ago, on what is involved in learning *ab initio* the meaning of the word 'love'. My own distinction between 'dangerous knowledge', knowledge which at least in principle threatens the integrity of one's self-image, and knowledge of some piece of information, might at first sight seem reminiscent both of Cavell's distinction between knowing and acknowledging and of Martha Nussbaum's distinction between the dispassionate knowing characteristic of science and the self-knowledge born of suffering and disconfirmation.

There are the resonances I have indicated, and no doubt others, but not identity. The difference which my distinction is meant to capture is not quite the same as those which Nussbaum's and Cavell's distinctions (which, for that matter, are not quite congruent with one another) aim at expressing. The kind of self-knowledge which can be mediated, I want to argue, by our experience of literature has in it, if I am right, more in the way of knowledge of the world, knowledge of the richness of possibility inherent in things themselves, than either Cavell or Nussbaum, at least as I read them, seem to want to claim.

Cavell's 'acknowledgement', after all, is not a cognitive state at all, but something more in the nature of a performative: an admission or concession: 'From my knowing I am late, it does not follow that I acknowledge I'm late – otherwise human relationships would be altogether other than they are'.[16] Similarly, while it is central to Martha Nussbaum's position, as to mine, that the cognitive gains to be derived from literature elude formulation in terms of the intellectual progeny of the Platonic conception of knowledge, it is not clear to me that her conception of what lies outside the scope of such conceptions involves much more than the claim – certainly an entirely sound and reasonable one as far as it goes – that there are some things that we can only come to know about (where 'know about' includes access to knowledge of one's own part in and relationship to the things in question) by living through them. To affirm that much is at best to equip literature with a special subject-matter which can only be explored by its means.

Even granting the existence of such a subject-matter it still remains unexplained how any cognitive gain can result from the exploration of that subject-matter in a fiction. For Proust's treatment of Marcel's anguish to move me, one might argue, I must be familiar enough with moments of anguish of that kind to grant the psychological reality of Proust's description of Marcel's suffering discovery of the actuality of his love for Albertine; and if I am familiar with such moments, then I already possess the kind of self-awareness which Marcel at the outset of this episode lacks. There is nothing in Nussbaum's argument, so far as I can see, to suggest that, or how, the construction of a fiction might in an interesting way compete with, or constitute a critique of, the dominant paradigm of knowledge. Indeed, her strict separation of the cognitive spheres appropriate to 'the philosophical view' and 'the literary view' would seem precisely to rule out any such interaction between them.

What interests me, on the other hand, is the exploration of just that kind of interaction; and along with that the sketching of a rather different, though not necessarily competing, account from those sketched by either Cavell or Nussbaum of the contrast between the cognitive gains accruing from the pursuit of theoretical understanding and those accruing from the pursuit of literature. My argument takes off from the thought, recently popularized by Derrida, but already reworked in so many forms this past century that it has a good claim to be considered the *Grundgedanke* of Modernism, that no language we speak or could invent merely mirrors in its conceptual structure the conceptual articulations of Reality. All language, and all thought, puts a gloss on things, construes rather than transcribes (which is not to deny that some assertions are straightforwardly true and others straightforwardly false; but only to assert that there is always the in-principle possibility of other points of view from which other equally straightforward truths or falsehoods become available which may make the first lot appear not to constitute quite the final word on the matter in hand). There is always a gap, most of the time hardly perceptible, between our construals and what they construe. One of the functions of serious literature, I want to suggest, is to widen this gap, by setting our familiar words sedulously against one another in unheard-of contexts, until it yawns, allowing other, alternative possibilities of construal to jostle into view within it; possibilities previously hidden by our naïve conviction that the way we like to talk about things is exactly the way things are.

Like both Nussbaum and Cavell I want to suggest that the kind of insight great, or considerable, literature offers cannot be distilled into some collection of true propositions about Life. But my reasons are somewhat different from theirs. We cannot formulate what Sterne, say, 'teaches us' in *Tristram Shandy* as a body of generalizations couched in the language we ordinarily speak, I want to say, because the instructive experience to be gained from reading Sterne is that of being led (by the nose, in his case) to an appreciation of some of the points at which the language we ordinarily speak, the scuffed, second-hand and limited range of conceptual options and alternatives it offers, fail seriously to be adequate to the full range of natural possibility. What is instructive about this experience can only be put negatively and in detail, by going over once more each of the points in the book at which words fail one, and why; by explaining the force of Sterne's jokes, which are often pragmatic, in the sense that they depend upon interactions between text and reader.

To do this is merely to stud the text with markers whose purpose is to make it easier for a reader to get the experience I am talking about; it is not to formulate 'the cognitive content of' that experience. Nevertheless, though there is no way in which Sterne can be reduced to a purveyor of "Great Truths", the experience of reading him has, I want to say, cognitive value; mediates a cognitive gain: it reveals to us the limitations of a commonplace language which we might have continued to speak in all innocence of those limitations had we not read him. In this Sterne typifies the methods of literature as an art of limits, disconfirmations and *mises-en-abîme*, and offers an object-lesson in the reasons why since Plato it has been permanently at war with theory, and why its role is endlessly to exceed and transgress the insights and outlooks fostered by theory.

Talk of transgression and *mise-en-abîme* brings me finally, and perhaps appropriately, to the question of the propriety of the use my argument makes of Derrida. Derrideans with whom I have discussed the relevant chapters here, or who have read and commented on them, tend to fall into one or other of two sharply differentiated groups. One group accuses me of having wrenched Derrida out of the context of continental philosophy, and of having, as a result, largely failed to grasp the import of his thought. This group tends also to read me as attempting some kind of radical refutation of Derrida and deconstruction (they tend to take the title of Chapter 4 to describe the enterprise rather than the topic of the essay it heads, for instance); a refutation of a somewhat underhand kind, which compounds its unfairness by choosing to focus exclusively on the Derrida of *La Voix et le phénomène* – a Derrida, as they see it, already twenty years in the past. The second group tends to see nothing inconsistent with Derrida's thought in these pages, and a good deal that is derivative from and in general accord with it. What this group tends to say by way of criticism is that the kind of "humanism" I wish to extract from the founding moves of deconstruction was always, and obviously, implicit in them; and that Derrida's view of language can coexist quite comfortably with the Wittgensteinian-*cum*-Merleau-Pontyan one which I develop in Chapter 1.

My own view of what I am up to is certainly closer to the response of the second group than to that of the first. Far from having in mind some root-and-branch "refutation" of Derrida, I had not supposed myself to be attacking him at all (whether I have misunderstood him is of course another matter). I do, clearly, attack certain very common assessments of what Derrida's achievement amounts to. In particular I dissent from the widespread view that, despite the novelty of its arguments, deconstruction is really just another form of philosophical scepticism; one which tells us that texts, although they seem to have, at least at some levels, meanings upon which different interpreters might agree independently, don't. This seems to me just wrong as a way of summarizing the thrust of Derrida's arguments. Semantic nihilism is not without its attractions for a certain wing of American philosophy: one which includes, say, the Kripke of the sceptical portions of *Wittgenstein on Rules and Private Language* and the Rorty of the essay on Derrida in *Contingency, Irony and Solidarity*. But among literary critics it is more likely to lead to the conclusions recorded by Wendell V. Harris: 'But now, twenty years after *De la grammatologie*, many more or less antithetical directions are being pursued by critical movements that do not much trouble themselves with attempting to refute deconstructive arguments – radical scepticism can after all never be logically overthrown.'[17]

I do, therefore, argue that deconstruction has, or need have, nothing much to do with 'radical scepticism'. In other ways my argument depends crucially on parts, at least, of Derrida's. And in any case, I should not like it to go without record that I very much admire Derrida's work and have derived much pleasure from reading him. I hope I may have read him with profit as well; but that, of course, depends on my capacities as much as on his. What I chiefly find to admire in him is his insistence on the permanent possibilities of renewal and movement implicit in any text or any body of thought once we turn our attention from what it ostensibly affirms to what it suppresses and marginalizes. What I argue in this book is that such liberating and transforming attention to the marginal is not a function merely of a more or less suspicious scrutiny of the literary text, but is one of the central functions of the literary text itself.

Chapter 1
How to Reconcile Humanism and Deconstruction

One can have no idea of the power of language until one has taken stock of that working or constitutive language which emerges when the constituted language, suddenly off centre and out of equilibrium, reorganizes itself to teach the reader – and even the author – what he never knew how to think or say. Language leads us to the things themselves to the precise extent that it *is* signification before *having* a signification.

Maurice Merleau-Ponty, *La Prose du monde*

The whole race is a poet that writes down
The eccentric propositions of its fate.

Wallace Stevens, 'Men made out of Words'

I The Concrete Universal

Literary criticism, as every reader of literary weeklies knows, is and has been for the past two decades the arena of a sometimes bitter dispute between humanist and anti-humanist critics. Humanist critics still believe, to put it crudely, that works of literature have something to tell us about "life" or "reality", and that, to put it still more crudely, they put us in touch, with an immediacy and richness seldom achieved in everyday social intercourse, with the minds of their authors. Anti-humanist critics, most, though not all, adherents of some form of post-structuralism; most, though not all, accepting to some degree the Derridean methodology of deconstruction, believe (still speaking on the level of crude pastiche) that literary texts taken neat – read, that is to say, without benefit of some more or less reductive exercise of literary "theory" – put us in no cognitive relationship to anything outside themselves, their authors included.

19

In this book I argue that we are not faced, as most parties to the debate suppose, with a straight choice between the two positions thus crudely delineated. My argument converges on its conclusion from two opposite starting-points, one in humanism, the other in the theory of deconstruction. Proceeding in the first direction, I argue that critical humanism is not, contrary to present appearances, inseparable from the philosophical positions – logocentrism and the 'metaphysics of presence' – which deconstructionists rightly reject. Once extricated from these embarrassing philosophical commitments, a refurbished and rehabilitated critical humanism, significantly different from the old both in its outlook and in the kinds of critical enterprise it promotes, can be installed within the purlieus of deconstruction. Proceeding in the opposite direction, I argue that the philosophical position underlying the practice of deconstruction can be construed in two ways, only one of which is internally coherent. The incoherent version, while it is indeed hostile to any conceivable form of critical humanism, is disabled by its incoherence from making good the threat it poses. The coherent version, while it remains an effective bar to certain familiar forms of critical humanism, bears within itself theoretical potentialities which make it entirely possible for it to develop into a humanism in its own right.

Debate in this area, no doubt because it straddles philosophy and literary theory and tackles difficult and ambiguous issues in each, is bedevilled by the ease with which each side, often with a great show of pinning the other side down to the strict meanings of whatever form of words it appears to be nailing its flag to, can distort the intentions of its opponents to the extent of making them look fools and their claims transparently absurd. The first requirement of serious discussion here as elsewhere is, evidently, to exclude mere point-scoring of this description. In practice this can only be done by taking the slogans on which most debate hinges (for instance, the claim that literary language is 'referential', or Derrida's claim that 'Il n'y a pas d'hors-texte' – does this really mean, as Richard Rorty once appeared, and maybe still is, happy to accept, that only texts exist, or what, exactly?), teasing out the various theoretical positions – not always the same ones – which they may on one occasion or another be intended to articulate, and trying to see what can actually be said for and against each such position. Only thus, it seems to me, can we hope to get the issues sorted out. It may not always be possible to discover by this method what an individual theorist's position, finally, *is* (what he or she is *really saying*), simply because all we have to go on is the theorist's writtten words (in itself a Derridean point) and these words may just *be* capable of being taken in several ways. But what we can hope to achieve by these means is a clear view of what positions the theorist has available to him, and which of them can be sustained with any force or plausibility. This, then, is the method I shall pursue in this chapter as well as in Chapter 4.

I propose to take as the leitmotiv of the discussion in the present chapter a brief remark of A. D. Nuttall's, taken from his defence of mimeticism and critical humanism, *A New Mimesis*; a remark which seems to me ambiguous in ways sufficiently complex, and so central to the entire current debate in this area, both to invite and to repay extended discussion. The passage concerns Shakespeare's treatment of the exchange between Lear and Cordelia in *King Lear*, Act I, sc. i. Nuttall's Observation goes as follows:

> The audience is moved, not by triumphant fulfilment of, or brilliant divagation from a dramatic norm, but by what could be summed up, barbarously enough, as the parent-child-ness of it all. If parent-child-ness were not found in the world the scene would be empty. If the representation were less accurate it would be less moving. It pierces by its truth.[1]

Some people will be shocked to discover that I find this remark simply correct (*in a certain sense*, of course: later I shall say what that sense is), and will put aside the book at this point. Never mind. To begin with I want to examine an interpretation of its meaning on which I don't think it can come out as correct. This way of taking it fastens upon the phrase 'the parent-child-ness of it all', taking that as indicating *the logical type of the object or entity* which occupies, to put it clearly if clumsily, the world end of the representing relation which, Nuttall seems to be claiming, holds between Shakespeare's text and the world. The phrase 'the parent-child-ness of it all', if it picks out anything at all, can only, it seems, pick out the kind of entity which philosophers have traditionally called a universal. This immediately sites Nuttall's remark, needlessly and misleadingly as I shall argue, in a long tradition of Platonizing Romantic criticism going back immediately to Coleridge (ultimately, of course, its roots are far deeper). It will help in showing why Nuttall's horse will not run under these Platonic colours if we move the discussion at this point to a celebrated theoretical text of the New Criticism, W. K. Wimsatt's essay 'The Concrete Universal'.[2]

The object of Wimsatt's essay is to harmonize, at least upon the plane of theory, two discordant strains in Romantic criticism; the Coleridgean emphasis on the forging of unity and wholeness in the text, versus the preference for the concrete, the particular and the unresolved represented by, say, Blake's 'To generalise is to be an

Idiot' or Keats's praise (foreshadowing the Pythian tones of deconstructionism echoing from the dark cleft, or *abîme*, of unstoppably disseminating semantic plurality) for the capacity, in a poet, to be 'in uncertainties, mysteries, doubts, without any irritable reaching after fact and certainty' (letter to G. and T. Keats, 21 December 1817). The necessary enterprise, as Wimsatt sees it, is to unite the particularizing with the universalizing strain, while at the same time correcting the deficiencies of both, by explaining (a) how the power of literary language to frame "universals" differs from the ordinary generalizing power which language possesses *per se*, and (b) why the exercise of this special sort of generalizing power should depend essentially upon the representation of particulars. The explanation is that whereas the use of an ordinary general name like 'dog' or 'chisel' presupposes that one's hearers already grasp some corresponding concept or "universal", a work of literature "shows" or displays the structure of some concept or concepts not already verbally marked in our language, by the way in which it systematically connects the particular observations which constitute the material of the poem or the narrative (I fear that the *Aufhebung* which it is my intention to contrive will have the effect of restoring, not only Leavis's reflections on the moral seriousness of reading as an activity, but also this bit of Wimsattian doctrine[3] – though I don't think it can be sustained quite in the form Wimsatt gives to it – to vigorous if curiously transfigured life by the end of the book: see, for instance, my Chapter 5). Here is how Wimsatt puts it:

> The poetic character of details consists not in what they say directly and explicitly (as if roses and moonlight were poetic) but in what by their arrangement they *show* implicitly. . . .
>
> A literary work of art is a complex of detail (an artefact, if we may be allowed that metaphor for what is only a verbal object), a composition so complicated of human values that its interpretation is dictated by the understanding of it, and so complicated as to seem in the highest degree individual – a concrete universal.[4]

This masterly synthesis of the two, one would have thought fairly hopelessly discordant, wings of Romantic critical theory packs into a remarkably small space virtually all the main theoretical claims of New Criticism. They deserve to be unpacked. There is for a start the analogy between the meaning of a general noun, in the sense of the concept (universal, intension) which it picks out, and the 'meaning' revealed by the internal structure or organization of a poem or narrative. This analogy can be deployed on various levels of textual analysis. It is often put to work in a prima-facie relatively plausible way, for instance, in the common claim (defended, for example, by Owen Barfield in *Poetic Diction* and attacked by Donald Davidson in 'What Metaphors Mean') that the function of a metaphor is to forge a new meaning distinct from the pre-existing literal meanings of the terms involved in the metaphor. This issue is explored in Chapter 10, and need not detain us here. At the level on which Wimsatt deploys it, however, that of the text taken as a whole, the analogy is clearly under considerable strain from the outset.

A 'universal' in the strict sense is the meaning of a common noun. It is commonplace to distinguish 'meaning' in this sense from the propositional content of a sentence: the sense in which 'the meaning of' the German sentence 'Schnee ist weiss' is rendered by the English sentence 'Snow is white'. The 'concrete universal' which, according to Wimsatt, a literary work as a whole makes manifest cannot, presumably, be a *meaning* in either of these senses. We need a third sense of 'meaning', in which meaning is a function neither of the propositional content of sentences nor of the privileges of sentential occurrence of individual words, but a function of unspecified but *a fortiori* supra-sentential forms of organization peculiar to works of literature. Nevertheless Wimsatt is sure that such 'meanings' are univocally accessible to any reader willing to go to the trouble of reading with sufficient care to understand what he or she reads, since the complexity of a 'literary work of art' – a book worth reading in the first place, that is – is such that a plurality of readings is excluded by the simple fact that 'its interpretation is dictated by the understanding of it'. The coherence of a text and its meaning are, in other words, just as Coleridge taught us, functions of one another.

It is generally possible to state the meaning of a sentence by giving some sort of paraphrase, if only an approximate one buttressed by supplementary explanations. Is this going to be the case for the 'meanings' carried by a work of literature? There is a dilemma to be faced here. If we say that the meanings in question can be carried only by the words of the text arranged in the order in which they are in fact arranged we are saying, in effect, that such meanings are otherwise ineffable: that we can say, for instance, nothing true about the meaning of *Lear* save that it is the meaning the sentences of *Lear* carry, over and above their propositional content, in virtue of their being arranged in the order in which they are arranged in the text of *Lear*; a claim which, for all its admirable and punctilious restraint, fails to move the discussion forward. If, on the other hand, we say that it *is* possible to convey the meaning of the text in a paraphrase, we risk incurring the consequence that, the meaning of a work having once been extracted in this way, readers will thenceforward not unreasonably prefer the paraphrase to the work, since the power of each to enlighten will be *ex hypothesi* identical and the former will most probably be shorter and clearer. Wimsatt treads delicately between these unappetizing alternatives towards the end of his essay.

> The function of the objective critic is by approximate descriptions of poems, or multiple restatements of their meaning, to aid other readers to come to an intuitive and full realization of poems themselves and hence to know good poems and distinguish them from bad ones. ... The situation is something like this: in each poem there is something (an individual intuition – or a concept) which can never be expressed in other terms. It is like the square root of 2 or like pi, which cannot be expressed by rational numbers, but only as their *limit*. Criticism of poetry is like 1.414 ... or 3.1416 ..., not all it would be, yet all that can be had and very useful.[5]

Once again we see how closely, for Wimsatt, the notion of *the meaning of the poem* is bound up with the notion of the poem as a systematically articulated structure, which can be read with understanding in only one way. The notion of the meaning of a text as the *limit* of interpretation implicitly presupposes the notion of a convergence of all admissible (unforced, textually defensible) interpretations upon that limit. Wimsatt's characterization of such criticism as 'objective' clearly also depends upon the claim that the structure of the text as a whole will function to exclude a non-converging plurality of readings. The notion of objectivity at stake here, that is to say, is a version of the familiar notion of scientific objectivity which demands convergence of theories relative to observation and of different observers' reports relative to the same phenomenon.

The task of the 'objective critic' in providing a relatively adequate explanatory paraphrase of a given work is, then, to join with other critics in adumbrating by convergence the meaning of that work. This way of envisaging the critic's task adds a new complication to the notion of *the meaning of a text* by introducing a further distinction, this time between the meaning ascribed to the work by a given paraphrase and what one might call the *absolute meaning* of the work: the meaning upon which all such paraphrases, if textually defensible, ideally converge. This raises the question of how much reality, and of what kind, we are to ascribe to the absolute meaning of the text. The issue here is whether we are to take the fact that interpretations converge, if they do, as a basic, unexplained and inexplicable fact of life. By making *that* move we should be placing ourselves in a position to treat the concept of the absolute meaning of the text as a *mere* limit concept, corresponding to no reality external to the process of interpretation. Wimsatt is not, I think, to be read in this way, for two reasons. The first is that, as the last passage quoted above makes clear, no critical paraphrase is to be regarded as more than a stepping-stone to a *further*, and this time ultimate and definitive experience of meaning which can be obtained only from the text. The second lies in the status of the text as an *artefact*: that is, as something constructed by somebody precisely to do the job of embodying the ultimate, otherwise ineffable meaning which the reader guided by sound critical paraphrases apprehends in it. The text so read, that is, can be taken as embodying a meaning which is not just the impersonal meaning of some string of words, but *somebody's meaning*, the meaning of a person; namely, the author.

New Criticism's relationship to the author is not to be confused with the French tradition of *l'homme et son oeuvre*, as represented, for instance, by Proust's *bête noire*, the 'method' of Sainte-Beuve. New Criticism does not, that is, believe in the possibility of illuminating the text through extra-textual access to the opinions, life and character of its author; on the contrary, it treats knowledge of the author's intentions as something to be sought primarily through interpretative paraphrase of his text. This looks all right at first sight. It is, after all, natural and commonplace enough for one speaker to offer to explain, and to succeed in explaining, the import of another speaker's words, especially if the words in question happen to be groping or inarticulate. But there is a certain oddity, to say the least, in taking the service one speaker may offer to another in circumstances like that as the model on which to understand the service offered to the author by the literary critic. As Philip Thody puts it,

> The technique of *explication de texte* is traditionally based on the idea that a text has one central meaning which it is the duty of the critic or commentator to bring out with absolute clarity into the full light of day. It consequently sets out from the rather curious presupposition that writers have something to say but that they somehow never quite manage to say it. It assumes – admittedly without saying so in so many words – that the critic's relationship to the creative writer resembles that of the members of the *Conseil d'Etat* to any *député* sufficiently ill-advised to bring forward a private member's bill for approval by the *Assemblée Nationale*. This body not only checks such projects to ensure that they do not contradict existing law. It also modifies the texts submitted to it 'pour les rendre plus conformés tant au droit pré-existant, qu'à la volonté réelle mais mal exprimée de leurs auteurs' ['to bring them into line with pre-existing law and with the real but imperfectly expressed intentions of their authors'].[6]

Wimsatt, as his position stands, is not vulnerable to this objection. Evading it has a price, however. What gets Wimsatt past Thody's objection is, of course, his claim that what the 'objective critic' is after is not meaning in the sense in which the individual sentences of the text have meaning, but *the meaning of the text as a whole*. The relation of critic to writer is therefore not that of the *Conseil d'Etat* to the unfortunate *député*, for the critic is not attempting to make the *sentences* in which the author has chosen to express himself more conformable to their author's intentions. The *sentences* of the text are, as Wittgenstein would say, perfectly in order as they stand. What the critic is out to illuminate is, for that matter, something which cannot be expressed as the *propositional content of a sentence* at all, but only *shown* by the structure of the text as a whole.

Wimsatt's distinction between what a text says and what it shows is not Wittgensteinian, but is squarely within a long and influential tradition which Genette traces to Plato's distinction in Book III of the *Republic* between pure narrative (*haple diegesis*), in which the poet speaks in his own person, and imitation (*mimesis*), in which the poet 'delivers a speech as if he were someone else'. 'We know', says Genette,

> how this contrast – somewhat neutralized by Aristotle (who makes pure narrative and direct representation two varieties of mimesis), and (for that very reason?) neglected by the classical tradition (which in any case paid little attention to the problems of narrative discourse) – abruptly surged forth again in novel theory in the United States and England at the end of the nineteenth century and the beginning of the twentieth, with Henry James and his disciples, in the barely transposed terms of *showing* vs. *telling*, which speedily became the Omazd and the Ahriman of novelistic aesthetics in the Anglo-American normative vulgate.[7]

This distinction, though no doubt effective against the Thodyesque objection we have just considered, cannot be deployed in that role, now, without serious damage to the coherence of a position such as Wimsatt's. If the 'meaning' of a text is not something that the author *tells* us, in the sense in which Hardy tells us that Jude Fawley was born at Marygreen – if it is not the kind of thing that could figure as the content of a well-articulated sentence or the putative content of an ill-articulated one – then in what sense, exactly, can we think of it as a *meaning* or – even stretching the term a bit – a *universal* at all? And if the absolute meaning of a text cannot sensibly be described as a *meaning* (a rather canonical deconstruction of Wimsatt is clearly beginning to take shape at this point), then what is to be made of the claim that a good critical paraphrase captures that meaning, even approximately? Wimsatt's attempt to explicate the nature of the relationship which supposedly links paraphrase to absolute meaning in terms of the relation between a mathematical constant such as pi and the series of numbers which successively approximates to its value is not, in fact, of any help to him here. Such a relation holds between objects – numbers – of the same type. What is at issue here is precisely the question whether the absolute meaning of the text supposedly captured by a paraphrase is a *meaning*: that is, is the kind of thing that can (even roughly and approximately) be captured by a paraphrase.

Wimsatt still has, it seems to me, one shot left in his locker. He can argue, bringing into focus a thesis which is never very far from the surface of the argument in the last page or two of his essay, that the experience of what I have been calling the absolute meaning of a work of literature *goes beyond language*. Experiencing the unity and coherence of a work of literature, that is, is unlike experiencing the unity and coherence of a sentence, in that it is not just a matter of seeing that the words fit together syntactically and make sense. It is a matter of being led to perceive, *through* the connections made by the words of the text with one another, something which is not merely a mode of connection of words but something more like a Platonic Idea: a form or structure directly present to the mind in a mode of apprehension which, while it may be mediated by language, is not in its essence linguistic.

This move, of course, gets Wimsatt clear in one leap both of Thody-style objections and of my own niggles. There is nothing absurd in the suggestion that readers may need help to read a text aright, if reading a text is not merely a matter of grasping the propositional content of a string of sentences in a language both writer and reader understand perfectly well, but a matter of taking those sentences merely as a sort of ladder by which to ascend to a standpoint from which the reader can survey the essentially extra-linguistic structures of meaning which were present to the author's intention, and which he embodied in the work in the only way possible to him, given the essentially extra-linguistic character of the meanings in question.

At the same time, such a move commits us to finding intelligible the notion of an essentially extra-linguistic meaning. The idea that there is something deeply confused and incoherent about such a notion is, now, by no means one that can be dismissed as a freak of French-inspired critical theory. In fact, as analytic philosophers have recently begun to notice, rather an impressive body of opinion can be mustered, on both sides of the Channel and the Atlantic, and on a variety of grounds, in favour of just that conclusion. The names to be cited include those of Quine, Davidson and Wittgenstein as well as Derrida.[8] We can rest content for present purposes with Derrida's reasons. They are, roughly speaking, that access to such a meaning, envisaged as given to what Husserlians call the 'pure Present of consciousness', would have, if it were possible, to proceed entirely independently of language, and cannot. We cannot say what we apprehend in such a way unless we speak of it, and once we do so we infect the pure and unitary apprehension putatively given to consciousness with a linguistic 'supplement' which is not only fundamentally alien in character, but destructive of the unity, the finality and the timelessness of what we are allegedly trying to express.

For meaning arises in language through relationships of contrast between signs: its essence is *différance*, Derrida's portmanteau word which captures both the relationships of difference which generate meaning within language and the indefinite deferral of *closure* – of any *final* determination of meaning, and thus by implication any possibility of working back to an *originary* meaning; any meaning, that is, which might be identified with the meaning putatively present to the consciousness of the speaker – which the involvement of meaning in such relationships entails. For the purposes of our discussion of the Concrete Universal, Derrida's argument can be given the form of a dilemma: either the Concrete Universal is ineffable or something can be said about it. If the former it can be no more to us than the Kantian Thing-in-itself; if the latter the distinction between the absolute meaning of the text and the approximative or provisional meanings caught by critical paraphrase collapses. Wimsatt, on pain of committing criticism to silence, must choose the second horn of the dilemma. But that leaves him with nothing upon which differing critical paraphrases can be regarded as converging. The differences between differing paraphrases thus become, in accordance with Derrida's doctrine of *différance*, just differences.

But now Wimsatt's way of articulating the notion of an *objective* criticism collapses in turn. The 'objectivity' of criticism, remember, was to be conceived by analogy with scientific objectivity: that is to say, in terms of the ultimate convergence of differing accounts of a text. On this notion of objectivity depends in turn, of course, Wimsatt's whole notion of the extra-textual reference of the text. The idea is that literary texts refer beyond themselves to the members of a special class of entities: Concrete Universals (the class of entities to which Nuttall's 'the parent-child-ness of it all' appeared to belong). If no such entity is available for reference (or to put it more accurately, if reference is fatal to the putative integrity of any such entity) then, it appears, both Wimsatt's account of the objectivity of criticism and his account of the extra-textual reference of the text are vacuous. The object of critical enquiry, it seems, is nothing outside the text, but rather something purely internal to the text: namely the endless vistas of new meaning thrown up by the relationship of its signs to one another; a relationship which shifts and disseminates continually without ever either returning to an origin or ending in closure.

II   Logocentrism and Formalism: Just how hermetic is the text?

One effect of Derrida's arguments has been greatly to strengthen, in the minds of many critics, the case for formalism. 'Formalism', as Peter Steiner argues in his excellent book on Russian Formalism and Prague Structuralism,[9] is itself an ambiguous and contested term which, when one examines the writings of actual 'formalists', turns out to designate a loose aggregate of views related as much by contrast as by the common conformity to some party line which such pat labels are apt to suggest. It thus behoves anyone introducing the term to say what, precisely, he has it in mind to pick out by means of it. What I have in mind is the thesis that the meanings carried by the significant elements of texts derive wholly from relationships linking those elements to other significant elements of (the same or different) texts, and not at all from relationships linking significant elements of texts to anything which is not an element of a text. For the purposes of this definition the term 'element of a text' is meant to be as wide in scope as is necessary for it to be to cover everything from the minutiae of rhyme scheme, alliteration or pun to the generalities of trope, *topos*, plot, genre, or the structural regularities which Lévi-Strauss and his followers discern in myths and stories of widely different origin. As I have already suggested, following Steiner, it is quite unclear whether all those labelled 'Russian Formalists' were 'formalists' in this sense. Take, for example, Shklovskii's well-known notion of de-familiarization (*ostranenie*). De-familiarization as prac-tised in a work of literature is a matter of thwarting or overturning the expectations of the reader. If formalism as I have just defined it were correct, then de-familiarization as a literary technique could operate only upon *formal*, or literary, expectations. It could overturn our expectations about things like the conventions of the novel genre, as Sterne does, or about the *topos* of the *miles gloriosus*, as Cervantes does; but it could not overturn our expectations about *the world*, or about *real life* (where 'real' means, among other things, 'extra-formal'. Shklovskii, in his 1914 manifesto *The Resurrection of the Word*, accepts no such limitation, however.[10] The object of *ostranenie* for him – related claims will be defended here, though in a somewhat different way – is to counteract the deadening weight of habit and commonplace ways of thinking, in order to give us back a living experience '*of the world*' (my italics); to 'resurrect things and kill pessimism'.

> By now the old art has already died, but the new has not yet been born. Things have died too: we have lost the sensation of the world. We are like a violinist who has stopped feeling his bow and strings. We have ceased to be artists in our quotidian life; we do not like our houses and clothes and easily part with a life that we do not perceive. Only the creation of new forms of art can bring back to man his experience of the world, resurrect things and kill pessimism.[11]

The formalism abroad at the moment, however, is not, on the whole, animated by Shklovskii's desire to 'resurrect things'. On the contrary, it conforms fairly closely to the definition given above. A good instance of it, which slightly antedates the influence of Derrida, can be found in Frank Kermode's essay 'Literary Fiction and Reality'.[12] Kermode, like many others, sees modernism in literature as consisting largely in a new consciousness of the gap between reality and the formal devices of poetry or the novel. Musil, for Kermode a paradigm instance of modernism, was 'prepared to spend most of his life struggling with the problems created by the divergence of comfortable story and the non-narrative contingencies of modern reality'. But even before modernism, 'the history of the novel is the history of forms rejected or modified, by parody, manifesto, neglect, as absurd. Nowhere else, perhaps, are we so conscious of the dissidence between inherited form and our own reality.' Sartre, in *La Nausée*, raises the fundamental question, which echoes, but in a more telling and philosophically sophisticated form, the seventeenth-century puritan charge of mendacity: 'How can novels, by telling lies, convert existence into being?'[13] Story-telling, in other words, is the mendacious attempt to conceal the irreducible but painful contingency of real life under the satisfying but specious appearance of rational coherence created by the purely formal structures and devices of textuality. The consoling but delusive experiences of order and pattern which we derive from reading fiction never actually reach out to interact with "life", and perhaps transform it, because they cannot, deriving as they do solely from the hermetic self-referentiality of the formal structures of the text. Paul de Man, writing subsequently to the Derridean earthquake, puts the same point neatly, as follows:

> Literature is fiction not because it somehow refuses to acknowledge 'reality', but because it is not a priori certain that language functions according to principles which are those, or which are *like* those, of the phenomenal world. It is therefore not a priori certain that literature is a reliable source of information about anything but its own language.[14]

Let us return now to Nuttall's Observation, which ran, remember,

> The audience is moved, not by triumphant fulfilment of, or brilliant divagation from a dramatic norm, but by what could be summed up, barbarously enough, as the parent-child-ness of it all. If parent-child-ness were not found in the world the scene would be empty. If the representation were less accurate it would be less moving. It pierces by its truth.

Let us disregard the final clause of the first sentence, with its apparent invocation of the Concrete Universal, and turn our attention instead to the first sixteen words of the sentence, up to the third comma. This part of the sentence can be read, consistently with very much else in *A New Mimesis*, not as expressing a commitment to the metaphysics of New Criticism, but as expressing a denial of the truth of formalism, defined as I have just defined it.* The Formalist position is, in effect, that the pleasure we get from a text is either that of experiencing the flawless working out of a structure of purely formal literary devices (that willing self-immersion in the pleasing delusion that life is as rationally ordered as fictions make it, which for the Kermode of 'Literary Fiction and Reality' is the whole point of reading fiction, to the extent that conscience and common sense will allow us to do that); or else the pleasure of *ostranenie* stripped of the Shklovskiian ambition to resurrect the world and operating upon purely formal or literary expectations. Nuttall's point is that the pleasure we take in the exchange between Cordelia and Lear is of neither of these types. We are moved not because we relate what is going on on the stage to other plays, to dramatic conventions or to literary *topoi*, but because we relate it to the world; to what we know from our extra-literary experience about the relationship between parents and children.

---

* From this point on I shall capitalize the term, in order to tie it for present purposes to that definition.

'So what,' some will say. 'Surely, any such claim must fall to deconstructive arguments of exactly the same type as those which, a page or two ago, proved fatal to the logocentric metaphysics of the Concrete Universal.' Unfortunately this is just not, logically speaking, necessarily so. The denial of logocentrism does not *in itself* entail Formalism. Conversely, the denial of Formalism does not *in itself* entail logocentrism. As is evident from their content, logocentrism and anti-Formalism are not only distinct but logically unrelated doctrines. What the logocentrist holds is that meanings are not intrinsically linguistic entities; that *logos*, in the shape, for instance, of 'ideas', mental states, intentional acts or concrete universals, is prior to language; that the function of language is merely to provide, for purposes of communication, a conventional representation of *logos*; that the life of language consists not in the continuous dissemination of new meaning through changes in the relationships of signs, but rather in the status of the sign as the direct expression of thought, so that speech is in this sense more 'alive', more informed by *logos* than writing; that there is, or could be, a 'privileged' language which finally and correctly represents the world as a structure of possible meanings (the 'fully analysed languages' of Wittgenstein's *Tractatus* and Russell's *Lectures on Logical Atomism*, or Leibniz's *lingua characteristica universalis*, offer instances of logocentric projects of this kind); that the final, or original, or absolute meaning of a literary text is to be sought in an extra-linguistic *logos* (the author's intentions, the Concrete Universal to which the reader will be led by apprehending the text as a uniquely unified structure, etc.) which informs it; and so on. The anti-Formalist, on the other hand, is committed to none of this. All he maintains is that descriptions, whether in the diegetic or the mimetic mode, can be compared with experience, and that such comparisons enter into our response to a work of literature. The extreme weakness of this claim, which, while it certainly amounts to more than a trivial truism in the context in which Nuttall presents it, begins to approximate to one when one generalizes it as I have just done, throws into relief the extraordinary strength, and thus the inherent implausibility, of the Formalist's claim that response to a work of literature *cannot* consist in anything except pleasure in the consistent working out of a literary *topos* or pleasure in the brilliant undermining of such a *topos*.

Why, if anti-Formalism and logocentrism are simply distinct and logically discrete positions, having logically speaking no bearing on one another, should so many extremely intelligent people be so persuaded that the Derridean collapse of the case for logocentrism automatically establishes the truth of Formalism? As often happens in such cases people have perhaps fallen into error by paying closer attention to the concrete historical development of the debate than to the abstract logical relationships of the issues under discussion. The debate has been perceived as a debate between on the one hand a loose confederation of forces (New Critics, Practical Critics, disciples of Dr Leavis, *et al.*), all to some extent and broadly speaking committed to the kind of Romantic and logocentric metaphysic of meaning of which Wimsatt's chapter on the Concrete Universal conveniently provides such a pure instance; and on the other hand an equally diverse collection of voices (structuralists, post-structuralists, Marxists, feminists, etc.) all of whom need, or think they need, commitment to something like Formalism as I have defined it, at some point in the development of their respective positions. We thus seem to be faced with a contest between two rather clearly marked and apparently exclusive alternatives on the level of personal allegiance and the internal politics of the academic 'subject' called English Literature; and it is only natural in such circumstances that a blow to one of these should appear to be necessarily a blow in favour of the other.

That, however, is not all there is to it. The thesis of Formalism is that the objects of literary-critical study are purely intra-textual; that there is no opening from text to world; that the text is an hermetic system of meanings produced wholly internally to it. The thesis of anti-logocentrism is that the dissemination of meanings within the text is not under the control of anything in the nature of an extra-textual *meaning*. This point can be expressed, as Derrida expresses it, as the slogan 'Il n'y a pas d'hors-texte' ('The text has no exterior'; 'There is nothing outside the text'); and this appears to give the Formalist exactly the kind of textual hermeticism he needs. A strict logical entailment between anti-logocentrism and Formalism is thus often taken to be established. But, as a moment's thought reveals, such an entailment could only be shown to exist if it could be shown that the logocentric picture of the deployment of signs within a text as under the control of extra-textual *meanings* offers *the only conceivable way* of envisaging any sort of relationship between a text and an *hors-texte*.

What makes it easy not to perceive that the argument which gets us from anti-logocentrism to Formalism needs this extra premise if it is to work is, of course, the sociological fact that the most influential recent versions of anti-Formalism in Anglo-American literary theory have, as it happens, tended to involve logocentrism in one form or another. But this fact is in itself powerless to establish the entailment the Formalist needs if he is to extract his favoured conclusion from the collapse of logocentrism alone. For that a further step is required at the logical level; and once we face that difficulty it is not at all easy to see how the required step can be justified. For the anti-Formalist (in the present shape of Nuttall read according to our second interpretation) seems to dispose of a quite simple and watertight counter-argument to any such claim. The argument goes as follows. A fictional text is related to an *hors-texte* just in case there is some possibility of comparing the descriptions given in the text in any way with any aspect of extra-textual experience, and such comparisons enter in any way into the reading of literary fiction. Such a relationship relates the signs of the text not to extra-textual *meanings* but merely to natural features of the world. It follows that if there are any relationships of that type between literary texts and the extra-textual, then it is false that the relationship between signs and extra-textual *meanings* envisaged by the logocentrist offers the only possible way of conceiving the relationship between a literary text and an *hors-texte*. And commonplace reflection on the reading of literary texts (such as, for instance, Act I, sc. i of *Lear*) is sufficient to establish that such relationships occur.

We have made a start towards reconciling critical humanism and deconstruction. The humanist can grant the deconstructionist his victory over logocentrism without necessarily endangering the possibility of rebuilding his own position, if he is prepared to take his stand upon a non-logocentric version of anti-Formalism. How such a humanist position is to be developed remains so far unclear – the blank spaces marked by phrases like 'some possibility', or 'in any way' in the exceedingly skeletal statement of non-logocentric anti-Formalism credited in the preceding paragraph to the humanist redivivus still have to be filled in in a way which will not lead us back inadvertently into logocentrism. But we have at least gained a bridgehead from which that campaign can be mounted.

Or have we? Two suspicions remain. One is that the assertion of any relationship, of any type whatsoever, between a text and an *hors-texte* must involve an assertion of *closure* – of the final determination of textual meaning which Derrida's arguments against logocentrism demonstrate to be impossible. The second is that any such assertion must simply have failed to reckon with the full force of the claim, common to Derrida, Saussure, Merleau-Ponty and Wittgenstein, that meaning is determined by relationships between signs, not by a relationship between signs taken singly and bits or aspects of the world. We shall have to examine these two suspicions, in the two immediately following sections, before we can be quite sure of our ground.

III Closure and iterability

The denial of *closure* is normally taken to rest on the denial of
logocentrism. Wimsatt's convergent paraphrases, for example,
would tend to close the question of the meaning of the text to the
extent that it became apparent what vision of the meaning of a text
as a whole they were converging upon. Other forms of logocentrism
envisage the closure of that question by appeal to authorial intention,
to 'essences' in the Husserlian or the Kripke-cum-Putnam sense of
'essence', to Platonic Ideas, and no doubt in many other ways. Anti-
logocentrism denies that the question of what a text means can be
settled by appeal to *meanings* considered as entities constituted
externally to the signs of the text. It denies this because it denies that
reality presents us (as Wittgenstein, for instance, believed at the time
of the *Tractatus Logico-Philosophicus*) with a ready-made array of
possible meanings (in the case of the *Tractatus*, possible propositional contents), and that textual signs acquire meaning by mirroring
or representing, through their relationships to one another, that
natural order of real conceptual possibilities. Far from propositional
signs acquiring meaning through a correspondence between their
relationships to one another and the externally-given structure of
some realm of extra-textual meanings, the anti-logocentrist contends, meaning is fabricated, originated, within language, *by* the
relationships in which we place signs with respect to one another
relative to some specific context.

It is not my concern here to defend the anti-logocentrist's contention. Rather, my concern is with what are, or what are thought to be,
its implications. Some writers on deconstruction conclude from it,
rashly in my opinion, that textual meaning is *radically indeterminate*:
that there can be no uncontroversial assertion about the meaning of
any significant element of a text. It can quite simply be shown,
however, not merely that the radical indeterminacy of textual meaning fails to follow from the denial of the possibility of closure, but
that the logical conjunction of the two is incoherent. Consider the
following four ways of construing the meaning of 'A knows what T
means', where T is any body of text:

(i)   A has present to his consciousness in a manner not essentially
        mediated by language some object of consciousness or other
        which just is *the meaning of T*.

(ii)   A is in possession of some totalizing verbal formula, say a
        dictionary definition or a paraphrase or a philosophical anal-
        ysis in the style of early Russell, which precisely captures the
        meaning of T.

(iii)   A knows, without necessarily being able to express his knowledge verbally, what interpretations of T, or any semantically or syntactically significant elements of T, are possible interpretations, and which are not possible interpretations. He knows because his judgements in this respect display a very high degree of agreement with the independent judgements of other competent speakers.

(iv)   A is able to specify descriptively what guides his judgements concerning the possibility of interpreting T or its elements in such a way as to make clear to some considerable extent the nature and grounds of those judgements to other speakers of the language in which T is written.

(i)–(ii), it will be readily apparent, are incompatible with the anti-logocentrist's denial of the possibility of closure; (iii)–(iv), equally evidently, are not. The bare assertion that it may in a given case be uncontentious that signs standing in certain relationships to one another in a given context will bear certain interpretations but not others, is simply neutral with respect to the issue of whether the *ground* of the possibility of ascribing to those signs, so related and in that specific context, just those possibilities of interpretation is to be sought internally or externally to language. Nor does acceptance of the determinacy of textual meaning in sense (iii)–(iv) commit one to the thesis that Reality presents us, in advance of the constitution of language, with an eternal and unchanging array of possibilities of meaning which a language can only passively mirror in the possibilities of significant articulation of its signs. Somebody who holds that textual meaning is determinate in senses (iii)–(iv) can perfectly consistently also hold that there is no theoretical limit to the range of meanings that can be constituted by relating the signs of a text to one another in different ways relative to different contexts. What he asserts in asserting the determinacy of textual meaning is simply that *these* signs, standing in *these* relationships to one another in *this* context, can bear *these* possible interpretations but not *those*.

Not only is the assertion of the determinacy of textual meaning in this limited sense consistent with anti-logocentrism, the assertion of at least that degree of determinacy of textual meaning is essential to the deconstructive enterprise, in the sense that, without it, it would not be possible to give a coherent specification of that enterprise. On the level of theory it is, as I argue in Chapter 4, essential to Derrida's argument against logocentrism that a text be readable, or as Derrida puts it *iterable* – iterable in repeated readings, in the absence or after the death of its author. A text can only be *iterated* in this way, as a structure of possibilities of meaning independent of reference to its author's intentions or conscious states, if the words on the page, at least to some limited extent, restrict their own possibilities of interpretation. For if they do not – if the signs themselves allow absolutely *anything* to count as an interpretation – then what we are confronted with is either not a text at all, but, say, a piece of mock-calligraphy in a non-existent script, or else a text in some private cipher or shorthand for the rules of interpretation of which we might have no option *but* to consult the author.

On the level of deconstructive practice the case is even clearer. Take for instance a moderately celebrated instance of deconstructive analysis: Paul de Man's suggestion that by taking the last line of Yeats's 'Among School Children', 'How can we know the dancer from the dance?', not as a rhetorical question but as a literal questioning of the possibility of adequately separating two actually distinct things, and restructuring the poem accordingly, 'two entirely coherent but entirely incompatible readings can be made to hinge on one line whose grammatical structure is devoid of ambiguity but whose rhetorical mode turns the mood as well as the mode of the entire poem upside-down.'[15] How could this entire enterprise get off the ground if it were not uncontentious not merely that the two possibilities of taking the rhetorical mode of a question upon which de Man's entire analysis hinges are available ones, but that the multifarious possibilities of reading which make each of the two resulting readings 'entirely coherent' are also uncontentiously available? Deconstruction is not, in short, to be equated with the thesis that texts can mean anything you like, but with the thesis that texts can always turn out to mean more than you might prefer them to mean, which as we shall see is a very different matter.

Non-logocentric anti-Formalism thus emerges unscathed from the criticism that the contraband of closure may be concealed in its baggage. All that the non-logocentric anti-Formalist contends is that, in assessing the possibilities of interpretation of signs standing in specific relationships to one another in a specific context, reference to familiar features of everyday experience, such as the relationship between parents and children, is not necessarily excluded. But the Formalist still has one shot left in his locker. He can object that such a stand is inconsistent, not with the deconstructive position on closure, perhaps, but with the deconstructive position on *différance*. What the non-logocentric anti-Formalist, on this account, has failed in his blindness to perceive is the force of Saussure's arguments (not to mention, as I noted earlier, those of a number of other equally formidable names) for the conclusion that meaning is a function of relationships between signs and other signs, not between signs taken singly and bits or aspects of the world. To this argument, therefore, we must now turn.

IV Two ways of taking Saussure

The principle of Saussure's upon which the Formalist bases his case is perhaps his most fundamental; namely, the principle of *l'arbitraire du signe* (the arbitrariness of the sign). Saussure considers this a principle '[que] domine toute la linguistique de la langue; ses conséquences sont innombrables' ('which dominates the whole of the linguistics of *langue*: its consequences are innumerable').[16] On the simplest level the principle states merely that there is no natural, non-arbitrary relationship between a concept (Saussure's *signifié*) and the 'acoustic image' (Saussure's *signifiant*) which represents it. There is more to the principle than this, however. According to Saussure the concept (*signifié*) attached to a given acoustic image cannot be identified independently of it: concept and acoustic image are not fully independent entities, but simply aspects of a single complex entity: the linguistic sign. Moreover the identity of the *signifié* associated with a given sign is a function of relationships between that sign and other signs in the language. Meaning cannot be studied word by word, in the fashion dear to eighteenth-century theorists of language, as a function of some presumed relationship between a word and something extra-linguistic: a distinct "thought", or "idea", or "object". On the contrary, it is a function (Saussure's thought is here reminiscent of Duhem or Quine) of the entire system constituted by all the signs which make up a language together with the relationships between them. 'Les autres institutions humaines . . . sont toutes fondées, à des degrés divers, sur les rapports naturels des choses' ('Other human institutions . . . are all founded, in differing degrees, on the natural relationships in which things stand to one another').[17] Language is the exception. It is a pure construct in the sense, firstly, that the relationship between a sign and its meaning is not a natural relationship but one brought into being by language, and secondly that meanings themselves are not natural, extra-linguistic entities, but are themselves constituted by relationships between signs.

The consequence of this is that the relationship between concept and acoustic image is in a certain sense *groundless*. It is not, that is, guaranteed and held firm by any set of stable natural relationships obtaining extra-linguistically. Hence the relationship between concept and acoustic image is inherently and radically unstable. 'Une langue est radicalement impuissante à se défendre contre les facteurs qui déplacent d'instant en instant le rapport du signifié et du signifiant. C'est une des conséquences de l'arbitraire du signe' ('A language is radically powerless to defend itself against the factors which, from moment to moment, displace the relationship between signifier and signified. This is one of the consequences of the arbitrariness of the sign').[18]

If this last remark of Saussure's sounds somewhat reminiscent of Derrida, well, so it should. Derrida's notion of *différance* is more or less directly derived from *l'arbitraire du signe*, a principle which, as Derrida points out, unites the notions of arbitrariness and differentiating contrast between signs. 'Arbitrariness can occur only because the system of signs is constituted by the differences between terms and not by their fullness.'[19] In the same essay, Derrida cites the following passage from the *Cours*:

> Si la partie conceptuelle de la valeur est constituée uniquement par des rapports et des différences avec les autres termes de la langue, on peut en dire autant de sa partie matérielle. . . . Tout ce qui précède revient à dire que *dans la langue il n'y a que des différences*. Bien plus: une différence suppose en générale des termes positifs entre lesquels elle s'établit; mais dans la langue il n'y a que des différences *sans termes positifs*. Qu'on prenne le signifié ou le signifiant, la langue ne comporte ni des idées ni des sons qui préexisterait au système linguistique, mais seulement des différences conceptuelles et des différences phoniques issues de ce système. Ce qu'il y a d'idée ou de matière phonique dans un signe importe moins que ce qu'il y a autour de lui dans les autres signes.*[20]

Derrida comments as follows:

The first consequence to be drawn from this is that the signified concept is never present in itself, in an adequate presence that would refer only to itself. Every concept is necessarily and essentially inscribed in a chain or system, within which it refers to another and to other concepts, by the systematic play of differences. Such a play, then – différance – is no longer simply a concept, but the possibility of conceptuality, of the conceptual system and process in general.[21]

---

*   ('If the conceptual part of the value of a sign is constituted solely by the connections and differences obtaining between it and the other terms of the language, the same may be said of the material part. . . . The whole of the foregoing amounts to this: *in language there are only differences*. More important still: a difference normally presupposes positive terms between which the difference in question subsists, but in a language there are only differences *without positive terms*. Whether one takes the signified or the signifier, language presents us with no idea or sound whose existence precedes that of the linguistic system, but solely with conceptual and phonic differences issuing from the system. What a sign contains in the way of idea or phonic material matters less than what surrounds it in the other signs of the language.')

Saussure's conception of language as a system of differences without positive terms gives us, in other words, the Saussurian principle of *l'arbitraire du signe*, which carries with it the idea that the relation between signifier and signified, being unsecured by any natural, extra-linguistic relationship, is radically unstable and inherently liable to displacement, and this in turn gives us Derrida's denial that meaning is ever given to the mind in full phenomenological presence, and his consequent notion of the processes of *différance* – difference-cum-deferral of meaning – which allow meaning to disseminate endlessly along chains of mutually referring and displacing signs.

What holds together this entire collection of arguments is, of course, Saussure's contention that in language there are no positive terms but only differences. This idea has become widely accepted in phonology, but it is not initially easy to see how it could work as a theory of meaning. The difficulty here is this: it seems as if language can only have any bearing on the extra-linguistic world if its signs, or at any rate some of them, refer to extra-linguistic objects whose existence and nature are independent of the operations of language. To put it another way, a language whose referring expressions picked out only entities constituted by relationships of difference between the signs of the language would not seem to be capable of referring to anything outside the language. And in claiming that language allows us to refer to no conceptual content which exists prior to the constitution of the linguistic system, and that its conceptual repertory consists solely of 'différences conceptuelles...issues de ce système', Saussure does appear to be embracing just such an implausibly hermetic conception of language.

Saussure, however, is by no means as simple-minded as this perfectly sensible but premature Positivist objection would make him. In Ch. 4 §2 of the *Cours*, entitled 'La valeur linguistique considérée dans son aspect conceptuel' ('Linguistic value considered in its conceptual aspect'), he recognizes the 'paradox' that, '...d'un côté, le concept nous apparaît comme la contre-partie de l'image auditive dans l'intérieur du signe, et, de l'autre, ce signe lui-même, c'est-à-dire le rapport qui relie ses deux éléments, est aussi, et tout autant la contre-partie des autres signes de la langue' ('...on the one hand, the concept appears to us in the interior of the sign as the counterpart of the auditory image, while, on the other hand, the sign itself, that is to say the relationship which connects its two elements, is also, and to just as great an extent, the counterpart of the other signs of the language').[22]

The problem here is that Saussure has already (*Cours*, p. 99) defined the sign as the union of a concept and an acoustic image.

How can the 'value' (one meaning of *valeur* in French is the meaning of a word) of a sign, considered as something dependent on relationships between signs, combine with (*se confondre avec*) the concept which is the counterpart, within each sign, of the linguistic image? Saussure's answer rests on a parallel between the determination of linguistic value and the determination of economic value (which is the other main meaning of *valeur*). The value of a coin, for instance, is established in one of two ways: either by exchange against dissimilar things (goods, other currencies, e.g.) or by comparison with similar things (other amounts in the same currency). In a parallel way the semantic value of a word is established in two ways: either by 'exchange' against 'something different', such-and-such a concept, or else by comparison with something 'of the same nature', another word.

The first process, Saussure contends, is not alone sufficient to establish the meaning of a term: 'Sa valeur n'est donc pas fixée tant qu'on se borne à constater qu'il peut être "échangé" contre tel ou tel concept, c'est-à-dire qu'il a telle ou telle signification; il faut encore le comparer avec les valeurs similaires, avec les autres mots qui lui sont opposables. Son contenu n'est vraiment déterminé que par le concours de ce qui existe en dehors de lui.' ('Its [i.e., a word's] meaning remains unfixed in so far as one limits oneself to noting that it can be "exchanged" against this or that concept, that is to say, that it has this or that signification: one must also compare it with values which are comparable, with the other words which are opposed to it. Its meaning is only fully determined as a function of what exists outside it.')[23]

As examples of the latter process, Saussure offers the following:

le français *mouton* peut avoir le même signification que l'anglais *sheep*, mais non la même valeur, et cela pour plusieurs raisons, en particulier parce qu'en parlant d'une pièce de viande apprêtée et servie sur la table, l'Anglais dit *mutton* et non *sheep*. La différence de valeur entre *sheep* et mouton tient à ce que le premier a à côté de lui un second terme, ce qui n'est pas le cas pour le mot français.

Dans l'intérieur d'une même langue, tous les mots qui expriment des idées voisines se limitent réciproquement: des synonymes comme *redouter, craindre, avoir peur* n'ont de valeur propre que par leur opposition; si *redouter* n'existait pas, tout sa contenu irait à ses concurrents. Inversement, il y a des termes qui s'enrichissent par contact avec d'autres; par exemple, l'élément nouveau introduit dans *décrépit* ('un vieillard *décrépit*' ...) resulte de la coexistence de *décrépi* ('un mur *décrépi*'). . . .

... Si les mots étaient chargés de représenter des concepts donnés d'avance, ils auraient chacun, d'une langue à l'autre, des correspondents exacts pour le sens; or il n'en est pas ainsi. Le français dit indifféremment *louer* (une maison) pour 'prendre à bail' et 'donner à bail', là où l'allemand emploie deux termes, *mieten* et *vermieten*; il n'y a donc pas correspondence exact des valeurs. Les verbes *schätzen* et *urteilen* présentent un ensemble de significations qui correspond en gros à celles des mots français *estimer* et *juger*; cependant sur plusieurs points cette correspondence est en défaut.*[24]

Are we, now, to interpret Saussure, on the basis of these examples and clarifications, as advancing the claim which the positivist, rightly to my mind, finds absurd: that none of the signs of the language refer to entities external to 'the linguistic system'; that language is referentially hermetic? Call this the Strong Interpretation of Saussure. Texts can indeed be extracted from Saussure's discussion and brandished as evidence for the Strong Interpretation. But they, and much else, can equally well be brandished as evidence for what I shall call the Weak Interpretation. In its weak form Saussure's thesis on the concepts to which a language gives access states merely that the conceptual content of a statement in a given language cannot be identified without reference, not merely to linguistic conventions, but to linguistic conventions and resulting conceptual relationships specific to that language. The Weak Interpretation in no way commits Saussure to the Formalism implicit in de Man's remark that 'it is not a priori certain that literature is a reliable source of information

---

*   ('French *mouton* may have the same signification as English *sheep*, but not the same value, and for several reasons; in particular because in speaking of a piece of meat prepared and brought to the table the Englishman says *mutton* and not *sheep*. The difference in value between *sheep* and *mouton* is a matter of the first having flanking it a second term, which is not the case with the French word.

'In the interior of a single language, all the words expressing neighbouring words limit one another reciprocally: the synonyms in a list such as *craindre, redouter, avoir peur*, possess specific value only through their opposition to one another; if *redouter* did not exist, all of its content would go to its concurrents. Inversely, there are terms which enrich themselves by contact with others; for example the new element introduced in *decrepit* (a *decrepit* old man . . .) results from the simultaneous existence of *décrépi* ["divested of plaster". Tr.] ("a wall divested of plaster").

'. . . If words were charged with the task of representing concepts given in advance, each of them would have, from one language to another, exact correspondents in point of sense; but such is not the case. The Frenchman says indifferently *louer (une maison)* to mean indifferently "to take on lease" or "to lease out", whereas German employs two words *mieten* and *vermieten*; there is thus no exact correspondence of values. The verbs *schätzen* and *urteilen* present an array of significations which correspond in broad outline to those of the French words *estimer* and *juger*; however on several points the correspondence is defective.')

about anything but its own language'. Under it, Saussure is not committed to the absurd claim that the language in which we talk about sheep is not a reliable source of information about the animals which the term 'sheep' picks out, but only about some abstract intra-linguistic entity which also happens to go by that name, and is indeed, given the referentially hermetic character of language, the only thing going by that name which we are actually in a position to refer to and make informative statements about. He is committed only to the modest, and prima-facie entirely sensible claim that we cannot be certain of the scope of the array of feature-clusters (which is what I propose to call the distinct recurrent clumps of features presented to experience by, say, sheep and roast joints of mutton) ranged over by the English word *sheep* unless we take account of the fact that in English the word for *mouton* is flanked by (*a à coté de lui*) another term, *mutton*, which divides with it the array of feature-clusters over which French *mouton* ranges. Generalizing this, the weak interpretation commits Saussure to the thesis that *the extra-linguistic reference of terms in a given language is in part under the control of sign/sign relationships specific to that language.*

The unrepentant logocentrist, who wishes to defend logocentrism by presenting it as the only alternative to what he considers, rightly no doubt, the manifest absurdities of Formalism, will at this point protest that Saussure must be committed to the Strong Interpreta-tion, and thus to Formalism, because Saussure's work is habitually read (by Derrida, for instance) as favourable to anti-logocentrism, and anti-logocentrism can only be served by the radical, paradoxical Saussure who emerges from the Strong Interpretation.[25] I have already argued that anti-logocentrism can perfectly happily cohabit with anti-Formalism; now I propose to argue that any interpretation of Saussure, Weak or Strong, yields anti-logocentrism as a con-sequence. Logocentrism requires the thesis, as I shall say, that the relationships which determine meaning be *strongly external to language*, that they are relationships holding, in fact, not between signs but between things. Formalism, on the other hand, requires the thesis that the relationships which determine meaning be *strongly internal to language*, that they be relationships which can be stated without mentioning anything external to what Saussure calls 'the linguistic system'. The Strong Interpretation credits Saussure with a version of this thesis. The Weak Interpretation credits him merely with the thesis that the relationships which determine meaning are *weakly internal to language*. They are relationships linking sign to sign in differential structures all right, but the relationships in question run by way of, can only be stated by mentioning, things external to the linguistic system; things such as, for instance, sheep and joints of meat.

Logocentrism, now, cannot coexist with any account which makes the relationships determining meaning *in any way* internal to language, whether the internality in question is of the strong or the weak variety. Any degree of internality, even the weak kind, is sufficient to free the relationship between *signifiant* and *signifié* from the absolute subservience required by logocentrism to the task of passively mirroring an altogether extra-linguistic structure of meanings, leaving it, as Saussure puts it, 'radically powerless' to resist displacement. It is important, and will become crucial to the argument I am developing here, to see that Saussure's claim that such displacements are *arbitrary* (a consequence of *l'arbitraire du signe*) in no way commits him to the claim that they are *gratuitous*, in the sense of lacking any explanation connecting them to human purposes or differences of practice and outlook, or in general to the concrete material circumstances of human life (such an interpretation is, indeed, just another way of bending Saussure to the requirements of Formalism). Even an *arbitraire* which is not in that sense gratuitous, however, is sufficient to unleash the movement of Derridean *différance*, ending with that movement both the possibility of a uniquely privileged language whose conceptual articulations mirror the conceptual articulations of Reality itself, and the correlative possibility of closure.

The nature of the reply which the non-logocentric anti-Formalist should make to the Formalist's suggestion that he should pay more attention to Saussure's demonstration that meaning is a function of relationships between signs will now be clear. The non-logocentric anti-formalist should retort that that meaning is indeed a function of relationships between the signs of a linguistic system, but that the sign / sign relationships in question can plausibly be construed only as weakly internal to language. On the one hand, construing them in that way gives the anti-logocentrist all he needs; while on the other, construing them as strongly internal to language neither offers a plausible interpretation of Saussure, nor credits him with a seriously defensible position.

v   Referential and constitutive language

The arguments of the last three sections have left the critical humanist still obstinately clinging by the skin of his teeth to a reduced but still substantial version of his fundamental claim: that Formalism is false; that a relationship of some sort, as yet unspecified, subsists between literature and the Real World, and that therefore there may yet be something to be salvaged from the idea that reading fiction offers readers, even without benefit of reductive criticism, something that might be termed a cognitive gain. It might seem at first sight that what my argument allows the humanist to retain of his intellectual patrimony is, even so, little more than a pittance. I shall now argue that this appearance is a misleading one; that from the bridgehead thus gained the humanist is free to move out in several interesting directions. The question now is merely which one he should take.

Let us return once more to Nuttall's Observation:

> The audience is moved, not by triumphant fulfilment of, or brilliant divagation from a dramatic norm, but by what could be summed up, barbarously enough, as the parent-child-ness of it all. If parent-child-ness were not found in the world the scene would be empty. If the representation were less accurate it would be less moving. It pierces by its truth.

It seems to me that if there is such a thing as a just critical judgement, this is one. But what are we to make of the last three sentences? There is certainly a pre-theoretical way of taking them which raises few problems. We cotton on to the tensions between Lear and Cordelia. We recognize at once what is going on between them from our own familiar experience of the moral and psychological conflicts which have arisen between us and our own parents, or our own children, just as one might quickly enough cotton on to the nature of the conflicts being expressed in a quarrel one happened to stumble upon in the street. And cottoning on in that way is essential to being moved in the way that we are moved by the scene. Our interest in what is going forward on the stage is not merely the interest we feel in the working out or the transforming of a formal pattern. Certainly this seems true and unproblematic enough, and yet it is important that it should be pointed out, since it is part of what the Formalist denies.

Problems begin to arise, though, over the word 'representation'; for this commits the anti-Formalist to a specific account of the mode of aesthetic functioning of his postulated text /world relationships, and beyond that to an account of the general function of literature in our lives. One way of construing the thought here would be this: the content of a work of literature is constrained by what is the case, just as a zoological description of, say, sheep is constrained by what is the case. And the criterion of adequacy of the description is the same in each case: truth. Accurate scientific description informs us by its truth; accurate literary representation moves us, 'pierces us', by its truth. The first worry that occurs to one, perhaps, is to wonder what the predicate 'moves us' is doing here at all. As Hume taught us, opening his grey, fatal Druid's bag of arguments to our loss, truths inform us; they cannot, of themselves, move us. How, then, can literary, representational 'truth' move us to the point of being 'piercing'? We need, it seems, to find some way of advancing literary representation a little further, at least, from straight forensic or scientific description.

Nuttall's strategy at this point is to invoke the ground of Aristotle's distinction between history and poetry at *Poetics* 1451a: while history tells us 'what Alcibiades did', poetry tells us 'the kind of thing that would happen'. The applicability of this to Lear and Cordelia on the pre-theoretical level canvassed above is evident enough. But does it do much to resolve the growing knot of problems about literary truth and representation? If we say that what moves us is a *true* representation of 'the kind of thing that would happen' we still have not answered Hume's demand to know how any kind of *truth* can move us. And then, *what kind* of thing, exactly, are we representing in representing 'the kind of thing that would happen'? To sharpen the question, is 'kind of thing' supposed to pick out a type, a universal of some sort, or an absolutely particular event, action or relationship?

This would no doubt be merely a metaphysical quibble if it did not project us into the historically important and perhaps not yet exhausted critical issue, which fuels Wimsatt's reflections on the Concrete Universal, of whether we are to read Shakespeare, say, in an Augustan or a Romantic frame of mind. If the former, we shall hold with Imlac that the business of the poet is not to number the streaks of the tulip or describe the different shades in the verdure of the forest, but rather to examine not the individual but the species; to remark general properties and large appearances. If the latter, we shall agree with Blake that general knowledges are the knowledges of Idiots, and take Hamlet, Lear and Cordelia to be admirable precisely as representations of unique individuals. Nuttall's preference for a general description, 'parent-child-ness', to identify *what* is truthfully represented in Act I, sc. i suggests a move in the direction of Imlac. But this, as we noted in §1, is a move in the direction of logocentrism. The view which Johnson is putting into Imlac's mouth seems to be one which finds a late expression in Wittgenstein's *Tractatus* and (for the most part) in Husserl's phenomenology: that Reality offers to our inspection a system of timeless possibilities of Being. Imlac's poet, for instance, much like a Husserlian phenomenologist preparing to discard the natural attitude in the interests of phenomenological reduction, must 'disregard present laws and opinions and rise to *general* and *transcendental truths* which *will always be the same*'

(*Rasselas*, ch. 10). On such a view meaning, so far as it partakes of truth, is firmly yoked to Being: there can be no dissemination of signs within the text into a new meaning having any bearing upon Reality.

Logocentrism is perhaps avoidable (surprisingly enough, considering the widely shared idea that Romanticism *per se* presents the ripest of targets for deconstruction) if one goes with the strand in Romanticism which links Blake, Keats and Nietzsche. It is perhaps plausible that literary texts both constantly disseminate new meaning and that in some sense what they explore is real possibility if what they explore are not general possibilities of Being but absolutely determinate and contingent possibilities of particular existence. But then, what would be the *point* of such representation, its function in our lives? (Rebecca West: 'A copy of the universe is not what is required of art; one of the damned thing is ample.') And why, coming back one more time and finally to Hume's dispiriting but perfectly reasonable question, what could explain our finding such a representation *moving*?

I have briefly canvassed a range of familiar problems about the notions of truth and representation in literature which have, of course, been exhaustively canvassed many times before. My suggestion is that we should simply take the message: the problems in question are in principle insoluble. The notions of reference and truth have no coherent application to literature. This, of course, is music to the ears of the Formalist anti-logocentrist; less so to his humanist opponent. Without access to the notions of reference and truth, how can he retain any grip at all on the idea that literary fictions stand in any *cognitively* significant relationship to reality; that the un-"theorized" reading of narrative fiction, for instance, has any cognitive gains whatsoever to offer readers?

As Wittgenstein taught us to see happens often in philosophy, our sense of what theoretical options are open to us, or between what theoretical options we must choose, is being constrained here, not by how things stand in the world, but by a persuasive *picture*, to which we perhaps do not even realize that we subscribe, of how things stand in the world. In this case the picture is a picture of the workings of language as we imagine them to be. The picture presents things in the following way. The sentences of a language are able to refer to, and to convey true assertions about, reality, because the basic signs of the language are conventionally correlated with elements of Reality. (It does not matter for the purposes of the picture whether the basic signs are supposed to be words or sentences, or whether the 'elements of Reality' in question are envisaged metaphysically, in the style of Russell's 'logical atoms' or the Objects of the *Tractatus*, or naturalistically, in the style, say, of Quine's 'stimulus meanings' or Putnam's rigidly designated samples of natural kinds.) The conventional correlations in question are the *sole* source of *cognitive meaning* in the language, where under the term 'cognitive meaning' we intend to include all those kinds of meaning which have any bearing upon the reference of terms and the truth or falsity of sentences. Strictly speaking, the words of a language can be combined into sentences with other ends in view than the articulation of cognitive meaning; but all such uses of language are controlled purely by linguistic convention, not by fidelity to the task of representing how things stand in the world: they represent a free field for the operation of conventions internal to language in its relation to our social and ideological concerns, rather than our descriptive or scientific ones. This picture of how language works is of great antiquity. Most recently it has been characteristic of Logical Positivism (think, for instance, of the Positivist's claim that the sentences of ethics or theology have no cognitive meaning but only a social function, in expressing and controlling emotion or structuring some cognitively entirely gratuitous religious outlook), and it exercises a determining influence still upon the thought of such neo-Positivist writers as Quine or Davidson (think of Quine's doctrine that there is no objective 'fact of the matter' about the way in which the terms in a language divide their reference,[26] or Davidson's denial of cognitive meaning to metaphors [see below, Chapter 10]).

The Formalist interpretation of Derrida and Saussure essentially endeavours to assimilate them to this Positivist paradigm. It takes the claim that meaning arises out of differential relationships between signs to entail that meaning so established cannot in principle relate signs to the real world, that *différance* defines a free field for the intervention of precisely those forces of arbitrary self-expression, social convention and social control which, according to the Positivist picture, hold power everywhere in language except in those small but sophisticated provinces, of science, mathematics and logic, which remain under the control either of 'cognitive meaning' or of the kinds of regimentation characteristic of formal systems. Marxists, feminists, Freudians, Foucaultians, also like to talk (not always, perhaps, but very often) as if, wherever it is not simply controlled by the demands of factual description, the movement of signs in the text must be controlled by essentially non-cognitive forces arising from conflict within society or the individual. Such visions of literature as intrinsically and necessarily under the control of ideology, or the Freudian mechanisms of the unconscious, or the kind of relationships between power and knowledge which interest Foucaultians and some feminists, share in fact – however much they would resist the suggestion that they have anything in common with Logical Positivism – much common ground with the Positivist picture of how language works.

As I argued in §4, however, this Positivist interpretation of Saussure (and by extension of Derrida) stands him on his head. Saussure's point is not that the relationships between signs in a language, as those affect 'the linguistic value of signs considered in their conceptual aspect', work to make language referentially hermetic, to separate it from referential contact with the extra-linguistic, but precisely the reverse: that the referential relationships which make possible informative discourse in a language are invariably mediated in part through relationships between the signs of the language. Indeed, if Saussure's view were not this one, but the version of the Positivist picture of language credited to him by the Formalists, then Saussure's position would not even be an anti-logocentric one; since the Positivist picture of language is one of the oldest and most canonical versions of logocentrism, holding as it does that meaning in a language, so far as that is not merely the outcome of a shuffling of signs against signs in response to entirely non-cognitive demands, results from the establishment of merely associative links between language and the extra-linguistic.

In §4 I argued that the relations between sign and sign which the mechanisms of *différance* displace cannot be, as the Positivist picture requires, relationships strongly internal to language. Saussure's examples leave us no option but to construe them as relationships only weakly internal to language. They are, that is, relationships saturated with implicit reference to the extra-linguistic. Thus, when they shift against one another, what changes is necessarily not merely the relationships of signs to one another but the relationships of the implicit extra-linguistic references carried by the signs. Language working upon itself in this way, shifting and reordering the relationships between its own signs in a manner which necessarily also shifts and reorders the relationships of the extra-linguistic, as that is implicitly adumbrated in the ordering of signs relative to one another, is functioning as what Merleau-Ponty, in *La Prose du monde*, calls *constitutive language*. Constitutive language conforms exactly to the terms of Merleau-Ponty's ambiguous remark, which might serve as an epigraph for the whole of the post-structuralist movement: 'In a sense language never has anything to do with anything but itself.'[27] Constitutive language is language occupied solely with itself. It is not, that is, language functioning to *inform*. It refers to nothing actual, it makes no statements: reference and truth in the ordinary senses of those terms are not its business.

Its existence, however, suffices to disprove the assumption implicit in the Positivist picture that it is only via the route provided by truth and reference in the ordinary senses of the terms that language can relate us to reality, can offer us what are recognizably cognitive gains. For constitutive language is only *in a sense* occupied solely with itself. What constitutive language does for us is to make *the workings of our own language* visible to us. It does this by setting it against an alternative language, another way of talking about the same things. It shows us our familiar ways of talking, that is, as *arbitrary* in the Saussurian sense (another transformation of *l'arbitraire du signe*); as constituting a language which is not logocentrically controlled by necessities of conceptual organization originating in the world it describes (a language, that is, which does not simply adhere to and mirror reality as the fully analysed propositions of the *Tractatus*, say, adhere to and mirror the contents of the logical space of possible facts), but which rests upon ways of construing the world linguistically which could in principle give place to other, though equally provisional, ways of construing the same world linguistically.

The cognitive gains offered by constitutive language are of two kinds. On the first and simplest level they are gains in self-knowledge. As such they are of an essentially negative kind. They disturb the self in its natural but mistaken conviction that the terms in which it habitually construes the world are the only terms in which the world is capable of being construed, simply by displacing the language, the system of connections and differences between terms which articulates and constitutes that habitual way of looking at things. In the process of achieving this (non-trivial and certainly not merely stipulative) shift of perspective, constitutive language necessarily, since the sign / sign relationships it reorders are only weakly internal to language, passes from reordering its own signs to reordering, not *the world* precisely (how could *language*, after all, do that?), but our perception of the limits and scope of natural possibility.

A vast amount of commonplace knowledge of the world is simply built into the relationships between the signs of our language. As those relationships shift, new possibilities come into view whose existence we would otherwise never have suspected. 'The constituted language,' as Merleau-Ponty says, 'suddenly off-centre and out of equilibrium, reorganizes itself to teach the reader – and even the author – that he never knew what to say.'[28] Constitutive language, in itself, never asserts that the possibilities it reveals are actualized:

assertion is not its business. Cognitive gain, however, is not – this is the fundamental error implicit in the Positivist picture of language – just a matter of augmenting the list of true statements known to us. The grasping of a new possibility, a vision of how things, perfectly feasibly, might be, can also constitute a cognitive gain.

My suggestion, then, is that the critical humanist, anxious to secure his fundamental claims, that literature stands in some sort of relationship to reality and that it can be a source of cognitive gain to the reader otherwise than through reductive criticism, has been setting about that task in the wrong way. Under the spell of the Positivist picture of how a language must work and how it serves the purposes of cognition, literary humanists from generation to generation have tried repeatedly and vainly to assimilate fictional narrative or poetry, somehow or other, to the model of scientific discourse, to show that it is, in some strained sense or other, 'referential', in some strained sense or other 'true'. Latterly, still willing, if inexplicably, conscripts to the cause of Positivism, critical humanists have bent manfully to the task of resisting at all costs the deconstructionist's suggestion that literary language 'never has anything to do with anything but itself'.

It is time to show the fly the way out of the fly-bottle. Literary language, the language of narrative fiction and poetry, is, root and branch, constitutive language. As such it is non-referential and it makes no statements. It does not even assert (as the Aristotelian phrase 'the kind of thing that would happen' suggests) that the possibilities it presents are, or might in practical terms be, actual. Its claim is merely that they are coherent: it just adumbrates them. It is language entirely occupied with itself, *in a sense*. The mistake promoted by the Positivist vision of language is to suppose that that sense can be absolute. Language is everywhere hopelessly infected by the extra-linguistic: the relationships between its signs run ineluctably by way of the world. So there is, just as the critical humanist has always maintained, a strong connection between language and Reality; only it does not run by way of referentiality and truth. Rather, it permeates the thickness of the language we speak in ways we only begin to guess at when constitutive language sets seismic convulsions going in that thickness which allow the relations between sign and sign, long confirmed by habit, to dissolve and reform in new patterns, creating the possibility of the kinds of cognitive gain I sketched in the preceding page or two.

Constitutive language, in short, shows us Reality only by showing us ourselves: it does this by showing us what our relationship to Reality has been. It can make that apparent to us only by making us aware of how language has mediated our relationship to Reality, and it can do that only by shifting and re-forming the sign / sign relationships which have functioned to accomplish that mediation. This means that the cognitive gains it offers are of a radically different kind from those offered by the ordinary language – the 'constituted language', Merleau-Ponty would say – in which reference and truth play their accustomed roles. Constituted language treats itself as invisible: as a neutral device for recording what is the case. It offers us knowledge which does not put the selfhood of the possessor in question, and which can thus be enjoyed as an amenity. Constitutive language, on the other hand, makes constituted language visible, by displacing its categories and internal relationships. It is always possible that the shifts and deformations it produces may affect sign / sign relationships in which the reader has invested many ordinary assumptions about life, and thus some portion of the structures of his or her self. Constitutive language thus always and intrinsically poses a potential threat to the continued integrity of the self of the reader. This is why, it seems to me, narrative fiction and poetry are important, and dangerous; why they have the power to change us and even to produce experiences of conversion; why Shelley's 'Poets are the unacknowledged legislators of the world' is only up to a point rodomontade.

Much of the remainder of this book is given over to exploring the implications in terms of actual narrative fictions of this way of re-articulating Merleau-Ponty's vision of literary language as constitutive. Not much more can be fruitfully achieved on the level of philosophy and literary theory until we have access to some exemplary investigations of that kind. But one or two things can still usefully be said at this stage. The first is this: The notion of literary language as constitutive, sketchy and skeletal though it still remains at this point in the development of the argument, seems to me to give the literary humanist most of what he has always wanted to assert about the connection between fiction and reality and about the reading of fiction and poetry as a source of possible cognitive gains. It is important to see that these benefits accrue to humanism in a way which is not merely consistent with the central insights of deconstruction, but depends crucially upon those insights. The possibility of constitutive language is a simple consequence of the falsity of logocentrism: it arises, in other words, just because the relationships between signs in a language are not guaranteed, fixed immutably, by the nature of some *hors-texte*. It is because there *is* no *hors-texte* that, in Saussure's words, 'Une langue est radicalement impuissante à se défendre contre les facteurs qui déplacent d'instant en instant le rapport du signifié et du signifiant'. The possibility of literature is not threatened, but guaranteed, by that radical powerlessness.

It is with this in mind that I suggested at the start of this chapter that the reconciliation of humanism and deconstruction must involve a double movement, on the one hand divesting humanism of its traditional logocentric commitments, on the other drawing out the humanistic implications of deconstruction. Those implications, oddly enough, cluster around the thoroughly Romantic issue, dear also to Lawrence, to Leavis and to Friedrich Nietzsche, of what it is to *live*. Philosophers since Descartes have constantly been drawn back to a division of the spheres of life and death which makes life a unique prerogative of consciousness. One corollary of the Cartesian view is that the body and the material world are lifeless tools and adjuncts of consciousness. Another is the philosophical version of antinomianism which holds that language is dead, and only the thought – the mental acts – informing it alive. Wittgenstein, Derrida, Merleau-Ponty are all three in various ways opposed to this strain in Cartesianism.

At one point late in *La Voix et le phénomène* Derrida argues that the 'life' of the pure transcendental consciousness dear to Husserl is actually a kind of death, since its description condemns it to a language, a 'pure speech', which can neither inform nor change, because its function is merely to mirror the timeless intentional life of pure consciousness. Derrida contrasts this language (*la voix*) with ordinary written language, subject as it is to all the vicissitudes of displacement and *différance*, and comments: 'Une voix sans différance, une voix sans écriture, est à la fois absolument vive et absolument morte.'[29]

If one reads this from the standpoint of the Positivist picture of how language works, then the 'life' which is here being claimed on behalf of *écriture* – of literary language, for example – is no more than a febrile and vapid dance of signs. If one reads it from the standpoint of the distinction between constituted and constitutive language, then what is being affirmed is the possibility of a living literary culture: a culture whose life involves the constant destabilization, through *différance* constitutively considered, of habit and conformity, and the kind of self which rears its kind of life upon the twin pillars of habit and conformity; and the perpetual dissemination of thought and feeling into new forms. It is perhaps something of the sort that Shklovskii, that unlikely candidate for the label 'Formalist', had in mind in speaking of the purpose of art in our lives as the resurrection of things and the killing of pessimism.

VI Cordelia's refusal

I began the last section by discussing one way of taking the last three sentences of Nuttall's Observation. That led us into canvassing some familiar problems concerning the application of the notions of representation, reference and truth to literature, among them the problem that if literature offers us merely true statements and accurate representations of natural phenomena, then, for Humean reasons, it becomes difficult to see how or why it should have, any more than a scientific treatise – in the present case, perhaps, one on Interpersonal Problems of the Multi-Sibling Family – the power to move, to 'pierce' us. The subsequent turn taken by the discussion left these questions hanging. It is time to return to them and to justify my repeated claim that there is a sense in which Nuttall's Observation expresses a just – a transparently true – critical judgement. At the same time we shall have the opportunity to pick up a second dropped thread: the issue of how general and particular are related as objects of literary and critical interest.

We have before us three ways of construing Nuttall's Observation:
(1) The exchange between Lear and Cordelia in Act I, sc. i of *Lear* would not move us as much as it does unless we were able to bring to its reading some knowledge, gained neither from the text nor from other texts, of relations between parents and children.
(2) The exchange between Lear and Cordelia moves us because it is an adequate representation of a Concrete Universal, 'parent-child-ness'.
(3) The exchange between Lear and Cordelia moves us because it is an adequate representation of our everyday experience of actual parent-child relationships.

(1) is entirely unexceptionable, but a blank cheque. To fill in the cheque we need to know in more detail what role extra-textually-gained knowledge of parents and children plays in the context of our response to the scene. (2) and (3) offer two oppositely theoretically loaded ways of addressing this question, both of which lead to severe philosophical difficulties. Let us attempt another way of filling in the blank spaces in (1).

(3) is tempting as an account of what is going on because of what seems to us the realism of Shakespeare's presentation of the exchange. Partly, I think, this is a result of the very sharp contrast between the formal courtesies of the opening and the extremely sudden descent into raw conflict and recrimination initiated by Cordelia's response to Lear's invitation to her to quantify her love for

him. This is what we all feel ourselves to have lived through before, many times, in real life. If we draw back from this a little and look at the scene as a whole, (3) becomes, I think, much less tempting. What militates against it is the sheer *extraordinariness* of both Lear and Cordelia as characters. Aristotle's *the kind of thing that would happen* is, as we have already noticed, ambiguous as between a generalizing and a particularizing interpretation. Here, given the entire and concrete particularity of Lear and Cordelia as people, the movement of interpretation has got to be towards the particular: if the text can be said to 'truthfully represent' anything conforming to Aristotle's dictum, it will have to be said to represent truthfully what these two extraordinary monsters *would say and do*. But saying that makes the supposed connection between world and text via the representing relation collapse: we cannot say now that the text is 'truthful' in respect of the representation it offers of something to be found in the world, since no original of Lear or Cordelia *is* to be found in the world: their habitation is the text.

If we want an explanation of the persuasiveness (at least to some of us: at least to me) of Nuttall's 'It pierces by its truth', then plainly we must look elsewhere for it. Perhaps, instead of attempting an explanation in terms of some analogue of factual discourse, we should look in the opposite direction: at the textuality, the fictionality of Lear and Cordelia: not, in other words, at what relates them to, but at what divides them from, the parents and children familiar to us from everyday life.

Present-day readers have available to them plenty of instances of children who entertain objections on moral grounds to making formal social gestures demanded of them by their parents. But in general the moral high ground thus occupied is ground originally enclosed by Rousseau, and involves the assertion of such values as simplicity, equality and the refusal of social artifice, coupled with a claim on the part of the child to independence and moral self-determination. Shakespearian audiences were no doubt also familiar with related kinds of conflict over parental notions of what dutifulness involves. So much for 'parent-child-ness' so far as that is, empirically and contingently speaking, a constituent of Reality. I suspect, though, that neither the moralizing undutifulness known in real life to us, nor that known to Shakespeare's audience, ever took the form of the admission by the child of far-reaching responsibilities of 'love ... honour ... care and duty' to both parent and spouse, combined with the entirely reasonable plea that no duty owed to either can in duty be sacrificed in order to meet unreasonable because exclusive demands made by the other. Cordelia is not, in fact, a type of undutifulness; she is, like Kent, a type of dutifulness (and dutiful-ness, like Kent's, of a peculiarly absolute kind at that) manifesting itself as an apparent undutifulness because, in the circumstances, it has no other choice than to do so.

It is the combination of absolute love and duty towards Lear with blank resistance to his wishes, of course, which makes Cordelia so extraordinary; so much a creature *not* to be found in nature. But, on the other hand, Cordelia's strange brand of dutifulness certainly qualifies, given the meaning of the term, as *dutifulness*. And that suggests a different, non-Aristotelian way of accounting for the persuasiveness of Nuttall's 'It pierces by its truth'. We, like the members of Shakespeare's audience, have (though we are less ready to admit it) perfectly serviceable notions of the duty owed by children to their parents, of fidelity, of love. These moral concepts are framed, certainly, by relating signs to other signs, but the relationships in question, like those which differentially define our concepts of colour or the basic notions of Newtonian mechanics relative to one another, are relationships which pass by way of the extra-linguistic: by way of aspects and features of the real world. Into the ordinary workings of such systems of concepts there is built, that is (as is the case with all concepts), a certain limited conception of the range of possibilities we may expect to find instantiated in nature. We take it for granted in the case of dutifulness, for instance, as Lear does, that there is a quasi-necessary connection between dutifulness and responsiveness to parental wishes. What the opening exchange between Lear and Cordelia does is forcibly to break this connection. It does so by presenting a scene so fully imagined in both moral and psychological terms that we have no option but to grant at least the theoretical possibility of such a combination of absolute duty with absolute honesty. *It is true*, we say to ourselves, *such things might be*; and to have wrung such an admission from us with so slight an expenditure of words is a small but significant part of Shakespeare's title to greatness as a writer.

Why, now, has this purely hypothetical, purely textual species of truth, the mere demonstration of the *abstract* possibility of a thing which, if it existed, would force a certain admission from us, without any supporting proof that such possibilities are, or in practical terms could be, instantiated in the real world; this truth divested, in fact, of all the normal accompaniments of truth: assertion, referentiality, representation – why has truth in this diminished, largely, if not quite hermetically, intra-textual sense, the power to 'pierce' us? It has the power to pierce us, I think, because what the scene is forcing upon our attention is not reality (*that* we could contemplate with equanimity, as we contemplate with equanimity the most appalling real events on the television every day of our lives), but the nature, and the limitations, of our own representations of reality. The scene is anguishing to watch because, while the love and dutifulness of Cordelia and Kent is apparent to the audience, it is not visible to Lear. And it is not visible to Lear because Lear has the conventional expectations about dutifulness I mentioned a moment ago: *our* conventional expectations, in other words. We are involved in this spectacle of a man wantonly rejecting the love and fidelity addressed to him by others because Lear is responding to Cordelia as we would, very possibly, having the conventional notions of dutifulness and the respect owed to us by love which we share with Lear, respond to a child who spoke to us as Cordelia speaks to Lear.

As we contemplate the absolute unhinging of Lear's life and world which flows from this initial act of blindness, it is our world also which is unhinged. If we are moved, that is, it is because we enter the tragedy not as intelligent but disinterested observers who are about to enjoy a cunning and lifelike representation of things already familiar to them from the life they have lived outside the theatre, but as participants. We have paid the price of our ticket not, it appears, to receive in return some agreeable and economically calculable amenity, but to be taken to pieces. 'It is true,' we say, in the painful blurring of the boundaries between our selves and the 'self' of another who is merely a 'character', a tissue of words skilfully spoken on a stage, that we call *being moved*, 'love can be refused out of just such blindness and vanity.' And we say it thinking both of Lear and of ourselves. The cap that Shakespeare has made for us fits us, and that, not unnaturally, is something which has the power to move us.

Such a fiction does not use words to illuminate Reality (by referring to it, by representing it, by offering us '*general* and *transcendental truths* which *will always be the same*', or by offering us fictional biography; armchair tours around such non-existent particulars as My Father, the Mayor of Casterbridge or Odette de Crécy); it uses Reality to illuminate words, and, through illuminating words, to illuminate us. It cannot, of course, do this directly by showing us Reality as it nakedly and transcendently is. It has to do it by operating upon words with words. It constructs out of conceptual connections we know perfectly well how to deploy and assess in real life a fictional 'reality', by the light of which it becomes manifest that certain other conceptual connections upon which we also rely constantly without thinking much about it may not be as sound a guide to the limits of natural possibility as we think they are. In this way it makes us aware of the gap between Reality and the conceptual-cum-theoretical constructions which we habitually and with varying degrees of warrant, success and durability attempt to place upon it. The object of Theory is to close this gap (to arrive at a construction so adequate that it will no longer *be* merely a construction placed upon the facts but simply a neutral representation of *the facts*); the object of literature is to keep the gap open.

That such a gap exists and is unclosable is, of course, the central insight of Deconstruction. Partly because critics find it easier to focus upon the practices of other critics than upon those of writers, partly because of the dead weight of Positivist philosophy of language, word has got around that nothing can live in that gap, that literature just as much as theory spends its energies in a vain attempt to close it, and thus that the icy winds blowing from it are winds of nihilism fatal to both. Nothing could be further from the truth. Literature lives in, and by, the unclosable gap of *différance*, in the only apparently sterile logical vacuity between words and things. In that gap, by working the reality-soaked conceptual structures of our language ceaselessly against one another, literature works upon us, ceaselessly shifting and redefining, as Wallace Stevens suggests in 'Men made out of Words', our conception of what, and who, we are. It is because this is a process that can only work if its wheels grind upon a multitude of commonplace facts about the real world that the humanist critic is right to resist the Formalist's attempt to see the process as one in which pure signs (signs defined in terms of differential sign / sign relations strongly internal to language) work emptily upon other pure signs. It is because it is a process that is in no way limited or preconditioned by any *representative* or *referential* relationship to Reality that the deconstructionist is right to insist that 'Il n'y a pas d'hors-texte'. I have shown, I hope, that, and why, neither of these claims need be read as in any way exclusive of the other.

Back now, in conclusion, to the issue of general and particular in literature. Johnson and Blake too, it seems, were both, each in his own way, saying something true. Very often a considerable work of literature can be felt as changing our conception of what a word means. *Lear*, for instance, plays variations upon the idea of blindness; and 'blindness', of course, picks out a concept, a *general* notion. So it is easy to think of the play as *telling us something general about* ... After that *about*, of course, the confident theorizing voice falters: about what, exactly? Not, presumably, about how blindness figures in the imaginary world of an imaginary king and his imaginary daughters. Well, about Reality, then: or better, about *general fea-*

tures which Reality shares with the invented world of that invented king; and at once here we are again shaking hands with Imlac. We would have done better to go more slowly. For really, all that *Lear* has to do with is the particular: the particular sayings of (invented) particular people in a concrete world of invented but quite particular circumstances. And how could it be otherwise? For a story can only be about particulars, and it is the story alone which is doing the work of placing under pressure the tissue of confident generalities from our stance in the midst of which we confront the world.

In general, for instance, we are apt to think of birth as an involuntary, and in a certain sense demeaning, hurling into the world, and to credit ourselves as adults with a morally superior condition of freedom to act or to refrain, to continue with life or to end it. The point at which Edgar says, 'Men must endure / Their going hence, even as their coming hither', is one of strain for this general distinction. Suddenly we are made to feel the condition of the new-born infant as the type rather than the antitype of our adult condition; and the animal energy of the infant rather than the febrile, conscious, voluntaristic energy of the willed suicide as the living, the human thing. But this inversion of the generalities in terms of which we ordinarily think could not be achieved by Edgar's words if they themselves had only the force of a moral generality: a *sentence*. The words can only take on that force in virtue of the *particular* circumstances in which they are uttered: without the story of blinded Gloucester and his two sons they are nothing. I conclude that literature in itself has nothing to do with anything except particularities. It offers us, in itself, no '*general* and *transcendental truths*' whatsoever. It is we as readers who bring generalities to bear on our reading of fiction, and the fate of the generalities we bring with us is never to be confirmed, or replaced by better generalities garnered from the fiction (as a physics textbook might replace our casual generalizations about the natural world with more accurate and powerful generalizations), but always to be merely confuted, always merely deformed in some new direction, always disconfirmed.

This perhaps suggests, contrary to experience, that literature cannot sustain or confirm. Worse still, given one popular way of understanding Modernism, it might suggest that the account which I have just outlined can really only be appropriate to Modernism or its precursors: that it cannot have much to say about writing which does not consciously insist upon its own artificiality and on the gap between word and world.

These are not consequences which I would wish to follow from the account I have outlined here, and as far as I can see they do not. My central claim is that the disturbance and renovation of *language* is both the fundamental business and the fundamental technique of literature; and that the renovation of language is inseparable from the renovation of the vision of reality which we share as speakers, because it is, finally, impossible to separate the possession of a language from the ability to apply to experience a repertoire of responses and practices which embody at every point implicit assumptions about the range and limitations of natural possibility. It seems to me, now, that the renovation of language as the central business of literature cuts deeper than either the issue of 'Realism' versus 'Modernism' or the question of whether a given work is found by a given reader to be disturbing and unsettling, or on the contrary affirmative and sustaining.

Many readers, I suppose, would find something affirmative in the lines 'Men must endure / Their going hence, even as their coming hither'. They seem to have some power to steady the nerves, to make suicide seem a less appealing option, and so on. The question is, why they have such a power; or rather, how such a power can reside merely *in a way of putting things*; in a certain way of arranging words. It is that question, or its generalized version, which I take myself to have been mainly addressing in the foregoing pages: my suggestion is that the words have the power they do because, among other things, they disturb the customary pairing-off of courage and autonomy with maturity rather than infancy (something which has to do both with blind Gloucester's new dependence upon his son and with the ambiguous resonances of the word 'endure'); thus throwing the associations of those commonplace notions into a new and surprising pattern, from the perspective of which things look different. The energy of the words, their power, depending upon the reader, to console or to unsettle (a moment ago I invoked the possibility of finding them heartening, but one can surely as easily imagine a Christian reader who might find the vision of birth and death they offer both bleak and pagan) comes from the suddenness, the unexpectedness and the persuasiveness of this chiasmatic transposition.

I discuss a related example in Chapter 5. Many readers, I imagine, have found *Sense and Sensibility* deeply consoling and confirming as a defence of the former over the latter. The question is, again, how a mere fiction, an invented farrago, can possibly make any outlook on life seem more just, more in accordance with the way things are. The answer, according to me, lies partly in episodes like the one in which Elinor rescues from Marianne the right to use the word 'esteem' without derisory overtones. What underlies affirmation and reassurance, in other words, is once again the dislocation of a conceptual association, this time one on the verge of becoming customary, in the service of a motivated renovation and re-energizing of language.[30]

The evident differences between the stylistic and pragmatic mechanisms of 'Modernist' and 'Realist' fiction and poetry also seem to me to conceal an underlying conformity in the means – pre-eminently the dislocation and renovation of the customary associations and relationships of words – by which the characteristic effects of each are obtained. The remarkable 'realism' of *Pamela*, for instance, does not seem to me adequately explained by Richardson's choice of the epistolary convention. Why, after all, should we take these invented 'letters' as actual letters? That we do is, I think, not helpfully to be explained as a consequence of the faithful adhesion of the words which compose them to the (fictional) immediacy of the circumstances in which they flowed from Pamela's pen: we do, of course, need to pinch ourselves to remember that neither Pamela nor her pen actually exist, but not all that hard. Rather, it seems to me, the acute immediacy of the sense Richardson manages to induce in the reader of the peculiar and individual flavour of Pamela's consciousness as she writes, is itself partly dependent on the gap which rapidly opens up as we read between what Pamela makes of the wretched Mr B and the sort of 'actual' person we can readily imagine, given our everyday knowledge of the world, to be thus reflected in the distorting mirror of Pamela's prose and personality. But it would require far more space than I can spare here to drive home the argument; and in any case, the pervasiveness of supposedly 'Modernist' techniques in supposedly pre-Modernist writing is perhaps nowadays well enough established.

VII Puritanism and literature

'The puritans', as a recent critical theorist, Lennard J. Davis, notes with approval, 'did not like fiction and they did not like it for the main reason that it was not the truth. It was a pack of invented lies.'[31] As the title of Davis's book, *Resisting Novels*, suggests, a kind of puritanism is with us again; though I am not sure how much it has in common with the seventeenth-century kind. Its appeal, indeed, is moral in character; but the morality it promotes is hardly that of any recognizably Christian form of puritanism. Rather, it is that of the secularized puritanism which forms one of the more recognizable strands in the tradition of secular or philosophical moralizing which begins with the first decade or two of the eighteenth century, and which is a powerful element in the thought of Mandeville, Rousseau, Kant and Sartre. The chief moral value promoted by puritanism of this secularized variety is that of a personal authenticity to be achieved by self-scrutiny directed towards securing conscious control over any influence which might threaten the integrity and autonomy of the will.

There are two main areas of threat to the position of absolute voluntary power over his own self and its acts which the puritan seeks to occupy. The first and most obvious is the body and its lusts and appetites, which the religious puritan wishes to make obedient to the Will of God, the secular puritan to the command of Reason. The second is epistemological, and involves the threat and the avoidance of deceit and illusion. For the religious puritan the illusions in question are primarily the shows and deceits of the world. For the secularized puritan the threat comes rather from false consciousness in various forms, including those of *mauvaise foi* and ideology. Fiction appears to qualify on both counts; both, that is, as worldly and as a potent source of ideological deceit and false consciousness. It is the suspicions of the secularized puritan, however, which will chiefly occupy me here.

To read fiction with pleasure (this comes as no surprise to the puritan, who has always known that pleasure *per se* cloaks a dagger directed at the autonomy of his will), it is necessary to abandon oneself to one's author, to enter trustingly into an imagined world of which one is not, oneself, the inventor or the master. The puritan has, or thinks he has, an argument which very simply demonstrates the dangers and the corruption implicit in such self-abandonment. Even to read critically, having accepted the author as one's master and guide, is to think in fetters. And though the fetters may be self-imposed, for the purpose of securing the enjoyments of reading, their acceptance may have consequences beyond the space of time during which the reader sits absorbed in his or her book, because it involves partial forgetfulness of the duty to take responsibility, in the real world, for one's beliefs about that world. As Davis puts it:

> Some people get bored with their marriages, but Emma Bovary turns the emotion into a flood of unbearable passion and destruction. In projecting unacceptable emotions into characters, we are doing the very thing we cannot do without damage in real life – we are blurring the distinction between fact and fiction. The space of novel-reading obviously provides a safe place to allow reality testing to go haywire. However, part of my critique of the novel has to do with this point that we can impair, to a certain extent, our ability to test reality.[32]

The same thought underlies the large body of recent work which takes the concept of ideology as the key to the joint enterprise of demythologizing literature and turning literary criticism into a respectable body of knowledge. Thus de Man: 'What we call ideology is precisely the confusion of linguistic with natural reality.'[33]

The stance of the critic of ideology is not without an Achilles' heel of its own, as Howard Felperin has recently pointed out.[34] The student of ideology must in the nature of things claim not merely to occupy a standpoint, shared with the deconstructionist, from which he can unmask the text in the merely negative sense of demonstrating the self-defeating character of its putative claim to represent 'natural reality', but also to occupy a further standpoint which belongs to him alone, from which he can unmask the text in the further, positive sense of revealing the real though covert relationships between social and political reality and the production and consumption of texts. The position of the critic of ideology, to put it bluntly, is that although literary texts lack the relationship to reality which liberal humanist criticism would like to persuade us they have, they do nevertheless *have* a relationship to reality, however obscure, esoteric and alien to the uninstructed or 'surface' reading of the text, about which the critic of ideology is in a position to inform us definitively. The difficulty with this, as Felperin points out, now, is that of seeing how the deconstructive scepticism characteristic of the first of these claims can fail to erode and undermine the putative omniscience which characterizes the second.

The problem is not, as Mannheim, for instance, saw it,[35] that of explaining how the theorist, or that part of the intelligentsia which he represents, can have achieved the emancipation from the power of ideology implied by his putative knowledge of the true state of affairs, but the deeper and more difficult one of explaining how there can be any 'true state of affairs' of the sort his theory requires. The outlook of ideological criticism is essentially gnostic: it probes beneath the surface of the text for a hidden but 'real' and 'final' meaning. The message of deconstruction, or of the unrelated but powerful arguments deployed by Frank Kermode in *The Genesis of Secrecy*, is that real and final meanings are unavailable. Closure is just not to be had: not at the level of the literary text and not, either, at the level of the canonical texts of Hegelian or Marxist *Geistesgeschichte*, upon which so much recent ideological criticism – that of Eagleton or Macherey, for instance – depends.

The epistemological difficulties for current ideological criticism which Felperin raises are real enough; but I think one can go deeper. The appeal of ideological criticism is largely to the kind of conscious-

ness for which to be undeceived, to have seen through the shows and
deceits of a culture felt to be an oppressive outgrowth of the power of
a corrupt establishment, is a central mark and guarantee of personal
authenticity: in other words, to the sort of consciousness for which
what I have called secularized puritanism is still a central, if not the
determining, constituent of morality. I doubt, now, whether either
the epistemological or the moral outlook of secular puritanism is
nearly as soundly based as each can, with proper rhetorical development, be made to appear.

Let us look more closely. Somewhere near the heart of the secularized puritan's position is the thought that to be in full command of
one's critical faculties *vis-à-vis* others one must be in the position of
confronting, upon an equal epistemic footing with them, a common
world given in experience. (Though the task of teasing out the
historical connections between the two would not be a brief or easy
one, this is clearly a thought which originates in the century, the
seventeenth, which gave rise both to the scientific revolution and to
secularized puritanism in its modern forms.) Most literature, now,
and certainly most pre-modern literature, proceeds on the assumption that author and reader do not, unlike two scientists working in
separate laboratories, confront a common world present to both, on
the properties and features of which each is in principle as competent
an authority as the other; but, on the contrary, that the author alone
is in a position to offer competent guidance to the imagined world to
which the fiction gives access. Into that world the reader must allow
himself or herself to be led, as Dante is led by Virgil; and at the outset
he must make Dante's act of submission:

> Tu se' lo mio maestro e 'l mio autore.

That act of submission is, of course, also an act of trust. It is that
trust on the part of reader towards author which Sterne has in mind
when he says, speaking for all writers, 'I would go fifty miles on foot,
for I have not a horse worth riding on, to kiss the hand of that man
whose generous heart will give up the reins of his imagination into
his author's hands, be pleased he knows not why, and cares not
wherefore' (*Tristram Shandy*, Bk. III, ch. xii).

If the secular puritan is correct such generosity is culpable: we
should never give up the reins of our imagination to another, for to
do so is to give up the responsibility we all bear to take reality
seriously: to tell the truth. But what if the truth is not all accessible
from any one viewpoint? The moral credentials of the authenticity
sought by the secularized puritan depend upon a strict separation
between world and self. On the one hand there is the world, capable

of being known exhaustively, truthfully and dispassionately from a single, neutral standpoint which is the same for any human being in his or her capacity as Knower. On the other hand there is the self as agent of moral choice and action, giver of meaning and bearer of responsibility. Authenticity consists in choosing a system of values in full cognizance of the facts.[36] This vision of things is fatally muddied if there just happens to *be* no single, neutral standpoint identical for any sentient observer from which *all* 'the facts' can be apprehended: if, in particular, the partial selection of facts available to any observer depends upon the structure of assumptions and presuppositions, estimates of natural possibility and of the range of possible alternatives available in a given context, which form the background, picked up by all manner of rational and sub-rational routes, to the choices, conscious and unconscious, which have made a given observer the person, the self, that he or she has become.

To such a creature, perched on the friable and constantly disintegrating isthmus of a middle state, the morality of authenticity as that has been envisaged is neither of exclusive nor immediate applicability. What is needed as a precondition for personal authenticity are older values: in particular those of humility and trust. The literary puritan's fundamental thought, expressed with engaging directness by Davis, is that narrative fiction 'provides a safe place for reality-testing to go haywire'. There is a certain oddity in the thought that anyone not a little unhinged would take imaginative fiction as a suitable sphere for *reality-testing*, haywire or otherwise, anyway: as Wittgenstein notes, we can justify a translation by looking up a word in a dictionary, but not by looking it up in a dictionary which exists only in our imagination (*Philosophical Investigations*, I. 265). But there is a deeper muddle here: the muddle of thinking that 'reality-testing' is an unproblematic notion: something each of us knows straight off (as a kind of God-given birthright?) how to do. One only has to contemplate this notion squarely for a moment for its inherent preposterousness to be evident. 'Testing Reality' always presupposes a standpoint from which, and a set of conceptual distinctions in terms of which, the test is to be applied and the results assessed. Neither can simply be read off from 'Nature' or 'Experience': each is open to criticism. Such criticism forms a large part of the history both of science and of culture in general.

But if one of the functions of serious literature is to unsettle the confidence of the self in the cognitive adequacy of the standpoint it happens to occupy, then the secularized puritan's moral objections to literature are simply misplaced. No threat to moral authenticity is posed by Dante's act of fealty to Virgil or by Sterne's demand that the author give up the reins of his imagination into his author's hands, because moral authenticity is not yet in question: its cognitive conditions have not yet been met. We are still at the stage of self-questioning: of a self-questioning which cannot in the nature of things be applied by the self to itself (which is what the puritan would most like), but must be suffered at the hands of another. To be willing to suffer that kind of self-questioning is to be willing to be silent, to listen, to trust, while the story unfolds; and it is only that kind of silence, of trust, which Dante offers Virgil and Sterne demands of his reader.

The strength of literary puritanism lies partly in the fact that its fundamental tenets have very frequently been, and still are, largely shared by critics who would not necessarily wish to draw all, or any, of the literary puritan's conclusions. One of the chief supports of literary puritanism, for instance, is the thought that, in real life, the business of narrative is to recount real events, and that literary fiction *per se* displays, therefore, a rather striking evasion of this responsibility. The nineteenth century produced a reply to this charge in the form of the theory of the Realistic, or True, Novel. 'Le public aime les romans faux: ce roman est un roman vrai,' proclaim the Goncourts in their Preface to *Germinie Lacerteux*. The habit of taking such claims seriously makes it very difficult to see those writers who trifle with the conventions of the *roman vrai* as anything other than tricksters. These, the suspicion insinuates itself, are fellows sufficiently lost to their moral responsibilities not to believe in the *vérité* of the *roman vrai*, and very possibly not to believe in truth itself either. The problem arises most obviously with the major modernists, but as has long been recognized it does not stop there. Swift, Fielding, Sterne, Dickens, Trollope; the list is endless of writers who never seem quite sure whether they are composing a *roman vrai* or sharing with the reader a joke rather more than half at the reader's expense about the inherent absurdity of any such enterprise.

Something vaguely disreputable of this sort takes place, of course, when the real Florentine poet Dante Alighieri, through his fictional act of submission to the imagined shade of the real Latin poet Virgil, endows himself with the role of a character in his own fiction. Gérard Genette discusses this curious narrative technique, in which the boundaries between fiction and reality grow hazy; and gives it a name: *narrative metalepsis*. Genette finds disturbing, just as does Davis, the way in which narrative metalepsis disturbs the stability of the boundary between reality and the imaginary worlds conjured up by narrative: 'The most troubling thing about metalepsis indeed lies in this unacceptable and insistent hypothesis, that the extra-diegetic is perhaps always diegetic, and that the narrator and his narratees – you and I – perhaps belong to some narrative.'[37]

If the account of the functions of serious literature and the nature of its relationship to reality which I have outlined in this chapter is correct, then we should find nothing anomalous or troubling in narrative metalepsis, and should in no way be surprised to find it cropping up everywhere in literature both before and after the brief reign of the *roman vrai*. Nor should we see Modernism as a failure of nerve, a loss of belief in the possibility of *serious* fiction, or, more absurdly still, wonder whether the opening shots of Modernism were not fired in 1750, or 1250. Rather, we should see literary Modernism, the Modernism of Proust, or Joyce, or Beckett or Virginia Woolf, as a rediscovery of what it *is* to be properly serious about the composition of a fiction, as distinct from a piece of reportage; and we should even try to get used to the idea that the jokes of Sterne or Fielding, or the metalepses of Dante, are *serious* jokes and *serious* metalepses. For metalepsis, the unhinging of the reader's sense of where reality ends and fiction begins, is not only essential to narrative fiction but morally salutary. It is both of these things because the point of telling a story seriously is the morally salutary one of unhinging the reader from his self and its web of assumptions and complacencies about what he calls 'Reality'. The 'Reality' to which the reader genuflects every day of his life, after all, never *is* Reality *per se*, but to some very large extent is itself a more or less fictional construct (in this sense Genette's troubling thought is simply correct: author and reader *are* both characters in some fiction).

J. L. Austin's observation to the effect that philosophical theories are apt to depend upon a very few, carefully chosen and highly artificial, not to say impoverished, examples is equally true, after all, of a great deal of what we ordinarily believe. Even God cannot let in the light of Reality Itself upon the darkness which that sort of selectivity contrives for us; but a fiction of genius, though it too cannot show us Reality Itself and may not reveal, even to the most intelligent reader, anything at all, at least stands a chance of opening a chink, by suddenly making apparent to the reader the gap, of *différance*, between what he has always presumed to be the relationships governing situations of a given kind and what he already knows on evidence elsewhere available to him, had he ever given it a moment's thought, of what such relationships might actually be.

Through the gap thus opened between the world and alternative ways of construing it Reality shines for a moment; makes itself apparent in what is probably, for creatures constituted as we are, the only way it can. The literary puritan's mistake is to suspect and reject such showings, for fear of being swindled out of a moral autonomy which, in reality, he could only come to exercise through their agency.

The puritan longing for a single, neutral standpoint, from which the whole of reality would be cognitively accessible without danger to the present constitution of the self, sometimes expresses itself in worries about the constitution of 'the canon'. If literary fiction itself is a force for ideology and false consciousness, the promulgation of a list of fictions certified as 'great' can hardly be anything else. Canons, in short, are the arbitrary constructions of cultural élites which thereby both express and enforce their social and economic power. This idea sometimes mutates into the milder one that the chief value of literature lies in its power to cement, by celebrating, the cohesion and the collective consciousness of social groups; a view expressed, for instance, by Professor Marilyn Butler in a recent Inaugural Lecture at Cambridge:

> The surprising feature of the Yale-Cornell canon is how many of the essential features of the old British-built canon it retains. In the future, and surely very soon, now that most readers of English are in India and China, we shall want to replace the old thin line of national heroes with a richer and more credible notion: *that writers represent groups and attitudes within the community*, and therefore from time to time come dynamically into contention with one another [my italics].[38]

At first glance these sentiments appear refreshingly liberal and progressive; but closer inspection reveals a darker side to them. Only a very little unfairness to Professor Butler is required to reparse the position she expresses here into the following one: Great writers are, taken just as individuals, quite frivolous and unimportant souls with no sustainable pretensions whatsoever to contribute to the march of knowledge; but they can be saved from utter uselessness by being co-opted into the service of our various rancid nationalisms and communal animosities, which are, unlike literature, to be taken seriously, presumably, because they animate very large masses of more or less bewildered people.

My response to this will be evident from the whole course of the argument so far. Writers do not *represent groups and attitudes within the community*: they represent nothing but themselves. The service they do us is not to reinforce our sense of sociological solidarity with those who think, equally unthinkingly, the same rubbish that we think (that would hardly be a service, though it is one some people think needs performing and one some writers are ready to perform for pay); but to introduce into our heads the suspicion that much of what we think may indeed be rubbish. That, after all, is why writers are so frequently the subject of persecution by the very 'groups' and 'communities' which they have the misfortune to be taken as 'representing'. If such readers had their way the 'canon' would indeed be swiftly and thoroughly 'reconstituted' by fiat, as it has been for much of this century, though impermanently and without effect for large numbers of readers, in Eastern European countries. In fact, as that experience shows, canons are not formed by the fiat of influential groups, whether inside or outside the academy. Though they may be helped on their way, or restored to public knowledge if forgotten, by critical fan clubs, texts themselves decide the issue of their canonicity, and they decide it by continuing to demonstrate, for successive generations of readers, some, no doubt, skipped, their power to bring the reader up short, to challenge, to unhinge his assumptions, to provoke resentment and the thought that resentment breeds: to take the reader, as we say, 'out of himself'.

What I have against, not attempts to enlarge the canon, which if they succeed are on my view by that very fact to be regarded as valuable, but against sociologically reductive analyses of the concept of canonicity itself, is that they arrogate cognitive significance to the constructions of theoretical knowledge at the cost of denying cognitive significance and power to literature. The same could be said, of course, of a very great deal of current critical theory, from Lévi-Straussian Structuralism to the analyses of the alleged ideological functions of literature propounded from a wide variety of viewpoints from Foucault on the one hand to de Man on the other. My chief object in this book is to combat as far as I can this draining of cognitive force from the literary text itself into some theoretical, and generally savagely reductive, reconstruction of it. The book can be read as a kind of artillery barrage from batteries quite widely spaced around a battlefield of indeterminate extent. In this opening salvo I have tried to show that deconstruction, far from being one of the props of that kind of reductionism, is our strongest weapon against it. Later chapters will carry the theoretical argument to other parts of the field. Others again will be occupied with the attempt to restore to specific texts their power to command a reading of the sort Sterne solicits: a reading, that is, which takes them, not as dead bodies of words served up for theoretical dissection, but as living bodies having the power another human being has to astound, to silence words on the tip of the tongue, to confute and disconfirm, to show things in an utterly new light, and by so doing to bring down in temporary ruin the pillars that uphold the self.

Chapter 2
The Defence of Wit: Sterne, Locke and the Particular*

I write a careless kind of a civil, nonsensical, good-humoured
Shandean book, which will do all your hearts good——
– And all your heads too, – provided you understand it.

Sterne, *Tristram Shandy*, VI.xvii

Les situations prêtent moins à confusion que les mots.

Henri Fluchère, *Laurence Sterne*

I

How one reads Sterne can depend on how one construes his attitude
to the great Locke, by turns Sterne's hero and his butt. According to
one widely accepted account, which derives from a number of
sources, including John Traugott's *Tristram Shandy's World* and to
some extent also Henri Fluchère's *Laurence Sterne*, Sterne and Locke
found common cause chiefly in distrust of the speculative intellect:
'both Sterne and Locke found primary energy in reflection on learned
trumpery and its utter success in the world.'[1]

From this point of agreement, however, their paths divide. What
Locke pits against idle learning is Newtonian science. In the service
of that kind of clarity and objectivity he defends on the one hand a
'plain historic method' which tests the validity of every concept by
asking whether its content can be explained in terms of sensory
experience and, on the other hand, an ideal of plain speaking and

* An earlier version of this paper saw the light at a meeting of the Renaissance Seminar at the
University of Sussex in April 1987. The present version has profited from the discussion at
that meeting.

writing founded upon accurate definition and the avoidance of metaphor and all other literary devices calculated more to decorate and charm than to clarify and instruct. Sterne, so it is said, disliked the rather arid rationalism of Locke's scientifically disinfected plain language, and set out to show that it would not work as a medium of communication. According to Traugott, Sterne's characters 'are so made that, operating on Locke's premises, they completely foil his rational method for communication'. Fluchère goes further, and speaks of the *faillité de la logique et des arts du langage* which manifests itself in the dialogue of the deaf which prevails between My Father and uncle Toby on any rational or intellectual level.[2]

One line of Sterne criticism, pioneered by the Russian formalist Shklovskii, develops this way of taking Sterne's intentions towards Locke into the familiar view of Sterne as a precursor of the formalist strand in Modernism, and the man who deconstructed the conventions of the Realist novel before they had properly become established. I want to concentrate here, though, on another, indigenous, line of criticism which pursues the relationship with Locke a little further.

Locke's philosophy of language was a variant of what literary critics have recently learned to call *logocentrism*. Locke believed, that is, that the meaning of a word was a mental state – an 'idea' – in the mind, or better, the consciousness of a speaker; and that language is only necessary because we cannot inspect the ideas in one another's minds. Being thus metaphysically isolated from one another, so Locke's story goes, we are forced to communicate by means of verbal tokens, each of which stands for a determinate idea or complex of ideas. A speaker, in effect, encodes his ideas into a string of words and transmits them to a hearer, who decodes the string by calling up in his own mind the simple or complex idea associated with each of its component words.

Locke, because of his logocentrism, was haunted by the thought that, since there can be no *direct* inspection of the contents of one mind by another, communication between minds would be metaphysically impossible if it did not proceed by means of verbal tokens in the manner he outlines. Sterne critics have proceeded to draw the inference – a very rash one, in my estimation – that Sterne was haunted by the same thought. They have not, on the whole, considered the possibility that Sterne might have broken with Locke's logocentrism; rejecting with good reason both Locke's Cartesian conception of the mind as a non-physical realm without essential dependence upon the body, and his doctrine that words acquire meaning by coming to stand by association as tokens for events or states in that realm, and thus freeing himself not merely from the detail of Locke's theory of language, but also from the metaphysical dilemma which motivated it; despite the fact that there is, as we shall see, plenty of textual evidence that Sterne rejected both that conception and that doctrine. Here, for instance, is J. B. Priestley drawing the fatal inference:

A satirist, loathing his species, could have taken such tragicomical little creatures, each in the separate mechanical box of his mind, and made out of them a scene or narrative that would have jangled the nerves of a dozen generations. Sterne, however ... preserves the balance by emphasizing what we might call the kinship of his people. If the Shandies cannot share one another's thoughts, they can share one another's feelings. ...[3]

Notice how smoothly Priestley manœuvres Sterne from the stance of one who really believes that the human predicament includes the tragic isolation of one Cartesian consciousness from another, into the stance of a sentimentalist intellectually credulous enough to imagine that the sharing of 'feelings' could possibly get us out of that predicament, if we were in it. The dangers to Sterne's reputation of this way of reading him have been ably drawn out by A. D. Nuttall. Nuttall accepts the thesis that Sterne's characters illustrate the Cartesian isolation of one mind from another:

Tristram Shandy stands as a marvellously rich and detailed embodiment of the Cartesian view – mediated by Locke – that the mind is a mysterious, fugitive, invisible substance, interpenetrating and acting upon the extended world of matter. ... We receive a vivid sense of the imprisoned souls of the Shandys, eccentric ghosts, fluttering inside mechanically determined machines.[4]

His way of developing this thesis is, however, destructive of Sterne's claim to be regarded as a proto-Modernist, turning him instead into a boringly representative embodiment of all that was most reactionary and glibly anti-intellectual in his age. Where Shklovskii and others see in Sterne a Modernist sense that the book is an artificial construct, a play of rhetoric and convention, Nuttall sees in Sterne's determination to keep his writing on the rhetorical surface of things a simple reflection of an age whose ultimate wisdom and most representative voice was Hume's. In Hume the medieval and Renaissance vision of the world as a rationally intelligible order gives way to one couched in terms of what Nuttall aptly calls 'chaotic determinism'. Chaotic determinism sees the world as a wilderness of natural accidence, beneath the phenomenal surface of which Reason has no power to penetrate, and which is hence susceptible only of that

minute, vapidly unsatisfying style of description of what is immediately given to experience which Hume recommends on philosophical grounds as constituting the ultimate ground and limit of
possible knowledge; but which only Sterne among the major writers
of his day transformed into a literary device. What Traugott sees
as a Lockeian dislike of 'learned trumpery', Nuttall thus sees as a
pessimistic conviction of the impotence of reason to compose our
differences or improve an essentially chaotic human condition.

> It is no accident that the writer who first mapped the farcical universe of
> interlocking trivia should also be the prophet of intellectual abdication. . . .
> Sterne has merely achieved a vague echo of that more incisive irony of
> Hume's whereby the completed principles of empiricism were to quell the
> ambitions of empirical science.

Nuttall's Sterne is a pessimist also about morality. Like Priestley,
Nuttall takes it that Sterne's answer to pessimism about the possibility of communication on the level of thought and rational discourse *has to be* optimism about the possibility of communication on
the level of feeling:

> The lamp of reason is virtually extinguished, but the sub-rational faculties
> of feeling, humour, social intuition and affection irradiate the world from
> below. What heart so chilled with scepticism that it cannot be warmed
> with contemplation of the good Toby? No book which so successfully
> combats intellectual despair with a faith in human charity should be
> described as pessimistic. So runs the argument.

Nuttall argues persuasively that this 'argument' is a very bad one.
How much has 'feeling' of the sort purveyed by Priestley's Sterne to
do with morality anyway?

> Perhaps it is because charity means more than a warm heart that we sense
> a breath of nihilism behind even the most affectionate exchanges of the
> brothers Shandy. We may even begin to suspect that real morality, so
> far from being preserved by the power of sentiment, has rather been
> discarded together with the competent intellect. Uncle Toby is a dear
> good soul, but it would be rash to call him a saint. Is this as high as
> human nature will reach? It is curious that before the eighteenth century
> the good characters in literature tend to unite an intelligent perceptiveness
> with a keen moral sensibility. Lear's moral regeneration on the heath
> involves an opening of the eyes. After the close of the seventeenth cen-
> tury, however, the road divides. One way leads to the warm-hearted,
> lovable innocent, the other to the moral vigilante – naturally, for it was

in this century that subjective feeling was firmly divorced from cognitive sensation.[5]

Sterne, Hume's literary double in his antipathy to reason, is in morals also a pale shadow of the Hume for whom the sphere of knowledge includes only matters of fact and relations of ideas, and who considered that in morals, 'Reason is, and ought to be, the slave of the passions.'

Everything about Nuttall's argument except its conclusion seems to me admirable. Of particular importance, it appears to me, is his insistence that any account of moral goodness worth taking seriously must in some way unite moral sensibility with something in the nature of knowledge. I would go further, indeed, and question whether a 'sensibility', however 'keen', which is not in any way disciplined by 'intelligent perceptiveness' can really be described as *moral* sensibility at all. Even here, however, a doubt creeps in. The thought that there is a gulf between maudlin sentiment and anything one would want to describe as moral sensibility is not a particularly obscure or difficult one, and it is not easy to believe that it never occurred to Sterne. So it comes as no surprise to come upon the following, in the peroration to Yorick's sermon on conscience:

—No, God and reason made the law, and have placed conscience within you to determine;—not like an Asiatic Cadi, according to the ebbs and flows of his own passions,—but like a British judge in this land of liberty and good sense, who makes no new law, but faithfully declares that law which he knows already written. (II.xvii.155)[6]

It is not easy, though, to discern in this staunchly morally objectivist and rationalist, and I think wholly unironic, passage the siren-voiced sceptic of Nuttall's indictment, beckoning us seductively up the garden path trodden by the Man of Feeling towards the heaven of the Asiatic Cadi by way of a Humean divorce between reason and the passions, feeling and cognition. In fact Nuttall's conclusions seem to me to embody a profoundly misled and misleading view of Sterne. The fault lies not in his argument but in its premises. He takes for granted the view of Sterne's intentions towards Locke shared by Priestley and many academic critics, and shows very persuasively that that view offers us a Sterne who is in essence a Humean pessimist about both reason and morality. The trouble is that the reading Nuttall takes over from Priestley, Traugott and others is wildly, though not simply, mistaken.

The simplicity of the canonical reading is, indeed, its strength. Sterne did agree with Locke in disliking the pretensions of learning.

He did, also, disagree with Locke's theories about language and the nature of communication. The trouble is only that there is so much *else* in Sterne's text. *Tristram Shandy* is thickly strewn with references to and jokes about Locke. They have become erudite in the century and a half since Locke's *Essay* became a book to be studied but not read; but many of them have been picked up individually by recent critics. What is not so easy, however, is to grasp how they fit together into a coherent response to Locke. My object in this essay is to trace some of the connections between them; and in so doing to reopen our eyes to the Sterne whose comedy is a vehicle of systematic deconstructive resistance to the philosophical dogma of his age. Reading Sterne with an eye to the full range of his response to Locke allows us, I shall argue, to place him in his century without making him merely its representative; and allows him to address some of the preoccupations of Modernism without getting cast as its precursor or patron saint. The Sterne who emerges from such a reading is one who is sceptical about Locke's theory of communication but not at all sceptical about the possibility of communication *per se*; who, far from being a Cartesian dualist, believes that mind and body are necessary 'co-sharers' in human individuality; whose whole thesis about morality is that the good man combines sensibility with an accurate perception of others: in short, a Sterne who, far from being one of the architects of the Eliotean dissociation of sensibility, is fighting a rearguard action against it from which we can still learn something.

Hume, I am afraid, is a red herring here, for two reasons. Nuttall rightly dismisses the first: that although the *Treatise* appeared twenty years before *Tristram Shandy*, Sterne is unlikely to have been familiar with it. Hume was famous in England in the 1750s not as a metaphysician but as an historian. While this suggests that any relation between Sterne and Hume could not have been one of influence, however, it of course leaves parallel responses to related issues as a possibility. The second reason is the important one. It is that Hume's achievement as a metaphysician consists in having drawn out to their logical conclusions just those aspects of Locke's philosophy which Sterne, as we shall see, found suspect.

The Sterne I hope to bring into focus in this essay can sometimes be encountered lurking, a shadowy figure, in the margins of more canonical accounts of his work. Thus Nuttall notes that

There is a sort of embryonic Wittgenstein inside Sterne, who constantly emphasizes those situations in which language is not a separable picture of the world, but rather a special mode of acting, or doing within the world. That this should happen anywhere in the eighteenth century is astounding.[7]

This embryonic Wittgenstein, like the embryonic existential phenomenologist sketched by James A. Swearingen,[8] is none other than the actual, adult Laurence Sterne who did not, in fact, faithfully mirror the logocentrism of his age, but, in a manner of speaking, deconstructed it. Traces of him abound in Fluchère. But these hints and intimations need articulating and bringing together into a coherent account of the novel, if they are to stand any chance of displacing the canonical account. To this task I now turn.

II

Sterne's obsession with Locke included both dissent and admiration. Why the latter? What was it that Sterne found liberating in Locke's philosophy? One obvious though unexplored answer is: its nominalism. Locke is a nominalist both in his ontology and in his theory of knowledge. On the first count he holds that 'All things that exist . . . [are] . . . particulars' (*Essay*, III.iii.1), and that 'General and universal are creatures of the understanding' (*Essay*, III.iii.11). On the second count he held that all knowledge 'concerning the existence of anything answerable to an idea' (knowledge of whether anything that exists corresponds, for instance, to such ideas as those of 'an elephant, phoenix, motion or an angel, in my mind . . .') is knowledge 'only of particulars' (*Essay*, IV.xi.13). Claims as abstract and metaphysical as these might appear to have little bearing upon the mundane concerns of the novelist. But just because of the dominating generality of such a view its implications tend to ramify, becoming more specific as they do so. And because such a view concerns what we are to regard as ultimately real, its implications, as they proliferate, partition the areas into which they ramify between the putatively real and the putatively unreal, imposing a systematic 'vision' of how things stand in the world; in this case a nominalist one. Thus the distinction between particular and universal which defines metaphysical nominalism easily gives rise to further distinctions of a generally, though not metaphysically, nominalist stamp; such as those which define the essentially nominalist stance of political individualism, with its claim that it makes no sense to speak, say, of the Church, or the Aristocracy, or the Royal College of Surgeons as really existing entities, since they are at best conceptual fictions, 'creatures', to use Locke's phrase, 'of the understanding', ways in which the mind groups together for its own convenience the things which *really* exist, that is to say, particular human individuals.

Sterne nowhere pays explicit reverence to Locke's metaphysical nominalism. But it is at the heart of Locke's philosophical position, and the whole tenor of *Tristram Shandy* is in sympathy with the vision which it dominates. For Sterne, the things which truly exist in the human realm are not institutions or organizations (or ideas or theories) but particular human individuals, and whatever abstracts from their unshakeable and ultimate reality is the coinage of the mind. Christopher Ricks, accepting the canonical view that *Tristram Shandy* is haunted by the spectre of metaphysical privacy, turns that into a virtue by construing the novel as enforcing a sense of humility before the unknowable inwardness of another person: the obverse of Guildenstern's attitude to Hamlet.[9] While I think Ricks is right to take the book as a serious call to an essentially Christian humility towards one another, it seems to me that what this humility is supposed to be exercised about is not the unknowable inwardness of another person, but rather her or his concrete particularity, as that is made visible from the outside by his or her words and deeds. There is a running contrast in the book between what a person is when taken as a particular individual, and what he or she may appear to be when viewed as the bearer of a social role. Social role in Sterne always represents a way of masking, a form of deceit, and thus an evasion of the duties of the Christian life, whether the evasion takes the form of assuming a superior role or of transfixing another in an inferior one. By contrast, the revelation of one's own naked particularity, or the apprehension of the naked particularity of another, is always seen as the most fundamental kind of honesty: as both type and guarantor of virtue. If there is a Shakespearian parallel to Sterne's moral position it is to be found (significantly enough, given the moral contrast Nuttall seeks to establish between *Tristram Shandy* and *Lear*) not in Hamlet's rebuke to Guildenstern, but in Lear's vision of Edgar as manifesting the essence of humanity: 'Thou art the thing itself; unaccommodated man is no more but such a poor, bare, forked animal as thou art.'

The contrast between accommodated and unaccommodated man is to be seen, for instance, in Sterne's portrayal of Yorick and of Slop. Yorick is introduced as having

> made himself a country-talk by a breach of all decorum, which he had committed against himself, his station, and his office; ——and that was, in never appearing better, or otherwise mounted, than upon a lean, sorry, jack-ass of a horse, value about one pound fifteen shillings; who, to shorten all description of him, was full brother to Rosinante, as far as similitude congenial could make him; ...   (I.x.47)

Out of modesty Yorick offers all kinds of humorous excuses for this eccentricity; but the real reason for it is that every good horse he buys is borrowed by some neighbour upon some 'piteous application' and ruined, so that in the end the expense of continually buying new horses becomes such 'as to disable him from any other act of generosity in his parish' (I.x.50).

Yorick's object in riding a spavined horse is, in other words, to regain his power to bestow charity upon other, and perhaps needier, objects than self-appointed ones. To achieve this end he is prepared to sacrifice the conventional dignities and appearances of his social role. His eccentricity, because it deprives him of the overt trappings of the parsonical role, reduces him in the eyes of many of his neighbours from a parson to a mere individual man, and one, moreover, contemptible by reason of the broken-down horse he rides. The dangers of this abandonment, in the pursuit of *imitatio Christi*, of the comforts and immunities of appearing to others less as a man than as a concept, are compounded by his indifference to the 'great wigs' who control preferment; for Yorick, while no enemy to 'gravity as such', has declared 'open war upon' the sort of gravity which serves to mask the vices of the individual beneath the solemn generalities of the type, so that 'whenever it fell in his way, however sheltered and protected, he seldom gave it much quarter'. It is the mark of his indifference to the masks of false gravity that he appears 'as heteroclite a creature in all his declensions . . . as the kindliest climate could have engendered and put together' (I.x.55).

We thus have in Yorick a version of Chaucer's poor parson turned Christian martyr: a holy fool who, because he is prepared, in the service of the Christian life, to give up concealing his naked particularity beneath the generalities of social role, is destroyed by those for whom the social universal and its dignities are indispensable tools of deceit. The Shandys stand with him in their refusal of masking and the gains to be derived from it. It is because none of the family would ever wear 'my great-aunt Dinah's old black velvet mask', which had grown 'a little bald about the chin by frequently putting off and on, *before* she was got with child by the coachman . . .', that 'in all our numerous family, for these four generations, we count no more than one archbishop, a Welch judge, some three or four aldermen, and a single mountebank——' (VIII.iii.517). Slop, on the other hand, is a monster of jealous professional pride, whose concern for the dignities of his role go to the length of venting Ernulphus's curse (obligingly furnished by My Father, who is fascinated to see how far he will go) upon the head of Obadiah, for no better reason than that the latter, by his clumsiness in tying the knots of the green baize bag, has made Slop look a fool.

Two preliminary points need making. The first is that Sterne's moral preference for the plainness and honesty of unadorned individuality is entirely Lockeian. Oddly enough, it is in this very spirit that Locke attacks metaphor as a device for veiling the plain truth of things in a cloud of fictitious universals; and this will bear remembering when we come to enquire into the exact nature of Sterne's defence of 'wit' and rhetoric against Locke's strictures. The second is that a moral preference for the Christian who, like Yorick, prefers the reality of charity to its appearance has more to do with the morality of respect for truth and sound judgement than it has to do with the morality of sentiment. Yorick at least does not go in for ecstasies of moral emotion; he gets down to the business of freeing himself to do what he conceives to be his job by the quickest route and without fuss; and since he is clearly as much part of the moral backbone of the book as Toby, any decent reading must make room for him.

A second aspect of Locke's philosophy with which Sterne is wholly, and this time explicitly, in sympathy is Locke's rejection of Cartesian dualism, embodied in the remark, famous in its time, that it is

> not much more remote from our comprehension to conceive that God can, if he pleases, superadd to matter a faculty of thinking, than that he should superadd to it another substance with a faculty of thinking; since we know not wherein thinking consists, nor to what sort of substances the Almighty has been pleased to give that power.... (*Essay*, IV.iii.6)

Voltaire refers to this passage with warm approval in the *Lettres philosophiques*. Sterne makes the issue it deals with one of those contested between Nosarians and Antinosarians:

> God's power is infinite, cried the Nosarians, he can do any thing.
> He can do nothing, replied the Antinosarians, which implies contradictions.
> He can make matter think, said the Nosarians.
> As certainly as you can make a velvet cap out of a sow's ear, replied the Antinosarians. (IV, Slawkenbergius' Tale, 266)

Sterne here is echoing Locke: there is no weight to the argument that, since matter could not be supposed to have the power of thought, the soul must be an immaterial substance, having no essential connection with the body, because the properties and powers of substances lie beyond the limits of possible human knowledge. Such questions are idle ones, fit only to be debated between Nosarians and Antinosarians.

I want to suggest, now, that this is one of the points – there are plenty of others, as we shall see, and their effect is cumulative – at which Sterne distances himself from the solipsism, and the consequent pessimism about communication on any rational level, which has so frequently been attributed to him in this century. Solipsism is the child of Cartesian dualism: it is those who believe that body and mind are distinct ontological realms having no essential connection between them who, when they reflect that all commerce with another is commerce with his or her body, are led ineluctably to the conclusion that all our conjectures about what is passing in another's mind are tragically and irremediably underdetermined by the *type* of evidence we have for them.

There are, though, two objections to this way of exonerating Sterne from solipsism which deserve to be considered. The first is that Locke's point against dualism is a negative one only; that to doubt whether it is possible for us to know the truth or falsity of dualism need not commit one, and did not in fact commit Locke, to any positive doctrine (of a Wittgensteinian or Merleau-Pontyan kind, for instance) affirming the essential unity of mind and body. This is perfectly correct as regards Locke, but misleading as regards Sterne; for Sterne did push beyond Lockeian doubt about dualism to a positive affirmation of an essential connection between body and mind:

> Lodovicus Sorbonensis makes this entirely an affair of the body (ἐξωτερικὴ πρᾶξις) as he calls it—but he is deceived: the soul and body are joint-sharers in every thing they get: A man cannot dress, but his ideas get cloathed at the same time; and if he dresses like a gentleman, every one of them stands presented to his imagination, genteelized along with him—so that he has nothing to do, but take his pen, and write like himself. (IX.xiii.587–8)

The second objection is that Locke, whatever doubts he may have entertained about dualism at the level of metaphysics, is firmly committed to it at the level of his epistemology, philosophy of language and philosophy of mind, and that his central commitment to 'ideas', which are certainly mental states in a sense agreeable to Cartesian dualism, as the objects about which all an individual's cognitive processes are ultimately exercised and in terms of which all the words he uses are ultimately defined, is quite sufficient in itself to commit him to some form of solipsism. Of course, Locke himself did not regard himself as a solipsist because he thought, absurdly, that words defined solely in terms of essentially private

objects could nevertheless serve as vehicles for public acts of communication; but it is not necessary to know that one is a solipsist to
be one.

Once again, though, even if this argument, sketchy as it is, is more
or less on the right lines as a critique of Locke, it does not necessarily
follow that the critique contained in it transfers *pari passu* to Sterne.
For Sterne, as we shall see, rejected the thesis that to understand how
another speaker uses a word it is necessary to call up in one's mind a
mental content – an idea – matching the corresponding mental
content in the mind of the speaker. With it, of course, he necessarily
rejected the thesis that the cognitive processes of each individual
operate solely upon events private to that individual. One reason
why *Tristram Shandy* has been taken as expounding some such view
is that it is, in one aspect, an extended *reductio ad absurdum* of just
that way of looking at things.

So far I have been drawing attention to aspects of Locke's nominalism which chimed in with Sterne's sense of the primacy, and in a
certain sense the concreteness, of the individual person. There are
other aspects of Locke's individualism which did not appeal to
Sterne. Locke's theory of knowledge shares with his political theory a
type of individualism which it would not be unfair to call 'pro-
pertarian'. Both are from one point of view theories of *justification*;
they explain what it is to *have a right to* one's opinions or one's
property. The explanations offered in the two cases are not dissimilar. Locke's political theory derives the individual's right to
property from an original right to his own body and its powers which
morally excludes both slavery and the surrender of absolute power to
a sovereign. It is on the one hand the impossibility of separating the
activity of the body, considered as labour, from what it has once been
'mixed with', and on the other hand the need to secure a material
basis for independence of conscience, without which an individual's
power to determine his own acts would be forfeit, which requires the
extension of the original property right which an individual enjoys
over his body to cover the fruits of his labour. Similarly, what gives a
man the right to his opinions is his own mental labour, guided by
familiar kinds of puritan virtue: independence of mind, disinclination
to repose one's own views idly and slavishly upon those of others,
refusal of the pleasures of metaphor and allusion in favour of the
intellectual virtues of truthfulness, exact discrimination and sound
judgement. The propertarian metaphor is directly applied to knowledge at the outset of Locke's *Essay*, when Locke characterizes the
Reader he wishes to address as 'he who has raised himself above the
alms-basket, and not content to live lazily on scraps of begged

opinions, sets his own thoughts on work, to find and follow truth . . .'
(*Essay*, Epistle to the Reader).

Sterne not only notices this propertarianism of the mind, but
explicitly mocks it: 'my father . . . picked up an opinion, Sir, as a man
in a state of nature picks up an apple. – It becomes his own – and if
he is a man of spirit, he would lose his life rather than give it up – '
(II.xxxiv.228). Elsewhere a mixture of Locke's theory of property
and associationism is brought in to explain how it is that a woman of
substance like Mrs Wadman cannot sit in her own house and think of
a man without insensibly coming to regard him as her property:

> here, for her soul, she can see him in no light without mixing something of
> her own goods and chattels along with him—till by reiterated acts of such
> combination, he gets foisted into her inventory ——
> —And then good night. (VIII.viii.522)

Sterne's point, it hardly needs to be said, is that Locke's ideal reader
is not to be found in nature. Our opinions are not, on the whole, the
fruit of intellectual industry: we pick them up like apples or fall into
them through habit; and the pertinacity with which we defend them
is a comic parody of the righteous energy with which Locke's heroic
individual defends, as the material basis of his exercise of independence of conscience, that with which he has mixed his labour.

Sterne's dislike of Locke's propertarian epistemology forms, I
think, the background, necessary to full understanding, of his attack
on Locke's distinction between Wit and Judgement. The two topics
are certainly connected in Locke, the distinction forming an essential
part of Locke's account of how the individual should order his
dealings with language and with nature if he is to rise above the
'alms-basket' and set his own thoughts to work in pursuit of truth.
The distinction is a very simple one. Wit, according to Locke,
consists in 'the assemblage of ideas, and putting those together
with quickness and variety wherein can be found any resemblance
or congruity, thereby to make up pleasant pictures and agreeable
visions in the fancy' (*Essay*, II.xi.2). Wit aims, in other words, not at
truth but at pleasure. It is unhinged from the Reality Principle, and
thus akin to madness, a connection which Locke draws explicitly in
the chapter 'Of the Association of Ideas' which he added to the
fourth edition of the *Essay*:

> Some of our ideas have a natural correspondence and connexion one with
> another; it is the office and excellency of our reason to trace these, and
> hold them together in that union and correspondence which is founded in
> their peculiar beings. Besides this, there is another connexion of ideas

wholly owing to chance or custom: ideas that in themselves are not at all
of kin, come to be so united in some men's minds that it is very hard to
separate them. . . . When this combination is settled, and whilst it lasts, it
is not in the power of reason to help us, and relieve us from the effects
of it.   (*Essay*, ii.xxxiii.5/13)

The role of Lockeian judgement 'lies quite on the other side, in
separating carefully one from another ideas wherein can be found the
least difference, *thereby to avoid being misled by similitude*' (*Essay*,
ii.xi.2; my italics). The task of Judgement, in other words, is to
pierce through the deceits of Wit to those plain facts of 'natural
correspondence and connexion' which 'it is the office and excellency
of our reason to trace'.

Why did Sterne think this seemingly rather sensible distinction so
pernicious? One reason, as he makes clear in the Author's Preface,
with its engaging analogy of Wit and Judgement as two knobs on the
back of the same chair, which would look absurd without either, is
that Locke's way of distinguishing them turns Wit and Judgement
into irreconcilable opposites, so that it becomes hard to see, if one
accepts the justice of what Locke says, how one and the same mind
could lead both the Life of Judgement, as it were, and the Life of Wit.
But I do not think this goes quite to the heart of the matter. Locke's
account of Judgement describes, in a rough-and-ready way, the
characteristic stance of a trained scientific observer whose job is to
record natural regularities. From this it is a short step to the thought
that the members of a community wholly dedicated to the life of
Lockeian judgement would not be sharply differentiated, or easily
differentiable, as individuals. For what could differentiate them?
What Lockeian judgement does for us is to make us into efficient
recording devices; and to the extent that a recording device *is*
efficient – unpolluted, for instance, by the inanities of Lockeian wit –
it will say exactly the same thing as any other efficient recording
device.

But how am I to enter into any sort of human relationship with a
being which, because it has opted exclusively for Lockeian judgement, operates exclusively like that? Normally, when I am addressed
by another human being, I encounter a sharply differentiated personality whose uniqueness expresses itself in the style of every
utterance and gesture: a being 'heteroclite in all its dimensions'.
The conversation of a being exclusively given over to Lockeian
judgement, since it would consist entirely in the recital of types and
instances of 'natural correspondence and connexion', would afford
no such possibilities of differentiation. But now we see the oddity

inherent in the idea of entering into ordinary human relationships with *either* the Lockeian Man of Judgement *or* the Lockeian Man of Wit. If I cannot be *addressed* (but only informed) by a barometer in good working order, neither can I be addressed by a deranged barometer.

I do not, of course, think that this thought occurred to Sterne in just this form. But we have textual evidence that a thought did occur to him which comes to much the same thing. Sterne, notoriously, prided himself on the 'dramatic' qualities of his sermons. Such a sermon, like *Tristram Shandy* itself, is a work of pathetic Wit. But the object of such a sermon is not to give pleasure; rather its purpose is to hold up a mirror to the congregation which hears it; to invite them to reflect seriously on themselves, to *see* themselves *in a new light*. The author of such sermons is thus less well placed than most people to accept Locke's contention that the aim of Wit is not truth but pleasure. In the Author's Preface Sterne makes just this sermon-writer's claim for the cognitive aims and powers of Wit: it holds up a mirror; not, admittedly, to extra-human Nature, but to its hearers and readers as individual human beings.

> Didius, the great church lawyer, in his code *de fartandi et illustrandi fallaciis*, doth maintain and make fully appear, That an illustration is no argument,—nor do I maintain the wiping of a looking-glass clean, to be a syllogism; — but you all, may it please your worships, see the better for it. . . .   (III.xx.203)

The reference to the looking-glass here provides compelling textual evidence that Sterne's reason for disliking Locke's denigration of Wit is not merely the trade-union one that it makes life difficult for 'poor Wits', but the philosophical (to be precise, epistemological) one that Lockeian judgement, while it may suffice to reveal natural regularity in the physical world, cannot focus upon the particular beings that we are. Wit, like a looking-glass, in other words, is needed to *show us ourselves*, to allow us to bring into focus what is particular and idiosyncratic about our mental physiognomies, in order that we may become less like Phutatorius or the 'great wigs' who persecute Yorick, who appear in their own estimation less as individual men than as beings so clothed in the dignified generalities of status and role as to resemble so many perambulating universals.

If we put this together with Sterne's mockery of Locke's pro-pertarian theory of knowledge, and with his insistence that Wit and Judgement are complementaries rather than opposites, we see what he would be at. As individual human beings we are creatures of Wit, our minds formed not by intellectual labour directed towards the accurate tracing of natural regularities, but by the accumulation over time of ideas picked up in ways determined by all the hazards of personal predilection and circumstance. Our tenure of the acres of the mind is not *de jure* but only *de facto*. Only Wit – exercised with judgement – can offer such creatures a mirror in which to perceive themselves. Wit so understood, however, is not Locke's *Wit*: a pleasant verbal game for intellectual wastrels with the real possibility of a resulting madness lurking in the background. I think it is perhaps because of the Lockeian assimilation of wit to madness that the family name of the Shandys is a dialect word for a madman or eccentric: it is to point the moral that human life takes over from the recording of natural regularity at exactly the point at which, for Locke, madness (or Wit) takes over from Judgement. But the whole point of this seemingly perverse grasping of the Lockeian nettle is, as we shall see, that there is a way of understanding the nature and role in human life of the verbal devices of wit which altogether blunts its sting, and makes wit not the opposite but the necessary partner of judgement. To pursue that understanding, however, we must turn to Sterne's treatment of language and the meaning of words.

III

Toby and Mrs Wadman are at a standstill over the different meanings they attach to the word 'place'. Sterne's authorial voice intervenes: 'This requires a second translation:——it shews what little knowledge is got by mere words – we must go up to the first springs' (IX.x.595). Is what we are witnessing in this passage Fluchère's *faillite de la logique et des arts du langage*? Does it, and others like it, offer evidence for Nuttall's suggestion that, 'while Locke retained his faith in the intellect and mistrusted the sub-rational part of the human mind, Sterne may be said to have presented the opposite view'?[10]

In one sense the tenor of the passage is entirely Lockeian. Abuse of medieval and Aristotelian philosophy for trifling with words, and an accompanying parade of mistrust of language *per se* is an intellectual fashion that comes into England with the Renaissance and the first stirrings of the scientific revolution. Bacon, Hobbes, Locke, Berkeley; all have their ritual expressions of mistrust of language, and all affirm in one way or another that 'we must go up to the first springs'. Locke, in his chapter 'Of the Imperfection of Words', observes that 'The imperfection of words is the doubtfulness of their signification' (*Essay*, III.ix.4). Doubtfulness of signification has various causes. The ideas words stand for are sometimes very complex; the ideas brought together under a single name sometimes have no 'certain connexion in nature', and so no 'settled standard any where in nature existing to rectify and adjust them by', and so on. Locke's remedy for these and other imperfections is the apparently sound and scientific one of giving exact definitions and sticking to them. By definition, after all, we may hope to make it absolutely clear and determinate which ideas are supposed to be called up by which word.

The object of purifying language in this way is to transform it into the fit instrument of Lockeian judgement: a neutral recording device by whose means everything in the world can be made known and rendered intelligible to anyone, no matter what his or her individual standpoint. But to formulate the Lockeian ideal of a perfect language in this way is at once to reveal that it is in a certain respect self-defeating. Language so purified can render an account and mediate an understanding of every particular in the world save one: another individual speaker. For to encounter another speaker is precisely to encounter a use of words, a connection of word with idea, different from my own. And the difference is not merely that he or she labels familiar groups of ideas in an unfamiliar way: says 'refute' where I would say 'rebut', or something of the sort. If that were the extent of the difficulty, Lockeian punctiliousness in the definition of terms could suffice to deal with it.

The difficulty goes deeper: it is that the Other *connects up ideas* in a different way: perceives different patterns of connection and relationship in the world. Sterne rubs the reader's, and Locke's, nose in this difficulty in the celebrated passage in which news of Master Bobby's death reaches the servants' hall:

> ——My young master in London is dead! said Obadiah—
> ——A green satin night-gown of my mother's, which had been twice scoured, was the first idea which Obadiah's exclamation brought into Susannah's head.—Well might Locke write a chapter upon the imperfections of words. (v.vii.354)

Why should one not read the last sentence of this absolutely straight, as an entirely unironic comment on the impossibility of communication by means of language given the difficulties of engineering a stable transmission of 'ideas' from one mind to another by words alone? What militates against such a reading is, of course, the fact that there can be no serious question here but that Susannah has *understood perfectly well what Obadiah is saying*. If she had not grasped the import of his words – that Bobby is dead – her mind could not have leapt, as it does, to the green satin nightgown she expects to be given as a consequence of Mrs Shandy's going into mourning. So, in the sense Locke has in mind of an impediment in the smooth transmission of factual information from speaker to hearer, Obadiah's words suffer from no 'imperfection' at all; on the contrary, they have performed their task admirably. What is imperfect must then be – can only be – Locke's account of how the transmission of information by means of words is accomplished. It cannot, that is, be by means of the standardized, machine-like binding of idea to word which Locke postulates, and which allows no difference in the reconstruction of the world as a network of connections of ideas between one rational mind and another, since the entirely idiosyncratic but entirely plausible dance of associations in Susannah's mind shows us, by the way in which it not only fails to impede her understanding of what Obadiah is saying, but actually depends upon that understanding, that that must be nonsense; and so serves to remind us once again of the gap between plausible philosophical theorizing and the everyday facts of human experience and the everyday functioning of language.

But if language as we have it functions perfectly well, what can Sterne mean when he says, apropos of Toby and Mrs Wadman, 'it shews what little knowledge is got by mere words'? If that is not an expression of mistrust of language, what is it?

Well, Sterne certainly does warn us (like Fielding, another sceptic where lexicography was concerned) not to trust *definitions*; but he mistrusts *them*, it appears, because *they* manifest in turn a mistrust of the ordinary confidence in the workings of language which, in most of the occasions of everyday life, we share with one another, and which is an expression, perhaps, of deeper kinds of trust in one another. 'Eugenius, said I, stepping before him, and laying my hand upon his breast, – to define – is to distrust' (III.xxi.225). Definition and translation, as Quine has taught us, are close kin in so far as each comforts our inability to understand words by offering us other words. What Sterne is saying about Mrs Wadman's 'I will not touch it' is that in such a case definition – 'translation' – besides being mistrustful is no help: '——we must go up to first springs'. Going up to first springs here can only mean grasping the nature of Mrs Wadman's worries about Toby's wound. Locke, in his chapters upon the imperfections of words and their remedy, assumes throughout that rational discourse and thought are only possible if it is in the power of *the word alone* to determine which ideas it will evoke in a reader's mind. It is in the attempt to give words this power, in effect to nullify what Derrida calls *différance* or *dissémination*, that Locke embarks upon the first of many empiricist programmes for the purification of language.

But, of course, words can have no such power. As I have, in effect, argued in Chapter 1, what 'ideas' a word evokes must depend partly upon the situation of its users and hearers, so that the connection between word and idea in each particular case can only be grasped by coming to understand that situation.[11] I need to know a person's history – how he or she has come to inhabit the particular standpoint from the midst of which she or he speaks and understands, before I can know how word and idea will come together in his or her mind. It is to this end that Sterne offers us in *Tristram Shandy*, though in a very different sense from Locke, 'a history . . . of what passes in a man's own mind'. The history uncovered by Locke's 'historical plain method' is, as I noted earlier, a history of *justification*: a tale told to establish a right, to own property or to lay claim to knowledge. Sterne's history is not that. Rather, it is a tale told in order that we may understand what the words in which it is told mean to the teller; and understanding that, understand him.

The need to unfold such histories is one of the main motors of Sterne's digressiveness. Thus uncle Toby is left at the outset suspended at the start of a sentence, because 'to enter rightly into my uncle Toby's sentiments upon this matter, you must be made to enter first a little into his character . . .' (I.xxi.87). But 'entering into his sentiments', as Sterne understands it, is not a matter of being told a few psychological generalities. We must be made familiar with Toby's entire life to date. We must learn of his conduct at the siege of Namur, of his convalescence, of his relationship with Trim and the origins of his hobby-horse, before we are equipped to understand a word he says.

Two things are to be noticed here. The first is that these narrations, to be effective, require the concurrence of both wit and judgement: wit because it is the faculty which detects congruity, and what we have to grasp are the alien congruities which have impressed another as important; judgement because it is the faculty which assesses difference, and what we have to assess is the gap of difference which separates another, 'heteroclite in all his dimensions', from us and from his fellows. The second is that, when we have heard, and with a due exercise of wit and judgement understood, Toby's history, we really are in a position to understand what he says: 'to enter rightly into his sentiments'. This is the ultimate, clinching reason why I find in Sterne no trace of the tragic sense of the isolation of separate Cartesian consciousnesses detected in him by Priestley, Nuttall and so many others. For Sterne the issue is never how we are to penetrate to a character's *consciousness*, conceived in classical Cartesian fashion as a theatre of purely spiritual events having no essential connection with the body; but simply how we are to make sense of what he or she *says*. Hence Sterne's refusal of the aid of Momus' glass, by whose aid we might have 'viewed the soul stark naked'. We do not need it, because we can 'draw my uncle Toby's character from his HOBBY-HORSE' (I.xxiii.98). And again, when Toby sends his humble service to Slop under the impression that the latter is making a bridge not for Tristram's nose but for Toby's fortifications,

> Had my uncle Toby's head been a Savoyard's box, and my father peeping in all the time at one end of it, —it could not have given him a more distinct conception of the operations of my uncle Toby's imagination than what he had. . . . (II.xxvi.221)

There are, in short, plenty of highly particularized subjects in Sterne, but no trace whatsoever of the Cartesian *présence* on which all literary celebration of the individual is supposed in some quarters to depend. There is plenty of verbal confusion dividing one character from another, true enough. But, first, to be divided from another person momentarily by a different way of taking words is not at all the same thing as being divided from others *per se* in the *in principle* irremediable way envisaged by the type of philosophical sceptic who has been with us since Descartes. And, secondly, it is precisely the verbal confusions to which Sterne's characters fall victim which, when taken in the context of situation and standpoint, make the workings of their minds transparently clear, both to us as readers and to other characters in the novel.

But what, it will be asked, is My Father, if not an object-lesson in the impotence of language and rationality to achieve genuine communication between differently constituted individuals? He is an object-lesson in the impotence of the verbal, and of a style of reasoning which restricts itself to the shuffling of words against other words, to achieve that; which is not quite the same thing. As such he constitutes, among other things, a Lockeian deconstruction of Locke's contention that judgement lives by opposition to wit; for the more My Father tries to live by Lockeian judgement alone, the more he becomes a monster of Lockeian wit, the weeded garden of his mind continually foundering under the luxuriance of his private fantasies and obsessions.

Mutual incomprehension is not, as a matter of fact, either a constant or a universal condition of life for the inhabitants of Shandy Hall. Toby and Trim, generally speaking, understand one another perfectly. Mrs Shandy understands her husband well enough to allow him absolute precedence in verbal disputation while keeping all practical matters of concern to the good order of the household entirely under her own control. And both Yorick and Toby, on occasion, understand Walter's metaphysical conceits well enough to rebuke him for them. What injures My Father's understanding, and his ability either to understand or to make himself understood by others, is simply his desire to reduce everything, including the death of one son and the upbringing of the other, to words. He believes implicitly in the Lockeian ideal of language as a neutral recording device by means of which all knowledge and all understanding may be conveyed to a man without his ever needing to change the standpoint from which he looks at things; a view of language which, as we have seen, comes to be sharply at odds both with Locke's empiricism and with his nominalist respect for the particular the moment we attempt to apply it to the special case of knowledge and understanding of other human individuals. I cannot understand another without admitting the possibility of a standpoint alien to my own. I cannot understand her, or him, if I insist that the words in which that understanding is to be formulated must be my words, honouring just those conceptual distinctions which my discourse honours, resonant with just those connotations with which they have always resonated for me.

One way of replying to this would be to argue that the Other has no grip on the language I use, because what words mean depends not on their intersections with the lives, interests and predicaments of individuals, but simply on other words. My Father, not unlike some recent critics, is, though passionately interested in the intersection of language with itself, profoundly uninterested in its intersection with the extra-linguistic. When Toby, frustrated by his inability to explain to his visitors in words the technicalities of fortification, finds 'his life . . . put in jeopardy by words' (ii.ii.108), he takes the obvious step of securing a large map of the fortifications of Namur and having it pasted down upon a board. He thus restores his lines of communication with others by considering how words are involved with things and doing what is necessary to make his tale comprehensible to others *from their point of view*; while incidentally laying the foundations of the hobby which secures both his physical recovery and his future mental health. One feels that the response of his brother, faced with the same difficulty, would have been to settle down to write a treatise analogous to the *Tristrapaedia*, which would have settled the exact definition of terms in fortification, but would have left the problem of communication with visitors exactly where it stood when Toby bought his map.

It seems to me, in short, that what differentiates the two Shandy brothers in the novel is not the contrast between reason and feeling, the rational and the sub-rational; but rather the contrast between two types of rationality, one verbal, self-enclosed and trusting more in the power of definition to regiment the meanings of words than in the possibility that an attentive and inquiring attitude to others might allow their meanings room to emerge; the other more interested in empirical enquiry than in disputation; prepared to let words and their meanings wait upon the investigation of things and their properties. It is, of course, commonplace for the New Philosophy of the century preceding Sterne to distinguish in its own favour between its own mathematical and empirical interests and the allegedly merely verbal and disputatious pursuits of the Schoolmen. One thinks of the stinging abuse heaped on the Aristotelians by Hobbes in the chapter 'Of Darkness through Vain Philosophy' in the *Leviathan*; or of Locke's self-effacing praise of the 'mighty designs' afoot in 'an age that produces such masters as the great Huygenius and the incomparable Mr Newton, with some other of that strain' in the Epistle to the Reader which opens the *Essay*. Readers who take uncle Toby's hobby-horse to be no more than an engagingly dotty obsession with as much and as little claim to be taken seriously as Walter's parallel obsessions with Noseology or the *Tristrapaedia* miss something here, I think. For when we turn to Sterne's list, in Volume II, of the reading undertaken by Toby in pursuit of his interest in warfare we find not only that it is very heavy reading indeed, in the mathematics of ballistics and the practical engineering of fortifications, but that it includes many of the leading natural scientists of the day, including Galileo and Torricelli:

> Towards the beginning of the third year ... my uncle Toby found it necessary to understand a little of projectiles: – And having judged it best to draw his knowledge from the fountain-head, he began with N. Tartaglia ... He proceeded next to Galileo and Torricellius. ...
>
> (II.iii.110)

Sterne ends this passage with a gesture of mock horror at the intricacy of the mazes into which Toby's reading is leading him, ' – O my uncle! my uncle Toby'; but the point is made all the same. Toby's reading, and the systematic urge he displays to penetrate further and further into the mathematical intricacies of the physical world mark him as a man of the new age as surely as Walter's obsession with words and definition marks him as a figure rooted in the medieval past as viewed from the perspective of the New Philosophy. One of the things Sterne wishes us to note, I think, is the way in which Toby's interest in the facts of ballistics is of a piece with his interest in the facts of other people's lives – his willingness to sit patiently and listen while the Other unfolds his story – and contrasts with Walter's tendency to reduce everything to a skein of words emptily mirroring other words.

It is worth pointing out once again that the moral predilections Sterne displays here, just as in the case of his preference for Yorick's unadorned plain Christianity over the pomp of the 'great wigs' who destroy him, are thoroughly Lockeian ones. Locke, after all, is in his period the philosopher above all others who recalls us from mazy verbal speculation to attentive enquiry into the empirical and the particular. Sterne's modest point is merely that the great philosopher's epistemology and theory of language, while perhaps well adapted to secure these admirable aims in the study of the natural world, are ludicrously ill-adapted to secure them in the study of our fellow creatures, and so provide not only a fit but a proper object of ridicule for a ludic novel which, none the less, has its moral dimension. This brings me, finally, to the crucial issue of the moral outlook of *Tristram Shandy*, and its alleged exaltation of the passional over the cognitive in morals.

IV

Volume VIII contains two vignettes which are seldom discussed but which seem to me to touch the nerve of Sterne's moral outlook. In the first, Trim is about to begin his story of the King of Bohemia and his seven castles when Toby notices – 'the eye of goodness espieth all things', interjects Sterne's narratorial voice, neatly making precisely the connection between virtue and cognition which critics allege to be absent from the book – that Trim's Montero-cap, which he values intensely because it was a present from his brother Tom before the latter was gaoled by the Inquisition, is lying on the grass instead of decorating Trim's head. Toby touches it interrogatively with his cane, and Trim picks it up, but

> casting a glance of humiliation as he did it, upon the embroidery of the fore-part, which being dismally tarnished and frayed moreover in some of the principal leaves and boldest parts of the pattern, he laid it down again betwixt his two feet, in order to moralize upon the subject.
> —'Tis every word of it but too true, cried my uncle Toby, that thou art about to observe—
> —'*Nothing in this world, Trim, is made to last for ever.*'
> —But when tokens, dear Tom, of thy love and remembrance wear out, said Trim, what shall we say? (VIII.xix.535)

This introduces a long passage of wonderful, crazy and intimate conversational meandering between Toby and Trim, in which they wander from the story of the King of Bohemia and his castles (which never gets told) to various details of their own campaigning, in the course of which Trim tells the history of his own wound and his convalescent relationship with the fair Beguine, his first experience of love. Sterne's capacity to depict servants as real, individual people, with neither sentimentality nor condescension, touched on already in the case of Susannah and Obadiah, shows to good effect here.

The second vignette also involves Trim's Montero-cap. My Father is expressing scepticism about the prospects of a marriage between Toby and Mrs Wadman. Trim loyally stands up for his master:

> I would lay my Montero-cap, said Trim—now Trim's Montero-cap, as I once told you, was his constant wager; and having furbished it up that very night, in order to go upon the attack—it made the odds look more considerable—I would lay, an' please your honour, my Montero-cap to a shilling—was it proper, continued Trim (making a bow), to offer a wager before your honours—
>
> —There is nothing improper in it, said my father—'tis a mode of expression; for in saying thou would'st lay thy Montero-cap to a shilling— all thou meanest is this—that thou believest—
>
> —Now, What do'st thou believe?　　　　　　　(VIII.xxxiv.562–3)

Note how here, as in other passages at which Sterne sets the wisdom which reveals itself in Trim's untutored conversation against My Father's settled conviction of his brother's servant's near-idiocy, My Father's tolerant contempt puts Trim in his social place. My Father accepts neither Trim's freedom of speech nor his apology for it. Nor does he *waive* the proffered apology; he merely dismisses it as unnecessary on the grounds that Trim's offer to wager his Montero-cap is in any case little more than unmeaning blather. Trim is, in effect, reduced from the status of a fellow human being, whose apologies one either waives, rejects or accepts, to that of a natural phenomenon whose babblings are not to be taken seriously as demanding a response in kind, but are more properly to be treated as subjects for dispassionate and objective intellectual analysis on the part of Trim's intellectual and social superiors.

The analysis to which My Father proceeds to subject Trim's remark is, moreover, of an entirely verbal kind, somewhat redolent of an entry for an Analysis competition in the heyday of what used to be called Ordinary Language Philosophy. Its thesis is that 'I will wager my Montero-cap to a shilling that p' means the same thing as 'I believe that p'. In one sense of 'means' this is fair enough: My

Father's analysans does more or less catch what its analysandum *comes to*. But there is more to catching another person's meaning than the ability to say what his remarks, literally speaking, come to. What My Father's bit of reductive analysis leaves out is what the Montero-cap means to Trim. It is his constant wager because of its associations for him. He swears by what he is; by all that he feels for his brother Tom. Swearing by that before Toby, moreover, he swears before and on behalf of someone who knows and understands by what he swears; who is intimate with Tom, the Jew's widow, the fair Beguine and the other figures who people Trim's narrative imagination and make him what he is, as the figures who people Tristram's narrative imagination make *him* what *he* is. In choosing his Montero-cap as his wager Trim aligns his trust in and admiration for Toby with what is for him the paradigm of confidence, his trust in his relationship to his brother Tom. All this is invisible to Walter, because, as usual, he is more interested in chopping words than in paying attention.

The moral to be drawn from the contrast between these two episodes, it seems to me, is that while Toby's capacity to feel for others is certainly a part of his goodness, it is not the whole of it, and not as central a part of it as his capacity to observe and listen. 'The eye of goodness espieth all things.' Toby's goodness is not just a matter of Humean sentiment, but includes an essential cognitive component. There is nothing 'sub-rational', for instance, about the way in which Toby anticipates exactly what Trim is about to say about the state of his cap, unless one is prepared to say that insight into what is passing in another's mind stemming from an intelligent and compassionate interest in that person's history and situation is not an exercise of rationality. Occasionally, of course, this capacity for putting himself in another's place goes over the top, as in the frequently quoted passage in which Toby apostrophizes the fly and sets it at liberty. But even this is not just an excess of *feeling*, but an attempt to push the comprehension of alien *situations* beyond all feasible limit. The case contrasts with the other frequently cited episode in which Tristram feeds a macaroon to an ass. This, it seems to me, is to be read, not as Sterne guiltily noticing how easily high-flown moral sentimentalism shades into moral self-indulgence and trying to pass it as a joke, but as part of the status of the book as a *memorial* to Toby and Yorick. It is essential to this side of the book that Tristram should not appear as the moral equal of Toby. In the case of the ass the difference is precisely that whereas Tristram finds himself all too self-consciously caught up both in the pleasures of benevolence and in the oddity of seeing whether an ass will eat a macaroon, Toby, as in the case of the fly, would have been wholly preoccupied with the job of grasping and responding to the situation of the ass.

Toby's interest in understanding others' situations brings it about that for him, as for Sterne himself, the unit of meaning is the complete conversational transaction, taken in the context both of immediate situation and of the personal histories which lie behind it. So for him, the pursuit of understanding involves turning towards people, hearing out their stories – that of Le Fever is another example – and so 'entering into their sentiments': into the particular inflections of meaning and connotation that words and things acquire in the context of a personal history.

My Father pursues a different conception of understanding, founded upon the hope of mastering the human confusions of Shandy Hall by exhaustively describing and explaining them in some neutral and universal language of scientific explanation: a language, to use Derrida's words, '*sans différance . . . à la fois absolument vive et absolument morte*'.[12] Thus his first thought, when presented by Mrs Shandy with a son to bring up, is not to turn towards the child, to listen to what he will say, to hear what strange twist of *différance*, of Wit, he will give to language; but to turn away from him towards words, towards the petrified, witless language of Lockeian judgement, and to compose a manual for the child's education: a *Tristrapaedia*. But the fate of the *Tristrapaedia* is identical with that of Tristram's project of recounting his life in the novel we are reading. Life moves on, and overflows the toils of language. Tristram is effectively brought up by Mrs Shandy, and My Father is left, at what I find the bleakest moment of the book, 'drawing a sun-dial, for no better purpose than to be buried under ground' (v.xxi.369).

My Father's urge to desert the concrete trials of the relationship between father and son by sublimating it into words goes with a more generalized Manichaean contempt for the concrete, the bodily and the particular. He is happiest with the mental and the universal, which no doubt goes far to explain his son's love-affair with Locke. Nuttall is right, I think, to discern in Sterne a fundamental disrespect for the distinction, which so mesmerized the Augustans, between the rational and the animal part of our natures. But where Nuttall sees a slack and rather shifty disregard for a distinction still worthy of respect, I see a deliberate and largely successful attempt to subvert an intellectual delusion. When Walter, platonizing after Ficinus, attempts to instruct Toby and Yorick in the distinction between two kinds of love, one rational, the other natural, Toby (this is one of the points at which he catches Walter's drift perfectly adequately) responds, 'Pray, brother, what has a man who believes in God to do with this?' My Father does not believe that 'soul and body are joint-sharers in all they get'. He wants soul to be in the saddle, and adopts Hilarion the hermit's way of speaking of his body as his ass; an eccentricity which with poetic justice leads him into the public appearance of having made a coarse and brutal jest calling into question his brother's sexual powers when Toby innocently takes this odd turn of phrase to embody a kindly enquiry concerning his wound.

This anti-Manichaean burlesque of Sterne's seems to me, as I suggested a moment ago, very much of a piece with his admiration for Locke. Besides the obvious Lockeian echoes – the redirection of attention from universals to particulars, the scepticism about dualism, the insistence on the importance of accurate attention to the empirical detail of things – which I have now, perhaps, stressed *ad nauseam*, there is a deeper Lockeian flavour to this aspect of Sterne's comedy. The aim of Locke's philosophy is to reconcile the impulse towards theory with the practical and empirical side of our life by showing that all effective theorizing is rooted in the latter and cannot in the end transcend it.

> Men may find matter sufficient to busy their heads and occupy their hands with variety, delight, and satisfaction, if they will not boldly quarrel with their own constitution, and throw away the blessings their hands are filled with, because they are not big enough to grasp every thing.   (Essay, i.i.5)

A parallel reconciliation seems to me to be the central aim of Sterne's comedy: the heart of the Shandyan vision of things. From a Shandyan viewpoint we are not rational spirits tethered to the bodies of brutes. We are creatures formed by accident and circumstance; our very language constituted as much by Wit as by Judgement. But we can nevertheless hope to achieve something in the way of order, community and mutual understanding if, instead of turning away to the endless, deserted vistas of verbal analysis and explication which invite us when we attempt to treat ourselves as objects for scientific or pseudo-scientific dissection, we turn towards one another and listen, while a story is told, a history unfolded. This, rather than the Humean assertion of the priority of something called 'feeling' over something called 'reason', is what seems to me to be at stake in *Tristram Shandy*. As I have tried to show, the moral outlook of the novel is less schematic and also less banal than that. It is an outlook from which we ourselves could learn something.

Chapter 3
Forster and Moore

I

The influence of Moore on the young Forster is vouched for by Leonard Woolf: 'That is the point: under the surface all six of us, Desmond, Lytton, Saxon, Morgan, Maynard and I, had been permanently inoculated with Moore and Moorism. . . .'[1] The search for traces of Moorism in the novels, however, has turned up relatively little. P. N. Furbank in his *Life* (1977) is skeptical about even the likelihood of literary gold in these bleak philosophical uplands: 'Too much has been made of the influence of G. E. Moore on him, for he never read Moore; but the epigraph to Moore's *Principia Ethica*, "Everything is what it is, and not another thing", hits off his own idea of the Cambridge "truth".'[2] Respect for truth and for Reality — for the hardness and solidity of the actual – are certainly to be gained from reading Moore, and no doubt these things are part of what Forster and his friends did gain from him. Woolf again: 'The main things which Moore instilled deep into our minds and characters were his peculiar passion for truth, for clarity and common sense, and a passionate belief in certain values.'[3] But these admirable if rather generalized virtues might be imbibed from any number of philosophers of stature. Did none of Moore's peculiar and characteristic doctrines exert any permanent influence on those 'inoculated with Moore and Moorism'?

S. P. Rosenbaum, in an interesting and ingenious article,[4] argues for the direct influence on *The Longest Journey* of some of Moore's epistemological doctrines – those expressed in his famous article 'The Refutation of Idealism'. Moore claims there *inter alia* that there is an irreducible difference between what is perceived and the perceiving of it, and Rosenbaum connects this kind of Realism with the ethical kind which consists in distinguishing carefully between the ideas we

98

are tempted to form of others and what they are, and are like really. There is something in this, and Rosenbaum is sustained not only by the fact that Realism was of the essence of the revolution in philosophy wrought by Moore and Russell in the Cambridge of Forster's youth, but by Forster's own account of the influences that went into the novel: 'There was the metaphysical idea of Reality ("the cow is there"): there was the ethical idea that reality must be faced (Rickie won't face Stephen) . . . .'[5]

But the connection thus established between metaphysical and ethical Realism seems more curious than fruitful; it is not clear in the end how much it can be made to contribute to our reading of the novel. Rosenbaum himself sees the problem: 'It is, of course, not necessary to know anything about Moore's "The Refutation of Idealism" to see that *The Longest Journey* is a novel about appearance and reality. What an awareness of Moore's philosophy can do for criticism of the novel is to help it avoid misinterpretations.'[6]

Unfortunately the 'misinterpretation' which Rosenbaum offers as a test of his reading is the generally accepted reading which makes Ansell as nearly the embodiment of truth as critical rigour, force of intellect and sound human sympathies can make a man. If Forster was at the time of writing the novel the consistent Moorean Realist that Rosenbaum wishes to make of him, then this cannot be, for Ansell fails to get his fellowship because he has read too much Hegel, and is in other ways tainted with Idealism. Rosenbaum's way around this is to treat Ansell as a flawed character whose 'sense of reality' needs to be 'corrected and completed by Stephen Wonham'. I find this unconvincing, as does Furbank: 'the trouble with this is that, whenever Ansell's philosophical inconsistencies are noted in the novel, Forster's tone suggests that they do not matter in the least – Ansell's position, humanly speaking, is absolutely sound.'[7]

The effect of this is to relegate 'the metaphysical idea of Reality' to Forster's 'quarry': to the status of an idea which influenced the shape of the novel rather than one which figures in it. What matters *in* the novel is merely that 'sense of reality' of which, as Russell once observed, philosophers, stand in more need than ordinary men; not the kind of metaphysical grounding for Realism which some philosophers, including Moore, have seen as the special function of their subject to provide. The technical machinery, the *arguments*, which make up the substance of Moore's contribution to epistemology have no place in *The Longest Journey*, nor is it easy to see how they could have, unless Forster had chosen to make his characters merely mouthpieces for metaphysical disputation – as those in, say, Berkeley's *Three Dialogues*.

For all that, however, I do not think that the effect on Forster of being 'inoculated with Moore and Moorism' did lie merely in the acquisition of a respect for truth. There is profit to be gained from reading Forster with some awareness of the more abstruse technicalities of Moore's philosophy. But to this enterprise a number of preliminary caveats are necessary. First, I think the technicalities in question are more likely to be those associated with Moore's ethics than those associated with his epistemology. Here again I am in agreement with Furbank:

> Rosenbaum persuades me that I have underestimated Moore's influence on E. M. Forster. However, the influence that I now think I see is of a slightly different kind from what he suggests, and certainly much less direct. It was, as we know, characteristic of Moore that he should approach Ethics by way of a survey of 'intrinsic' goods or things that are good in themselves. ... And this was so much Forster's own attitude to life and ethics – he so explicitly repudiated the 'Wilcox' approach, which concerned itself with things merely as means and with the use they could be put to; and he attached so much importance to the discrimination of the various intrinsic goods offered by the universe – that I would suspect we can detect in him the general climate of thought of Moore's Cambridge.[8]

Second, and again following Furbank, I do not think that Forster's engagement with Moore was a direct one. He encountered Moore's work not as a body of philosophical arguments, but as a body of effects which those arguments were having on the minds of his contemporaries. We have confirmation of this from Forster himself: 'I did not receive Moore's influence direct – I was not up to that and have never read *Principia Ethica*. It came to me at a remove, through those who knew the Master. The seed fell on fertile, if inferior, soil, and I began to think for myself.'[9] Hence in what follows I shall be concerned as much with J. M. Keynes's account, in 'My Early Beliefs', of the impact of *Principia Ethica* at Cambridge as with that work itself.

Third, and here I depart from both Rosenbaum and Furbank, I doubt if Moore's effect upon Forster was, in the ordinary sense, wholly a case of 'influence'. The term suggests a simple transfer of ideas or ideals from one writer to another who receives them with conscious or unconscious complaisance and proceeds to embody them in his work. The supposition that the relationship between Moore and Forster fits this pattern seems to me to underestimate the power and seriousness of the latter's work. Forster, already as Keynes drily puts it 'the elusive colt of a dark horse',[10] was not simply a complaisant publicist for the Moore-inspired outlook which he encountered among his friends at Cambridge. Some things he took from it; in other respects he was, like Keynes, a severe and searching critic.

This must, though, raise the question of how one can make critical headway against a philosophy by writing a novel. Novels, as I have just been arguing myself, do not – unless their characters are just animated metaphysical positions like Hylas and Philonous – contain any *arguments*. How then can a novel engage with the technicalities of a subject which consists of nothing but arguments?

The answer is, I take it, that a philosophy isn't *just* a body of arguments. A philosophy establishes itself by arguments, certainly; the question is, though, what exactly is being established? Thomas Nagel has distinguished between claims about reality which are 'objective' in the sense that they embody no reference to any particular point of view, and claims which, while they may correctly pick out some real aspect of things, pick it out in a way which is inherently tied to some special point of view.[11] Boyle's Law would be an example of the first kind of claim; examples of the second kind would include claims about what it is like, say, to be a bat, or to see colours as human beings see them. Philosophical claims for the most part, it seems to me, fall squarely into the second of Nagel's categories. What philosophical argument tries to establish, that is to say, is the intellectual credentials of some special point of view or other. Philosophy thus has a dual status: it exists on the one hand as sets of arguments, and on the other hand as the points of view such bodies of argument tend to establish. Professional philosophers tend to perceive their subject under the first of these aspects: they are more interested in the technical detail of the arguments than in the viewpoints the arguments are meant to establish. They tend to see these latter merely as motives for attempting to argue in a given direction: as mere starting points or limiting conditions for the subject, and thus as things lacking in interesting internal complexity. Another way of putting the same point would be to say that, for the professional philosopher, the internal complexity of a philosophical point of view *is* simply that of the body of arguments for and against it.

To the non-philosopher, on the other hand, the positions attacked and defended by philosophers are complex in their own right, and the complexity they exhibit is not identical with that of the technical arguments for or against them, though these will generally need to be taken into account to some extent if we are to say what such a position *is*: what its content consists in. To the non-philosopher a philosophical position is simply a rather abstract way of representing an outlook on life: a point of view which ordinary, actual persons may adopt, and even try seriously to live by. From this direction the complexity of a philosophical position is a matter of what it does for, and to, people who adopt it in that way. It is in this way that philosophy comes to be of interest to the novel; for one of the things in which novelists are professionally interested is the question of how far our intellectual and moral ambitions – our more grandiose and general theories about life, and the feelings, impulses and acts which go with them – can be made to cohere with, to stand up to, the predicaments and experiences forced on us by life.

Novels, in short, can chart the pitfalls which confront the intellectually confident holder of a philosophical position when he or she moves from argument to commitment and from commitment to action. If it is objected that the resulting critique does not engage directly with philosophy under its aspect as argument, the answer is that this is not the only aspect, nor even finally, perhaps, the most important one, under which philosophy presents itself to us.

It is in this sense, at any rate, that I want to claim Forster is a critic, as well as a disciple, of 'Moorism'. Before getting on with the argument, however, there remains a fourth and final caveat, and a further respect in which what I have to say here will depart from the paths trodden by the small amount of recent discussion of Forster's relationship to Moore. This is that I do not think the place to look for Forster's settling of accounts with Cambridge and 'Moorism' is necessarily, or at any rate primarily, the obvious one. Most critics have looked for the influence of Cambridge philosophizing in *The Longest Journey*, because that novel is partly set in undergraduate Cambridge, opens with a philosophical discussion redolent of the Cambridge Apostles, and contains one character who is an embryonic philosopher. I think it may prove more fruitful, at least at the outset, to look instead at the work closest in date of publication to Forster's Cambridge years: *Where Angels Fear to Tread*.

II

Moore's ethics is a version of utilitarianism. It retains the most striking feature of utilitarianism, and the one which makes many ordinary unphilosophical people uncomfortable with it, once they have grasped its implications; namely, its consequentialism. The consequentialist holds that whether an action is morally right or wrong depends solely on its consequences: on the nature of the state of affairs which it brings into being. This differs sharply from the common view that the rightness or wrongness of actions depends on what one might call their *moral constitution*: that what matters is whether a given action *constitutes* the keeping of a promise, *constitutes* a betrayal, *constitutes* a kindness or a piece of cruelty: that, in short, it is the nature of the act and not its consequences which makes the difference morally. Consequentialists of course have ways of squaring their position with this commonly held view of the matter. The most usual is to argue that society trains us to feel that acts having a given moral constitution are right or wrong in virtue of having that constitution, for the very good reason that *in the general run of cases* the moral constitution of an act is a reliable guide to the utility or disutility of its consequences. But, or so consequentialists from Mill onward have argued, these ingrained non-consequentialist intuitions are liable in certain circumstances to lead us seriously astray morally, either because they conflict with one another, or because under certain extreme conditions refusing to act because of the moral constitution of the act demanded of one may require one to accept very bad consequences indeed. In such cases, the consequentialist argues, our everyday intuitions about the moral constitution of acts must yield to consequentialist considerations, which shows that such considerations are, after all, the nerve of morality.

None of this commits the utilitarian to any disrespect for ordinary moral rules in the general course of everyday life, for it is part of the utilitarian's position that in the general run of cases respect for the generally accepted rules can be relied upon to produce the best possible consequences. But it does set him apart from the ordinary, unenlightened person, whose respect for the commonly accepted dictates of morality is automatic, unthinking and unconditional in a way in which the utilitarian's can never be. The latter's theory places him under a moral obligation to decide for himself, by appealing to his own estimate of the relative weights of the competing utilities, in which cases ordinary moral considerations should be respected and in which they should not.[12] Utilitarianism as a moral outlook is thus of a piece with that peculiarly Protestant, peculiarly English form of individualism which consists in demanding for oneself as an individual not the right to do as one pleases but, more subtly and more dangerously, the right to decide for oneself, in the last analysis, what is Right. In *Where Angels Fear to Tread* Harriet most obviously represents the Evangelical form of this tendency, but it is one to which all the English characters, in one way or another, ultimately subscribe.

Utilitarianism so characterized might seem to exemplify what Furbank calls 'the "Wilcox" approach' to life: an approach concerned more with the practical consequences of action than with ultimate questions of value. This would be a misunderstanding. Merely in order to define his notion of utility, the utilitarian has to give some account of what sorts of things are ultimately worthy to be brought into being. This is where Moore's philosophy comes into its own. Bentham, the father of the theory, held that the only intrinsically valuable thing is pleasure. This is open to a great many objections, of which only two need concern us here. The first is that it commits the utilitarian, implausibly, to the claim that the only things which ultimately have value are mental states. The second – Moore's objection – is that it forces the utilitarian to deny what seems to be a truth of logic: that even if it is granted that no state of affairs could have any value if it contained no pleasure, it does not follow that the value of a state of affairs is proportional to the quantity of pleasure it contains. A given quantity of pleasure derived from having grasped just such a logical truth, for instance, may possess more value – more worthiness-to-be-brought-into-being – than the same quantity of pleasure derived from imagining some hideous revenge, even though the revenge in question remains unacted. Earlier utilitarians failed to notice this logical gap, Moore argues, because they tacitly, and mistakenly, assumed the *non-natural* property *goodness* to be simply identical with whatever *natural* property it is – the property of *being pleasant*, for instance – that confers value upon states of affairs. Moore baptized this error, if error it be, 'the Naturalistic Fallacy'.

Moore's own account of intrinsic value is founded upon the rejection of ethical naturalism. Its fundamental claim is that the property *goodness* is not identical with any of the natural properties which confer goodness (value; worthiness-to-be-brought-into-being) upon states of affairs. (This is the point of Moore's Butlerian epigraph, *Everything is what it is, and not another thing*.) The enquiry into what is of ultimate or intrinsic value thus divides into two distinct questions. First, there is the question of what natural properties of things do in fact confer value upon the situations in which they occur. Moore's answer to this question is well known: among the most important intrinsic sources of value in life are friendship and the contemplation of beauty. Second, there is the question of how much value these natural features of things confer, in each case, upon specific states of affairs. Answers to both questions, Moore argues, are to be sought by a common method. The method involves carefully comparing, in imagination, one thing with another, leaving out of account any causal consequences or antecedents that either may have, and considering each simply for what it is in itself. In answering questions of the second type, what have to be compared are states of affairs, taken as internally related 'organic wholes' whose intrinsically valuable and non-intrinsically valuable elements work together to yield whatever value the state of affairs possesses, in such a way that there is no possible mode of further analysis which would allow one to assign responsibility for the resultant sum of value to one element of the total situation rather than another.

Moore's account of intrinsic value might appear to constitute, technically speaking, no more than a minor, though interesting and important, adjustment to utilitarian theory. Moore himself called his theory 'Ideal Utilitarianism'. But we are interested in its impact on young, literate readers who were not technical philosophers. What attracts such readers to philosophical theories of ethics is, I suspect, the light they expect such theories to throw on the nature of the moral life. They want, like most people but more especially young people, to know how to live. What they look for in a philosopher, therefore, is some clear and arresting statement about what it is to be moral: about what it is that specifically characterizes the moral standpoint.

Now, the account of what is characteristic of the moral standpoint to be gleaned from Moore's 'Ideal Utilitarianism' is markedly different from that to be gleaned from most other forms of the doctrine. The impression one gains from most versions of utilitarianism is that the moral standpoint is pre-eminently a practical one, in which the energies of the virtuous mind are more or less wholly given over to assessing the consequences of actions or policies with a view to selecting those most productive of some reasonably straightforwardly and uncontroversially defined good labelled 'general happiness', or 'welfare'. This is not the impression one gains from *Principia Ethica*. The focus of the entire book is on the question of how we are to determine what things are intrinsically valuable: worthy to be sought for their own sake alone. Inevitably, as we read the book, this comes to seem the central issue which we confront as *moral* beings; and questions about how we are to achieve the realization of intrinsic goods, once we have determined which those are, seem to relegate themselves naturally to the subordinate status of '*merely* practical' questions: questions, that is, whose solution requires no peculiarly *moral* insight, but merely empirical knowledge and everyday practical nous.

The (fairly extraordinary) claim that moral consciousness, strictly defined as such, excludes the practical from its sphere is not, one supposes, one which Moore would have accepted, let alone one which he would have wished to defend. The fact remains that the impression left by an enthusiastic reading of *Principia Ethica*, especially one which dwells lovingly on chapter VI, is that the moral standpoint is a quasi-aesthetic one, consisting largely in the possession and exercise of informed connoisseurship with regard to the discrimination of intrinsic value.

If we are to trust J. M. Keynes, this is very much the way in which Forster's young contemporaries read Moore:

> Now what we got from Moore was by no means exactly what he offered us. He had one foot on the threshold of the new heaven, but the other foot in Sidgwick and the Benthamite calculus and the general rules of correct behaviour. There was one chapter in the *Principia* of which we took not the slightest notice. We accepted Moore's religion, so to speak, and discarded his morals. Indeed, in our opinion, one of the greatest advantages of his religion was that it made morals unnecessary – meaning by 'religion' one's attitude towards oneself and the ultimate and by 'morals' one's attitude towards the outside world and the intermediate. To the consequence of having a religion and no morals I return later.   (p. 82)

A little later Keynes describes the content of 'the religion' as follows:

> Nothing mattered except states of mind, our own and other people's of course, but chiefly our own. These states of mind were not associated with action or achievement or with consequences. They consisted in timeless, passionate states of contemplation and communion, largely unattached to 'before' and 'after'. Their value depended, in accordance with the principle of organic unity, on the state of affairs as a whole which could not be usefully analysed into parts. For example, the value of the state of mind of being in love did not depend merely on the nature of one's own emotions, but also on the worth of their object and on the reciprocity and nature of the object's emotions; but it did not depend much on what happened, or how one felt about it, a year later, though I myself was always an advocate of a principle of organic unity through time, which still seems to me only sensible.   (p. 83)

It will now perhaps become clear why I see *Where Angels Fear to Tread* as something more than a black social comedy about national character and suburban class pretensions. Though it would be false to the book and to Forster to read it with solemnity, nevertheless the novel has a serious as well as a black side to it. It is in part an exploration of what is liable to happen to people who attempt to live, as Keynes puts it, with 'a religion and no morals'.

Before pursuing this, however, we should pay attention to one final, methodological, feature of Moore's moral philosophy: its intuitionism. As Keynes indicates, Moore's way of settling questions of intrinsic value involved holding a given state of affairs before the mind, in the shadowless light of consciousness, and asking oneself whether one could, or could not, will to bring *that* into being. The essence of the method is that one has to put both the causal antecedents and the consequences of the state of affairs entirely out of one's mind, and consider it simply in itself. The acquisition of moral knowledge, in other words, is conceived as analogous to the acquisition of knowledge through sensory perception. Just as I know with simple, immediate certainty that *this* is my hand, so I know with simple, immediate certainty that *this* (love, say, or the contemplation of beauty) is intrinsically valuable.

One has, I think, to get into a rather special state of intellectual exaltation to find plausible the suggestion that knowledge of ultimate good and evil is as easily accessible as this, and accessible on such a purely private and intellectual level. Common sense tells us that the difference between right and wrong, good and evil, is only to be learned by slower and more painful means; means which intrinsically involve relationships with others, much experience, many nasty shocks to the system, and above all the passage of time: that, in short, such knowledge is taught not in the singing school of the soul, but only in the school of hard knocks. Experience teaches us, moreover, that our views about what is ultimately good and bad are liable to change as a result of experience.

Moore's deeply Cartesian methodology makes no allowance for any of this. It proceeds on the assumption that the final truth about what is to be valued in life is already, timelessly, settled; and that we can come to know what it is merely by directing the inward eye of consciousness in the right sort of way upon sufficiently carefully specified objects. Seen from this angle, Moore's ethics partakes of the *logocentrism* which Jacques Derrida regards as the most enduring and characteristic feature of the Western metaphysical tradition. This is apparent from Moore's treatment of the two predicates 'is good' and 'is yellow' as analogous in respect of being unanalysable and ultimate in our conceptual scheme. Just as the meaning of 'yellow' is an object – a property – directly accessible to consciousness in sensory experience, so the meaning of 'good' is a property directly accessible to consciousness through the peculiar species of thought-experiment by which we assess the intrinsic value attaching to an organic whole. The task of the philosopher *as writer* – of Moore's celebrated sixth chapter, for instance – is merely to transcribe the truths about intrinsic value which consciousness so directed reveals.

The Cartesianism of Moore's view comes out in another, closely related way. His moral epistemology, like Descartes's general epistemology, makes the acquisition of knowledge, in this case moral knowledge, at least in its most adequate and ultimate form, the outcome of processes of reflection internal to the individual mind. 'Moorism' about intrinsic value thus provides a further way of intellectually articulating that distinctively English, distinctively Protestant strain of individualism I mentioned earlier, which reserves to the individual mind the right and the power to determine for itself, by the exercise of an inner light proper to it, what is Right.

III

Where Angels Fear to Tread is on the face of it a tragicomedy of manners, about a raw English suburb and an ancient Italian town, neither of which comes out of the book particularly well. The English characters include Mrs Herriton, a wealthy Sawston widow, her fiercely Evangelical daughter Harriet, and her lawyer son Philip. The values with which Philip enters the novel are clearly meant to embody a version of Cambridge 'Moorism'. 'By far the most valuable things, which we know or can imagine,' Moore has written, 'are certain states of consciousness, which may be roughly described as the pleasure of human intercourse and the enjoyment of beautiful objects.'[13] Philip, weak on the first of these moral absolutes, is strong on the second, which he opposes to what he sees as the philistine rule-worship practised by Sawston in general and his sister Harriet in particular. 'At twenty-two he went to Italy with some cousins, and there he absorbed into one aesthetic whole olive trees, blue sky, frescoes, country inns, saints, peasants, mosaics, statues, beggars. He came back with the air of a prophet who would either remodel Sawston or reject it. All the energies and enthusiasms of a rather friendless life had passed into the championship of beauty' (p. 61).[14]

Given the obsessive discussion of the moral properties of organic wholes recorded by Keynes among the Cambridge Apostles, I doubt if Forster's choice of the phrase 'into one aesthetic whole' is accidental. And if it is not, it is certainly satirical in intent. An organic whole, to be the seat of a moral absolute, should be, one feels, more coherent than Philip's hodgepodge.

Loosely connected to the Herriton clan is Mrs Herriton's daughter-in-law, Lilia Theobald, left widowed and socially, if not entirely financially, dependent on the Herritons by another son, Charles. There are also Irma, Lilia's daughter, and Caroline Abbott, a friend of the family, on whose shifts of moral position much hangs.

Lilia is a vulgar, bouncy woman of a type uncongenial to the

Herritons, whose unsuitability consists in part in a tendency to encourage unsuitable suitors. As the novel opens she is being packed off at Philip's suggestion for an extended tour of Italy in the company of Caroline Abbott, with the object, from the Herritons' point of view, of getting her away from the latest of these suitors. Philip's hopes for the tour nicely catch the way in which moral and aesthetic considerations freely interpenetrate one another in his mind.

'I admit she is a Philistine, appallingly ignorant, and her taste in art is false. Still, to have any taste at all is something. And I do believe that Italy really purifies and ennobles all who visit her. She is the school as well as the playground of the world. . . .'

He found the situation full of whimsical romance: there was something half-attractive, half-repellent in the thought of this vulgar woman journeying to places he loved and revered. Why should she not be transfigured? The same had happened to the Goths. (p. 9)

Solicitous for Lilia's aesthetico-moral redemption, Philip advises the pair to spend some time in the ancient and beautiful Tuscan hill town of Monteriano. There Lilia meets and falls in love with her most unsuitable suitor yet: an Italian dentist's son by the name of Gino Carella. Gino is twenty-one, Lilia considerably older. Miss Abbott, whom the Herritons know as a prim young spinster devoted to Church causes and the care of an elderly father, might have been expected to discourage such a rash attachment. But alas, Caroline Abbott turns out to have a romantic streak of her own, and sees in it Lilia's last chance of freedom and happiness. The news reaches the Herritons in a cautiously worded letter from old Mrs Theobald announcing Lilia's engagement, in which Gino, thanks to the remoter ramifications of his extended family, has been transmogrified into a member of the Italian nobility. Mrs Herriton is quite able to read between lines as far apart as these, and Philip is dispatched by the night train to put a stop to the engagement. He arrives too late: Lilia and Gino are already married. Lilia tells him exactly what she thinks of the Herritons' attempts over twelve years to train her into conformity with Herriton ideas of propriety, and Gino laughs at him and ends what should have been a serious interview by pushing him over backward. Philip returns much discomfited to Sawston, and Mrs Herriton duly severs relationships with Lilia, refusing even to let her write to Irma.

There matters might have rested. But in Monteriano Lilia discovers the disagreeable side of marriage to an Italian. The social circle to which she has access is extremely limited; it is thought improper for

her to continue her English habit of going for long walks alone. She is
virtually confined to home and church. Finally, to cap it all, she
discovers that Gino is unfaithful to her. She makes various hopeless
attempts at escape, then after a long illness dies in childbirth, leaving
Gino a son.

Reactions in Sawston to this news are various. For Philip it
constitutes a spiritual crisis.

> . . . Lilia's marriage toppled contentment down forever. Italy, the land of
> beauty, was ruined for him. She had no power to change men and things
> who dwelt in her. She, too, could produce avarice, brutality, stupidity –
> and what was worse, vulgarity. It was on her soil and through her
> influence that a silly woman had married a cad. He hated Gino, the
> betrayer of his life's ideal, and now that the sordid tragedy had come, it
> filled him with pangs, not of sympathy, but of final disillusion.   (p. 62)

Mrs Herriton's impulse, and Harriet's, is to let sleeping dogs lie, and
keep the existence of a Herriton baby in Monteriano a secret,
especially from Irma. It is Caroline Abbott who once again troubles
the waters. She reveals to Philip how much she is responsible for
Lilia's second marriage: how she had felt about Lilia's treatment by
the Herritons over the years, and how she said to Lilia one warm
night in a hotel bedroom in Monteriano, 'Why don't you marry him
if you think you'll be happy' (p. 66). Not surprisingly Caroline now
feels guilty and responsible for Lilia's child. She has the impertinence
to ask Mrs Herriton 'what is to be done' about it, and threatens to
take an interest in any expedition to rescue it. This is too much for
Mrs Herriton. A letter is sent to Gino offering to adopt the child;
when this fails, Philip is sent off once more to Monteriano, this time
with Harriet in tow to see that weakness does not get the better of
him.

Before Philip and Harriet have got far into Italy, they are quarrelling in the heat, and Philip's spiritual malaise has begun to pass off,
leaving in its place a renewed pleasure in Italy and renewed doubts
about the moral credentials of Sawston.

> 'Because he was unfaithful to his wife, it doesn't follow that in every
> way he's absolutely vile.' He looked at the city. It seemed to approve his
> remark.
> 'It's the supreme test. The man who is unchivalrous to a woman–'
> 'Oh stow it! Take it to the Back Kitchen. It's no more a supreme test
> than anything else. The Italians never were chivalrous from the first. If
> you condemn him for that, you'll condemn the whole lot.'
> 'I condemn the whole lot.'

'And the French as well?'

'And the French as well.'

'Things aren't so jolly easy,' said Philip, more to himself than to her.

(pp. 86–7)

In Monteriano, nothing goes according to plan. Caroline Abbott is there before them, but Gino is out of town. Caroline, who has already met Gino, conveys to Philip his apologies and sorrow for having treated Philip so rudely the previous year. This completes Philip's re-conversion to Italy, and he proposes that the ill-assorted party fill in the time on its hands with a visit to the Monteriano opera house. There, in the course of an evening which deeply scandalizes Harriet, he meets Gino in the company of some other young Italian bloods, and they carry him off to the café with them, thus completing the ruin of his intention to 'rescue' the child from Gino.

Caroline Abbott spends an uneasy night, however, and in the morning goes to visit Gino. While she is waiting for him, he returns, and puts her completely off her stroke by his charm, his inconsequentiality and, as will appear, his masculinity. While she is still reeling, he tells her of his plan to marry again so that the baby will be properly cared for, and draws her into the protracted business of giving it a bath, something he will no longer trust the servant Perfetta to do because she 'is too rough', and to do which he has cheerfully torn himself away from the café. Caroline Abbott is entirely unmanned by this display of maternal instinct, and is still seated in the loggia with the dripping baby on her knee when Philip arrives, to perceive the scene as 'the Virgin and child, with Donor', by Bellini.

Philip stays to proceed, quite unsuccessfully, with the negotiations for the adoption of the child by the Herritons. Caroline Abbott leaves, in turmoil. The issue, as she puts it to Philip in the church of Santa Deodata later that day, is clear to her: '... I do expect you to settle what is right and to follow that. Do you want the child to stop with his father, who loves him and will bring him up badly, or do you want him to come to Sawston, where no-one loves him, but where he will be brought up well.'

She repents again, this time of ever having goaded the Herritons into interfering with the child's future, and wants Philip to be decisive and call off Harriet. But Philip is in no state to be decisive. Exercising the same genial tolerance towards Harriet as towards Gino, he goes off for one final attempt, in the Caffé Garibaldi, to persuade the latter to part with the child, and when that fails he prepares to leave Monteriano. Harriet, however, will not give up so easily. She makes mysterious arrangements with Philip for the carriage to pick her up not at the hotel, but at the Siena gate near Gino's house; and when she enters the carriage she is carrying the baby. On the way down the hill of Monteriano in a sudden thunder-storm the carriage overturns and the baby is killed.

Philip, who has broken his arm, goes to take the news to Gino, who is both inconsolable and violent, and who tortures Philip by grinding the broken bones of his arm together until Caroline Abbott puts a stop to it. But this is the end of the enmity between Philip and Gino, who has 'the southern knack of friendship', and to whom Philip is soon 'bound by ties of almost alarming intimacy' (p. 152). With Caroline Abbott he is not so lucky. When he proposes to her on the train ascending from Italy towards the St. Gotthard tunnel, she reveals that she is in love, sexually and physically in love, with Gino, but that nevertheless she is going back to Sawston to resume her loveless life there.

IV

In *Where Angels Fear to Tread*, as in other Forster novels, it is not altogether easy to say whose side Forster is on. One inviting way of reading the novel is to take it as a satire on the prosaic, hypocritical and selfish values of Sawston, conducted from the standpoint of Romance, represented by Philip Herriton, Caroline Abbott, and Monteriano. Thus Norman Kelvin suggests that of the two main themes of the novel, the first is that engagements between people can also be engagements with 'culture and history', while the second is 'that romance, reserved for a few, easily confused with a "spurious sentiment" superficially resembling it, is paradoxically in the light of its élitist connotations, essential for all life.'[15]

There are many difficulties with this. First, Sawston and its representatives are not unrelievedly condemned in the book. To Caroline, passing a sleepless night after the opera, it is revealed as Poggibonsi, from whose rule Monteriano emancipated itself in the twelfth century, 'a joyless, straggling place, full of people who pretended'. But that is Caroline's vision, not Forster's; whereas it *is* the authorial voice of the novel which ends Harriet's quarrel with Philip in the hot, dusty train like this: 'She kept her promise, and never opened her lips all the rest of the way. But her eyes glowed with anger and resolution. For she was a straight, brave woman, as well as a peevish one' (p. 87). That same voice also tells us that when Harriet vanishes just before the final departure from Monteriano with the baby, she leaves her prayer book on her bed open at the words, 'Blessed be the Lord my God who teacheth my hands to war and my fingers to fight'. We are reminded sharply, if we are prepared to be reminded, that Harriet is on her way to rescue a child for whom, however belatedly, she has assumed responsibility, from a man she considers, not without evidence, to be a brute and a lecher. Harriet, in short, is a figure of some moral substance, not just a figure of fun. For that matter Sawston itself, seen through the remorseful Lilia's tears, resembles an earthly paradise:

> One evening, when [Gino] had gone out thus, Lilia could stand it no longer. It was September. Sawston would be just filling up after the summer holidays. People would be running in and out of each other's houses all along the road. There were bicycle gymkhanas, and on the 30th Mrs Herriton would be holding the annual bazaar in her garden for the C. M. S. It seemed impossible that such a free happy life could exist.
>
> (p. 55)

I see no reason at all why we should take this Betjemanesque idyll as merely the expression of Lilia's jaundiced view of Monteriano. For one thing, Lilia's view of Monteriano is by this point in the novel understandably jaundiced. For another, Forster expends quite as much loving care in depicting the warts of Monteriano as in depicting those of Sawston, from the absurd superstition of its cult of Santa Deodata to the opera house 'thoroughly done up, in the tints of the beetroot and the tomato', from the 'horrible sighings and bubblings' of the dumb idiot who brings Harriet's message requesting Philip to meet her at the Siena gate to Gino's friend Spiridione's chilling advice on how best to settle Lilia down into her new role:

> 'Is she a Catholic?'
> 'No.'
> 'That is a pity. She must be persuaded. It will be a great solace to her when she is alone.'   (p. 47)

Then again, just as the novel resists our efforts to turn Harriet into a figure of unrelieved bigotry, so it resists our efforts to turn Philip Herriton into a convincing hero or Caroline Abbott into a convincing heroine. Certainly both in different ways stand for Romance, in opposition to the values of Sawston; but just because those two are its representatives it is not easy to construe the function of Romance in the book as anything but that of a principle of comic disorder. Philip's romantic aesthetico-moralizings are what send Lilia to Italy in the first place. Later, the revival of his romantic vision of Italy contributes to his nervelessness in the face of Caroline Abbott's appeal to him to be decisive about the fate of Gino's child. Caroline really does not do much better. It is her moment of romantic enthusiasm at somebody else's expense which assists Lilia up the flowery path to her appalling marriage with Gino; and the later feelings of guilt which lead to Caroline's prodding the Herritons into doing something about the child are, while in one way honourable, in another thoroughly sentimental and self-regarding. Caroline's claim to be the real heroine of the novel rests, of course, on her belated honesty: her capacity in the final pinch to put aside all sentimental moralizing in the face of a real human encounter. This is a serious claim: the episode in which she and Gino bathe the baby clearly is the moral centre of the novel. But her unsentimental acceptance of the reality before her eyes, and of her own solidly physical reaction to it, is the opposite of the romantic, 'aestheticizing' moral sensibility she partly shares with Philip. And though she rises to this occasion, she does not rise far enough.

In short, I cannot find any textual grounds in the novel for regarding Romance as a principle of life. On the contrary, as the plot unfolds, Romance consistently lights the way to graves as fine and private as any dug in Sawston.

Why, then, should Forster have chosen to construct the novel around the contrast between Sawston and Monteriano? It is here, I think, that Moore and Keynes can help us. From Keynes's account we know that Forster found dominant among his Cambridge friends a way of taking Moore's version of utilitarianism which exalted knowledge of the intrinsic values of things into a religion, and tended rather to look down on 'morality', meaning by that, as Keynes puts it, 'one's attitude towards the outside world and the intermediate'. I have suggested that there are links at the level of theory between this outlook and the long tradition of English puritanism and moral individualism. Keynes confirms those links at the level of feeling: 'Our religion closely followed the English puritan tradition of being chiefly concerned with the salvation of our own souls. The divine resided within a closed circle. There was not a very intimate connection between "being good" and "doing good"; and we had a feeling that there was some risk that in practice the latter might interfere with the former.' ('My Early Beliefs', p. 84)

The basic comic situation in *Where Angels Fear to Tread* consists, I take it, in the juxtaposition of Philip Herriton, who believes, in the style of the Cambridge Apostles, that he has a far keener insight into the intrinsic values of things than the dull souls around him, with the suburban, puritan rule-morality which he affects to despise. The comedy arises from the evident fact that Philip's values are not only no sounder than those of his family, but are in crucial respects the same values. What I have in mind here is not merely Philip's tendency throughout the early part of the novel to relapse at any moment of stress into attitudes characteristic of the average young Englishman of his class and period. More importantly, Philip shares with his mother and Harriet a certain coldness. For all three of them morality is primarily an inward condition—a matter of inner fidelity to high and commanding abstractions: in Philip's case, Italy and Beauty; in Harriet's, the requirements of Low-Church rectitude; in Mrs Herriton's, those of social order and respectability. The common feature linking all the English characters in the book is that none of them, with the sole exception of Caroline Abbott, ever feels the need to set his or her own values aside in order to respond directly to the needs and condition of another. Examples of the refusal to make the least move outward from an entrenched moral position abound in the book, not least in the Herritons' unsympathetic treatment of the unfortunate Lilia. But Philip is as prone to this as the rest: when news of Lilia's 'sordid tragedy' reaches him, 'it filled him with pangs, not of sympathy, but of final disillusion.' Even Lilia runs her life more in response to her inward dreams and fantasies than in response to what is actually going on around her, and from this comes her downfall, when she chooses to treat Gino not as another human being, with desires and values of his own, but as a pretty Italian boy whom she can fascinate and control. One of the running ironies of the book, I take it, is that Philip's own inner condition, as revealed in action, is not half as remote from Lilia's as he thinks it is. This shows, for instance, in his response to the baby-bathing episode, which leaves Caroline morally disturbed in her purpose, but which Philip simply assimilates wholesale to his dream of Italy:

> There she sat, with twenty miles of view behind her, and he placed the dripping baby on her knee.... For a time Gino contemplated them standing. Then, to get a better view, he knelt by the side of the chair, with his hands clasped before him.
>
> So they were when Philip entered, and saw, to all intents and purposes, the Virgin and the Child, with Donor. 'Hallo!' he exclaimed; for he was glad to find things in such cheerful trim.   (p. 122)

If the negative pole of the novel is the moral self-absorption of English puritanism, whether in the form of commonplace suburban philistinism or in the intellectualized mandarin form represented by 'Moorism' in one of its aspects, what is its positive pole? Its positive pole, I take it, is Friendship, that most Moorean as well as most Forsterian of values. So far as Philip makes any spiritual progress at all (and even then it is hardly to be described as growth, more as an involuntary pitchforking at the hands of life from one state to

another) it is progress in the direction of friendship. He begins
unpromisingly: 'All the energies and enthusiasm of a rather friendless
life had passed into the championship of beauty' (pp. 61–2). But he
ends 'bound by ties of almost alarming intimacy' to Gino; and he
even manages to hear out Caroline Abbott's confession of her
feelings for Gino and take well her 'You're my friend forever, Mr
Herriton, I think'. It looks, oddly, as if Philip has simply passed
from championship of one of Moore's two 'most valuable things',
to, if not exactly championship of, at least forcible immersion in
the other.

No doubt the young Forster did draw sustenance from Moore's
elevation of friendship to the status of one of the two most valuable
things 'which we know or can imagine'. Nevertheless, Forster's idea
of friendship is not quite the same as Moore's. Moore's 'most valuable things' are described by him as 'certain states of consciousness',
one sub-set of which 'may be roughly described as the pleasures of
human intercourse'. This way of putting it, because it invites us to
think of the enjoyment of a friendship as the enjoyment of *states of
consciousness* resulting from it, does suggest rather strongly that
friendship is nothing more than a cultivated amenity, a refined and
purely mental gratification offering no serious threat to the integrity
of the self. And, once again, Keynes can be called to testify that the
young men of Forster's Cambridge generation read Moore this way.
'Nothing mattered except states of mind ... timeless, passionate
states of contemplation and communion.'

It is a noticeable feature of *Where Angels Fear to Tread* that
friendship in the book is not treated in quite this light. Friendship
with Gino, or for that matter any unguarded and direct encounter
with him, tears apart all three of the English characters who come
into contact with him. In Philip's friendship with Miss Abbott as well
there is as much pain as pleasure, as much loss as gain. What is lost
for both, and for Lilia as well, is the firm complacent hold, with
which each sets out, upon a system of largely theoretical but quite
unquestioned and untested moral values and assumptions in terms of
which each defines his or her self. Friendship breaks the defensive
crust of inwardly generated values, sets the still waters of the self in
motion towards change or towards destruction. Forster's point, I
take it, is that friendship is not just an amenity, a refined gratification, because it is not ultimately controllable in its effects upon them
by those who enter into it; and that it is not controllable because it is
not purely mental in its nature, not just a matter of *states of
consciousness*. It reaches into the physical side of our being: into the
facts of our embodiment which both puritanism, in its drive towards

perfect purity and integrity of the self, and Cartesian philosophy endeavour to deny.

Keynes, looking back on Moore and 'Moorism', finds it a blend of seriousness and comedy: impressive in its philosophical detachment and its concern with ultimate goods, absurd in its capacity for *ad hoc* armchair moralizing:

> It was a purer, sweeter air by far than Freud cum Marx. It is still my religion under the surface. I read again last week Moore's famous chapter on 'The Ideal'. It is remarkable how wholly oblivious he managed to be of the qualities of the life of action and also of the pattern of life as a whole. He was existing in a timeless ecstasy. His way of translating his own particular emotions of the moment into the language of generalized abstraction is a charming and beautiful comedy.
>
> ('My Early Beliefs', p. 92)

It would be difficult to find better words to describe the mental condition in which the younger English characters in *Where Angels Fear to Tread* approach the world beyond their native shores. Like Moore, but without his seriousness, they 'exist in a timeless ecstasy'; that is to say, they endeavour sedulously to ignore the concrete, the physical and the temporal aspects of life. Like him, but without his innocence, they display a suspicious facility in 'translating [their] own particular emotions into the language of generalized abstraction'. They want, above all things, to be moral, but they want morality to remain confined to the realm of thought and talk.

Monteriano and Gino possess the at times almost grotesque physicality which Forster bestows upon them because, I take it, they are meant to stand in comic contrast to the fastidious Manichaean refinement with which the four English characters approach their respective Italian Waterloos. The crucial moments of the novel all draw their moral energy from the intensity with which they confront their English protagonists with the concrete physical facts of life, and the inescapable interplay of mind and body. Gino's absurd half-assault on Philip in the hotel room; the 'great clods of earth, large and hard as rocks', over which Lilia stumbles in her attempt to catch the *loggia* and escape; the baby's body lying in the rut in rain and darkness; Gino's torture of Philip, and the gesture with which he drinks the warmed milk intended for the dead child and 'either by accident or in some spasm of pain', breaks the jug to pieces, all come to mind as examples. The terms in which Caroline Abbott invites Philip to consider whether the baby is to be loved and badly brought up in Monteriano or well brought up and unloved in Sawston are not without significance here. She says to him, 'Settle it. Settle which side you are to fight on' (p. 130). Meaning: settle it for yourself, settle it *in your mind*. But Caroline has not 'settled' it for herself, by any process of thought – it has been settled for her by the physical, tangible presence of Gino's love for the child in the bathing episode, reinforced no doubt by the equally physical attraction she feels towards Gino.

From this point of view we can make sense of something which has puzzled some critics of the novel: Forster's ironic moral approval of Philip's readiness to be flattered into altogether abandoning his moral condemnation of Gino at the first hint of an apology from the latter.

> What did the baby matter when the world was suddenly the right way up? Philip smiled, and was shocked at himself for smiling, and smiled again. For romance had come back to Italy; there were no cads in her; she was beautiful, courteous, lovable, as of old. And Miss Abbott – she, too, was beautiful in her way, for all her gaucheness and conventionality. She really cared about life, and tried to live it properly. And Harriet – even Harriet tried.
>
> This admirable change in Philip proceeds from nothing admirable, and may therefore provoke the gibes of the cynical. But angels and other practical people will accept it reverently, and write it down as good.
>
> (pp. 97–8)

Norman Kelvin suggests that Forster is here allowing his own approval of Philip's easygoing attitude to the situation to stand in contradiction to Caroline Abbott's well-founded condemnation of it and that this constitutes a failure in the moral coherence of the novel.[16] I see no incoherence. The whole drift of the book is that redeeming impulses do not come from conscious moralizing, which is as often as not self-interested, but from concretely and directly encountering others in ways which bring into play aspects of ourselves which our reflective consciousness can neither wholly grasp nor wholly control. Philip is being betrayed out of his previous rather pompous stance towards Gino by just this kind of impulse. And it does lead him towards a more adequate, a more realistic perception of how things stand. It jerks him out of the absurd disillusionment with his former values into which the failure of Lilia's marriage plunged him, and it does not simply reconstitute those values. If it leaves him something of a moral relativist, able to look down with amused tolerance on the values of both Sawston and Monteriano without accepting either, well, it is also preparing the overthrow of the cheery moral agnosticism which constitutes the second phase of Philip's reaction to the loss of his Moorish faith in the virtual identity of aesthetic and moral sensibility, since it is preparing him for friendship with Gino.

V

Philip's anthropological relativism, the new-found belief upon which he lectures Harriet in the train to the effect that what is a mark of vileness in Sawston is not necessarily so in Monteriano, brings me back in conclusion to the issue of Forster's 'Realism'. Rosenbaum's claim is that Forster's interest in 'the ethical idea that reality must be faced' derived directly from the metaphysical Realism of Moore. The conclusion towards which I have been arguing is that, on the contrary, it developed from Forster's uneasiness about certain aspects of the Moorean ethical Realism which so impressed his Cambridge contemporaries. The worry is the one which most philosophers nowadays would cite as their reason for relegating Moore's doctrine of intrinsic value to the status of a historical curiosity, and on which Keynes unerringly puts his finger forty years on: 'How did we know which states of mind were good? This was a matter of direct inspection, of direct unanalysable intuition about which it was useless and impossible to argue. In that case who was right when there was a difference of opinion?' ('My Early Beliefs', p. 84)

There is, of course, no answer to this one, and Keynes goes on amusingly to detail the various ruses by which members of the Apostles strove to veil the embarrassing outlines of this unfortunate fact: 'In practice, victory was with those who could speak with the greatest appearance of clear, undoubting conviction.... Moore at this time was a master of this method – greeting one's remarks with a gasp of incredulity – Do you *really* think *that*, an expression of face as if to hear such a thing said reduced him to a state of wonder verging on imbecility,... Oh! he would say, goggling at you as if either you or he must be mad: and no reply was possible' (p. 85). Such, in all seriousness, is the degree of moral certainty upon which it is good form to presume in Sawston; and it is precisely the effortless English assumption of the immediate evidence of at least some ultimate moral propositions to all but the manifestly mad or wicked (though some difference of opinion over which these are may be tolerated, if not exactly welcomed) which meets its Waterloo in Monteriano. God knows what truths about the nature of the good Caroline Abbott would have discovered had she applied Moore's method before meeting Gino, but it seems doubtful whether they would have included the proposition that love between father and child morally trumps all considerations of upbringing.

The conclusion towards which Forster's narrative seems to be leading us is that what appears to trump what is morally very much a matter of where we happen to be standing. There is nothing particularly Realist about this conclusion; indeed, it is rampantly Idealistic. We must, however, distinguish between two types of Idealism. There is, on the one hand, the Absolute or Dialectical kind which goes in for degrees of truth. One negative thesis associated with that kind of Idealism says that there is no standpoint from which we can finally, absolutely, grasp and write about the realities of our situation. This thought is present in Forster's work from the beginning, it seems to me. It accounts, indeed, for the occurrence of motifs drawn from Oriental religion long before *A Passage to India*, for example, the mandala in *The Longest Journey*, of which Rickie asks whether it is real, to be told by Ansell that only the undrawable, ungraspable centre is. If I am correct about the working out in *Where Angels Fear to Tread* of the thought that we cannot view our existential situation from a standpoint external to it, then we should not be at all surprised that Ansell, who has the root of the matter in him, should have read Hegel, or imagine that Forster nodded to or displayed his ignorance of Cambridge philosophy in making him so, when in fact the way Forster chooses to draw Ansell shows that Forster was ignorant neither of philosophy nor Cambridge. Finally, of course, the notion that we cannot get outside our situation has a good claim to be regarded as the ur-thought of Modernism; and I think Forster's interest in it may account for the feeling many readers have that despite the scrupulously pre-Modernist form of his fiction, it is in some not easily definable way engaged with Modernist themes and problems.

On the other hand, however, there is Idealism of the other, Berkeleyan kind, which identifies being with appearing and which yawns invitingly at the feet of anyone who dabbles in Idealism of the first kind. If *Where Angels Fear to Tread* can be read as I have suggested, that possibility yawns at Forster's. In philosophical terms, the alternative to intuitionism of the type defended by Moore is generally thought to be some form of non-cognitivism. And although gallant efforts have been made in some quarters to base a belief in the objectivity of moral judgements upon purely logical foundations, it remains hard to see how a non-cognitivist can avoid some version of moral relativism: the doctrine that moral judgement is wholly relative to the customs and expectations of a particular society or social group. This is the position into which Philip, showing an impressive capacity to anticipate the direction to be taken by academic philosophy over the coming half-century, has settled by the time we find him lecturing Harriet on the historical absurdity of condemning an Italian for unchivalrousness. We need, I think, to understand Philip's subsequent behaviour in Monteriano in the light of this earlier passage: not simply as *frivolity* (for which there is no particular warrant elsewhere in the novel), but as issuing from a new-found conviction that one cannot judge one society by the lights of another – that what separates people of different moral outlook is not *error* about the topography of a moral landscape accessible to both, but simply empty space. One can imagine an equally amusing, though slighter, version of the novel being written with this as its central thesis. But clearly it is not the central thesis of the book we have: Philip's moral relativism is not the last word.

What Forster is out to demonstrate in the book, it seems to me, is that even if relativism should happen to have the last word on the level of theorizing about morality, what has the last word at the level of moral commitment and change of outlook is not theory but relationship. Two remarks of Furbank seem to me of particular value here. The first concerns 'the extraordinary precipitateness and swift-ness of transformation of his [Forster's] narrative. . . . Hardly any characters exchange two sentences before they have changed in relation to each other, and also changed in themselves, often for ever.'[17] The second is Furbank's observation that for Forster 'what supremely mattered was human relationships . . . people mattered, but only relatively, for people are inevitably in a ceaseless state of flux and dissolution; the thing which may contain more reality and permanence is found in *relationships* between people.'[18]

Why does relationship have the power to change people 'in them-selves'? The answer, I take it, lies in the way in which the confident moral conclusions which we derive from solitary, inward reflection are apt to die on our lips when we measure them against the acts and words of the alien Other. The moral objectivities we encounter on such occasions are admittedly of a rather negative, not to say Popperian, kind–they afford us knowledge only of what Will Not Wash, morally speaking, not of what will – but that does not make them any the less objectivities. And they afford us as much in the way of moral objectivity as we are ever likely to obtain. Of course, if we are to enjoy even this much grasp on moral objectivity, it is essential above all things that we do not falsify the Other. It is primarily for this reason, it seems to me, that Forster wanted to insist upon the importance of 'the ethical idea that reality must be faced'. In so far as he was a Realist, he was a Realist about personal relationship; not, or not primarily, about cows or tables. And this, of course, is how it comes about that the bathing of Gino's little son can provide *Where*

Angels Fear to Tread with a moral centre which has the power to transcend, and through Caroline Abbott to rebuke, Philip's moral relativism. In that episode both Caroline Abbott and the reader are forced to reckon with the physical, undeniable presence of a love to which Gino has cheerfully sacrificed the pleasures of the café that morning, and to which he manifestly intends to go ahead and sacrifice those of the single state. As Caroline discovers, there is not much arguing with that. It has indeed, as Rosenbaum suggests, something of the blank Reality of Moore's two hands, though, as I have tried to suggest, the workings of Forster's mind in the novel are perhaps a little more complicated than that.

Chapter 4
Deconstructing Derrida

Je n'ai jamais dit qu'*il n'y avait pas* de 'sujet de l'écriture'. Je n'ai jamais dit non plus qu'il n'y avait pas de sujet.

Jacques Derrida, Positions[1]

I   The Pervasiveness of Logocentrism

New Criticism, we are told, believed in the text as 'verbal icon': a closed structure of meanings which it was the business of the critic to display in all its subtle articulations, thereby revealing not, perhaps, the author's *intentions* (these might safely be left out of account) but the living consciousness of the author as manifested in his work.

Newer criticism, in its rush to dissociate itself from the 'liberal humanism' of such views, has embraced some desperate doctrines. The following, for instance, might serve as a basic statement of the critical theory of 'deconstruction', as that term has come to be understood among English-speaking literary critics:
1. No text has a determinate meaning.
2. A text, though it may refer to other texts, refers to nothing extra-textual.
3. Equally legitimate interpretations of a text may be incompatible with one another, or just have nothing in common.
4. Since a text gives no access to the consciousness of its author, it gives no access to authorial consciousness *tout court*, and therefore cannot be taken as in any sense a *communication* from author to reader.
5. The job of the critic is not to explain what a text means, but to elaborate it into a new text.

Not all critics conventionally labelled 'deconstructionist', of course, would wish to accept theses (1)–(5) just as they stand here. Some would wish to dissent from one or another, or to diminish – or sharpen – by qualification the paradoxical appearance of others. Each, however, can claim one or more serious practical critics among its defenders, while in the secondary literature of deconstruction something like the whole position outlined by theses (1)–(5) is frequently offered as constituting a new critical orthodoxy.

At the same time, although the resulting orthodoxy can claim some basis in practical criticism (Barthes, Bloom, de Man, Fish, Miller *et al.*), it is not primarily recommended by its defenders as the *ad hoc* theoretical precipitate of some interesting criticism. It is recommended primarily on philosophical grounds, and the philosophical support in question is taken to come most importantly from the work of Jacques Derrida.

Derrida's work has so far received little attention from English-speaking philosophers. The exception is John Searle, whose pugnacious dismissal of Derrida's claims to serious philosophical attention has only served to increase the disinclination of analytic philosophers to undertake the task of penetrating a style and a background of philosophical reference which they find, to say the least, unappealing.

I have not myself found Searle's dismissiveness compatible with any extensive reading of Derrida's work. I have not the slightest doubt that Derrida is an important philosopher. What I do doubt is whether his work provides much philosophical support for theses (1)–(5). In fact I would put it more strongly than that. Theses (1)–(5) can be shown to be strictly incompatible with Derrida's philosophical position, if his work is read as a connected body of thought, rather than just used as a convenient quarry from which to extract exhilaratingly sceptical *obiter dicta*.

My object, however, is not to take possession of Derrida's thought on behalf of a more conservative ideology of criticism, or of 'philosophy' departmentally considered (as what Richard Rorty likes to call *a Fach*); or even to accuse some distinguished critics of having got philosophically out of their depth. Something more interesting than any of that is at stake: something having to do with the transmission of Derrida's thought into an English-speaking academic culture; something, also, which Derrida's thought itself equips us to understand.

To invert the terms of an ingrained conceptual dichotomy is, as Derrida frequently reminds us, not at all the same thing as escaping from the influence of that dichotomy. Theses (1)–(5), however, represent a position arrived at by simple denial of what Derrida calls 'logocentrism'; thus a position which, because it accepts the polarities of logocentrism as the condition of its self-definition, remains profoundly, if obscurely, logocentric. No doubt this has something to do with the ingrained empiricism of English-speaking philosophical and literary culture. We can come to grips with a view which says that there is a solid extra-linguistic reality which language passively represents, or with an opposed view which denies language any commerce with reality at all; but we lack ready access to, and find difficulty envisaging, views, like those of Heidegger or Merleau-Ponty, say, which aim (however imperfectly, if we are to accept Derrida's estimate of Heidegger) at transcending that sort of opposition.

Be that as it may, any reading of Derrida which systematically and straightforwardly reinterprets him in terms of (1)–(5) imports into his position a covert logocentrism which opens it to the sort of accusation (of denying logocentrism in terms which require logocentrism to support them) which Derrida himself levels at Lévi-Strauss:[2] makes it, in other words, itself open to deconstruction. It is this phenomenon which I propose now to examine in detail.

II   Meaning and *Différance*

To begin with, let us take the thesis (1), that a text has no determinate meaning, and the correlative theses (3) and (5) that equally legitimate interpretations may have nothing in common and that the task of criticism is to elaborate, not elucidate, texts. Equivalent claims are not hard to find in the literature of deconstruction. Here, for example is Christopher Norris:

> Writing, for Derrida, is the 'free play' or element of undecidability within every system of communication . . . [it] is the endless displacement of meaning which both governs language and places it for ever beyond the reach of a stable, self-authenticating knowledge. . . . If meaning could only attain to a state of self-sufficient intelligibility, language would no longer present any problem but serve as an obedient vehicle of thought. To pose the question of writing in its radical, Derridean form is thus to transgress – or 'violently' oppose – the conventional relation of language and thought.[3]

And here is Rorty on 'strong textualism', a view which Rorty (who, unlike at least some literary critics, is well aware of some of the complexities in Derrida's thought which I propose to unravel here) thinks Derrida upholds in his better – i.e. least constructive – moments:

> The second sort of textualist – the strong textualist – has his own vocabulary and doesn't worry about whether anybody shares it. . . . He

recognizes what Nietzsche and James recognized, that the idea of *method* presupposes that of a *privileged vocabulary*, the vocabulary which gets to the essence of the object, the one which expresses the properties which it has in itself *as opposed to those which we read into it* [my italics]. Nietzsche and James said that the notion of such a vocabulary was a myth – that even in science, not to mention philosophy, we simply cast around for a vocabulary which lets us get what we want.[4]

Finally, Norris again, drawing the consequences for interpretation of the alleged indeterminacy of meaning:

> Having done away with the Author as transcendent source of authenticated meaning, one is left with a limitless free play of textual potential, open to a reading which asserts its creative independence of all traditional sanctions. Derrida and Barthes have been the most outspoken in their choice of this second, more joyous and vertiginous mode of deconstructive thinking.[5]

How far can this kind of thing be defended by appeal to Derridean arguments? A good place to start is *La Voix et le phénomène* (*Speech and Phenomena*); for Derrida, 'peut-être l'essai auquel je tiens le plus.'[6]

Speech and Phenomena is a reflection on a few pages of the first of Edmund Husserl's *Logical Investigations*: pages in which Husserl elaborates a few 'essential distinctions' which embody an account of the nature of the linguistic sign. The resulting theory of language turns upon the claims (which it shares with a very long metaphysical tradition extending from the *Cratylus* to early Russell) that the physical apparatus of language, though it is essential to the *expression* of meaning, contributes nothing to the *constitution* of meaning. Meaning has nothing essential to do with the manipulation of signs, in fact, but is apprehended directly in the immediate presence of consciousness to itself.

Derrida does not attempt a direct demonstration of the falsity of this thesis. What he does is to show, elegantly and persuasively, that the thesis cannot be coherently propounded in the first place; that the more Husserl struggles to get it formulated, the more he involves himself in absurdities and contradictions: that, in short, the thesis 'deconstructs' itself.

The thrust of Derrida's deconstruction of the notion of meaning as manifest in the self-presence of consciousness is profoundly anti-Cartesian and anti-Platonic, in that Derrida is opposing to the idea of the mind as a system of non-material, timeless, closed meanings a conception which views mentality as essentially involved with the physical and the temporal. This is the background to Derrida's talk of 'effacing the difference between signifier and signified' (*signifiant et signifié*). What he has in mind is not the exclusion from discourse of all concern with or reference to the extra-textual, but the erosion of the Platonic/Cartesian distinction between the intelligible and the sensible.

> Car il y a deux manières hétèrogènes d'effacer la différence entre le signifiant et le signifié: l'une, la classique, consiste à réduire ou à dériver le signifiant, c'est-à-dire finalement à *soumettre* le signe à la pensée; l'autre, celle que nous dirigeons ici contre la précédente, consiste à mettre en question le système dans lequel fonctionnait la précédente réduction: et d'abord l'opposition du sensible et de l'intelligible.*[7]

A related thought lies behind the Derridean reversal of the traditional (e.g. Rousseauian) view of writing as secondary to speech: a matter of representation rather than of primary utterance. The primacy of speech in the traditional view, according to Derrida, is related to its presumed status as the direct expression of thought. In listening we are confronted with another living subject. In reading all we have is the text, in its naked and humble conventionality. But, Derrida wants to say, the moment one reflects on the alleged poverty of the material – the text – confronting the reader, one sees that that poverty is illusory: that the text is *readable (lisible, itérable)* despite the absence – the non-*présence* – of its author. That seen, the point transfers back to listening, and we see that access to *présence*, to the full and living immediacy of another consciousness, is quite inessential even to the understanding of speech. So writing, which had been thought to belong on the side of the sensible, the accidental, the material, the temporal, the conventional, turns out to be the primary mode of language (of discourse), while speech, which had been classed as closest to thought, as the direct expression of the living and eternal *logos*, turns out to be, not secondary to, but no less conventional, accidental, sensible, material, etc., than writing.

Having arrived at the view that meaning is constituted within language, or within *writing (écriture)*, Derrida needs a way of representing the results of this constitution. He chooses to adopt for this purpose Saussure's characterization of linguistic objects as

---

*   ('For there are two quite different ways of effacing the difference between signifier and signified. One, the classical, consists in reducing or deriving the signifier; that is to say, finally, in subordinating the sign to thought. The other, which we are deploying here against the former, puts into question the system within which the former reduction operated; *and questions first of all the opposition between the sensible and the intelligible* [my italics].')

structural or *diacritical*: constituted, like phonemes, purely in terms of the relationships of contrast holding between them.

From this Saussurian perspective, meaning within language appears as a system of 'differences' (contrasts) between one sign and another. Derrida now argues, plausibly enough, that once we cut language free from the control of a 'transcendental signified' (*signifié transcendentale*) we are left with no means of limiting the array of potential contrasts which can contribute to the meaning of a sign. In consequence we never arrive at a complete, final and totalized meaning for a sign. The goal of a complete and final meaning flees endlessly before us as a given sign passes into new contexts and new relations of contrast: is always *deferred*, as a consequence of the fact that meaning is *difference*. Derrida coins the famous compound *différance* to express the intimate relation between difference and deferral.

The Cartesian metaphysics of *présence*, as manifested, for example, in the Husserlian ἐποχή, can now be seen as offering the delusive hope that human life might escape from temporality and perpetual becoming into a 'pure consciousness' which would be a realm of *meanings*, but of closed, and so eternal meanings. The central message of Derrida's thought is that there can be no such closure of meaning, and thus no escape from the perpetual reformulation of ourselves and our concepts whose image is the process of endless projection and augmentation of meaning through text after related text which Derrida calls 'dissemination' (*dissémination*).

These arguments provide the basis for the interpretation of Derrida which enlists him on the side of those who want to claim that a text has no determinate meaning, that 'creative' interpretation is the only kind there can be, and so on. Two thoughts should make us pause before accepting this interpretation.

The first is the thought that such an interpretation depends covertly on the very 'logocentrism' which Derrida attacks (which in turn should prompt the cautious reader to recall Derrida's frequent complaints, in *Positions*, in *Limited, Inc.*, and elsewhere, that his critics accuse him of defending the very positions he attacks, using arguments drawn from his work: 'Là encore, on me prête ce que je dénonce, comme si l'on était moins pressé de me critiquer ou de me discuter que de se mettre d'abord à ma place pour le faire' ('Here, too, what I denounce is attributed to me, as if one were in less of a hurry to criticise or discuss me, than first to put oneself in my place in order to do so').[8] The logocentrist thinks that strings of linguistic signs can be perceived as determinately meaningful only because their order or structure can be seen as representing or mirroring the structure of external reality. If it is shown to everyone's satisfaction that this is not so, and that the ascription of specific meaning to a text cannot be controlled by any appeal to extra-linguistic meanings residing in the very structure of Reality, it is thus precisely the *logocentrist* whose tendency will be to conclude that, in that case, the ascription of meaning to a text cannot be controlled by anything at all, but must be to all intents and purposes arbitrary: that, as Rorty tells us, there is no difference between reading and reading-in.

This transition of thought is of course a *non sequitur*. It simply does not follow from the assertion that the ascription of meaning to a text is not controlled by a 'transcendental signified' (by meanings directly apprehended in the Husserlian 'living present of consciousness', or something of the sort) that it is not controlled by anything at all. Which brings us to the second of the two thoughts which the cautious reader of Derrida should bear in mind. It is this. Suppose we take seriously the idea that all reading is reading-in; that the Derridean 'opening' of meaning really does betray us into 'the abyss of an endless regress of ever-promised, never-delivered meaning'.[9] Don't the notions of *text* and *écriture* themselves begin to disintegrate under us?

We cannot, after all, cut the text loose from the 'transcendental signified' unless we can somehow retain the possibility of distinguishing between a text and a random string of marks or sounds. Once the 'transcendental signified' has gone, what basis for such a distinction remains available to us? The only possible one, it seems to me, is that different readers can, in the case of a text but not in the case of a random string of marks, give independently of one another accounts of the semantic features of the text, and the semantic mechanisms operating in it, which agree with one another. But to avail ourselves of this criterion of textuality we need to maintain a rather rigid distinction between reading and reading-in. If we *both* do away with the 'transcendental signified' *and* refuse to maintain the distinction between reading and reading-in, then we are left with a position which is simply incoherent – or, to put it modishly, which 'deconstructs itself' – because, as I have just tried to show, it is itself deeply, if covertly, logocentric.

It is no doubt for this reason that Derrida insists everywhere, in a way rather reminiscent of Wittgenstein, on the *publicity* of the mechanisms of *dissemination*. In the celebrated passage in *Éperons*, on the fragment 'I have forgotten my umbrella' found among Nietzsche's *Nachlass*, for instance, Derrida is concerned to argue only that the words give us no clue to Nietzsche's intentional states, not that they lack determinate meaning: 'Sa transparence s'étale sans pli, sans réserve. . . . Chacun comprend ce que veut dire "j'ai oublié mon parapluie"' ('Its transparence displays itself without fold or reserve. . . . Everyone knows what "I have forgotten my umbrella" means').[10]

Perhaps all Derrida has in mind is that 'Everyone knows' what words *literally* mean. But no; in 'Signature Event Context' the claim of publicity is extended by implication to all the rhetorical mechanisms of *dissémination*, to every 'organon of iterability', for reasons which have to do with the central move of Derrida's position: the severing of textuality from psychic *presence*:

> Une écriture qui ne serait pas structurellement lisible – itérable – par-delà la mort du destinataire ne serait pas une écriture. . . . Imaginons une écriture dont le code soit assez idiomatique pour n'avoir été instauré et connu, comme chiffre secret, que par deux 'sujets'. Dira-t-on encore que, à la mort du destinataire, voire des deux partenaires, la marque laissée par l'un d'eux est toujours une écriture? Oui, dans la mesure où, réglée par un code, fût-il inconnu et non linguistique, elle est constituée, dans son identité de marque, par son itérabilité, en l'absence de tel ou tel, donc à la limite de tout 'sujet' empiriquement déterminé. Cela implique qu'il n'y a pas de code – organon d'itérabilité – qui soit structurellement secret.*[11]

It is not difficult to show, either, that the publicity of the mechanisms of *dissémination* is not a mere afterthought, but is essential to Derrida's position. I have the impression that English-speaking readers tend to see parallels between Derrida and Sartre; perhaps not surprisingly, since Sartre is the one philosopher in the phenomenological tradition whose ideas have penetrated fairly deeply into English-speaking literary culture. They tend to equate Derridean *présence* with Sartrean *Being* (or, as one perhaps should say, with Sartre's bizarre glossing of Heidegger's notion of Being), and thus to see the operations of Derridean *dissémination* as roughly equivalent to those of Sartrean *anéantissement*: as a process, that is, in which an absolutely arbitrary act of denial or exclusion results in an equally absolute and arbitrary creation of meaning. This is to stand Derrida

---

*   ('A writing that is not structurally readable – iterable – beyond the death of the addressee would not be writing. . . . Imagine a writing whose code would be so idiomatic as to be established and known, as secret cipher, by only two "subjects". Could we maintain that, following the death of the receiver, or even of both partners, the mark left by one of them is still writing? Yes, to the extent that, organized by a code, even an unknown and non-linguistic one, it is constituted in its identity as mark by its iterability [*itérabilité*], in the absence of such and such a person, and hence of every empirically determined "subject". This implies that *there is no such thing as a code – organon of iterability – which could be structurally secret* [my italics].')

on his head. Derrida's insistence on the *materiality* of language – his reduction, in effect, of the intelligible to the sensible – aligns him not with Sartre's intensely Cartesian, not to say Manichaean, theory of consciousness, but with the sort of objections brought against it by Maurice Merleau-Ponty, which in another way question the feasibility of a radical distinction between the sensible and the intelligible.

Thus, in *Positions*, Derrida insists on the 'regulated' character of *différance*. The 'play' (*jeu*) of *différance*, it appears, involves not just change, but *transformation*:

L'activité ou la productivité connotées par le *a* de la *différance* renvoient au mouvement génératif dans le jeu des différences. Celles-ci ne sont pas tombées du ciel et elles ne sont pas inscrites une fois pour toutes dans un système clos, dans une structure statique qu'une opération synchronique et taxinomique pourrait épuiser. Les différences sont les effets de transformations et de ce point de vue le thème de la différance est incompatible avec le motif statique, synchronique, taxinomique, anhistorique, etc., du concept de *structure*. Mais il va de soi que ce motif n'est pas le seul à définir la structure et que la production des différences, la différance, n'est pas astructurale: elle produit des transformations systématiques et réglées pouvant, jusqu'à un certain point, donner lieu à une science structurale. Le concept de différance développe même les exigences principielles les plus légitimes du 'structuralisme'.*[12]

Some readers may merely see in this evidence of vacillation or the simple desire to have it both ways.[13] Surely a system governed by *rule* must be one in which the rules determine everything beforehand, in which nothing is left to chance. And conversely, once we begin to talk of 'openness' or 'play' surely we must be speaking of an activity not, or no longer, governed by rules.

In fact there is no inconsistency. The key to Derrida's thought at this point lies in the word 'productivity'. Derrida is claiming, in effect, that a sign system is *productive* in the sense that the rules of use which we lay down initially, and which *in one way* entirely

---

* ('The activity or productivity connoted by the *a* of *différance* refers to the generative movement in the play of differences. The latter are neither fallen from the sky nor inscribed once and for all in a closed system, a static structure that a synchronic and taxonomic operation could exhaust. Differences are the effects of transformations, and from this vantage the theme of *différance* is incompatible with the static, synchronic, taxonomic, ahistoric motifs in the concept of structure. But it goes without saying that this motif is not the only one that defines structure, and that the production of differences, *différance*, is not astructural: it produces systematic and regulated transformations which are able, at a certain point, to leave room for a structural science. The concept of *différance* even develops the most legitimate principled exigencies of "structuralism".')

determine the meanings of the component signs of the system, may turn out to yield surprising and unexpected possibilities of combination and extension of meaning when projected into unfamiliar contexts.

This view of the 'activity or productivity' of *différance*, of course, specifically excludes arbitrariness or subjectivity in interpretation. *That* is not at all the kind of 'activity' at stake. (In general, in Derrida, it is *the text*, the actual signs themselves, which is conceived as 'active', not the subjectivity of the interpreter.) It is not hard to see why this is so. If reading and reading-in were one and the same thing, the 'activity' of the text would not be a matter of 'productivity' or 'transformation' at all, but simply one of *change*: not *différance*, but merely difference.

This is why Derrida speaks in *Of Grammatology* of the *trace* (what is produced by the movement of *différance*): 'comme l'unité d'un double mouvement de protention et de rétention' ('as the unity of the double movement of protention and retention').[14]

The commonplace meaning of a sign, which it carries with it into a new context (*rétention*) is what enables the reader to grasp the nature of the transformation, semantic or rhetorical, which the sign is producing in a new context (*protention*). If there were no retention, then, since it would not be possible for the reader to recognize the text produced by his reading as standing to an 'original' text in a relationship of transformation (i.e. systematic reordering of structure), there would be no protention either.

All this seems closely related, as I suggested a few paragraphs ago, to the account Merleau-Ponty gives of reading in *La Prose du monde* and elsewhere:

> Je sais, avant de lire Stendhal, ce que c'est qu'un coquin et je peux donc comprendre ce qu'il veut dire quand il écrit que le fiscal Rossi est un coquin. Mais quand le fiscal Rossi commence à vivre, ce n'est plus lui qui est un coquin, c'est le coquin qui est un fiscal Rossi. J'entre dans la morale de Stendhal par les mots de tout le monde dont il se sert, mais ces mots ont subi entre ses mains une torsion secrète. A mesure que les recoupements se multiplient et que plus de flèches se dessinent vers ce lieu de pensée où je ne suis jamais allé auparavant, où peut-être, sans Stendhal, je ne serais jamais allé, tandis que les occasions dans lesquelles Stendhal les emploie indiquent toujours plus impérieusement le sens neuf qu'il leur donne, je me rapproche davantage de lui jusqu'à ce que je lise enfin ses mots dans l'intention même où il les écrivit.... Des mots communs, des épisodes après tout déjà connus – un duel, une jalousie – qui d'abord me renvoyaient au monde de tous fonctionnent soudain

comme les émissaires du monde de Stendhal et finissent par m'installer sinon dans son être empirique, du moins dans ce moi imaginaire dont il s'est entretenu avec lui-même pendant cinquante années en même temps qu'il le monnayait en ses œuvres. C'est alors seulement que le lecteur ou l'auteur peut dire avec Paulhan: 'Dans cet éclair du moins, j'ai été avec toi'.*[15]

All this is no doubt very remote from 'deconstruction' as practised, say, by J. Hillis Miller, or Stanley Fish, or even Harold Bloom. But it is very close indeed to Derrida. The following words, from *L'Écriture et la différence*, which virtually repeat the substance of the above passage, should suffice to demonstrate Derrida's affinity with Merleau-Ponty:

Le sens doit attendre d'être dit ou écrit pour s'habiter lui-même et devenir ce qu'à différer de soi il est: le sens. C'est ce que Husserl nous apprend à penser dans *l'Origine de la géométrie*. L'acte littéraire retrouve ainsi à sa source son vrai pouvoir. Dans un fragment du livre qu'il projetait de consacrer à *l'Origine de la vérité*, Merleau-Ponty écrivait: 'La communication en littérature n'est pas simple appel de l'écrivain à des significations qui feraient partie d'un *a priori* de l'esprit humain: bien plutôt elle les y suscite par entraînement ou par une sorte d'action oblique. Chez l'écrivain la pensée ne dirige pas le langage du dehors: l'écrivain est lui-même comme un nouvel idiome qui se construit...'. 'Mes paroles me surprennent moi-même et m'enseignent ma pensée', disait-il ailleurs.

C'est parce qu'elle est *inaugurale*, au sens jeune de ce mot, que l'écriture est dangereuse et angoissante.†[16]

---

* ('Before I read Stendhal, I know what a rogue is. Thus I can understand what he means when he says that Rossi the revenue man is a rogue. But when Rossi the Rogue begins to live, it is no longer he who is a rogue: it is a rogue who is the revenue man Rossi. I have access to Stendhal's outlook through the commonplace words he uses. But in his hands these words are given a new twist. The cross-references multiply. More and more arrows point in the direction of a thought I have never encountered before, and perhaps never would have met without Stendhal. At the same time, the contexts in which Stendhal uses common words reveal even more majestically the new meanings with which he endows them. I get closer and closer to him, until in the end I read his words with the very same intention that he gave to them. ... Common words and familiar events, like jealousy or a duel, which at first immerse us in everyone's world, suddenly function as emissaries from Stendhal's world. Although the final effect is not for me to dwell within Stendhal's lived experience, I am at last brought within the imaginary self and the internal dialogue Stendhal held with it for the fifty years he was coining it in his works. It is only then that the reader or the author can say with Paulhan, "In this light at least, I have been with you."')

† ('Meaning must await being said or written in order to inhabit itself, and in order to become, by differing from itself, what it is: meaning. This is what Husserl teaches us to think in *The Origin of Geometry*. The literary act thus recovers its true power at its source. In a fragment of a book he intended to devote to the *Origin of Truth*, Merleau-Ponty wrote: "Communication in literature is not the simple appeal on the part of the writer to meanings

One can agree, I think, with A. D. Nuttall: 'Certainly, if one reads Derrida with Merleau-Ponty in mind, certain passages suggest not so much free-floating formalism as a peculiarly tense engagement with reality.'[17] An engagement also, one might add, with language, considered not as the garden of relaxedly burgeoning parasitical kudzu vines recently evoked in Derrida's name by Richard Rorty,[18] but something rather more like a gymnasium, or possibly a minefield.

III   The author as 'effect of *différance*'

Let us turn now to the second and fourth of the five 'deconstructionist' theses with which we began. Here again, we find plenty of commentators ready to cite Derrida in their favour.

'Our traditional commitment to the voice as the primary communicative instrument also commits us, in Derrida's view', according to Terence Hawkes, 'to a falsifying "metaphysics of presence", based on an illusion that we are able, ultimately, to "come face to face once and for all with objects". That is, that some final, objective, unmediated "real world" exists, about which we can have concrete knowledge.' According to A. D. Nuttall, 'in his [Derrida's] writing as in the earlier work of Sartre there is a bias towards idealism'. 'It is in Derrida that the dissolution of the subject is most complete.' Richard Rorty, assessing 'textualism' as 'the contemporary counterpart of idealism', assures us that 'textualists', among whom he includes Derrida, 'write as if there were nothing but texts'.[19]

Against the weight of this Anglo-Saxon chorus, in which disciples and opponents stand for once united, Derrida's 'Je n'ai jamais dit qu'il n'y avait pas de "sujet d'écriture". Je n'ai jamais dit non plus qu'il n'y avait pas de sujet' ('I never said there was no "subject of writing". I never said either that there was no subject') takes on a certain pathos. And yet he never has said either of those things. What has gone wrong?

One fruitful source of misunderstanding lies in the terms (of Saussurian origin, but now universal in French philosophy of language) *signifiant* and *signifié*. They are invariably translated 'signifier' and 'signified'. For English-speaking readers, because of

which would be part of an *a priori* of the mind; rather, communication arouses these meanings in the mind through enticement and a kind of oblique action. The writer's thought does not control his language from without; the writer is a kind of new idiom, constructing itself. . . ." "My own words take me by surprise and teach me what to think", he said elsewhere.

It is because writing is *inaugural*, in the fresh sense [*sens jeune*] of the word, that it is dangerous and anguishing.')

the way in which English thought has, since the eighteenth century, turned centrally upon the issue of idealism versus realism, the term 'signified' can only mean the 'external' real-world object which is (in Russellian terms, for instance) the *designatum* of the sign: the *real tree*, for example, to which I refer when I point and say, 'there is a tree'. This is not at all what *signifié* means in Saussure, or in subsequent French linguistic or philosophical discussion. For Saussure the term *signifiant* refers to the 'acoustic image', the sign-*vehicle*, that is, while *signifié* refers to the *concept* evoked by the *signifiant*. *Signe* (sign) designates the union of sign-vehicle and concept.[20]

Thus, when Derrida says that we have no access to a *signifié transcendentale* ('transcendental signified'), what he means is not, absurdly, that we have no access to trees but only to texts on trees. He means that *meanings*, or concepts, are elaborated solely within the text, through the transforming activity of *différance*. As reference to the preceding context of the passage will confirm, it is only this that is at stake in the famous slogan 'Il n'y a pas d'hors-texte' ('there is nothing outside the text'). Plainly, nothing in the claim that 'meaning must await to be spoken or written' ('Le sens doit attendre d'être dit ou écrit') in order to exist *as meaning* entails any form of philosophical idealism. In using language to refer to and talk about what exists, extra-textually, in reality, we are not, after all, using it to refer to and talk about *meanings* (about, that is, the Saussurian *signifié*). On the contrary, the meanings (concepts) which we elaborate *within* language are just what serve to give us common referential access to the extra-linguistic, or real, *world*.

So much for Derrida's alleged idealism. Related, but more interesting issues arise over the status of the author in Derrida's theory of reading. He holds that the reader of a text is acquainted with its author as an 'effect of *différance*':

> Rien – aucun étant présent et in-différant – ne précède donc la différance et l'espacement. Il n'y a pas de sujet qui soit agent, auteur et maître de la différance et auquel celle-ci surviendrait éventuellement et empiriquement. La subjectivité – comme l'objectivité – est un effet de différance, un effet inscrit dans un système de différance.*[21]

M. H. Abrams concludes from this that, 'since they lack a ground in presence',[22] such effects must be illusory. But this does not

---

* ('Nothing – no present and in-*different* being – thus precedes *différance* and spacing. There is no subject who is agent, author and master of *différance*, who eventually and empirically would be overtaken by *différance*. Subjectivity – like objectivity – is an effect of *différance*, an effect inscribed in a system of *différance*'.)

necessarily follow. When I am confronted with another person, what confronts me is not the 'living present' of his consciousness, but the 'text' of his words, deeds, gestures and expressions. His or her responses to the contingencies of life are apprehended by me as those of a single, unique person, not because I have access to the metaphysical unity of a Cartesian substance underlying them (even the knowledge, which the nature of his or her responses forces upon me, that the Other is *conscious*, does not entail the kind of meta-physical self-identity which Cartesian metaphysics – the metaphysics of *présence* – demands as a condition for ascribing personhood), but because those responses confront me as a *system*: a unique order of transformations effected in the structure of physical and perceptual capacities, notions of morality, social and linguistic conventions, which is common to all of us. And this system develops over time: transforms itself in ways which are not always foreseeable, but which can be seen in retrospect to constitute transformation and not just change; to have come about by just that 'double movement of pro-tention and retention' in terms of which Derrida characterizes the *trace*. The person who confronts me in life confronts me, just like the author of the book I am reading, 'comme un nouvel idiome qui se construit'.

Sterne, who saw deeply into these issues at a time when they were less familiar, turns the tables on the Lockeian sceptic in just this way in the chapter of *Tristram Shandy* which begins with Momus's glass and ends with my Uncle Toby's hobby-horse. If 'the fixture of *Momus's* glass in the human breast, according to the proposed emendation of that arch-critick, had taken place', we could 'have taken a chair and gone softly, as you would to a dioptical bee-hive, and look'd in, – view'd the soul stark naked; – observed all her motions, – her machinations; – traced all her maggots from their first engendering to their crawling forth; . . . '.[23]

Alas, this is not possible. Cartesian *présence* is inaccessible in the case of the Other. Are we to conclude, sceptically, that others, including my Uncle Toby, unfortunately inhabit that 'final, objective, unmediated "real world"' of which, according to Terence Hawkes, 'we can have no concrete knowledge'? Certainly not. Sterne, after considering various increasingly elaborate and alarming ways of penetrating my Uncle Toby's dark backward and abysm, concludes that no such metaphysical surgery is necessary:

> To avoid all and every one of these errors, in giving you my Uncle *Toby's* character, I am determined to draw it by no mechanical help whatever; – nor shall my pencil be guided by any one wind-instrument which ever was

blown upon, either on this, or on the other side of the *Alps*; – nor will I consider either his repletions or his discharges, – or touch upon his Non-Naturals; – but, in a word, I will draw my Uncle *Toby's* character from his HOBBY-HORSE.[24]

It is, of course, much to the point that my Uncle Toby's hobby-horse is a *game* (a *jeu*), just as *Tristram Shandy* itself is a game, of words. Don't we reveal ourselves, precisely, in the games we play?

'Not if the way we play them is incoherent, subject to radically exclusive interpretations', the deconstructionist may want to reply, playing once more the third of his supposedly Derridean cards. So let us look at this move again.

The notion of 'incoherence' at stake here is clearly going to have to be a pretty strong one, if it is to do the work the deconstructionist requires of it. Mere logical inconsistency will hardly do. When a fellow philosopher says something logically inconsistent with something he said a moment ago, that in itself has no tendency to make me doubt – indeed it may confirm me in my belief – that one and the same person, familiar over many years, is continuing to address me. Christopher Norris, arguing against Hirsch, commits a pair of *non sequiturs* when he says:

> The author is not simply *there* in the text, a self-authenticating 'voice' of intent, as Hirsch (in his more sanguine moments) would have us believe. One might expect some such assurance from the homely narrative address of a novelist like Fielding, or the intimate soul-baring style of Wordsworth's poetry. Yet Fielding is as cunning a narrative tactician as any, his 'voice' a shifting multitude of ironies and ploys; while Wordsworth manages a complex and selective rhetoric of memory which (as recent critics have shown) by no means communicates the 'unmediated vision' of purely personal address.[25]

To show that the 'voice' operative in Fielding's novels cannot be ascribed to Fielding, Norris would need to show that his 'multitude of ironies and ploys' is not merely 'shifting', but as incoherent as those of a madman to whom we can attribute no single stable personality; while to suppose that 'rhetoric' excludes self-revelation (rather than serving, as it often does, as its instrument) is just to take at face value the Romantic opposition between the naïvely direct and the rhetorically opaque which Norris supposes himself to be questioning in the case of Wordsworth.

Again, when we have read and understood Derrida's deconstruction of Rousseau's *Essay on the Origin of Language* we do not feel ourselves, when subsequently reading that text, any the less in the presence of Rousseau, considered as an 'idiome qui se construit'. Derrida has shown, indeed, how Rousseau's text 'differs' within itself. To show that is indeed to show that the text is not a closed, final, plenitude of meaning, that there are tensions within it capable of starting it moving, along paths of further development, parody, citation to one end or another and so on. But these tensions, or rather the way in which they are held in an unstable and dynamic balance with one another, in a discourse caught in the act of fabricating meanings which are not a mere reflection of the timeless finality of the *logos*, but exist only in this never-ending coming-to-birth in the act of writing, which is always further projectible: they and their shifting and always provisional resolutions *are* – constitute – the idiom of Rousseau's mind. Talk of the author as an 'idiom which constructs itself' is perfectly compatible with talk of the text as something which deconstructs itself, just as continuity of the person is compatible wtith the strains, inconsistencies and uneven accommodations and self-transcendences of everyday life.

But isn't *parody* one of the Derridean modes of *différance*? And isn't every reading in one sense a parody, if only in that it emphasizes and associates some aspects of the text while neglecting or dissociating others? And does not that make every reading false not just to authorial intention but to any stable reconstruction of the author's mind or outlook?

One can make two answers to this. The first is that different readings generally more resemble different artists' sketches of the same cathedral than sketches of different cathedrals. Fish, de Man, Kermode and others have attempted to provide instances of more radically alternative readings than this. They deserve separate discussion. My concern here is merely (mostly) to show that the thesis of the 'death of the author' receives no general, philosophical, support from the work of Derrida.

The second answer takes the objection by the horns. Doesn't *actual* parody depend for its effect not on a rupture with the author as 'idiome qui se construit', but precisely on a continuity between his idiom and that of the parody? And doesn't *that* mean that there is a sense in which a parody, far from demonstrating the possibility of a 'free play' of signs which annihilates the author by the mere fact that it can proceed in his absence, actually *belongs* to the author parodied, at least in the capacity of an albatross hung around his neck, or a chicken come home to roost?

Take, for example, Max Beerbohm's killing parody of a Barrack Room Ballad:

> Then it's collar 'im tight,
>   In the name o' the Lawd!
> 'Ustle'im, shake 'im till 'e's sick!
>   Wot, 'e *would*, would'e? Well,
>   Then yer've got ter give 'im 'Ell,
> An' it's trunch, trunch, truncheon does the trick.[26]

This *is* Kipling, though of course a Kipling gone very much over the top. But doesn't the fact that Kipling's characteristic mannerisms, and not just of style but of tone and moral impulse, can be transformed by *différance* in this way, show something about Kipling? Doesn't all first-rate parody show something about its target? And doesn't that mean that the evanescence of the author under the impact of *différance* is not quite the self-evident consequence it has been taken to be, *even* when the activity of *différance* is being carried on by another mind, be it that of a parodist or that of the reader?

In general there are (at least) three senses in which we can put the question 'What did A mean by "p"?' We may want to know what 'p' *says*: what the ordinary meaning of the words is. This is the sense in which, as Derrida says, 'Everyone knows' ('Chacun comprend') what 'I have forgotten my umbrella' means. Secondly, we may want to know what were A's *intentions* in saying 'p'. Pretty evidently, this is a psychological rather than a hermeneutic question, and, as Derrida rightly points out, one which, once a text has left its author's hand and embarked upon a public career, rapidly becomes matter for mere speculation.

Thirdly, we may wish to know *what A has said in saying 'p'*. This *is* a hermeneutic question. We can answer it only by taking the measure of the text; and not just by drawing out its logical implications (though certainly in part by doing that), but by examining the transformations which overtake its characteristic structures and polarities when we project these into new contexts. The author may never have envisaged those contexts: may never, therefore, have *intended* (psychologically speaking) that his words should be taken in quite that way. But does nothing of *him*, of his mind and characteristic way of looking at things, project into the new context along with his words? If meaning is constituted within the text, don't we *have* to say, in fact, that the structures of meaning which constitute an author's textual personality *just are* what we project into a new context?

But surely his *textual* personality is to be distinguished from his *actual* personality, present to him if to him alone, through the 'privileged access' of consciousness?

Is that so clear? Don't we recognize the unclarity of such claims when we recognize in everyday life the power of our own words to depart from us and yet to retain a hold upon us, to drag us with them into a new context, within which we would vastly prefer not to have to reconstrue either them or ourselves? One need only think of the telling force with which words once lightly said and since forgotten can be recalled when circumstances have changed. 'That is not what I intended', we say, logocentrically: but does that absolve us?

It is only if 'taking the measure of the text' in new contexts is a process of arbitrary invention, rather than one of 'transformation' in the structural sense of that term, that words once spoken can depart absolutely from their speaker. But such a view is false to everything we know about speaking, writing and reading. Certainly, as I have tried to show here, it receives no philosophical support from anything in Derrida. It seems to, for English readers, only because the Cartesianism ingrained in an empiricist outlook makes it quite easy for us to miss or blur the distinction between the second and the third of the senses distinguished above in which one can ask 'What did A mean by "p"?'

iv   Reconstructing Derrida

So far I have been doing my best to separate Derrida from everything which is thought on this side of the English Channel to stamp him as a radical literary theorist. And yet plainly Derrida *is* a radical thinker, whose work does have implications for the practice of criticism. So I shall end by offering a brief reassessment of what these might amount to.

Derrida has, by and large, been billed in England and America as a 'free floating formalist' (Nuttall) and an enemy of American 'New Criticism'.

In fact, I take it, Derrida's primary literary-critical target is not New Criticism but the type of French structuralism known as 'semiology'. Derrida objects to the semiological notion of literary work as a closed system of structural relationships, and also to the way in which the 'static, synchronic, taxonomic, ahistoric' aspects of semiology participate in the Cartesian 'metaphysics of presence'.

Of course there are New Critical echoes in this: in the notion of the work as a closed structure of meanings, explicable with finality, for instance. But the arguments in Derrida which oppose them are equally opposed to formalism. Derrida is opposed to any kind of criticism which seeks to put the reader in an epistemologically dominating position, from which the text can be exhaustively and finally explained, irrespective of whether the explanation proposed is a formalist one, in terms of semiological structures, or a 'thematic' one, in terms of, say, Marxist or Freudian theory. Indeed, Derrida sees both formalism and thematic criticism (rightly, I think) as equally conditioned by the 'metaphysics of presence'; as the alternatives within which such a metaphysics constrains us to restrict our critical options:

> une critique du simple contenu (critique thématique, qu'elle soit de style philosophique, sociologique, psychanalytique, qui prendrait le thème, manifeste ou caché, plein ou vide, pour la substance du texte, pour son objet ou pour *sa vérité illustrée*) ne peut pas plus se mesurer à *certains* textes (ou plutôt à la structure de certaines *scènes* textuelles) qu'une critique purement formaliste qui ne s'intéresserait qu'au code, au pur jeu du signifiant, à l'agencement technique d'un texte-objet et négligerait les effets génétiques ou l'inscription ('historique', si vous voulez) du texte lu *et* du nouveau texte qu'elle écrit elle-même. Ces deux insuffisances sont rigoureusement complémentaires. On ne peut les définir sans une déconstruction de la rhétorique classique et de sa philosophie implicite. . . .*[27]

What has been thought to stamp Derrida himself as a 'free floating formalist' is his supposed commitment to the indeterminacy of textual meaning and to the 'death of the author'. If, as I have been trying to show, these alleged commitments are misunderstandings engendered by a reading directed by the very logocentrism which Derrida attacks, what follows?

First of all, I think, we have to see Derrida as recommending that we drop, or cease to worry about, the distinction between 'Realist' and 'Formalist' *writing*; between writing, that is, which because of its Lockeian plainness seems to put us directly in contact with Reality, and writing which because of its artificial, rhetorical character, seems to refuse the challenge of what Dr Leavis liked to call 'Life', in favour of remaining on a level of 'pure play', or talk for its own sake; between *Clarissa, Sons and Lovers* or *Germinal* on the one hand, say,

---

* ('a criticism concerned only with content (that is, a thematic criticism, be it in philosophical, sociological or psychoanalytic style, that takes the theme – manifest or hidden, full or empty – as the substance of the text, as its object or as its *illustrated truth*) can no more measure itself against *certain* texts . . . than can a purely formalist criticism which would be interested only in the code, the pure play of signifiers, the technical manipulation of a text-object, thereby overlooking the genetic effects or the ('historical', if you will) inscription of the text read *and* of the new text this criticism itself writes. These two insufficiencies are rigorously complementary. They cannot be defined without a deconstruction of classical rhetoric and its implicit philosophy. . . . ')

and *Tristram Shandy, Tom Jones* or *To the Lighthouse* on the other. 'Textuality' rules: no text is any less 'textual' than any other.

This in itself, of course, is a thought which has already penetrated quite deeply into the consciousness and practice of English-speaking critics. But the assimilation is generally taken to run one way (is so taken by Christopher Norris, for instance, in the passage on Fielding and Wordsworth quoted earlier), towards the idea that all writing is equally remote from Reality, equally *play*, in the somewhat pejorative sense (*not* equivalent to Derridean *jeu*) which a traditional logocentrism makes available to us.

What I want to suggest is that the assimilation can just as easily (and more faithfully to Derrida) be made to run the other way. If meaning is brought to birth within the text, then the text itself is the bearer of all the Reality that inheres in meaning; and that, when one thinks about it, is, while by no means all the Reality there is, quite a good portion of that part of Reality which matters to us. On such a view, to read *Tristram Shandy*, say, as a field of reverberating and self-mirroring rhetorical devices is not to forget Sterne and his world, but precisely to encounter Sterne, and the world as strangely transmuted, but also strangely recognizable, in his vision. The vision, and the world, are not *behind* but *in* the rhetoric.

Secondly, we have to see Derrida as recommending an 'active', disseminative style of reading. Again this thought is already deeply entrenched in the minds of critics, especially American ones, who see it as a valuable counterbalance to the New Critical insistence on the scholarly pursuit of a single, privileged, final elucidation of the text. But here again, 'activity' is very often construed in terms of 'free floating' subjectivity; in part, I suspect, because that is the way in which 'activity' in interpretation, as opposed to 'passive' delineation of the Real, is marked within the scheme of conceptual distinctions which characterizes an only formally renounced logocentrism.

'Active' reading does not for Derrida, as I have been trying to show, mean subjective reading. It means the projection of the structures and polarities of the text by a public 'organon of iteration' into new contexts. What that will yield, doubtless, is a fan of alternative readings, with no means of stopping the fan from opening still further. My suggestion, however, is that if we attend carefully to what Derrida has to say about the nature of *itération, dissémination, différance* and the rest, we shall be led to see the alternative texts generated by disseminative reading not just as *other texts*, having no connection (or at best a causal one) with the text from which they sprang, but as refractions or transformations of that original text, each of which catches an aspect of its potential for significance. Of course, we have equally to consider each of these aspects as coming to birth as fully *explicit* structures of meaning in the new texts which elaborate them as such – but I have already done my best to rid that thought of its supposed idealist implications.

Such an account of reading displaces us as readers (this, it seems to me, is Derrida's most fundamental thought) from epistemological dominance over the text. It is worth noticing in this connection that such dominance is just as much assured by a stance of pure subjectivism towards the text as by the pursuit of a canonical eluci-dation. We have to see ourselves neither as inventively fooling around with texts nor as 'decoding' complex ciphers, but as generat-ing a reading of the text by a process which, because it involves an intercourse between our concerns and those of the text of a kind whose outcome we cannot altogether control (we may indeed find ourselves 'read' by the text), has more in common with a relationship between persons than with the scientific scrutiny of a natural object. For such a reading, what is required is just that combination of trust,[28] honesty, self-scrutiny and readiness to catch hints which is required in personal relationship.

Chapter 5
Muriel Spark and Jane Austen

I

Here are some reasons for disliking the novels of Muriel Spark. First, that she is, as the mother of a friend of mine put it, a girl of slender means. Her books are too spun-out. They seem all surface, and a rather dry, sparsely furnished, though elegant and mannered surface at that. The one exception is *The Mandelbaum Gate* (1965), which offers us, as the blurb-writers say, a vivid panorama of contemporary Israel. But *there*, if you like, is a book which lacks moral profundity. A serious young man once told me that he could find nothing but distaste for a writer who, confronted by the Arab–Israeli conflict with all its tragic moral and political dilemmas, chose to treat it all, as he put it, merely as the background for a trivial love story.

'Trivial.' The word is out. Yet Muriel Spark's novels seem, while one is reading them, to be profoundly, if obscurely, preoccupied with morality, not to say moral theology. Indeed they seem to be about nothing else. But there is no denying the obscurity. One is reminded of F. R. Leavis's remark about Henry James:

> We have, characteristically, in reading him, a sense that important choices are in question, and that our finest discrimination is being challenged, while at the same time we can't easily produce for discussion any issues that have moral substance to correspond.[1]

The trouble with James, however, is presumably that the nerve of morality often seems finally to be obscured by the very detail of the dissection through which James tries to expose it. In Muriel Spark obscurity has an exactly opposite source, in what is felt by many readers as a kind of studied inconsequentiality which pervades her work, and which is also a prime source of the felt 'thinness' of the novels.

Partly the air of inconsequentiality stems from Mrs Spark's authorial tone of voice, which is characteristically cool, level and uninvolved, and occasionally enigmatically flippant. Listen to the transition between the murder of Merle Coverdale by Mr Druce in *The Ballad of Peckham Rye* (1960), and the next section of the chapter:

> He came towards her with the corkscrew and stabbed it into her long neck nine times, and killed her. Then he took his hat and went home to his wife.
>
> *
>
> 'Doug dear,' said Miss Maria Cheeseman. (p. 136)

This is very elegant: but is the blood real? And what of the enigmatic Dougal Douglas, whose unfathomable machinations have led to this death?

> Much could be told of Dougal's subsequent life. He returned from Africa and became a novice in a Franciscan monastery. Before he was asked to leave, the Prior had endured a nervous breakdown and several of the monks had broken their vows of obedience in actuality, and their other vows by desire; Dougal pleaded his powers as an exorcist in vain. Thereafter, for economy's sake, he gathered together the scrap ends of his profligate experience – for he was a frugal man at heart – and turned them into a lot of cockeyed books, and went far in the world. He never married. (p. 142)[2]

Is this, as it seems, indulgent amusement at Dougal's goings-on, or is something deeper at stake? The glancing reference to Catholicism – Dougal's becoming a Franciscan novice – suggests the latter. But then how serious is Muriel Spark's Catholicism? Barbara Vaughan in *The Mandelbaum Gate* is, after all, prepared to marry without the consent of the Church, though she would prefer not to have to do so. When that knot is finally cut her marriage still rests, unbeknown to her, on the bottomlessly insecure foundation of a forged birth certificate; and this state of affairs is apparently taken by the narrator, and by one of the priests whom Ricky consults to try to get at the reasons for the failure of Joe Ramdez's well-laid plot, almost as a sign, or a gratuitous grace.

> The priests all said in effect, 'Well, if both parties remain in ignorance and the Church is satisfied, then it's a valid marriage.'
> 'According to the logic of the Catholics, that seems impossible.'
> No, they mostly said, it was quite logical if one started from the right

premiss. Others said, well, logic or no logic, that was the case. One of them replied, 'With God, everything is possible.'[3]

All this has a merry ring of Chestertonian paradox about it. But for Chesterton paradox was a device – paradoxically – for enforcing upon over-sophisticated minds the claims of an orthodoxy which he believed not merely to constitute the central tradition of Christianity but also to correspond to the ultimately sane, and naïvely realist, perceptions and sentiments of a child or a simple man.[4] In Muriel Spark paradox is not a means of leading us to an emphatic re-discovery of 'orthodoxy' or of the world as it 'really' and 'objectively' is. It seems rather to be sought for its own sake. But that raises the question of whether what underlies it is not the bottomless relativism Chesterton feared. Seen in this light the 'lightness of touch' for which Mrs Spark has been praised may seem all too explicable: mere intellectual shiftiness; a paper screen concealing an abyss.

Once raised, the charge of shiftiness can be extended all too easily to plot and characters. Nothing is ever full explained or given depth. When, at crucial points, the puzzled reader demands explicit en-lightenment, he is invariably fobbed off with an authorial giggle or a significant silence. Or novels suddenly peter out into scraps and fragments of action and conversation, as at the end of *Jean Brodie* or *The Comforters*, and the reader is left to work out for himself why these particular fragments have been shored against the ruin of what had appeared until then, at least in long stretches, to be almost a conventional plot. If you see these things merely as failures of conception conveniently licensed by the canons of a fashionable 'modernism', then it is easy to see the most recent novels, *The Driver's Seat, Not to Disturb, The Hothouse by the East River* or *The Abbess of Crewe* for example, as representing the final decay of a small and over-praised talent. On this view, surface and fashionable enigma have finally won out: there is nothing to be seen but what is to be seen, and that is precious little, though terribly stylish.

II

There, bluntly and acidly stated, is a case against Muriel Spark which one often hears put in conversation but which I, at least, have seldom if ever come across in print. No doubt it rests on a superficial and unperceptive reading of her work; but still, I think, it expresses what many intelligent readers feel in their hearts; and hence there may be some practical utility in stating it clearly and meeting it head-on. It must be answered, and not pushed aside, if we are to arrive at a more adequate reading.

One answer, of course, is that these are not 'traditional' novels. But that in itself gets us very little further. Even if 'the traditional novel' is a real category, its principle of unity is clearly likely to turn out to be rather complex. Such a principle can be clearly formulated only by means of a good deal of discussion conducted upon a far more modest level of generality, and it is to this discussion that I wish, in part, to contribute at present. If we are to see where, and why, Muriel Spark's fiction departs from the canons of the traditional novel we need a concrete example of a 'traditional' technique of fiction, and some reasonably clear idea of what such a technique achieves, and how.

For this role I shall select Jane Austen. Her major novels are everything that Muriel Spark's seem not to be: both morally and psychologically they are impressively achieved and coherent structures[5] into which a vast amount of concrete detail is incorporated without arbitrariness or loose ends.

At the same time there are parallels. Like Jane Austen, Muriel Spark is a moral satirist. Like her she paints with fine strokes upon a small canvas, and yet achieves at her best a power and universality which transcend the littleness and provinciality of her characters and their world. Both are, in some sense which is at least partly the same sense, anti-Romantic writers. Both nourish a preference for the concrete over the general, for what is actually, materially given over idealizing fancy.[6] Both mistrust antinomian individualism, and the rejection of familial or personal ties (and, in the logical extreme, of the whole fabric of what is concrete, given and intractable to the individual will about our existence) which springs from it. Neither has much time for sentimental moralizing; that is, for moralizing which is not under the control of a moral intelligence which is exact and discriminating precisely because it is exercised about some concrete and intimately known set of circumstances.

The most obvious disparity lies in the overt clarity and coherence of a Jane Austen novel. We feel in reading her indeed that 'our finest discrimination is being challenged'. And in fact it is. I think we can use this sonorous phrase of Leavis's with absolute literal appropriateness in her case. But what does the phrase mean? What is it to have one's finest powers of moral discrimination 'challenged' by a novel? It obviously cannot mean, I think, just that the characters are sufficiently well drawn to excite a moral response. For the response in question might be a facile and conventional one, like the boos that greet the appearance of the wicked stepmother at a pantomime. A more satisfying debunking interpretation, particularly tempting since the phrase is Leavis's, is that by 'finest powers of (moral) discrimination' we are to understand merely the conventional moral responses of a better class of person than the average pantomime-goer; the responses, let us say, of a clever, puritanical Cambridge don with a taste for acid wit.

But, unhappily for the devoted literary polemicist, this won't do either. Anyone who embarks upon the reading of Jane Austen with an open mind is likely to encounter a phenomenon which is both familiar and yet, when one thinks about it, very odd, not to say startling; and which makes perfect and unexceptionable sense of Leavis's phrase. It is this: that in reading a Jane Austen novel one's accustomed habits of moral response may be altered by the book. It is not merely that one may be forced to revise one's estimate of a particular character; that one may pass from thinking Emma a good deal nicer and kinder than most people around her to thinking her a self-indulgent snob and manipulator, gravely in need of Mr Knightley's restraining hand; or from thinking Fanny Price a dreary, priggish mouse to seeing her undue seriousness and passivity as faults wholly separable from her kind-heartedness and her quick perception of other people's suffering, which is in the end inseparable from her perception of their moral flaws. Beyond that the novel may succeed in altering, for a time or even permanently, one's whole moral outlook. It may in short make one aware of the possibility of just moral distinctions which one had never noticed, or had been blind to, before: that is why talk of 'challenging our finest discrimination' is in order.

But now, this is very queer. It is obvious how one can find one's moral outlook shaken or changed by life. But how can it be changed or even shaken by a fiction? Emma and Fanny Price are – and it is a measure of the power and strangeness of what is happening that one needs to take a grip on oneself to remember it – not real; they never existed. They and all the characters and events of the novels in which they figure were made up by Jane Austen out of her head from beginning to end. Equally clearly the domain of moral discrimination is life: the real actions of real people. How can it possibly be challenged by the imaginary doings and sayings of creatures of fantasy; creatures, after all, who are just not subject to the constraints of reality; who can be made to do and say anything their inventor chooses.

It is, I think, possible to give a fairly short and clear answer to this question if we look closely at the mechanisms by which Jane Austen constrains our moral assent. Put generally, the technique by which she achieves this consists of the arrangement of the fictional 'facts' of the novel, so that whenever we endeavour to put a moral construction on events different from the one Jane Austen intends, we are driven back from it – unless we wilfully refuse to see certain things which are 'there' in the text – by the remorseless pressure of 'reality': that is, of the fictional reality presented to us by the novel.

Take, for example, Knightley's insistence that Harriet Smith is fitted both by background and natural parts for the society of the Martins and nothing more. Suppose we try to see this, not as clear-sighted and realistic concern for Harriet's happiness but as snobbish and exclusive social pigeon-holing. We are obstructed at once by the contrast with Mrs Elton's eternal babble of Maple Grove (if *that* is what we take as our standard of snobbery then Knightley is very far from it) and by Knightley's own transparent kindliness as manifested in his rebuke to Emma on the excursion to Box Hill. Then again there is the manifest factual justice of Mr Knightley's estimate of Harriet. Her simplicity, docility and slowness of uptake are evident through-out the book. Contrariwise, indeed, these characteristics and the facts of Harriet's background cast doubt on the quality of Emma's concern for her friend. If Harriet were brighter, less biddable and of better family there would be more of true friendship and less of Lady Bountiful in Emma's relationship to her, and the way would not be prepared, as it is through most of the novel, for Emma's painful discovery of the nature of her own motives and desires.

What we must notice here is that the attempt to construe Knightley as a cold snob is being turned and defeated not by any single piece of countervailing evidence, but by the whole structure of the novel. If we see Knightley simply as a cold snob we have indeed no explana-tion for his rebuke to Emma on Box Hill (simple countervailing evidence); but in addition we have the ambiguities of Emma's relationship to Harriet, by contrast with which Knightley seems such a paragon of directness and plain justice of vision. Emma and Knightley, that is, are each known to us in the end by the relationship in which they stand to Harriet, and thus indirectly to one another. Each makes the character of the other intelligible as the opposite term of a moral polarity which can be grasped only if we attend to each not as he or she stands in isolation, but in relation to the other. Again, what sustains the polarity, and gives it a firm foundation, is the fact that we have independent knowledge (knowledge indepen-dent of what either Knightley or Emma say on the matter, that is) of Harriet Smith's simplicity and lack of sophistication or social *éclat*.

In short the reader who, following his own private moral predilec-tions, classes Knightley as a cold snob (just as he might do if he ran into Knightley in real life at one of Mr Woodhouse's dinners) finds himself not merely up against a countervailing anecdote (Box Hill), but up against a moral structure in which Knightley's character,

Emma's character, and Harriet Smith's independently known nature are held in a tension, a polarity, which defines not merely Emma's and Knightley's characters but a general outlook on the world. You can look at matters other than Harriet Smith's prospects in terms of that contrast between a superficially benevolent and attractive romanticism and a dry pessimism which is the kinder just because it is the more honest and realistic. Indeed you can make out of it a vision, a philosophy and a way of life; and a long and important tradition of broadly liberal conservatism in English letters and English moral feeling has done so. In *A Passage to India*, for example, Fielding's sense that 'the British Empire really can't be abolished because it's rude'[7] seems to me a late and rather enfeebled expression of this tradition.

It is because they are concerned with the construction and exploration of a moral outlook of great potential generality that Jane Austen's novels, although profoundly concerned with morality, are not didactic fictions or moral fables. A moral fable simply illustrates a moral. It may illustrate, for example, how mere idleness, without any malicious intention, may cause great harm. It may show this as happening through a very plausible train of events and circumstances. But however plausible the fiction, and however strong the moral horror of idleness it produces in the reader's mind, the reader can always say, putting down the book and recollecting himself, 'But this is just a story; it never happened: and even though it *might* happen that does not show that idleness must have such consequences.' In short, moral fables suffer not only from being special pleading, but from being special pleading *founded upon a fiction*.

What we have in *Emma* is not at all this proving of a case, however plausibly, upon made-up evidence. We have the construction, through fictional exemplification, of a system of moral polarities and categories in terms of which we can, if we will, exhaustively partition and reduce to order the whole of our moral experience. The relationship of fictional 'fact'-making to the moral concerns of such a novel is quite different from its relationship to the moral concerns of a didactic fable. The 'facts' about Harriet's simplicity do not, any more than the 'facts' about who eventually married whom, support a 'moral'. They provide the foundation for a system of moral distinctions and oppositions which is not officiously pressed upon the reader, but which a candid and diligent reader learns and discovers as he reads the book, through learning by experience the ways in which the novel restricts his power to regard the characters otherwise than as Jane Austen intends. For this to happen, the fabric of the novel must be a seamless unity, so that no matter how the reader attempts to find footing for some 'private' view of his own, to the effect that Knightley is a cold snob or that Emma's wit and charm come to the same thing as moral intelligence, his foot will find no purchase.

In addition novel-readers possess a great mass of miscellaneous knowledge drawn from everyday life about character and conduct. None of the 'facts' selected and assembled to form the 'reality' of the novel must be *ultimately* inconsistent with any of this: that is, inconsistent without an explanation internal to the novel which *is* consistent with it. That in turn means that the moral outlook which the reader learns from the novel must be one which the novelist can apply systematically throughout the fabric of the novel without either breaching the internal coherence of the outlook in question or, in pursuit of the coherence of his outlook, committing himself to events or characters which breach the canon of plausibility. Only a serious and powerful moral outlook can meet these demands; and indeed the capacity to organize a very complex and 'plausible' fictional structure can quite properly be taken for that reason as a species of empirical test of the seriousness and weight of the outlook in question, even though the material so organized is, strictly speaking, fictional.

We may, of course, if we are out of sympathy with Jane Austen's outlook, feel discomfort as we read her, and snipe in a limited and ineffectual way at her position. But to do more than snipe, to effect a real escape from the ordering polarities of her moral vision, requires an effort of creative imagination as serious and sustained as her own. And for that reason we are under a constant temptation to take her voice as the voice of morality *tout court*. The student who persists in seeing Harriet Smith as a working-class heroine provokes our impatience. He isn't *reading the novel*; he is letting 'external' moral considerations come between him and the text; in effect he is treating Emma and Mr Knightley as if they were real people whom he had just met, like the man who jumped on the stage during a performance of *Hamlet* to warn the Player King of the approach of the poisoner.

And we are right: this is not the way to read a novel. But there is another temptation: to take the moral polarities which the characters and events of the novel define as the form of morality itself, and the moral insights which it is possible to define within these polarities as the content of morality. Jane Austen does not tell us what to think about morality; we learn it; it proves itself upon the events of the novel, and these events are wholly plausible, and compose a naturalistically imagined world of great complexity, within which one can constantly stumble upon new insights which one missed on a previous reading. But learning the moral geography of this world is not learning the only moral geography there can be, or the moral geography of *the* world.

III

Because fiction and reality are held together in a Jane Austen novel by the tensions and constraints of simultaneously maintaining the plausibility of a complex fiction and the coherence of an organizing moral viewpoint, readers feel that they 'know where they are' with Jane Austen, whereas with Muriel Spark they don't. Opening her novels one enters a world governed by ascertainable moral laws, by a viewpoint which proves itself exhaustively upon the events of the novel. To every question there is an answer, because Jane Austen has made sure that there will be. The moral distinctions and polarities about which the novel turns govern its interior world as geometry and classical mechanics govern the world of Newtonian physics. To try to think oneself outside them and still read the novel *as a novel* is like trying to think of a material reality outside space, or to think of space itself as curved without recourse to the general theory of relativity.

Similarly where the novel deals with moral growth, it is growth which proceeds against the background of, and is made intelligible by, this same Newtonian fabric of moral distinctions. When Emma discovers the ambiguity of her own motives, and by contrast the straightforwardness of Mr Knightley's, and knows at last to her chagrin that Knightley has always been right in their disagreements, she is discovering the inner logic of principles which her better self has held to all along, though blinded to their full implications by carelessness and self-indulgence. And this is no surprise: these principles are, within the novel, the only principles which can survive the scrutiny of an intelligent and clear-sighted critic: they *are* morality, and that is the end of it. Her self-discovery seems, indeed, less a confrontation with 'morality', conceived as a set of social norms of behaviour imposed upon life 'from outside', than a confrontation with reality itself. The greatness of the novel consists of its power to achieve this fusion of the form and the matter of morality; of values and the concrete realities of life which they nourish and organize.

But other novels offer other worlds, other air, which we can as easily learn to breathe as the air of Highbury or Mansfield. Opening *Le Rouge et le noir* or *Pamela* we encounter moral outlooks as serious and as impressively fused with the fictional 'reality' of the novel, and through it, via the canons of plausibility, with real life, as Jane Austen's. We feel no strain in passing from one to another: we learn to do it as we acquire the habit of reading and the love of literature.

And this is strange, for we *should* feel a certain strain. What fills the space between these worlds? If one did not encounter them safely enclosed between the pages of books; if one lived through the transition from one to the other, as people do live through experiences of conversion, or in a less conscious way and over long periods change their outlook on life through their particular experience of it, wouldn't one feel the very fabric of reality shifting beneath one's feet?

For obvious reasons the classical technique of novel-writing which we have been discussing will not easily permit you to deal with the experience of passing from one universe of values to another. It will not allow you to show the reader the gulf between a set of values taken together with the detail of the life, the *modus vivendi*, which they organize, and what gives life and content to all such partly conventional structures: the formless magma of human potentiality. But this, it seems to me, is Muriel Spark's peculiar subject-matter. In *The Mandelbaum Gate* Barbara Vaughan, a half-Jewish Catholic spinster on a pilgrimage in Israel, is questioned with flamboyant persistence about the ambiguities of her religious and racial identity by an Israeli tour guide:

> Barbara thought, 'Who am I?' She felt she had known who she was till this moment. She said, 'I am who I am.' The guide spoke some short Hebrew phrase which, although she did not know the language, quite plainly signified that this didn't get them any further in the discussion. Barbara had already begun to reflect that 'I am who I am' was a bit large seeing it was the answer that Moses got from the burning bush on Mount Sinai when he asked God to describe himself. The Catechism, it was true, stated that man was made in God's image chiefly as to the soul. She decided, therefore, essentially 'I am who I am' was indeed the final definition for her.   (p. 28)[8]

But she cannot leave it there.

> He was demanding a definition. By the long habit of her life, and by temperament, she held as a vital principle that the human mind was bound in duty to continuous acts of definition. Mystery was acceptable to her, but only under the aspect of a crown of thorns. She found no rest in mysterious truths like 'I am who I am'; they were all right for deathbed definitions, when one's mental obligations were at an end.   (pp. 28–9)

The last few sentences of this might serve as a general epigraph to the works of Muriel Spark. Her books are exercises for the reader in continuous redefinition. To see this it is easiest to begin with one of several books, *The Prime of Miss Jean Brodie*, *The Girls of Slender Means* or *The Mandelbaum Gate*, for example, which deal explicitly with conversion and the transcendence of a point of view. I shall concentrate for reasons of space on one of them, *The Prime of Miss Jean Brodie* (1961). It is a curious feature of this book, which it shares with *The Girls of Slender Means*, that although it concerns a crisis in the beliefs and personality of one character, Sandy Stranger, as she emerges from childhood, the character in question is treated merely as one more character, and often a rather peripheral character, in the novel. We are not treated to a ringside view of Sandy's inner life, as we are to Emma's. At the same time we *know* in a rather external way all sorts of curious extrinsic facts about her. We know, for example, that when she slept with Teddy Lloyd 'she left the man and took his religion and became a nun in the course of time'. But we know nothing of Teddy Lloyd beyond his blond handsomeness and his capacity to turn every portrait into a portrait of Miss Jean Brodie. Of his *mind*, and thus of Sandy's mind from that source, we know nothing. Why does she become a nun in an enclosed order? What about her strange book of psychology, *The Transfiguration of the Commonplace* ('on the nature of moral perception')? Why put any of this in at all?

There are two answers, which are at first sight contradictory. The first is that the enigmatic and incomplete fragments of information which the novel drops casually concerning Sandy are meant to puzzle and irritate; to create in the reader a spirit of nervous dissatisfaction, of not knowing quite where he is going or what he is supposed to see when he gets there, which will make him work towards a reconstruction of Sandy's mind from the bits and pieces of information which the novel offers him.

The second and more important answer, which seems at first sight to contradict the first, but in fact complements it, is that the enigmas are there to obstruct the establishment of that systematic and unblemished unity of conception which it is of the essence of Jane Austen's genius to create and of her readers' pleasure to explore, and which makes possible the liberating, constantly surprising play of wit and moral perception that informs the interior of the novel precisely by the very rigour with which it restricts the range of what can enter the bounded, though not finite, world it creates. The technique of a Muriel Spark novel is in fact exactly opposite to Jane Austen's: it works by continual *dislocation*, by setting up a fabric of faults and cleavages from one side of which the events of the novel can be construed in one way, while from the other they fall irrevocably (although we can recapture our first innocent vision by an effort of imagination) into another pattern. The pleasure of reading her lies in the unexpectedness and yet the justice of these discoveries. It is the pleasure of continually breaking out into a new-found world – a new level of sophistication – whereas the pleasure of Jane Austen is the pleasure of finding that each new vista, however surprising, is a vista of the same well-ordered park, and fits naturally and ineluctably with all the others. Muriel Spark's technique is inherently inimical to the setting-up of a single 'authorial' or 'ultimate' point of view from which alone everything in the novel can ultimately be seen as cohering with everything else (that point of view in a Jane Austen novel from which we stray only by dint of misreading or by ceasing to read the novel *as a novel*); although of course one can have a reading of a Muriel Spark novel which is *from a technical point of view* ultimate and 'complete' in the sense that it catches all the force (although perhaps not all the reverberations) of all the dislocations.

The Prime of Miss Jean Brodie is in this sense organized round Sandy's betrayal. Read straightforwardly from the first page on, the book can for some time be taken as a piece of amusing but rather lightweight social satire about the startling effect of a flamboyant and strong-minded spinster upon the girls of a drably conformist Edinburgh school. Of course even on that level there is an undercurrent of resistance and discomfort stemming from the urbane, deadpan irony of the style (one can trace the acknowledged influence of Max Beerbohm here).[9] The book relies on one level on a stock response of liberal approval for the independent-minded, creatively subversive schoolteacher in order upon another level to subvert it, just as *The Girls of Slender Means* (1963) relies on and subverts a stock belief in the innocence and half-socialist community spirit of the war years and as Golding's *Lord of the Flies* relies on and subverts a set of stock responses deriving from the boyhood reading of *Coral Island*.

However, even discounting style, the social-satire reading of the Spark book runs steadily into choppier and choppier waters. We pass from the idyll under the tree in the grounds of Marcia Blaine School for Girls, with Miss Brodie handing out to her enthralled little girls her coloured, delightful, half-sinful scraps of knowledge of the exciting adult world (so much more real and alive than the school subjects), to the isolation of her set in the whispering, private world of their precocity, to the strange fruits of political and sexual craziness that grow so naturally in this microclimate, untouched by the frosts of Edinburgh winters. Throughout this there is a constant swell, as of wind and tide in opposite directions, of uncertainty about what we are to think of Miss Brodie. Something obscure and darker struggles against the cosy, collusive intimacy of the 'Brodie set', which the reader at this point largely shares.

After all, though, Miss Brodie *is* under attack from Miss Mackay and the governors.

> 'It has been suggested again that I should apply for a post at one of the progressive, that is to say, crank schools. I shall not apply for a post at a crank school. I shall remain at this education factory where my duty lies. There needs must be a leaven in the lump. Give me a girl at an impressionable age and she is mine for life. The gang who oppose me shall not succeed.'   (p. 112)[10]

And if she is a bit paranoid and has taken a leaf out of the Jesuits' book, well, she is under pressure. And she *is* a leaven in the lump. Doesn't she stand for independence of thought and for bold experiments in personal life?

> 'Interests you, forsooth,' said Miss Brodie. 'A girl with a mind, a girl with insight. He is a Roman Catholic and I don't see how you can have to do with a man who can't think for himself. Rose was suitable. Rose has instinct but no insight.'   (p. 123)

Admittedly she is a fascist and she encourages her girls to sleep with the lover she will not, or dare not, commit herself to sleep with; and she encourages one, insanely, to go and fight for Franco. But after all, independence of mind and a boldly experimental attitude to personal relationships are bound sooner or later to lead one into deep water if one is serious about them. . . .

The tolerant, easygoing voice in the reader's mind trails off. By the time we arrive at Miss Mackay's study, and Sandy's economical betrayal, we are mostly on Sandy's side, and the novel has turned retrospectively in our hands from a light social satire to a vision of metaphysical evil. Standing – like the half-adult Sandy – partly in and partly out of the Brodie set and its peculiar ambience, we are able to take Sandy's vengeful view of Miss Brodie as a secularized Calvinist.

> In this oblique way, she began to sense what went to the makings of Miss Brodie who had elected herself to grace in so particular a way and with more exotic suicidal enchantment than if she had simply taken to drink like other spinsters who couldn't stand it any more.   (p. 109)

And later on: 'She thinks she is Providence, thought Sandy, she thinks she is the God of Calvin, she sees the beginning and the end' (p. 120). On this view Miss Brodie has sought a private election. She

has sought to make the world intelligible on her terms by constructing a little world in which she can be, as none of us can in the real
world, the source of all enlightenment. (It is no accident that this
might also be a description of what a novelist does: on one level you
can see Muriel Spark either as writing about her own craft and its
predicament, or as using her own craft as a type of the human
condition.) In this world love is a sentimental fiction. Jean Brodie's
'renunciation' of Teddy Lloyd is no more a real renunciation than her
affair with Gordon Lowther is a real affair. Indeed it is hard to see
what *reality* either man has for her: in the end they are both objects
of her fantasies. To give body to this genteel, garish world of dream-
sophistication she makes real children its accessories and servants,
even to the extent of making them her sexual proxies: her 'set' is thus
quite literally an extension of her person. And in other ways she
deprives her protégées of innocence and of contact with reality
(substituting for a knowledge of the real poor of Edinburgh her
absurd visions of Mussolini's Italy, for example), and in one case of
life itself. She has set herself in the place of God.[11]

Here at last is something which one might identify as the 'message'
of the novel, and a very proper Catholic message too, which we
can all greet with enthusiasm (especially if we are non-Catholics)
and relief, since once one has discovered the message one can put
the novel back, cheerfully unmoved like Miss Rickward in *The
Mandelbaum Gate*, on the shelf with all the other books. But, thank
God for Muriel Spark's intelligence, the novel's supply of concealed
trapdoors is not yet exhausted, and the floor once again gives way
beneath the reader's feet. The voice which delivers this impassioned
judgement on Jean Brodie is Sandy's, charged with all the vengeful
fires of adolescence, 'more fuming, now, with Christian morals, than
John Knox'. This is the girl whose virtuous brutality in the demoli-
tion of Miss Brodie contrasts to such fine comic effect with Miss
Mackay's genteel delicacy, no doubt rendered in a Morningside
accent:

> 'I shall question her pupils on those lines and see what emerges, if that
> is what you advise, Sandy. I had no idea you felt so seriously about the
> state of world affairs, Sandy, and I'm more than delighted –'
> 'I'm not really interested in world affairs,' said Sandy, 'only in putting a
> stop to Miss Brodie.'   (p. 125)

Here again, style is operating to disturb the reader's assurance
that he is on the right track at last. Little stylistic land-mines of this
sort pepper the concluding pages of the novel, and are the clue to
their fragmentary, apparently offhand character. Thus Sandy herself,

answering Jean Brodie's complaints about betrayal, sounds not, indeed, like the God of Calvin but like a cross between St. Ignatius Loyola and the Christ of the Apocalypse casting out the lukewarm: 'Sandy replied like an enigmatic Pope: "If you did not betray us it is impossible that you could have been betrayed by us. The word betrayed does not apply ..."' (p. 126).

But the real thrust of dislocation comes from Teddy Lloyd, who both loves Miss Brodie and sees through Sandy's newfound fanaticism.

> Teddy Lloyd continued reproducing Jean Brodie in his paintings. 'You have instinct,' Sandy told him, 'but no insight, or you would see that the woman isn't to be taken seriously.'
>
> 'I know she isn't,' he said. 'You are too analytical and irritable for your age.'   (p. 123)

The contrast between insight and instinct is, as we know, Miss Brodie's own. We are in no doubt that Miss Brodie prefers insight to instinct, which is indeed why she chooses Sandy as a natural confidante. Insight sets you above the mob; instinct plunges you into the ignorant darkness of passion and dangerous involvement. Sandy too, perched on her new-found rock of insight, finds love a dangerous enigma. It is for an answer to this that she rummages through Teddy Lloyd's mind.

To all this we have a footnote in the shape of Sandy's penultimate recorded judgement on Jean Brodie:

> When Jenny came to see Sandy, who now bore the name Sister Helena of the Transfiguration, she told Sandy about her sudden falling in love with a man in Rome and there being nothing to be done about it. 'Miss Brodie would have liked to know about it,' she said, 'sinner as she was.'
>
> 'Oh, she was quite an innocent in her way,' said Sandy, clutching the bars of the grille.   (p. 127)

In what way was Jean Brodie innocent? Well, there is a sense in which Jean Brodie is necessarily innocent: she has never *done* anything, has never *acted*. If you encounter the world as she does, only as shadows on the wall of your Platonic cave, then what you do to those shadows is in a sense not done to the people or things which cast them. The whole absurd charade of Jean Brodie's love-life is intelligible only as a series of devices to maintain an intangible barrier between the dream and the real world whose types and images figure in it: to ensure that no action passes this barrier. What happens to others as Miss Brodie tosses in her sleep is, poor innocent, not her fault. And it is significant that nothing much does happen to them. All the plain commonsensical girls like Eunice and Rose and Jenny pass through her hands unscathed. She harms only those who are like her: Joyce Emily Hammond, who shares her political romanticism, and Sandy, who loves day-dreams, secret knowledge and the superiority which comes from 'insight'.

What distinguishes Sandy from Jean Brodie is fear and desire. Edinburgh frightens her. To the man who comes to see her in middle age in her nunnery she says, 'I once was taken for a walk through the Canongate . . . but I was frightened by the squalor' (p. 34). As a child she does not go like the others to St. Giles, 'with its tattered blood-stained banners of the past'.

> Sandy had not been there, and did not want to go. The outsides of old Edinburgh churches frightened her, they were of such dark stone, like presences almost the colour of the Castle rock, and were built so warn-ingly with their upraised fingers. (p. 35)

It is because she fears it that Calvinism is not a joke to her, as it is to Miss Brodie, but an alien presence which cannot be assimilated to the commonplace unity of her life but sticks out like a sore thumb.

> Fully to savour her position, Sandy would go and stand outside St. Giles Cathedral or the Tolbooth, and contemplate these emblems of a dark and terrible salvation which made the fires of the damned seem very merry to the imagination by contrast, and much preferable. . . . All she was conscious of now was that some quality of life peculiar to Edinburgh and nowhere else had been going on unbeknown to her all the time, and however undesirable it might be she felt deprived of it; however undesirable, she desired to know what it was, and to cease to be protected from it by enlightened people. (p. 108)

Desire leads her into the affair with Teddy Lloyd; jealously she wishes to know how he can love Jean Brodie, and she searches his mind to find out. Calvinism and Teddy Lloyd's mind: these two thrusting obstructions tear at the fabric of a life made from a nice Edinburgh suburb and the Brodie set. They let in light, give Sandy new ground to stand on, a vantage-point upon which to erect her critique of Brodieism and from which to act against it.

Sandy's betrayal is thus precisely *not* innocent; in one sense, obviously, because it destroys Miss Brodie for good – ' "I'm afraid", Jenny wrote, "Miss Brodie is past her prime. She keeps wanting to know who betrayed her. It isn't at all like the old Miss Brodie; she was always so full of fight" ' (p. 127) – but more profoundly because Sandy knows and wills what she has done. It is the prime act of her liberation; it is the affirmation of her awakening from childhood and sleepwalking, from day-dreams of Alan Breck among the heather and all that fatuity of *la crème de la crème* stage-managed by Miss Brodie. And therefore Sandy needs – must have – assurance that she *is* awake, that in her new and pristine state she sees straight, perceives reality at last: the commonplace transfigured. It is scarcely surprising that she should feel the need to write a book on the nature of moral perception; as we have seen, she is, like Jean Brodie, a great one for insight: she likes to feel on top of things as Miss Brodie, once Sandy has finished with her, plainly no longer does.

The loss of any assurance of reality, of the finality of any vision of what is or of what has worth, is the underlying theme of all Muriel Spark's fiction. In *The Mandelbaum Gate* two long passages occur, one an account of part of the Eichmann trial, the other a sermon by a young English priest in the Church of the Holy Sepulchre on fake shrines and commercialism in Jerusalem, which seem inconsequentially placed where they occur but which have, I think, a good claim to be the central pillars of the novel. Barbara Vaughan is a pilgrim in a land clotted with ambiguous history, with endless shrines among which it is impossible to distinguish the true from the false; in which a trial is going on which resembles 'one of the new irrational films which people can't understand the point of, but continue to see; one can neither cope with them nor leave them alone'.

> The counsel for the defence consulted his document and drew his client's attention to specific names, Misters this and that and their sons, locked in reality. And his client, a character from the pages of a long *anti-roman*, went on repeating his lines which were punctuated only by the refrain, *Bureau IV-B-4*. Barbara felt she was caught in a conspiracy to prevent her brain from functioning.
> ... The man was plainly not testifying for himself, but for his pre-written destiny. He was not answering for himself or his own life at all, but for an imperative deity named Bureau IV-B-4, of whom he was the High Priest.   (*The Mandelbaum Gate*, p. 179)

Later Barbara is arguing with Susi the impossibility of making religion something separate from life: a little block of sacred certainties of absolutely clear purpose and implications, against which we may measure and correct all the uncertainties of life.

> 'Well, either religious faith penetrates everything in life or it doesn't. There are some experiences that seem to make nonsense of all separations of sacred from profane – they seem childish. Either the whole of life is unified under God or everything falls apart. Sex is child's play in the argument.' She was thinking of the Eichmann trial, and was aware

that there were other events too, which had rolled away the stone that revealed an empty hole in the earth, that led to a bottomless pit. So that people drew back quickly and looked elsewhere for reality, and found it, and made decisions, in the way that she had decided to get married, anyway. (p. 283)

Barbara's image of the empty grave catches the tone of familiar modern versions of the Victorian crisis of belief. God is dead, so everything is permitted; men's minds are transient sparks of consciousness adrift on the fathomless gulfs of time and space which confront us in the physical universe, a universe which is inanimate, springs from no ultimately assignable intelligible cause, is indifferent to human wishes and so on. We have an elusive sense that somehow Muriel Spark, through Barbara Vaughan, is making all this commonplace nihilism conned out of Nietzsche, or Bertrand Russell, look a bit vulgar and beside the point. But how? Surely just turning one's back smartly upon the empty tomb of Christ as manifested in the Eichmann trial, and deciding to get married in defiance of one's Church, is a grotesquely frivolous response to a genuine anguish?

Well, but it does not follow, because the Decalogue is not inscribed in the movements of the stars, that reality is an infinitely plastic substance which can be shaped to our dreams and desires in any way we please. That would be a real 'crisis of belief': to know that whatever we chose to believe or however we chose to live, the world would accommodate itself *without strain* to our wishes, so that anything we wanted could be made to cohere, without the need for any ingenuity, without the sacrifice of any other consideration, and without the need for any radical growth or maturing of our attitudes to things, with anything else whatsoever. Then we should really be in the padded cell. Philosophers sometimes manage to invent arguments which seem to show us to be in just such a position with respect to certain very special sorts of question. Do you see the things I see as green *as green*, or as blue? It can seem as if, provided the transposition were sufficiently systematic, no conceivable utterance or act of yours could reveal the difference, for whenever you see blue you will, after all, *call* it 'green'.

But the cases which lend themselves to plausible scepticism of this sort are very special ones. Normally reality obstructs the free construction of private worlds of belief and feeling, as Edinburgh's churches, Teddy Lloyd, and the grating disparity between what Jean Brodie tells the girls about her love-life and what that love-life as witnessed and in part lived out by Sandy as confidante and proxy actually amounts to, obstruct and impede the influence of the Brodie set over Sandy's mind. We know reality, in short, by the inarticulate, mute resistance it offers to the human will. It is indeed true that reality offers us no final guaranteed description of itself, nor any real possibility of constructing one. But it is also true that its nature perpetually 'shows' itself, to use a term of Wittgenstein's, in the nature of the resistance it offers to our successive attempts to describe it, and that the nature it reveals in this dumb and in one sense passive way is not intrinsically vague and wavering but perfectly definitive and final, and, in short, real.

From this point of view Eichmann belongs in *The Mandelbaum Gate* as the polar opposite of Barbara Vaughan. He is fighting a long rearguard action against the evidence: the eroding drift of individually trivial, obstructive facts 'locked in reality'. In the process he is ceasing to be Adolf Eichmann, a man. He is not 'answering for his own life at all'. He is becoming the creature of the very construction which formerly gave him life, significance and importance – Bureau IV-B-4. He scuttles now over the disintegrating surface of Bureau IV-B-4 and the world to which it belonged, patching it together against the terrible, unremitting inroads of small facts. His condition is analogous to Pincher Martin's at the end of Golding's novel, and he stands here as a type of all those, including Miss Brodie and perhaps in the end Sandy herself, who, having built a world, occupy it until it breaks apart rather than admit its intrinsic separateness from reality. This is a process by which the self – the self as potential, the self whose life is creation – buries itself in the debris of its own constructions: 'The man was plainly not testifying for himself, but for his pre-written destiny.'

The Mandelbaum Gate is, in fact, about *letting go* of the world you have made for yourself. Barbara Vaughan, who is neither Gentile nor Jew, lets go of her comfortable condition of spinster schoolmistress with a sub-lesbian friendship when she meets Harry Clegg. In the same way she is not prepared to treat the doctrines of the Church on marriage as authoritatively deciding the question of whether she is to marry Clegg or not. But that does not mean that she treats the doctrines of the Church as of no importance. She treats them with perfect seriousness *as an impediment* to her marriage. It is indeed as an impediment, as something having the resistance and solidity of reality, that she values the Church, and that is why she hesitates to marry Clegg and have done with the charade – which for that very reason is not a charade – of the request for annulment, knowing that she will not find it easy to live without the Church to measure her life against. If she did not live in this curious tightrope fashion, between belief and apostasy, if she relapsed into being a Jew or a Catholic, a schoolmistress or a whore, someone bound by the chains of an ancient and authoritarian religion or a simple suburban pagan, she would become indistinguishable from many of Muriel Spark's nastier or more pathetic characters. You can measure her condition, for example, against the voice of Rudi Bittesch in *The Girls of Slender Means*, telling Jane Wright, from his fount to desiccating worldly knowledge of the limited possibilities of café ideology, of Nick Farringdon's general unsatisfactoriness as a sound party man.

> Rudi said, 'You notice his words, that he says the world has fallen from grace? This is the reason that he is no anarchist, by the way. They chuck him out when he talks like a son of the Pope. This man is a mess that he calls himself an anarchist; the anarchists do not make all that talk of original sin, so forth; they permit only anti-social tendencies, unethical conduct, so forth. Nick Farringdon is a diversionist, by the way.'[12]

Here, I think, we can find an answer to the charge of intellectual shiftiness with which we began. Curiously enough, it is not Barbara Vaughan's inventive Catholicism, nor the voice of the young English priest as he lists with muscular cheeriness one fraudulent shrine after another to the chagrin of the elderly priests who wait their turn to say mass, which gives us the sharpest vision of the empty tomb and the abyss which lies behind the screen of words. It is Rudi Bittesch's voice dividing life between dry and circumscribed doctrines which between them exhaust the very possibility of a new thought; or Eichmann's voice cataloguing the duties and responsibilities of an office in which official duty itself has become no longer a living expression of human community but a vapid and murderous fetish.

It is, indeed, precisely the refusal to admit that reality escapes all human formulas and established modes of response, and hence must continually be rethought, responded to freshly and incessantly each day, that lets in the void, that rolls away the stone to reveal an empty tomb. It is from this that Barbara turns away, to decide, to act. And it is because she can accept mystery 'only under the aspect of a crown of thorns' that she can accept mystery.

Teddy Lloyd, like Barbara Vaughan, understands the possibility of simultaneously accepting and relinquishing a vision of the world. Teddy Lloyd's mind 'invents Miss Brodie on canvas after canvas'. She is for him not something fixed in any single vision of his, but something outside all visions, which can thus serve as a perpetual and inexhaustible source of new creation, and is known through the resistance it offers to imagination in the work of creation. The real Miss Brodie is what each new-minted picture has in common with all those that went before it: but *that* cannot be expressed in a picture. That is how he can know Jean Brodie to be just as ridiculous as Sandy makes her out to be, and yet still love her. Sandy's view of her is quite just, but it is not final: it has not the piercing security which 'insight' would have if it were not the epistemological chimera which it is.

Muriel Spark leaves open, I think, the question of whether Sandy cleaves to 'insight' to the bitter end. The fact that she tries to capture the nature of moral experience in a book suggests that she does, as does the final haunting image of her 'clutching the bars of her cell'. For if we cannot know the world from the standpoint of a single vision we cannot know it by detached contemplation at all. We can know it only through the experience of the resistance of the real, and to know that resistance we must commit ourselves, we must act, take chances. We find reality, as Barbara says, by making decisions.

The contrast between detached contemplation of the world, and exposure to the real in decision and action, runs as a connecting thread through all Muriel Spark's fiction. But it is also, I think, the clue to her style and technique as a novelist. When Caroline in *The Comforters*, that curious novel about writing novels and being a character in a novel, leaves at the end of the book to write her novel, she leaves her notes behind her. This, I take it, is because the act of writing, if it is a real engagement with the world, must break from the husk of whatever preconceptions, hopes and expectations she may have entertained about it like a dragonfly from its larval skin. For a related reason Caroline *the character* leaves the novel when she begins to write, as Sandy does not. For again the process of writing, if it is a real engagement with the world, will change her. In creating we partly create ourselves, as Muriel Spark's Eichmann has ceased to do.

Writing is here a metaphor for living, in all those who have not so far chosen to die, and for reading. The purpose of Muriel Spark's technique, I think, is to construct novels that have to be read with the same sense of engagement with a perpetually obstructing reality. Certainly in reading *The Prime of Miss Jean Brodie* one passes, as I have tried to show, through a series of dislocations, each of which disturbs one's former conception of the novel and transforms it into something new. In the process the reader finds himself living through the stages of Sandy Stranger's childhood and conversion, and is finally led to see, *through* the texture of the novel, as it were, something about the nature of our relationship to reality which mutely shows itself in the ambiguities of Sandy's final state and of her relationship to Teddy Lloyd. This is not something the novel could achieve if it possessed the luminous integrity of surface and depths which Jane Austen's novels have. For then it would possess and generate a moral climate, on which the reader could repose his judgement, and the kind of reading which Muriel Spark needs for her purposes would be excluded.

In short whereas Jane Austen's art occupies the interior of a very serious and powerful moral point of view, Muriel Spark's is busy precisely at the still point at which worlds of consciousness, each organized and dominated by such a moral vision, cleave from the still and speechless surface of reality. But come now, it may be said; while both are no doubt worth reading, one can surely ask, and say, which of them is better *as a novelist*. Can one? The force of the question depends, after all, on the idea that worthwhile fictions are comparable after their kind, thus that they belong to a single kind, and demand one kind of reading; and those are among the assumptions which, for better or worse, I have set out to challenge in this book.

Chapter 6
The Text as Interrogator: Muriel Spark and Job*

I

Muriel Spark's novel, *The Only Problem* (1984), is about a wealthy Canadian, Harvey Gotham, who has sequestered himself in a simple cottage in the Vosges in order to write a monograph on the Book of Job.

This sends the reader at once to the bookshelf for a copy of the Old Testament. But will he get much good of it? The idea is that here we have a text by Muriel Spark which explicitly claims some kind of relationship with a biblical text. We are now thoroughly accustomed to the idea that texts are meditations, transforming, re-ordering, decomposing, etc., upon other texts, and though one is not supposed to say that the texts involved in such relations of parasitism 'throw light upon' one another, a faint hope, not yet reconciled to the idea that there is something fundamentally wrong with the notion of light upon which such hopes depend, tempts us to imagine that here it might be so.

But what light can come from joke and enigma? *The Only Problem* is as 'Bristling with mysteries', as 'wickedly delicious' as the blurb-writer tells us it is, hinting thereby, I take it, that beyond noting that the prose seemed pretty crisp and witty he couldn't actually make a great deal of it. While Job, to which the reader turns for whatever enlightenment he still expects to receive, is of course widely credited with being the most puzzling book of the OT.

---

* An earlier version of this essay was given as a talk to a one-day conference on 'The Bible and Literature' at the University of Sussex, 18 March 1985. Comments from Dan Jacobson, A. K. Thorlby, A. A. H. Inglis, Gabriel Josipovici, A. D. Nuttall and others helped in the preparation of the present version.

Job is frequently taken to be about the Problem of Evil; that is to say, to address the question of what the believer is to make of the following inconsistent triad of propositions:

God is omnipotent.

God is good (merciful, just, etc.).

Suffering exists.

The believer wishes to affirm the first two; the third he can hardly deny. But he cannot consistently affirm all three at once. One or more of them must be false, but, and here is the rub, whichever of them is false it is clearly not going to be the third.

This is the problem to which Harvey Gotham takes the Book of Job to be addressed, and which is for him The Only Problem.

> . . . . he could not face that a benevolent Creator, one whose charming and delicious light descended and spread over the world, and being powerful everywhere, could condone the unspeakable sufferings of the world; that God did permit all suffering and was therefore, by logic of his omnipotence, the actual author of it, he was at a loss how to square with the existence of God, given the premise that God is Good.

'It is the only problem', Harvey had always said. Now, Harvey believed in God, and this is what tormented him. 'It's the only problem, in fact, worth discussing' (p. 19).[1]

But, notoriously, the Book of Job offers no clear answer to this question. 'Surely I would speak to the Almighty, And I desire to reason with God', says Job (13:3). And his wish is granted. But when God finally speaks it is, seemingly, to dismiss with contempt the idea that Job's sufferings deserve explanation, let alone apology. 'Who is this that darkeneth counsel by words without knowledge? / Gird up now thy loins like a man; for I will demand of thee, and answer thou me.' And there follows what appears to be merely a blank assertion of divine omnipotence, 'Where wast thou when I laid the foundations of the earth?' (38:2–4), and an extended hymn of praise to the glories and mystery of the Creation. This surely begs the *moral* question. But, mysteriously, Job himself accepts it as an answer. 'I know that thou canst do everything, and that no thought can be withholden from thee. . . . I have heard of thee by the hearing of the ear: But now mine eye seeth thee. / Wherefore I abhor myself, and repent in dust and ashes' (42:2–6).

Many honest people, and not just village atheists, find this revolting. If God's answer to the suffering, moral and natural, of the world is that we should be content to grovel before Him and forget about it, then perhaps such a god should not be worshipped. The believer who continues to affirm God's omnipotence and goodness begins, under this light, to look a little like Job himself: a grovelling, power-worshipping sycophant content, perhaps, not only to waive his own sufferings, but to ignore or minimize those of other people, provided he can bask in the charismatic presence of his omnipotent Leader.

This would be a perfectly sound way of debunking the claims of the Book of Job to 'mystery' or 'profundity', if it were not that the text continues beyond this point. Having downed Job, the Lord rounds on the comforters.

> ... the Lord said to Eliphaz the Temanite, My wrath is kindled against thee, and against thy two friends: for ye have not spoken of me the thing that is right, as my servant Job hath. / Therefore ... go to my servant Job, and offer up for yourselves a burnt offering; and my servant Job shall pray for you: for him will I accept: lest I deal with you after your folly, in that ye have not spoken of me the thing which is right, like my servant Job. (42:7–8)

What 'my servant Job' has been doing all along is to contend stoutly that he has done nothing to *deserve* the loss of his herds, the deaths of his children and his affliction of boils. Eliphaz and his two friends have been arguing equally passionately that for Job to stick in this way to what he perceives as the moral truth of the matter is in itself an act of impiety. It is they who argue that Job should adopt an attitude of abject submission to the inscrutability of God's will and condemn himself for no reason apparent to him: whatever the evidence to the contrary, if God is punishing him in this way He *must* be unjust. A fifth speaker, Elihu the son of Barachel the Buzite, angry at the failure of the comforters to convince Job of his unworthiness, states the nub of their objection to Job's conduct. His obstinacy in cleaving to the truth of his own moral perceptions is an implied affront to their own righteousness, and the right which it should confer upon them to interpret God's intentions to him.

Elihu is not afraid to present himself to Job as God's representative, confirmed in that role by his righteousness.

> My words shall be of the uprightness of my heart: and my lips shall utter knowledge clearly. / The Spirit of God hath made me, and the breath of the Almighty hath given me life. / If thou canst answer me, set thy words in order before me, stand up. / Behold I am according to thy wish in God's stead: I also am formed out of the clay. (33:3–6)

And, of course, there is a certain impious presumption in this stand itself, so that later, when Elihu rebukes Job's alleged impiety thus, 'Thinkest thou this to be right, that thou saidst, My righteousness is more than God's? / For thou saidst, What advantage will it be unto thee? and, What profit shall I have, if I be cleansed from my sin?' (35:2–3); it is unclear whether the alleged insult is to God's righteousness or to Elihu's, and beyond him to the validity of the accepted institutions for detecting and cleansing sin.

'I'm analysing the God of Job, as I say', writes Harvey to Edward late in the Spark novel. 'We are back to the Inscrutable. If the answers are valid then it is the questions that are all cock-eyed' (p. 180). If we construe the Book of Job backward from God's acceptance of Job and rejection of the comforters, rather than forward from the fact of Job's suffering, is it so clear that the poem is addressing itself to the Problem of Evil? Is it so clear that that is The Only Problem?

Perhaps because of the deep and lasting influence of utilitarianism, suffering has taken on a peculiar centrality in our moral thinking. It is reasonable to think that suffering, though it is sometimes valuable, is often meaningless, and sometimes appalling in its meaninglessness. What we tend to believe, however, is that suffering is not merely often but always and intrinsically bad: more, that it is that which is primarily bad, in the sense that only by partaking in it, or by a causal connection with it, do other things become bad. We like to think that it is the perception of the badness of suffering *per se*, and the consequent endeavour to remove it wholly from human life, that sets our morality in motion, gets us moving, as it were, as moral beings.

If we look closely at the Book of Job, however, we find that this familiar but rather recently invented point of view is shared by none of the characters. What the poem is grappling with is not the possibility that God does not care about suffering, construed as always and intrinsically an evil, but that He does not care about our *deserts*. Job, for instance, does not think suffering in itself a ground for reproaching God. When his wife says to him, 'Dost thou still retain thine integrity? curse God, and die', he replies. 'Thou speakest as one of the foolish women speaketh. What? shall we receive good at the hand of God, and shall we not receive evil?' (2:9–10). What is foolish is presumably precisely the idea that suffering can be wholly removed from life: that the goods of the kind of life we enjoy here could be had without any correlative evils.

What Job himself cannot stand is the apparent injustice of his sufferings.

My face is foul with weeping, and on my eyelids is the shadow of death; / Not for any injustice in mine hands: also my prayer is pure. / O earth, cover not thou my blood, and let my cry have no place. / Also now,

behold, my witness is in heaven, and my record is on high. / My friends
scorn me: but mine eye poureth out tears unto God. / O that one might
plead for a man with God, as a man pleadeth for his neighbour! / When a
few years are come, then I shall go the way whence I shall not return.

(16:16–22)

Even now, however, Job is so far from ceasing to trust in the eternity
of God's justice and truth that he appeals to heaven to justify him:
'my record is on high'. What if God keeps no records, perhaps
because He does not exist? Well, then, we shall have to rely for our
ideas of what is just and unjust on the comforters, or in other words
upon the social construction of reality, including moral reality.

The comforters seem, by the present-day standards I mentioned a
moment ago, grossly callous. They impute no moral significance to
suffering *in itself*. They seem to feel no temptation to take Job's
suffering as constituting, just *qua* suffering, a reproach to their
comparative ease and prosperity. They lack altogether our tendency
to speak in hushed voices in the presence of suffering: to treat it as
something intrinsically deserving of respect.

Job's complaint against them, however, is not this. His complaint
against them is that they will not claim fellowship with him, or
involve themselves in his sufferings, as one might involve oneself in
the sufferings of someone one loved. They will not plead for him with
God, 'as a man pleadeth for his neighbour'.

And Job answered and said, / No doubt but ye are the people, and
wisdom shall die with you. / But I have understanding as well as you; I am
not inferior to you: yea, who knoweth not such things as these? / I am as
one mocked of his neighbour. . . .   (12:1–4)

Not unnaturally, he prefers to take his chance with God.

Hold your peace, let me alone, that I may speak, and let come on me
what will. / Wherefore do I take my flesh in my teeth, and put my life
in mine hand? / Though he slay me, yet will I trust in him: but I will
maintain mine own ways before him. / He also shall be my salvation: for
an hypocrite shall not come before him.   (13:13–16)

This stance, of course, is exactly what irritates the comforters.
Their moral theology is what justifies them; by its light they are
righteous men, entitled by their righteousness to rebuke and exhort
Job. That Job refuses to play this game is thus felt as a personal
assault upon them.

Then answered Bildad the Shuhite and said, / How long will it be ere ye
make an end of words? Mark, and afterwards we will speak. / Wherefore

are we counted as beasts, and reputed vile in your sight? / He teareth himself in his anger: shall the earth be forsaken for thee?   (18:1−4)

God speaks, however, and the roles are reversed. The comforters, who would not plead for Job, 'as a man pleadeth for his neighbour', are now made dependent upon his pleading: only after they have sacrificed before Job, and Job has prayed for them, will they be acceptable to God. When Job has prayed for his friends, doing for them the office which they denied him, his 'captivity is turned', he becomes twice as prosperous as before and has seven sons and three daughters, the third of whom is quaintly named Keren-happuch, 'Box of Eye-Paint'.

I have been emphasizing, of course, those elements of Job which make it into something like a comedy of manners, about righteousness and its relation to social status and to reality, including the reality of suffering and the reality of other people as individuals. Out of these elements, I shall suggest, Muriel Spark has made *her* comedy of manners. But such a reading of Job, although by no means a very original or strained one, does put the thundering speech of God in chapters 38−41 in a somewhat different light, in two respects. First, God's blank reaffirmation of His originating power, which can seem like mockery of Job ('I made the world, and you: be content with it') can also appear as a genuine reassurance: 'I made the world and *it is real*: truth and falsity mean something, in the sense of being beyond human wishes and conventions: there is, after all, a record on high'. Second, there is the peculiar delight that the God of the poet of Job takes in His creation: a delight that seems to shine through and past all suffering. I shall come back to that in a moment.

II

Harvey Gotham has deserted his wife, Effie. On holiday Effie gets out of the car at a service station to buy two bars of chocolate. Later it turns out she has stolen these, as a measure of proletarian redistribution and a way of striking back at the multinationals. Effie at that time is extremely rich, on Harvey's money. Harvey, on learning that the chocolate was stolen, pulls in a little further down the *autostrada* and leaves the car, ostensibly to pee, actually to hitch a lift on a truck. He simply decamps, leaving Effie with the apartment, his personal belongings and the bills. The reason he offers later is that he could no longer stand the sketchiness and subjectivity of the political moralizing she goes in for. Harvey retires to a cottage near Epinal in the Vosges and immerses himself in the Book of Job. Effie becomes a terrorist, robs supermarkets and banks, involves Harvey in an investigation of his activities by the police and the international press, kills a policeman in Paris and is finally herself shot by the police at the scene of a second hold-up.

What has all this to do with the Book of Job? Consider, first, how close, in one way, Effie's moral universe is to that of the comforters. The world of the comforters' moral vision is populated exclusively by the righteous and the reprobate: the role of God is simply to exalt the one and cast down the other. The central moral concepts are desert, justice, reward, retribution. What stinks morally, what cries out for action to restore the moral balance of the universe, is not suffering but the unrebuked prosperity of the wicked; and the action called for is not action to alleviate suffering, but a retributive outpouring of suffering upon the heads of the unrighteous, who work iniquity.

Eliphaz the Temanite and his friends are content to leave the chastisement of the wicked in the hands of God. But suppose someone who shares their moral outlook comes to believe that God is dead. Will he or she conclude that 'everything is permitted': that the distinction between righteous and unrighteous has no basis in reality? Perhaps; but why should he? Will not the unpunished luxury of the wicked stink in his nostrils just as much as before? If God is dead, is it not better, perhaps, that men should take on the divine role of agent of wrath, rather than that the wicked should continue to rejoice in their prosperity? Someone who thinks like this will no longer be able to claim a theological basis for the distinction between righteousness and unrighteousness, of course, but he or she can just as easily found it upon a political outlook, which need only be quite sketchily developed as a body of ideas and analysis; enough to confuse opponents and satisfy doubters.

The point is that once such a person has founded the distinction between the righteous and the unrighteous in some such way, any action he or she undertakes in his or her capacity of agent of wrath against the unrighteous will be morally justified simply on the grounds that the unrighteous *are* the unrighteous, and so deserve all they get. In this way we arrive at the moral consciousness of Effie, of whom Harvey says,

> 'I couldn't stand her sociological clap-trap. If she wanted to do some good in the world she had plenty of opportunity. There was nothing to stop her taking up charities and causes; she could have had money for them, and she always had plenty of time. But she has to rob supermarkets and banks and sleep with people like *that*.' He pointed to a row of photographs in the paper.   (p. 124)

Harvey hasn't much time for justice as a self-authenticating moral imperative.

> 'A matter of justice. A balancing of accounts.' This is how Ruth put it to Harvey. 'I'm passionate about justice,' she said.
>
> 'People who want justice', Harvey said, 'generally want so little when it comes to the actuality. There is more to be had from the world than a balancing of accounts.'
>
> She supposed he was thinking of his character Job, as in fact he was.
>
> (p. 42)

But this doesn't mean that Harvey is not himself a painfully moral man: it is just that, like Job, he likes to stick in his moralizings strictly to the facts as they appear to him. With him it is actuality first, justice second.

Like Job, Harvey has his comforters. Indeed almost every other character in the book seems dominated by the desire to accuse Harvey of something, to dig out the root of his wickedness. And, as in the Book of Job, many of these accusations seem to have in them more of moral enthusiasm than of fidelity to fact or logic. Ruth, Effie's sister, is a case in point. Ruth is 'passionate about justice', but the style of argument by which she goes about establishing the justice of any actual moral claim is just one long *non sequitur*. Effie, after leaving Harvey, has a baby, Clara, by Ernie Howe, a computer expert. When, predictably, she leaves Howe, she settles the child on Ruth, now also divorced from her ex-curate actor husband Edward. Ruth decides in turn to go and settle both the baby and herself on Harvey. To the reader, who has been made privy to Ruth's attempt to blackmail Effie, through knowledge of her affairs, into sharing out some of Harvey's money by inviting herself and Edward, then still in his impoverished curate stage, on the ill-fated Italian holiday, and who has grasped also that Effie is the pretty, vivacious one, to whom men and affairs and money present no problem, the motives for Ruth's descent with Clara upon Effie's rich ex-husband seem simple enough. But to Ruth it is a matter of justice.

> 'It's a matter of justice,' Ruth said.
>
> 'How do you work that out?' said Nathan.
>
> 'Well, if it hadn't been for Harvey leaving Effie she would never have had a baby by Ernie,' Ruth said. 'Harvey should have given her a child. So Harvey's responsible for Clara; it's a question of justice, and with all his riches it would be the best thing if he could take responsibility, pay Effie her alimony. He might even take Effie back.'
>
> 'Effie doesn't want to go back to Harvey Gotham,' said Ernie.

'Harvey won't take her back,' Edward said. 'He believes that Effie boils down to money.'

'Alas, he's right,' said Ernie. (p. 41)

Ruth and Edward, both deeply conventional souls, use this kind of happy-go-lucky special pleading mainly to put a respectable gloss on what they propose to do anyway, and are not unaware of the resulting gap of credibility. Thus Edward, going to visit Harvey in his French cottage with the idea of getting him to agree to a profitable divorce settlement for Effie, wonders 'if there wasn't something of demonology in those confidences he shared with Ruth about Harvey; Ruth didn't know him as well as Edward did. They had certainly built up a case against Harvey between themselves which they wouldn't have aired openly.' (p. 10).

Edward finds Harvey difficult company, mainly because of an insistent, Job-like veracity which cuts Edward's actorly moral poses to ribbons.

> Edward used to confide in Harvey, and he in Edward, during their student life together. Harvey had never, to Edward's knowledge, broken any of these confidences in the sense of revealing them to other people; but he had a way of playing them back to Edward at inopportune moments. . . . So many sweet things seemed to have spilled out of his ears as soon as they entered them; so many of the sour and the sharp, the unripe and frivolously carping observations he made, Harvey had saved up in his memory-bank at compound interest; it seemed to Edward that he capitalized on these past confidences at a time when they were likely to have the most deflating effect on him; he called this a breach of confidence in a very special sense.
>
> (pp. 21–2)

The interview, not surprisingly, goes badly for Edward. Harvey concludes the discussion of Effie's affairs by giving Edward a sealed envelope to send to Harvey's lawyer when Edward gets back to England. Edward feels insulted by the fact that the envelope is sealed. When he arrives home he finds Ruth in the company of Nathan Fox, an ex-student who makes himself useful in their house, and who later ends up as one of Effie's terrorist accomplices.

Nathan's morality is happy-go-lucky in a more profound way than Ruth's and Edward's. 'Ruth', reflects Harvey at a later stage, is 'thoroughly bourgeois by nature; Effie anarchistic, aristocratic.' When she is told that she has gone off the rails, Effie says, 'What rails? Whose rails?' (p. 45). When she wants to get Harvey's address she has no compunction at all in doing it in a way which is both dishonest and lands an unsuspecting secretary in the soup. Nathan is a chip off this block. Like Effie he knows that everyday morality is merely a delusive glare which hides a deeper and darker geometry of justice and retribution. So he plays with Ruth's and Edward's preposterous scruples in a way at once elegant and ingenious; and when they do finally steam the objectionable letter open it is because Nathan has deftly, with a nudge here and there, shown them how to square it with their consciences.

> ... Nathan seemed to serve them like a gentleman who takes a high hand in matters of form, or an unselfconscious angel. In a way, that is what he was there for, if he had to be there. He often said things out of his inexperience and cheerful ignorance that they themselves wanted to say but did not dare. (p. 36)

So far, then, we have the following schema: a man with a Job-like preference for sticking to the facts, flanked by representatives of two quite different styles of sloppy moral reasoning, each governed by the determination to reach certain conclusions come what may, in the face of the facts if need be; and each related, though in different ways, to the comforters' obsession with justice and divine vengeance, and to their comfortable occupancy of a closed system of moral beliefs and arguments which makes sense of their world and assures them of their own moral worth.

From this point the novel moves into deeper waters. Harvey, like Job in his rectitude and his regard for truth ('perfect and upright, and one that feared God, and eschewed evil'), is quite unlike him in other ways. For one thing he does not suffer very much. Harvey himself worries about this, and is inclined to put it down to his wealth. Nobody tells him anything: his lawyers do everything for him.

> How can you deal with the problem of suffering if everybody conspires to estrange you from suffering? He felt like the rich man in the parable: it is easier for a camel to go through the eye of a needle than for him to enter the Kingdom of Heaven. (p. 64)

When Ruth persuades him to buy the château in whose grounds his cottage-hermitage stands, the same curious spring of inverted self-pity wells over again: we see why he likes the cottage, which has so far at least served to estrange him from the visible tokens of his wealth. '"Instead of disabusing myself of worldly goods in order to enter the spirit of Job I seem to acquire more, ever more and more," was all that Harvey said' (p. 57).

But is wealth all that is wrong with Harvey? Others know better. Edward, for instance:

And undoubtedly Harvey was often right. That he had a cold side was no doubt a personal matter. In Edward's view it wasn't incompatible with Harvey's extremely good mind and his occasional flashes of generosity. And indeed his moral judgement. Perhaps a bit too much moral judgement. (p. 22)

And bit by bit the fact of his own coldness begins to dawn on Harvey, either in the form of Freudian slips or outright pieces of self-analysis. The trouble is, he can't stand people, can't bear to pay attention to them, keeps wanting to get back to the solitude of his cottage and the puzzling moral geometry of Job.

Ruth didn't notice, or affected not to notice, a look of empty desperation on Harvey's face; a pallor, a cornered look; his lips were parted, his eyes were focusing only on some anguished thought. And he was, in fact, suddenly aghast: What am I doing with these people around me? Who asked this fool to come and join us for Christmas? What do I need with Christmas, and Ruth, and a baby and a bloody little youth who needs a holiday? Why did I buy that château if not for Ruth and the baby to get out of my way? He looked at his writing table and panicked.

'I'm going out, I'll just fetch my coat,' he said, thumping upstairs two at a time. (p. 60)

But later he reflects, 'I can't hold these women, . . . Neither Effie nor Ruth. My mind isn't on them enough, and they resent it, just as I resent it when they put something else before me, a person, an idea. Yes, it's understandable.' (p. 62)

A quasi-feminist polarity is emerging, between the amoral women, who must be attended to, and the bracing rectitude of Harvey's moral intelligence, thoroughly masculine but a bit arid. It is no accident that the grass around Harvey's cottage is dry and wilting, while the grass at the château, full of women and a baby, is greener. Harvey obscurely puts his finger on the heart of this matter in conversation with Stewart, his lawyer.

Stewert said, 'Lousy soil you've got here. Nothing much growing.'
'I haven't bothered to cultivate it.'
'It's better up at the château.'
'Oh, yes, it's had more attention.' (p. 127)

What Harvey prefers to attend to is the intellect, rectitude, the ethical. The reason why Job is such a torment to him is that it puts into the mouth of God words which deny the completeness, even the final validity, of such interests. Writes Harvey to Edward, 'I agree that Job endlessly discusses morals but there is nothing moral about the Book of Job. In fact it is shockingly amoral' (p. 67).

This, I take it, is the source of most of the suffering that Harvey endures for most of the novel. It is the source of the air of anxiety Edward notes during his visit: 'Anxiety, suffering, were recorded in his face; that was certain. Edward wasn't sure that this was not self-induced' (p. 27).

What, in God's name, is God trying to tell Job? It is to Muriel Spark's credit that she offers a kind of answer to this ancient and troubling question, though not quite the kind of answer Harvey thinks he is after. It is something to do with the way in which the fact that the universe is real, a place of concrete individuals which can never be fully reduced to intellectual schemata, both mocks our moral consciousness, our rectitude, in so far as *it* is something intellectual and schematic, a matter of abstract justice and balance of sin and retribution, and at the same time invites it to transcend itself, to share in the creative joy of God as well as His justice.

III

Part Two of the novel opens with Ruth, Harvey and Effie's baby, Clara, at the château: all quiet. Suddenly, pandemonium. Effie and her gang rob a string of supermarkets near the château. Harvey is arrested as a possible suspect, his studious privacy shattered.

There follows a long period of interrogation of Harvey, by the police, who think he may be financing the terrorists, by the press, who think he is a religious maniac and have no doubt that he is financing the terrorists, and by his Canadian Aunt Pet, who thinks he may be bringing dishonour on the family name. In all this Harvey, like all inexperienced interrogatees, reveals most about himself when he takes himself to be being most cleverly evasive, and stumbles towards some kind of better understanding of himself.

The key to this part of the book is, I take it, the painting of *Job visité par sa femme*, by Georges de La Tour, in the museum at Epinal. Harvey is looking at this work, trying to fathom it, when the police come to arrest him. It is a lovely, intimate painting. Job sits naked with his potsherd looking up with a rather childlike expression of trust and distress. His wife, bending over him in a crimson dress and a broad white apron lovingly thrown into light and shadow by the wax candle she holds in her right hand, is addressing him with serious concern. Yet in the Book of Job Job's wife jeers at him. The painting puzzles Harvey, not least because of the striking physical resemblance between Effie, Ruth, and Job's wife in the picture.

> ... what is she saying to him, Job's wife, in the serious, simple and tender portrait of Georges de La Tour? The text of the poem is full of impatience, anger; it is as if she is possessed by Satan. 'Dost thou still retain thine integrity?' She seems to gloat, 'Curse God and die'. Harvey recalled that one of the standard commentators had suggested a special interpretation, something to the effect, 'Are you still going to be so righteous? If you're going to die, curse God and get it off your chest first. It will do you good.' But even this, perhaps homely, advice doesn't fit in with the painting. Of course, the painter was idealizing some notion of his own; in his dream, Job and his wife are deeply in love. (p. 78)

As the police arrive, the unsuspecting Harvey continues to develop these thoughts. Job

> ... doesn't call her a foolish woman, he rather implies that she isn't speaking as her normal self. And he puts it to her, 'Shall we receive good at the hand of God, and shall we not receive evil?' That domestic 'we' is worth noticing, thought Harvey; he doesn't mean to abandon his wife, he has none of the hostility towards her that he has, later, for his friends. (ibid.)

That Job 'doesn't mean to abandon his wife', even if she does by his lights talk a little wildly and foolishly on moral and theological questions, is, I take it, the heart of the matter. For Harvey has abandoned his wife, on the *autostrada*, for doing just that; because he 'couldn't stand her sociological clap-trap'.

Inspector Chatelain, trying to gain Harvey's sympathy for the police in their efforts to trace Effie, graphically describes the effect of her latest murder on the victim's wife, incidentally putting strain on the comforter-like notion that desert is the bedrock of morals.

> 'If I was in your place,' said Chatelain, 'I would probably speak as you do. . . . I don't blame you for trying to protect your wife. You see,' he said, leaning back in his chair and looking away from Harvey, towards the window, 'a policeman has been shot dead. His wife is in a shop on the outskirts of Paris where they live, a popular quarter, with her twelve-year-old daughter who has a transistor radio. The lady is waiting her turn at the cash-desk. The child draws her mother's attention to a flash item of news that has interrupted the music. A policeman has been shot and killed in the eighteenth *arrondissement*. . . . Now this lady, the policeman's wife, is always worried when she hears of the death or wounding of a policeman. In this case the description is alarmingly close. . . . She hurries home and finds a police car outside her block of flats. It is indeed her husband who has been killed. Did she deserve this?' (pp. 142–3)

It looks at first sight, perhaps, as if Effie is the sole target here. She, after all, is the chief comforter of the book: the character to whom the application to real life of the idea that people have deserts, and should get them, appears least problematic. But is Harvey himself outside the scope of Chatelain's question? Did Effie, despite her moralizing prattle, deserve to be deserted on the *autostrada*?

Well, one might answer, yes. She was a terrorist and a murderer. Ah, but was she *then* a terrorist and a murderer? Well, she was the *same person* then. And that person's *nature* was to be a terrorist and a murderer. It just needed time for all that to come out.

There is something comfortably Cartesian about that way of looking at it. It suggests a reliably substantial notion of the self as something hard and solid, like a billiard ball, with a 'real essence', as seventeenth-century philosophers liked to say. Deconstructionist literary critics are not alone nowadays in feeling uncomfortable with that kind of view. Nor need we fetch our anti-Cartesianism from writers as relatively unfamiliar to the Anglo-Saxon reader as Derrida or Merleau-Ponty. Anti-Cartesian accounts of the self can be found much closer to home: in Hume, for instance, or in Gilbert Ryle's observation in *The Concept of Mind* that we come to know our own nature not by a Cartesian 'privileged access', but as it comes to be known to others, by observing the unfolding of the text of our own acts and sayings across time; or in John Stuart Mill's claim that we have free will because, although we have a nature, we can change it over time by attention to what we do, the habits we allow ourselves to form, and so on. It seems to me important to bring Mill in here, as one of the ways in which Muriel Spark's Catholicism shows itself is in a persistent interest in the freedom of the will. Free will, as one discovers by reading Spinoza, is not a concept accessible to anyone who adopts a consistently Cartesian conception of the self.

What tells intuitively against the Cartesian conception is simply the fact that people change as they reflect and as things happen to them. When Harvey is shown a police photograph of Effie, taken at the time of a shop-lifting episode in Trieste, some months after he left her, he finds difficulty in recognizing his wife.

'It looks like a young shop-lifter who's been hauled in by the police,' said Harvey.

'Do you mean to say it isn't your wife?' said Pomfret. 'She gave her name as Signora Effie Gotham. Isn't it her?'

'I think it is my wife. I don't think it looks like the picture of a hardened killer.'

'A lot can happen in a few months,' said Chatelain. 'A lot has happened

to that young woman. Her battle-name isn't Effie Gotham, naturally. It is
Marion.'   (p. 163)

So Chatelain's question, 'Did she deserve this?' does attaint Harvey:
sets him against the Job of the de La Tour painting, who trusts in his
railing wife as obstinately as he trusts in the God who afflicts him.
Harvey accepts that, and accepting it, his own failure to act as a
husband and a lover should have done towards Effie.

> 'Terrorist is out of the question,' he said. 'I left her because she seemed
> to want to go her own way. The marriage broke up, that's all. Marriages
> do.'
> 'But on a hypothesis, how would you feel if you knew she was a
> terrorist?'
> Harvey thought, I would feel I had failed her in action. Which I have.
> He said, 'I can't imagine.'   (p. 152)

Later, Pomfret returns to the attack:

> 'But why', said Pomfret, 'did you leave her? . . . You must already have
> perceived the incipient terrorist in your wife; and on this silly occasion,
> suddenly, you couldn't take it. Things often happen that way.'
> 'Let me tell you something,' said Harvey. 'If I'd thought she was a
> terrorist in the making, I would not have left her. I would have tried to
> reason her out of it. I know Effie well. She isn't a terrorist. She's a simple
> shop-lifter. Many rich girls are.'   (pp. 164–5)

Notice that Harvey will not accept Pomfret's phrase, 'implicit terrorist', with its Cartesian implications of a fixed essence waiting to
realize itself. In his reply he changes the form of words, to 'a terrorist
in the making', and suggests that she 'might have been reasoned out
of it'. Had he stayed with her: had he possessed some power to trust
in the capacity of human beings to respond to reason, as Job, in the
face of equally powerful countervailing evidence, trusts both his wife
and God.

IV

Harvey's intellectual abstraction, his distance from actual emotional
involvement with people, makes him, indeed, short on trust, long on
mildly paranoid suspicion. Anne-Marie, the policewoman planted
on him as a maid by the police, leaves him a vast bouquet of expen-
sive flowers from her sister-in-law's flower shop, because she feels,
maternally, that he may be missing Ruth and baby Clara, who have
been sent away to avoid press persecution. Distracted and over-

wrought, Harvey tears the flowers to pieces, looking for a bug ('I think you are not human,' says Anne-Marie, in tears next morning), although, as his more worldly lawyer Stewart points out, it would have been far easier for the police to plant the supposed bug almost anywhere else in Harvey's wholly accessible château. Here again Harvey differs from Job, whose leading characteristic is what the Hebrew text calls *tam*, translated 'integrity', but having additional connotations of innocence and simplicity.

Harvey also remains all too apt to suppose that the natures of others can be exhaustively captured by summary descriptions of role or essence. To Harvey Anne-Marie is primarily a policewoman, secondarily a maid. To the womanizing Stewart she is more than either.

> Stewart walked about the little room, with his scarf wound round his neck. 'It's chilly,' he said. He was looking at the books. 'Does Anne-Marie cook for you?' he said.
>
> 'Yes, indifferently. She's a police agent by profession.'
>
> 'Oh, that doesn't mean much,' said Stewart, 'when you know that she is.'   (p. 130)

But all this is changing. It changes because Harvey, under the stress of police interrogation, begins to admit to himself that he has not inwardly deserted Effie, but still loves her. As he comes to admit this, his peculiar and un-Joblike immunity to all save the most drily intellectual kinds of suffering begins to dissolve and desert him.

Now, why? Up to this point, Harvey's suffering has had a curiously metaphysical quality about it. Like the metaphysician, Harvey has tended to engage with the world not as an array of concrete, particular things and phenomena, but as an abstract totality, to be 'made sense of' by being brought into conformity with some abstract intellectual or moral schema.

An example of the metaphysical in this sense is, of course, The Only Problem itself. The problem of pain is not a practical problem, like the problem of how to build a bridge or how to conduct a marriage; it is a stumbling-block in the path of the mind's drive towards *total* comprehension, in this case theological comprehension, of the universe taken as a whole. The intellectual anguish arises because two magisterial claims of a totalizing theology, 'God is absolutely good' and 'God is omnipotent', will not cohere with the irritatingly plain and commonplace fact that suffering exists. The metaphysical impulse, scenting its own death in this impasse, batters its wings against the bars of the inconsistent triad like the fly in Wittgenstein's fly-bottle – and suffers. It hunts about, this being its nature, for some *general* solution to the problem, some *argument* which might even at this point save the face of natural theology. The history of rational theodicy, from Augustine to Leibniz and beyond, is fascinating enough, and impressive in some of its detailed arguments, but few theologians and no philosophers would want to claim nowadays that its achievement runs much beyond that of giving us a clearer view of the problem.

I think Muriel Spark wants to show us in Harvey a man who in some sense manages to get beyond this problem. But clearly the novel can't be offering us a new and *mirabile dictu* effective set of moves in rational theodicy. The 'getting beyond' has to be of a different kind; one with which the novel is by its nature fitted to deal.[2] Harvey gets beyond the problem not in his thought but in his life, though as we shall see the two are not wholly unconnected.

The clue to what is going on lies, I think, in the passages in which Harvey comes to recognize that he still loves Effie. At first, when asked point-blank by Chatelain whether he does, he tries to recover his balance, to retreat even now into his pose of studious distance: 'He was suddenly indignant and determined to be himself, thoughtfully in charge of his reasoning mind, not any sort of victim' (p. 141). But soon he is admitting his love for Effie to anyone who will listen, including the second, 'sympathetic' interrogator Pomfret:

> Harvey couldn't help liking the young man, within his reservation that the police had, no doubt, sent him precisely to be liked. Soften me up as much as you please, Harvey thought, but it doesn't help you; it only serves to release my own love, my nostalgia, for Effie. And he opened his mouth and spoke in praise of Effie, almost to his own surprise describing how she was merry at parties, explaining that she danced well and was fun to talk to. (p. 151)

The thing that strikes and moves one about this passage is the parallel between it and God's hymn of praise in Job 38–41 to His magnificent and amoral Creation. The voice of God, in the visionary language of the Job poet, delighting in the terrors of Leviathan and Behemoth, is echoed by the voice of Harvey delighting in a woman whom he knows in his heart (if he won't admit this to the police, he lets it slip casually enough to Stewart) to be a terrorist and a murderer.

The movement of the novel at this point reproduces the most intellectually infuriating aspect of the Book of Job: Job's apparently sincere conviction that he has been *answered* by God ('I have heard of thee by the hearing of the ear: but now mine eye seeth thee. /Wherefore I abhor myself, and repent in dust and ashes' [42:5–6]).

We want to say: there has been no *answer*, no *argument* offered; only a vainglorious trumpeting about Leviathan and Behemoth, and a blank assertion of Job's incapacity to receive the understanding he seeks. Similarly Harvey, the questioner of Job, has suddenly begun to sound like the God of Job himself. When later we learn that Harvey has arrived, after Effie's death, at some kind of intellectual accommodation with Job ('since he was near the end of his monograph on Job, he finished it' [p. 185]), we feel a certain frustration. We want to know what form that accommodation *took*, what Harvey *thought*, what *arguments* his experiences suggested to him; to look, in other words, *behind* the surface of the novel.

This desire to excavate, to get behind surfaces even when, as here, there is no *logically* conceivable depth into which we could excavate is, as Wittgenstein observed, one form of the metaphysical impulse. There *is*, after all, nothing behind the surface of the novel (we don't need *hypothesis* here, only thought). It is merely that Harvey's admission to himself of his love for Effie necessarily brings him into a state in which he feels for the first time the force of the two things God is undoubtedly saying to Job in Job 38–41. The first of these is that the very things which make for suffering in the world, wild beasts, for instance, or human beings, are proper objects of delight and love, as well as of terror and moral loathing. To really appreciate this duality, the brute fact of it has to be forcibly made present to one, as it now is to Harvey.

The second thing God has to say to Job is that human knowledge and understanding have their limits: that reality is, beyond a certain point, unfathomable. This is also something Harvey cannot help feeling, acceding as he does to the fundamental paradox of the splendour and dreadfulness of Effie. But a sense of epistemological inadequacy is also something enforced by the logic of Harvey's guilt over his desertion of Effie on the *autostrada*. For if Effie were *just* 'an incipient terrorist', there need be no guilt at having left her. It is only if she is (always and in principle) more than that; if she possesses the numinousness of flawed but infinite possibility; if in herself she is an abyss of possibilities that cannot be fathomed by human knowing, that there is that guilt. And vice versa. The physical similarity, the alternation, of Ruth, Effie and Job's wife in the de la Tour painting which strikes Harvey from time to time corresponds to something deeper: a sense of the three as being one and the same in that they represent alternative possibilities of becoming for one and the same person.

The effect of these revelations on Harvey is to dethrone (or, more modishly, to deconstruct) the masculine, judging, moral intellect, and

correlatively to let in suffering. Harvey begins as a man of rather
rigid rectitude, given, in Edward's sceptically perceptive summary, to
'moral judgement. Perhaps a bit too much moral judgement'. From
the point of view of this earlier self, strongly redolent of what
Kierkegaard called The Ethical, the new Harvey might appear something of a disaster: in love with a dead terrorist and sexually involved
with a living and pregnant blackmailer, definitively expelled from the
ascetic, quasi-religious seclusion of his cottage and installed in the
château surrounded by all the female mess of childbirth and child-
centred domesticity. Even his love for Effie is morally suspect. One
might be tempted to see in Harvey arguing for Effie's innocence to
the police an analogy with Job praying for the comforters. But is he,
perhaps, merely trying to defend himself from the realization of guilt
which will come with the realization that she really has become a
terrorist? In any event his love partakes of all the moral ambiguities
of earthly love. When it becomes certain that Effie lies dead in Paris,
shot at the scene of another attack on a policeman, Harvey feels a
guilty flash of relief at the thought that she is not alive in California
and in bed with Nathan Fox.

The new Harvey still has moral impulses, but they work in un-
Harveylike ways. Astonishingly, he is no longer closed to something
which, if he thought about its implications, he would recognize as the
world seen partly through Effie's eyes. Briefly encountering a poor
immigrant under some kind of investigation at the police station,
Harvey finds himself for the first time interested in a more than
intellectual way in the fact that people suffer. More curiously still, we
find him speculating that, instead of thought contriving somehow to
make sense of suffering, it may be that suffering makes sense of
thought, at least in so far as thought can be considered a part of life.

> Patience, pallor and deep anxiety: there goes suffering, Harvey re-
> flected. And I found him interesting. Is it only by recognizing how flat
> would be the world without the sufferings of others that we know how
> desperately becalmed our own lives would be without suffering? Do I
> suffer on Effie's account? Yes, and perhaps I can live by that experience.
> We all need something to suffer about. But Job, my work on Job, all
> interrupted and neglected, probed into and interfered with: that is experi-
> ence, too; real experience, not vicarious, as is often assumed. To study, to
> think, is to live and suffer painfully.   (p. 153)

The tone of this, riddled with qualifications, ifs and perhaps,
differs considerably from the confidently morally dissecting manner
of Harvey's earlier conversations with Edward, which now might
even look in retrospect not so very different from the manner of

Bildad the Shuhite and his friends. The magisterial note of epistemological dominance, of moral overview, has gone. Nevertheless there
is a kind of bedrock to Harvey's new attitude: a rooted distaste for
the cognitive imperialism of the notion that you can pin down
another human being in a phrase. Ernie Howe, Effie's lover and
Clara's father, makes no bones about doing this. Stewart *loquitur*, to
Harvey:

> 'He says if you want to adopt Clara, you can. He doesn't want the
> daughter of a terrorist.'
> 'How much does he want for the deal?'
> 'Nothing. That amazed me.'
> 'It doesn't amaze me. He's a swine. Better he wanted money than for
> the reason he gives.'
> 'I quite agree,' says Edward. 'What will you do now that you've
> finished Job?'
> 'Live another hundred and forty years. I'll have three daughters, Clara,
> Jemima and Eye-Paint.'   (pp. 188–9)

V

Part of the interest of *The Only Problem* lies in the way in which it
plays with some of the leading ideas of current critical theory. It
constitutes itself as a text, for instance, by systematically questioning
the meaning of another text. One line of reasoning would have it that
the possibilty of doing this destroys the possibility of supposing that
any text means, in itself, anything at all: meaning, on this view,
simply dissolves into 'inter-textuality'.

And yet it does seem, at least to this reader, that Muriel Spark's
novel offers one way of *making sense of* the Book of Job, and that the
sense it makes of it does actually *belong* to Job. Is this just an
illusion?

Before rashly concluding that it is, it is worth reflecting on the
extreme artificiality and complexity of the notion of meaning which
passes muster on both sides of the current critical debate, accepted by
both New Critics and deconstructionists as defining the differences
between them.

The notion of *the meaning of a text*, as understood in these
debates, has a double genealogy. On the one hand it is meaning as
defined by the theory of signs in Husserl's *Logical Investigations*
(the ur-theory against which Derrida primarily defines and distances
his own views). According to Husserl a meaning is a complex of
intentional acts exhaustively present to consciousness. It is thus

something outside history and outside the text: language *per se*, as a merely conventional technique of *representing* meaning, is inessential to the *constitution* of meaning. On the other hand *meaning* is also taken to mean roughly what it meant to the New Critics and to the line of Romantic theorizing which descends from Coleridge. According to this view there is a single correct interpretation of a text: the one which welds its sense and the operation of its rhetorical devices into the most complete and harmonious unity.

Despite their radically different origins and theoretical purposes, the two views exhibit certain superficial similarities. One can easily see why it should seem so natural and so tempting to take them as constituting a single, coherent theory of meaning, and then to line up for or against that theory. Nevertheless, a single coherent theory of meaning is exactly what they are not; and hence the central issues for critical theory cannot turn in any neat or orderly way upon the question of whether we are to affirm or deny the theory which they supposedly jointly constitute.

Take, for instance, the notion of meaning as something which 'belongs to' a text. On Husserl's view, meaning 'belongs to' a text only extrinsically, in the kind of way in which its meaning belongs to a message in code (i.e., because of some arbitrary associations recorded in the deciphering manual). This won't at all satisfy the Romantic critic, who, because he wants to think of writing as in some sense creating rather than simply mirroring reality, wants meaning to reside inherently in language. But here the Romantic critic finds himself suddenly hand in hand with Derrida, who also thinks of meaning as something whose habitation (*contra* Husserl) is not consciousness but the text, which thus becomes as the Romantics wished an instrument for the active production and dissemination of meanings, rather than for the mere representation of meanings already extant in the self-reflective Cartesian consciousness.

Derrida, of course, just because he holds that meaning is not something external to the text, holds that the meaning of an interpretative text is something which comes into being as that text is written (or 'writes itself': one needs the delicate ambiguity of the French passive voice to catch the right feeling of the meaning emerging wholly in and through the evolution of the text). Doesn't that, now, entail that the meaning ascribed by the interpreting to the interpreted text, being created *de novo* by the former, cannot *really belong to* the latter?

Well, no. It depends how you represent the process of interpretation, and, as I have argued in Chapter 4, it is only if you represent the process as wholly arbitrary that all content drains from any claim by an interpreting text to have elucidated a meaning which really belongs to the interpreted text. But you can only represent the process of interpreting a text as *wholly* arbitrary at the cost of ceasing to have any kind of conceptual grip on the notion of *text* itself. The meaning of a text *is* what issues from interpretation. It follows that if interpretation is entirely arbitrary (if a text can have any meaning anyone cares to assign to it), then there are no texts, only strings of marks on paper.

What does follow from Derrida's rejection of Husserl's Cartesian theory of meaning is that no interpretation of a text is privileged. There isn't any *single* real meaning, only an abyss of possibilities, just as, on Muriel Spark's view, there isn't any final account of a person, except as an abyss of possibilities. But the one vision in no way invalidates or renders hopeless the encounter between a reader and a text, any more than the other invalidates or makes hopeless the encounter between one person and another. What appears in response to thought and effort will in either case really belong to the Other, even though it might not be quite what someone else might have elicited from that Other.

The analogy between responding to a text and responding to a person returns me to my beginning. I began by asking whether a book as jokey as *The Only Problem* could possibly have anything serious to say about a biblical text, even one as jokey in some respects as Job.

Here again, it depends what you mean by interpretation. It isn't as if Muriel Spark were setting out to offer us *the meaning of* Job in the shape of some complex verbal formula allegedly expressing that. Her method is simply to trace the interaction, in Harvey's life, between Harvey and Job in a way which, through the use of characteristically 'modernist' narrative techniques, unsettles the reader and prods him into activity: invites and nudges him to feel his way through the complex pathways of his own reaction to Harvey's problems, and through them, to Job.

At one point *The Only Problem* touches explicitly on these issues. They arise all over again in connection with translation. We want, naturally, a translation which will enable the text to speak *correctly*, as it should, to every reader. But uneasiness with this demand is precisely what induces Harvey to stick with the Authorized Version: it lets you make a fresh approach, be your own translator. 'One can get to know the obvious mistakes and annotate accordingly' (p. 133).

'What about these other new Bibles?' said Stewart, pointing to a couple of new translations.[. . .]

'Messy,' said Harvey. 'They all try to reach everybody and end by saying nothing to anybody.' (pp. 132–3)

Chapter 7
Rhetoric and the Self

We derive as much dignity as we possess from our status as works of art.

Nietzsche, *The Birth of Tragedy*

Je ne peints pas l'estre. Je peints le passage.

Montaigne, *Essais*, Bk. III, ch. 2

I

The Death of the Author, I shall argue, has been much exaggerated. Only a weaker claim is seriously defensible: that the relationship between discourse and the self cannot be that sketched by one tradition of Western metaphysics. If that tradition offered the only possible way of conceiving of the relationship between the self, its utterances and the Other it addresses, the coffin of the author might all the same be well on its way to being nailed shut. But 'the Western Metaphysical Tradition' is not nearly as coherent and monolithic a body of intellectual constructions as writers like Rorty and Derrida, for good polemical reasons, like to make out. And even if it were, the formal constructions of metaphysicians are not the only means we have for making sense of our relationships to one another; even those mediated by talk; even, when it comes down to it, those mediated by talk which takes the form of poetry or narrative fiction.

It is certainly possible, at the cost of neglecting very substantial differences between individual writers and schools of thought, to formulate an (admittedly pretty skeletal) account of the self which unites at least the metaphysical tradition which extends from Descartes to Kant with some of its twentieth-century representatives such as Edmund Husserl or Bertrand Russell. According to this

188

account, the inner life of a person manifests itself as a temporal sequence of 'states of consciousness' (sensory states, desires, acts of will, moods, emotions, have all been considered 'states' in the required sense). The metaphysical problem is to say in what the *unity of the sequence* consists: what grounds there are for referring all the component 'states' of the sequence to a single 'subject.' Cartesianism, British Empiricism in its numerous versions, Kantianism, Husserlian phenomenology, offer, of course, radically different accounts of how the wished-for 'unity' is to be constituted. As so often in philosophy, it is only the bare form of a question (a 'problematic', as some people like to say) which serves as the glue holding together the work of such radically contrary minds in a single 'tradition of thought' on the topic. But, equally evidently, to see 'the problem of the self' in such a light is to grant certain assumptions about what it is to have, or to be, a self. One such assumption, hardly questioned before Wittgenstein questioned it,[1] is that the self enjoys perfect, doubt-free knowledge of the immediate character of its own states and acts as these present themselves to consciousness. Husserl, in this respect a characteristic representative of the tradition, thought indeed that awareness of the immediate contents of consciousness can be clouded by habits acquired through the 'natural attitude' – the attitude of ordinary sensory and scientific enquiry which takes for granted the accessibility of the physical world to consciousness – but equally that it can be restored through various techniques of *epoche*, Cartesian in inspiration, which involve setting aside questions of the objective reality of the objects of consciousness in order to become more fully aware of the structure of intentional acts through which each such object becomes accessible to consciousness.

Such an account of self-knowledge invites us to consider the relationship of language to the conscious life of the self as a mimetic one, in a rather straightforward sense of 'mimetic'. It suggests strongly that meaning itself is primarily a property, not of signs, but of states of consciousness, and that signs acquire meaning only secondarily, by being made to serve as arbitrary marks for mental contents which would otherwise be incommunicable. Such a view unites thinkers as diverse as Husserl (whose version of it in the *Logical Investigations* is brilliantly and savagely attacked by Derrida in *La Voix et le phénomène*), the early Russell and John Locke, in whom it finds expression in the following characteristically owlish passage:

> Man, though he have great variety of thoughts, and such from which others as well as himself might receive profit and delight; yet they are all

within his own breast, invisible and hidden from others, nor can of themselves be made to appear. The comfort and advantage of society not being to be had without communication of thoughts, it was necessary that man should find out some external sensible signs, whereby those invisible ideas which his thoughts are made up of might be made known to others. For this purpose nothing was so fit, either for plenty or quickness, as those articulate sounds which, with so much ease and variety he found himself able to make. Thus we may conceive how *words*, which were by nature so well adapted to that purpose, came to be made use of by men as the signs of their ideas; not by any natural connection that there is between particular articulate sounds and certain ideas, for then there would be but one language amongst all men; but by a voluntary imposition, whereby such a word is made arbitrarily the mark of such an idea. The use, then, of words is to be sensible marks of ideas, and the ideas they stand for are their proper and immediate signification. . . . That, then, which words are the marks of are *the ideas of the speaker* [my italics]: nor can anyone apply them, as marks, immediately, to any thing else but the ideas that he himself hath. *For this would be to make them signs of his own conceptions, and yet apply them to other ideas* [my italics]; which would be to make them signs and not signs of his ideas at the same time; and so, in effect to have no signification at all. 			(*Essay*, III.ii.1–2)

The tension between the privacy of 'thoughts' or 'ideas' and the publicity of words in this passage no doubt provides an object-lesson in the self-deconstructing character of logocentrism. Words have meaning only as marks of *the ideas of the speaker*, yet it is the very incommunicability of the speaker's ideas which led to the introduction of language. It follows that it is only if words can shake off Locke's postulated unique and exclusive connection with the conscious states of a particular speaker that they can function as vehicles of communication.

In this aporia are prefigured all the arguments currently used to establish the Death of the Author. The root difficulty, as critics and philosophers alike are apt to see it, is that a private language could not serve the purposes of communication, so that, conversely, a public language cannot *in principle* be adequate to express the personal. Thus, for instance, Gabriel Josipovici:

> Who . . . is the author of a work of literature? The man whose name appears on the cover? But by what authority does this author determine the meaning of what he writes, since he is after all deploying a language which belongs to his culture and not personally to him.[2]

Barthes, again, praises Valéry for constantly arguing for 'the essentially verbal condition of literature, in the face of which all recourse to the writer's interiority seemed to him pure superstition'.[3]

Beside this, as making essentially the same point, we can set Foucault's remark,

> Using all the contrivances that he sets up between himself and what he writes, the writing subject cancels out the sign of his particular individuality. As a result, the mark of the writer is reduced to nothing more than the singularity of his absence; he must assume the role of the dead man in the game of writing.[4]

or de Man's,

> ... are we so certain that autobiography depends on reference, as a photograph depends on its subject or a (realistic) picture on its model? We assume that life *produces* the autobiography as an act produces its consequences, but can we not suggest, with equal justice, that the autobiographical project may itself produce and determine the life and that whatever the writer *does* is in fact governed by the technical demands of self-portraiture and thus determined, in all its aspects, by the resources of his medium?[5]

or Derrida's arguments to the effect that the meaning of a text cannot be sought in the consciousness of its author since a text is always readable (*itérable*) in the absence or after the death of its author.

These arguments are often taken to entail conclusions which appear blankly counter-intuitive. They invite us, for instance, to take Derrida's well-known remark that the author is an *effet de différance* in a straightforwardly idealist sense: to take it as implying, that is, that the author as we encounter him in the text is a mere *appearance*: a simulacrum confected out of grammatical and rhetorical conventions which no more places us in the presence of the author than the sensory field in Berkeley places us in the presence of material objects, at least as conceived of by Newton or Locke. It follows from this that we are never in fact *addressed* by the author, as, for instance we certainly seem to be addressed, and rather movingly, by Fielding over the heads of his contemporaries, in the preamble to Book XVIII of *Tom Jones*.[6] One might be prepared to swallow this – after all the milder thesis that the author may on occasion take on the role of a character in his own fiction was a respectable critical truism long before post-structuralism was heard of – were it not that the same arguments seem to yield the conclusion that I cannot be *addressed*, either, by my wife in a letter – which after all is a text: a piece of *writing*. That in turn seems to imply that there can never be any communication of inwardness from one person to another. Not just the Author but the person dissolves into a depersonalized, socially constituted play of signs which bears upon its surface, continually dissolving and reconstituting themselves under the pressure of deconstructive analysis, simulacra which gesture towards a fictive origin in a Subject removed forever into *in-principle* inaccessibility behind the patterned surface of signs which is all a text offers to our inspection.

The possibilities of theory are not endless. The philosopher has always heard that one before somewhere. Argument of this strikingly metaphysical kind seldom concerns entities with which we become acquainted in everyday life, as distinct from the more august and capitalized Entities which populate philosophy books. So a philosopher is bound to feel a certain suspicion that the Subject which has just dissolved into the limpidly formal surface of the text is not the subject called Henry Fielding, still less the subject called Dorothy Harrison, but the Subject of Western Metaphysics, and more particularly the Subject of Descartes and Locke, whose disappearance into the abysm of *différance* is a simple consequence of the logocentric aporia into which a few paragraphs ago we observed Locke himself happily tumbling. The Self which retires into inaccessibility behind the text, that is, is the Cartesian Self, the self defined in terms of the unity across time of its 'inner states' and the epistemologically flawless presence to self-consciousness of the content of those states. The dissolution of that Self into the surface of the text is a simple consequence of the fact that the relationship between such a Self and language could only be the mimetic or specular one which Locke postulates. It follows that if the notion of a specular language is incoherent (a thought which both Derrida and Wittgenstein develop, though in very different ways), then language – the language we actually speak, not the specular language of logocentric theory – can offer no access to the (Cartesian) Self.

The effects achieved by deconstructive analysis, while startling, thus seem to depend, here as elsewhere, on the availability to the analyst of an already incoherent metaphysic whose predestined collapse in upon itself can be relied upon to produce the effects in question. This, no doubt, is why Derrida and his school are reluctant to announce the final demise of 'Western Metaphysics' (why Derrida, for instance, sustains the availability of familiar metaphysical concepts for both mention and use by adopting the typographical device of placing them *sous rature*). Deconstruction and 'Western Metaphysics' need one another. But are the resources of Western Metaphysics really coextensive with those of 'Western Metaphysics'? In the present instance, is the account given of the self by the Cartesian tradition down to and including, say, Russell and Husserl, really the only account of selfhood and its relationship to discourse which can be given? Dissident voices in our century and the preceding one, in particular those of Nietzsche, Merleau-Ponty and Wittgenstein, afford glimpses of a different way of thinking about these matters. The account I shall now offer owes something to all three, and to others.

II

It seems self-evident to me, as to each one of us, that I am a single self whose life extends continuously across time. Hume, on the other hand, was clearly right to argue that this assurance cannot be founded upon inner acquaintance with a special sort of *object*. What, then, is self-knowledge knowledge *of*? I want to suggest that it is, primarily, knowledge of *what I am about*. One reason for finding sense in this suggestion is that knowledge of what I am about can do duty for the Cartesian self-as-object in respect of its primary function, that of binding together the acts of one and the same self across time. It ties together, for example, the beginning of the movement of my arm towards the coffee cup on my table with the conclusion of the movement as my fingers close around the cup. But connectedness of that kind is resistant to analysis in terms of discrete, temporally located 'states of consciousness'. How many such 'states' occurred between the inception of the gesture of reaching for the cup and the closing of my fingers around the handle? The question is without a clear sense; hence without an answer; but without an answer we are left merely with the continuity across time of a bodily action continuously informed by one and the same intention. Moreover, the continuity of intention and purpose which such an act displays is not limited to the act itself. It spreads out to embrace the immediate context of the act. I am reaching for a sip of coffee because I have reached a momentary impasse in the composition of the chapter which I am sitting here in my room on a sunny Saturday afternoon to finish because . . . The intentionality of the act of reaching for the cup sites itself in a fabric of wider intentionalities whose boundaries also reach out until they become coextensive with the boundaries of my identity as a self. I am a *single* self, the self I am, not, as Kant thought, because the unity of my experiential field is both the ground and the mirror-image of the unity of the physical space I inhabit, but because of the uninterrupted continuity of the intentional space in which my acts situate themselves relative to one another.

To conceive of the unity of the self in this way (roughly speaking, in the spirit of Maurice Merleau-Ponty's version of existential phenomenology) is to abandon the *Cartesian* problem of the unity of the self by, in effect, abandoning the tacit assumptions about the human existential situation which underlie and generate that version of the problem. The Cartesian problem derives from Descartes's perception that there is nothing in my total state of consciousness at any given instant of time which could necessitate my existence at the next instant of time. Putting matters in this way invites us to conceive of time, as Hume was later explicitly to do, as a succession of discrete instants, each occupied by a distinct state of consciousness. The problem is now to say what holds the states occupying successive instants together as states of one and the same self. Descartes's answer is, in effect, that they all inhere in one and the same substance, and that substances just are continuants: just are re-identifiable across time. The answer which Hume developed from Locke's suggestions is that successive states of the self are held together by a fabric of contingent associative relationships. Hume's theory, like Locke's, makes *memory* fundamental to the unity of the self. Memory provides the field in which past instants of consciousness can be brought together to be compared with one another and with the present. Self-knowledge thus becomes in essence a reflection upon the contents of memory: its deliverances (to slide back briefly into a literary mode) a continual *memorializing* of the self: the endless composing of an *epitaph* upon one's past, and thus dead, selves.

To conceive of self-knowledge as in the first instance knowledge of what I am about, however, is to displace memory from the pivotal role it occupies in eighteenth-century and later Empiricist theorizing about the self. The focus of selfhood and self-knowledge moves immediately from the past to the present; from what I have done and been to what I am doing, and am. Even more crucially, it is no longer the (contingent or necessary) facts about past 'states' of my self which establish that I *am* the self which 'owned' those past states. Instead, what allows me to reconstruct my past as a coherent temporal sequence is the *intentional* unity of the self to which I have access *in the act* which occupies any given present in which I find myself, and which always has the potential of reaching out to organize an intentional fabric of which that act is the culmination and centre. It is the unfolding of the intentionality of the bodily act into a larger intentional context which allows me to reconstruct the temporality of my past: on occasion to recognize false memories as false, or even to recover, by patiently reconstituting the intentional structure of a past passage of my life, the recollection of what actually took place.[7]

If we follow empiricism in founding the unity of the self on memory, instead of vice versa, memory becomes an essentially magic, Faustian faculty, capable of making dead Helen live again, of piercing the veil which cuts off the living present from the already past and so non-existent moment which preceded it. A notorious epistemological worry arises here: how can memory pretend to offer me *knowledge* of what, being past, is already out of the range of any possible verification? If we take the primary form of self-knowledge to be knowledge of what I am about, then this problem also fails to get off the ground. A temporal reference is implicit in knowledge of what I am doing, but it is secondary to and dependent upon my grasp of the intentionality of my own doings. I know what I just *did*, and what I *did* just before that, because I know what I am *doing*. Conversely, if I forget or become confused about what I am doing it may become difficult or impossible to recapture the sequence in which I did what I just did. My primary self-knowledge is not fundamentally temporal in character but fundamentally intentional and only secondarily and derivatively temporal; and it is because this is so that self-knowledge manifested as memory can give me, as it were, a cognitive grip upon past events even though those events have passed beyond the range of any possible direct verification. The intentional structures which continuously unfold out of my moment-to-moment knowledge of what I am about, taken in their interaction with the vast body of everyday knowledge each of us possesses about the behaviour and characteristics of the natural world, form a rigid reference grid which allows me to carry out running checks on memory, and, in the end, to distinguish between what counts as a genuine memory-image and what does not.

Self-knowledge in the sense of knowledge of what I am about, however, while it will suffice to account for the felt unity of the self across time, is very far from constituting self-knowledge as that has been understood in the Cartesian tradition. Hume's discussion of the self, for instance, presents self-knowledge as if it consisted in the direct apprehension of past states of consciousness strung like jewels upon the thread of temporal succession. Viewed in this way the mind becomes a special realm, occupied by a special kind of natural furniture, 'mental states', to which introspection affords us what Ryle, in *The Concept of Mind*, called 'Privileged Access'. Husserl, because of the Cartesianism of his method, makes something not dissimilar of his structures of constitutive intentional acts: a special 'phenomenological' realm to which the various 'reductions' give access. An intentional account of self-knowledge need not go like that, however (it does not go like that in Merleau-Ponty, for instance). And if we divorce self-knowledge intentionally construed from the refined Cartesianism of Husserl's method it turns out to be oddly limited in scope. In particular it does not reach back beyond the inception of the act. As Wittgenstein made us see, explaining the difference between a thoughtful and a thoughtless act by taking the former to be the expression of a further, underlying 'mental state' (for which the very same distinction would need once again to be grounded in the presence of some yet deeper state) leads to a vicious regress. The same argument delivers the same conclusion for utterances. Utterance, whether spoken or written, does not mirror an underlying, 'purely mental', and only indirectly or inferentially accessible process of thought; it *is* thought. Speaking or writing, knowing what one is doing, is what thinking is.

From this Wittgensteinian perspective Derrida's much-quoted and to the humanist profoundly unsettling remark that the author is an 'effect of *différance*' begins to take on a new sense. So viewed, it says not that the text offers only a simulacrum of its putative author, but that the author is not in the end distinguishable from the text he or she writes, being like all men and women essentially involved in the intentionality of his or her acts and utterances.

Wittgenstein's argument suggests an account of self-knowledge going roughly as follows: I know from moment to moment what I am doing and what I am saying. That is, at any given moment I can relate what I am doing and saying at that moment, with reference both to my intentions and to the context to which my acts and utterances have been and continue to be intentionally and cognitively related, to what I was doing and saying a moment ago and to what, provisionally at any rate, I have it in mind to do and say a moment from now. To that limited extent I dispose of (or more precisely *am*) a self 'unified across time'. On the other hand it is entirely compatible with the unity of such a self that acts and utterances from time to time simply, as it were, erupt from me. In the heat of a quarrel, for instance, I blurt out an accusation which surprises even me. I know what I have just said (I know what those words mean in English, that is); and in a sense when I said it I knew what I was doing: I was quarrelling; the quarrel had arisen in a certain way, had taken a certain familiar course, I had lost my temper, and so on. What I am at a loss to explain is *what I meant by saying it*, where one part of answering that question would involve explaining how my having said it fits with the account I ordinarily give, to myself and to others, of the kind of person I am. At such moments of aporia, as one's self-image and the brute fact of a particular utterance having burst from one confront each other, one is apt to feel a type of anxiety not unrelated to Sartrean *angst*. It would be nice, at such times, if one could inspect one's Cartesian Self, under the impulsion of whose unchanging Essence the words presumably leapt into utterance, to discover there the real meaning, the correct interpretation, of those unfortunate words; since an interpretation so discovered, even if in some respects disquieting, would at least be coherent – and necessarily coherent – with the nature of my Real Self, and would thus at least free me from the sense of having in the heat of the moment lost track of my true identity. But unfortunately (here Hume, Wittgenstein and Derrida shake hands, as it were, over the prostrate forms of Descartes and Freud) I have no access to a Cartesian Self: that avenue is closed. There is, then, no saving 'true' meaning of my utterance, transcendentally guaranteed by its origin in pure Cartesian self-knowledge. I said what I said. The utterance stands there in all its grisly blankness and opacity, and if any sense is to be made of it it is the temporal 'I' of limited, merely intentional self-knowledge which must make it. The Self which might have the power to make sense of that utterance lies, in other words, not at its point of origin, but in the future.

We seem to have arrived, by way of Merleau-Ponty and Wittgenstein, at a position somewhat reminiscent of Nietzsche: the Nietzsche of the gnomic apothegm, 'What does your conscience say? – You must become who you are' ('du sollst der werden, der du bist' [*The Gay Science*, par 270]. Nietzsche, according to his best recent interpreter,[8] divides the self into a multiplicity of discordant drives and impulses. These are not the drives and impulses *of* any *thing*: we can begin to speak of a self only when, and to the extent that, a hierarchy of domination has been established amongst them. To achieve that, however, requires according to Nietzsche an effort of 'co-ordination'.

> *Weakness of the will*: that is a metaphor that can prove misleading. For there is no will, and consequently neither a strong nor a weak will. The multitude and disgregation of impulses and the lack of any systematic order among them result in a 'weak will'; their co-ordination under a single predominant impulse results in a 'strong will': in the former case it is the oscillation and the lack of gravity; in the latter, the precision and clarity of the direction.[9]

The freedom attained in this way is, as Nehamas puts it,

> ... not the absence of causal determination but a harmony among all of a person's preference schemes. It is a state in which desire follows thought, and action follows desire, without tension or struggle, and in which

the distinction between choice and constraint may well be thought to disappear.

But such serenity represents a limiting case only, for

> ... Nietzsche does not think of unity as a state of being that follows and replaces an earlier process of becoming. Rather, he seems to think of it as a continual process of integrating one's character traits, habits and patterns of action with one another.[10]

If his position, so set out, is not to collapse into incoherence, Nietzsche has two pressing questions to answer. Firstly, if the self has no being, but only a perpetual becoming, what organizes the becoming? Nietzsche's talk of 'co-ordination [of impulses] under a single predominant impulse' evades the question without answering it. It is easy enough to see how one impulse can dominate over other impulses (I want to sober up but want a drink more, e.g.) but to *co-ordinate* other impulses, now giving some rein, now restraining others, seems to require more similarity than is conceptually intelligible between an impulse and a person. For the same reason it is not easy to see how an impulse could audition, even in principle, for the role of what responds to the command of Nietzschean conscience – 'Du sollst der werden, der du bist' – unless that is to be interpreted as a *reductio ad absurdum* of the very idea of conscience: Don't even bother trying: you will become what chance makes you. Nor, although it seems to me to be moving in the right direction, does Nehamas's suggestion that 'Because it is organized coherently, the body provides the common ground that allows conflicting thoughts, desires, and actions to be grouped together as features of a single subject',[11] cut very much ice in this connection.

The second question a Nietzschean account of the self[12] must face is this: if the self is to arrive at any assessment of its own impulses and proclivities, in order to integrate them into some new structure, then (a) the impulses and proclivities of the self must have some sort of reality, however provisional, despite the non-existence of the Cartesian Self, and (b) the self must have some means of getting to know about its own impulses and proclivities, despite the non-availability of Cartesian privileged access.

As so often in Nietzsche when major metaphysical issues are at stake, we seem to have ended up head-on to a string of contradictions. But there is a way back to firmer ground. The difficulties faced by an account of the self as self-synthesizing which posits radical or ground-up synthesis are indeed insoluble. The move from thinking of the life of the self as a string of temporally discrete 'states of consciousness' (which, because in theory they might not be states of the same person, require some further step to establish that they are) to thinking of the self in terms of the intentionality of its acts,[13] however, removes the need for a ground-up synthesis.[14] A self which is capable of keeping track of the intentionality of its acts across even the short space of time needed to complete the simplest action is a self which is *already* unified in the required sense. Such a self, however, although thus provided with the minimal unity and coherence needed to make the notion of self-synthesis intelligible, still has plenty of self-synthesizing left to do. The reason for this is that, for a self constituted on the level of agency, an entirely adequate grasp of what it is about can coexist with the most blank inability to give any persuasive general account of its own motives and proclivities. Cartesianism forges an unbreakable link between the unity of the self and perfect self-knowledge. Construing self-knowledge as in the first instance knowledge of what I am about cleaves these two categories apart, giving a theoretical description of the self in which each of us, if he is honest, can recognize at least a former self: a self possessing an iron grip on its own unity and its immediate goals and strategies, coupled with a Lear-like slenderness of self-knowledge. Such a self is Nietzschean precisely in that, while it possesses the unity and the potential for domination and co-ordination which it must possess if it is to take on the Nietzschean role of organizing its impulses into a hierarchical order, it lacks cognitive access to itself as a transparent and purely spiritual realm of 'inner states'. Its horizons are near and contingent ones, bounded by what Nietzsche called 'physiology': the enigma and opacity of impulse, the unchosen but unignorable significances of the body, and an imperfectly faced and comprehended past.

For such a self, of course, the second of the two questions confronting Nietzsche is now pressing. The proclivities and personality patterns of such a self must on some level be real and enduring, and the self must have some cognitive access to them: must be able in some way to get to know about them if it is to change them. What is their habitation, if it is not the transparent abyss of the Cartesian Self? Only one answer seems possible. Their habitation is the text of the self's actions and utterances, taken in context. The acquisition of self-knowledge is more like reading a difficult and painful text than it is like gazing at a harmoniously proportioned and shadowlessly illuminated object. We come to know ourselves by coming to grasp the *effets de différance* which display themselves in the temporally extended text of our own past words and actions, taken in context, to whatever extent we can bring ourselves to scrutinize and assess that text dispassionately. We now need to look in more detail at the nature of the textual mechanisms which such scrutiny brings into play.

III

One version of the argument for the Death of the Author holds that the formal, rule-governed character of language, the *textuality* of the text considered as a play of rhetorical devices and inter-textual references, is alone sufficient to cut the tie holding together the self and its utterances. Another version, of Derridean inspiration, holds that it is primarily the presence of failures of coherence, aporias, *mises-en-abîme* in the text, which disconnects it from the self. Both arguments make sound enough sense from the standpoint of a generally Cartesian account of self-knowledge. From a Cartesian standpoint the relationship between language and inner life is specular. For that to be so the expressions of a language fitted to describe the inwardness of a speaker must have meanings fully and finally determined by reference to the inner states which it is the business of the language to describe. If the meanings of expressions in the texts we actually have to deal with are in crucial ways established by reference to other texts and through the play of rhetorical devices resting upon literary conventions antedating and quite independent of the author, then clearly, to whatever extent that is the case, their supposedly directly referential connection with states of their authors' Cartesian Selves thins and dissipates. Similarly, if different aspects of a text are at odds with one another, if meanings fissure, disseminate into alternative and incompatible readings, that too must place in question the claim of the text to offer an adequate representation of the Cartesian Self which is its supposed origin. The Self of the Cartesian tradition is nothing if not internally coherent, whether the style of its coherence is of the rational-causal, associative, transcendental or noetic-noematic variety.

It is less clear that either textuality or aporia is a bar to access, via the text, to its author, if the relation between the self and discourse is of the kind sketched in the preceding section. Proust, in *Du côté de chez Swann*, offers a good example of the kind of textual access to the self I have in mind.[15] The young Marcel is visiting a family friend, M. Legrandin, and happens to ask him whether he is on visiting terms with the Duchesse de Guermantes.

> I summoned up all my courage and said to him: 'Tell me, sir, do you, by any chance, know the lady – the ladies of Guermantes?' and I felt glad

because, in pronouncing the name, I had secured a sort of power over it, by the mere act of drawing it up out of my dreams and giving it an objective existence in the world of spoken things.

But at the sound of the word Guermantes, I saw in the middle of each of our friend's blue eyes a little brown dimple appear, as though they had been stabbed by some invisible pin-point, while the rest of his pupils, reacting from the shock, received and secreted the azure overflow. His fringed eyelids darkened and drooped, his mouth, which had been stiffened and seared with bitter lines, was the first to recover, and smiled, while his eyes still seemed full of pain, like the eyes of a good-looking martyr whose body bristles with arrows.

'No I do not know them,' he said, but instead of uttering so simple a piece of information, a reply in which there was so little that would astonish me, in the natural and conventional tone that would have befitted it, he recited it with a separate stress on each word, leaning forward, bowing his head, with at once the vehemence which a man gives, so as to be believed, to a highly improbable statement (as though the fact that he did not know the Guermantes could be due only to some strange accident of fortune) and with the emphasis of a man, who, finding himself unable to keep silent about what is to him a painful situation, chooses to proclaim it aloud, so as to convince his hearers that the confession he is making is one which causes him no embarrassment, but is easy, agreeable, spontaneous, that the situation in question, in this case the absence of relations with the Guermantes family, might very well have been not forced upon, but actually designed by Legrandin himself, might arise from some family tradition, some moral principle or mystical vow which expressly forbade his seeking their society.

'No,' he resumed, explaining by his words the tone in which they were uttered. 'No, I do not know them; I have never wished to know them; I have always made a point of preserving complete independence; at heart, as you know, I am a bit of a Radical. People are always coming to me about it, telling me I am mistaken in not going to Guermantes, that I make myself seem ill-bred, uncivilized, an old bear. But that's not the sort of reputation that can frighten me; it's too true! In my heart of hearts I care for nothing in the world now but a few churches, books – two or three, pictures – rather more perhaps, and the light of the moon when the fresh breeze of youth wafts to my nostrils the scent of gardens whose flowers my old eyes are not sharp enough, now, to distinguish.'[16]

Proust sums up the significance of this passage with the following strikingly anti-Cartesian observation:

Et certes cela ne veut pas dire que M. Legrandin ne fût pas sincère quand il tonnait contre les snobs. Il ne pouvait pas savoir, au moins par lui-même, qu'il le fut, puisque nous ne connaissons jamais que les passions des autres, et que ce que nous arrivons à savoir des nôtres, ce n'est que d'eux que nous avons pu l'apprendre.*[17]

The point of this observation, I take it, is that Legrandin's snobbery is not a matter of an inner state to which he might possess Cartesian guaranteed access, but something which displays itself in, among other things, a pattern of incoherences and aporias in the text of his remarks in response to Marcel's innocent question. His explanations of why he is not on visiting terms with the Guermantes are too numerous, and are inconsistent one with another. The discord arises because each successive explanation presupposes a certain *stance*, and with it a certain general description of the self supposedly offering the explanation, which simply fails to cohere with the stances and the correlative self-descriptions presupposed by the others. The old Radical, the *tête de jacobin* who would feel politically compromised in an aristocratic drawing-room, cannot easily be reconciled with the Epicurean hermit of the next sentence. Worse still – this, I think, is the clincher – there would not be the multiplicity of explanations, the solemn emphasis on words, the vehemence, the bowing of the head, the readiness all this manifests to take as an extraordinary state of affairs, requiring extraordinary feats of explanation, a social lacuna which seems entirely normal to the young Marcel (to whom the Guermantes are as remote and as majestically fabulous as figures in a tapestry), and which would excite as little wonder in a genuine *tête de jacobin* or a genuine Epicurean sage.

In so far as these incoherences invalidate Legrandin's claim to be offering a mimetically accurate description of his Cartesian inwardness we have here a palmary instance of deconstructive aporia. The trouble is that deconstructive aporia seems to be functioning here not as a means of severing Legrandin's words from any connection with Legrandin, but as a means of making both the fact and the nature of that connection clear. For if we ask ourselves: What is Legrandin, really? How is one to describe a man who offers, in response to a simple question, such an incoherent rigmarole as this? – only one answer plausibly offers itself: as a covert and deeply repressed snob, who feels keenly, *in propria persona*, the social exclusion which, in

---

*   ('Certainly that does not mean that M. Legrandin was not sincere when he inveighed against snobs. He could not know, at least of himself, that he was one; since we are only aware, ever, of the passions of others, and whatever knowledge we may come to have of our own can only have been acquired from them.')

the characters of *tête de jacobin* or elderly Epicurean, he would like to persuade his young listener that he does not feel at all. The conclusion that the stance from which Legrandin is really speaking is that of a snob is the only possible one because that hypothesis alone fails to disintegrate into aporia under deconstructive scrutiny. Note, too, that the knowledge of Legrandin's real feelings and character which Marcel, and we as readers, obtain from what essentially amounts to deconstructive analysis of the text of Legrandin's remarks is *definitive*, in a sense in which the 'knowledge' of himself upon which Legrandin supposes himself to be drawing in giving his explanation is not. For suppose someone were to say: 'After all, perhaps one should not base too much on a mere string of words. Isn't it possible that M. Legrandin's True Self, the self which is forever and in principle hidden behind the veil of his words and deeds, is in reality not, after all, a snobbish self?' Wouldn't we just ignore this as a contribution to the discussion? And wouldn't we be right to do so, since the hypothesis it propounds is an entirely empty one which could make no difference either way? In reality the way in which we come to understand *les passions des autres* is not by inspecting, or framing hypotheses about, their Cartesian selves, but by subjecting the text of their words and actions to exactly the sort of scrutiny to which Proust subjects the text of M. Legrandin's. That text is not a veil cutting us off from the self of its author, but a small portion of the vast web of talk and action in which that self lives and manifests itself.

The deconstructionist will want to protest that the concept of *différance* cannot simply be stood on its head in this summary way. Derrida's arguments show that the text – that *writing* – constitutes a sphere of pure textuality, hermetically sealed off from any 'outside' – any *hors-texte* – within which meanings disseminate and shift endlessly with no possibility of ever being brought to a halt, as Proust's deconstruction of Legrandin's reply comes to a halt in the fact of Legrandin's snobbery. This, of course, is just what is contestable. What Derrida's arguments in fact show is that logocentrism and the 'Metaphysics of Presence' are incoherent. The impossibility of any kind of interaction between text and *hors texte* follows from the incoherence of those doctrines only if they offer the only possible means of conceptually constituting the notion of an *hors-texte*. The main task of the argument in Chapter 1 and the present chapter has been that of showing this second assumption of conventional deconstructionism (I use the term 'conventional deconstructionism' because, while many of Derrida's literary disciples take this second step, it remains quite unclear to me whether Derrida himself is prepared to take it) to be false. My claim in Chapter 1 was that the relationships between sign and sign which constitute meaning within the text can only be weakly internal to the text. They relate sign to sign only via features and aspects of the extra-linguistic world. My contention in this chapter is that the way in which we test the sincerity of a speaker's account of himself in terms of the coherence of what he is saying with one or another account of the stance from which he may be supposed to be saying it, is a case in point of a sign–sign relationship weakly internal to language.

The notion of 'stance' which we employ in such cases is clearly replete with extra-linguistic reference. It takes for granted the intentional coherence of the acts and discourse of a normal human being. Taking that for granted in no way involves a commitment to logocentrism or the metaphysics of presence: it is no bar, for instance, to accepting everything that Saussure has to say about meaning as a function of relationships between signs, and thus everything that Derrida has to say about *différance*. It offers us, certainly, access to an *hors-texte* capable of bringing the movement of meanings to a halt, as in the case of M. Legrandin's reply; but (a) access to an *hors-texte* in that sense in no sense involves access to *presence* in the shape of M. Legrandin's 'inner states', and (b) the *hors-texte* in question, for that very reason, cannot be shown to be inaccessible by appeal to the arguments which demonstrate the incoherence of logocentrism. What, after all, would it be to doubt the intentional coherence of M. Legrandin's, or for that matter Proust's, acts and utterances? If such doubts could intelligibly be raised the immediate consequence would be to make it a real, and in principle undecidable question whether the string of sentences which compose the text of *A la recherche du temps perdu* should be regarded as constituting a *text* at all, rather than just a string of unrelated sentences. I can find nothing in Derrida to support a scepticism as whimsical as this; and even if there were, what would follow? We should, rightly, shrug our shoulders and carry on as usual.

If textual aporia interacts, in the way we have just observed, with the stance or stances from which a text is nominally produced to discredit the claim to authenticity of some putative stances and correlative characterizations of the authorial self while leaving others as residual legatees, as it were, of the text, then the mere *textuality* of the text, its status as a play of socially and historically locatable tropes and inter-textual references, offers no greater bar than aporia to the text's functioning as a manifestation, and as such a source of direct knowledge, of the self of its author. Legrandin's response, after all, is an entirely formal, literary construct, replete with allusions to genres as diverse as pastoral and the political tract; but this in no way prevents it from functioning as the vehicle of a self-revelation, however inadvertent. The counter-intuitive consequences of the arguments for the Death of the Author which we listed earlier included the impossibility of being addressed by the author through his text and the impossibility of a text's communicating an individual person's thoughts and feelings. To these we might add the odd conclusion that there is no reason for an author to feel in any way responsible for his text, since once it passes from his hand all connection between him and it is automatically severed. The temptation to say any of these things about the Marcel / Legrandin exchange is, I think, rather slight. Marcel is quite evidently being addressed by Legrandin despite the entirely fictional character of the explanation which Legrandin is addressing to him. Equally, Legrandin's little fiction certainly communicates to Marcel his thoughts and feelings, confused and self-indulgent though these are. Finally, it seems clear that Legrandin is responsible for his words, just in the sense that, since they do manifest one aspect of his self, he cannot detach them from him, or disown them merely on the grounds that they do so under the form of a flawed literary construct. It seems that the author may be alive after all, and living in the region in which New Criticism (which never, after all, subscribed to the Method of Sainte-Beuve) located him, namely, in the text.

IV

The critical consequences of taking the relationship between the self and its utterances to be either specular in character or non-existent are well displayed in Paul de Man's discussion, in his subtle and brilliant essay 'Autobiography as De-Facement',[18] of Wordsworth's *Essays upon Epitaphs*. De Man's reading, it seems to me, makes Wordsworth into more of a Cartesian than he is. To put it more precisely, while Wordsworth is apt, hardly surprisingly, to avail himself of Cartesian or Lockeian formulas when he wants a *general* way of characterizing the relationship between self and utterance, his detailed treatment of examples in *Upon Epitaphs*, and many of his occasional reflections, here and elsewhere, upon his own poetic practice, conform much more closely to the alternative account of that relationship sketched in the preceding two sections. A whole cluster of issues concerning Wordsworth's type of Romanticism and Romanticism in general, about Wordsworthian 'truth to Nature' and about what it is to take writing seriously, come to a head here.

De Man takes the stance of autobiography to be that 'The author declares himself the subject of his own understanding...'. The putative relation of autobiography to the self is specular, that is. To a philosopher within the tradition of Cartesian metaphysics that is the relation of all writing to the self. De Man accepts that, and thus accepts that the particular practice of autobiography

> merely makes explicit the wider claim to authorship that takes place whenever a text is stated to be *by* someone and assumed to be understandable to the extent that this is the case. Which amounts to saying that any book with a readable title page is, to some extent, autobiographical.[19]

There is already here, I think, a suspicion that de Man may be proceeding a priori from a half-acknowledged metaphysic to a conclusion about what the stance of autobiography, and by extension of literature in general, given the exclusive truth of that metaphysic, *must be*. Not only is it hard to find an express declaration of authorial self-understanding in Wordsworth's text; such a stance seems actually to be excluded by passages such as the following, from the address to the Friend in Book I of *The Prelude* (1805–6):

> Nor will it seem to thee, my Friend! so prompt
> In sympathy, that I have lengthen'd out
> With fond and feeble tongue, a tedious tale.
> Meanwhile my hope has been that I might fetch
> Invigorating thoughts from former years,
> Might fix the wavering balance of my mind,
> And haply meet reproaches, too, whose power
> May spur me on, in manhood now mature,
> To honourable toil. Yet should these hopes
> Be vain, and thus should neither I be taught
> To understand myself, nor thou to know
> With better knowledge how the heart was fram'd
> Of him thou lovest,...   (ll. 645–57)[20]

Here self-understanding is precisely not seen as a necessary precondition for the composition of *The Prelude*, but as something which might, though only chancily and with luck, result from it. The proposed method, too, is not the lapidary representation of a past life already understood in all its significances and consequences for a narrator speaking with all the authority of a self which at the point of utterance is stable and fully achieved. Rather, the object is, by reflection upon the past, to achieve stability of personal stance *in the present*: to 'fix the wavering balance of my mind' (a foreshadowing here of Nietzsche on strength of will!) by fetching 'invigorating thoughts from former years'. Altogether the stance of these lines is much more that of someone embarking upon an enterprise of self-examination in the interests of Nietzschean *Selbstbildung* than that of the achieved specular magus of de Man's characterization.[21] Of course one could try retorting that to talk about any subject, and hence to talk about myself, implies a claim to know what I am talking about. But this merely offers de Man the uninviting choice between a truism and a falsehood. I know *what happened* in my childhood if I can talk about it. What I may not know, and perhaps can only find out by attempting to talk or write about those events, is their significance for my present self: how they are or might be articulated into the structure of my present outlook and personality.

Wordsworth's theme in the third of the *Essays upon Epitaphs* is the Romantic opposition between Nature and Artifice. The 'artifices which have overrun our writings in metre since the days of Dryden and Pope' are contrasted with

> Energy, stillness, grandeur, tenderness, those feelings which are the pure emanations of nature, those thoughts which have the infinitude of truth, and those expressions which are not what the garb is to the body but what the body is to the soul, themselves a constituent part and power or function in the thought – all these are abandoned for their opposites, – as if our Countrymen, through successive generations, had lost the sense of solemnity and pensiveness (not to speak of deeper emotions) and resorted to the Tombs of their Forefathers and Contemporaries only to be tickled and surprized. (p. 84)[22]

Language, correctly used, is continuous with Wordsworthian Nature in its power for good: it is because words so used are a *part of Nature* (they must be, since they are a 'constituent part and power or function' of our thought – of our selves, that is – and we ourselves are a part of Nature), are 'external powers', that they are not to be 'trifled with'.

> Words are too awful an instrument for good and evil to be trifled with: they hold above all other external powers a dominion over thoughts. If words be not (recurring to a metaphor before used) an incarnation of the thought but only a clothing for it, then surely will it prove an ill gift; such a one as those poisoned vestments, read of in the stories of superstitious times, which had power to consume and to alienate from his right mind the victim who put them on. Language, if it do not uphold, and feed, and leave in quiet, like the power of gravitation or the air we breathe, is a

counter-spirit, unremittingly and noiselessly at work to derange, to
subvert, to lay waste, to vitiate, and to dissolve.   (pp. 84–6)

It is worth noting in passing, of course, that Wordsworth's observation that words which are not, in the sense intended, trifling are
'themselves a constituent part and power or function of the thought',
suffices in itself to make what is, finally, the central point of the
present chapter concerning the relationship between discourse and
the self.

After some further consideration of examples of epitaphs, the
third *Essay* ends with what is in effect a long verse epitaph
of Wordsworth's own composition, taken from *The Excursion*. It
concerns a Dalesman, made deaf in childhood, for whom books
remedy the silence of nature. The point is that words *give nature
voice*: Book and Nature work together in moral harmony.

> The dark winter night,
> The stormy day, had each its own resource;
> Song of the muses, sage historic tale,
> Science severe, or word of holy writ
> Announcing immortality and joy
> To the assembled spirits of the just,
> From imperfection and decay secure.   (p. 95)

From a post-structuralist standpoint this whole long passage of
distinction, analogy, lyric and prose exhortation is, of course, simply
logocentrism on stilts. The central distinction, between language as
analogous to the body (as 'incarnation of thought') and as analogous
to clothing, is easily 'placed' at first sight as a variation upon the
standard logocentric distinction between a language which mirrors,
with specular fidelity, the living process of thought (Derridean *speech*)
and a language (Derridean *writing*) which merely sets signs together
in dazzling and unexpected ways to 'tickle and surprize'.

Not surprisingly, then, it is the distinction between language as
clothing and as incarnation which de Man singles out (his p. 79
et seq.) as 'The main inconsistency of the text'. De Man's argument
is, in effect, that the second wing of the distinction collapses into
the first: all language is clothing. Ostensibly the thought here is
Derrida's: all language, including speech, is writing: there is no
language which neutrally and immediately mirrors the living presence of the self. But de Man's discussion infects this thought, the
native tenor of which is not epistemological but metaphysical (see my
Chapter 4, 'Deconstructing Derrida'), with the appearance / reality
doubts characteristic of philosophical idealism. De Man's deconstruction begins thus:

De Quincy singled out this distinction and read it as a way to oppose compelling figures to arbitrary ones. But incarnate flesh and clothing have at least one property in common, in opposition to the thoughts they both represent, namely their visibility, their accessibility to the senses.[23]

De Man takes Wordsworth's claim to be that 'a garment is the visible outside of the body as the body is the visible outside of the soul'. Of course Wordsworth cannot keep language-as-clothing and language-as-incarnation apart as distinguishable categories of discourse on this interpretation: 'The language of tropes (which is the specular language of autobiography) is indeed like the body, which is like its garments, the veil of the soul as the garment is the sheltering veil of the body.'[24]

No one, not even a Lake Poet, could be supposed altogether insensible to the discomfort of finding himself perched above a *mise-en-abîme* as vertiginous as this. De Man's next move, therefore, is to search the third *Essay* for signs of the discomfort produced by an obscure consciousness of *mauvaise foi*. They are not hard to find. The violence of Wordsworth's attack on Dryden and Pope is first singled out as suspiciously inconsistent with the former's expressed (and of course putatively logocentric) preference for what de Man characterizes as 'a lucid language of repose, tranquillity and serenity'. Wordsworth's choice of the coat of Nessus as a metaphor for the destructive power of a language that does nothing more than 'tickle and surprize' is itself evidence of lurking bad faith, since, given the impossibility of 'the specular language of autobiography', it is in reality not trifling language but language *per se* which obscures and de-faces the self.

> The coat of Nessus, which caused the violent death of Hercules, as narrated in Sophocles' *Trachiniae*, was given to his wife Deianeira, in the hope of regaining the affections from [sic] which she would soon be deprived. It was supposed to restore the love which she lost, but the restoration turned out to be a worse deprivation, a loss of life and sense.[25]

The story of Wordsworth's 'gentle Dalesman' is similarly ambiguous. The Dalesman's deafness, his dependence upon *writing*, does not represent the restoration of nature, but is merely the counterpart of the muteness of nature, which even at the height of a storm is 'silent as a picture'.

> To the extent that language is figure (or metaphor, or prosopopoeia) it is indeed not the thing itself but the representation, the picture of the thing and, as such, it is silent, mute as pictures are mute. *Language, as trope, is always privative* [my italics].[26]

V

De Man's argument depends upon the assumption that Wordsworth's distinction between language as dress and language as incarnation, to be sustainable at all, must be sustainable on conditions set by Cartesianism and by the philosophical idealism which is one natural terminus of Cartesianism. Is this really so? One thought which might give us pause is that if this had been the interpretation Wordsworth had in mind it would have been difficult for him to fail to perceive its incoherence.

Certainly twentieth-century philosophy has returned often enough to the thought that language *incarnates* being, including the being of the self. I am thinking here not merely of Heidegger's talk of language as the House of Being, but of Merleau-Ponty's version of existential phenomenology, with its denial of Cartesian (or Kantian, or Husserlian) intellectualism in favour of an intrinsic connection between language, consciousness and the body, and of Wittgenstein's denial that 'inner states' can intelligibly be abstracted from their bodily manifestations and functional context.[27] Is there textual warrant, perhaps, for siting Wordsworth's distinction as a fore-shadowing of this essentially anti-Cartesian (and certainly in some sense late Romantic) tradition, rather than as yet another manifestation of Cartesian logocentrism? I think there is, if we turn from the logocentric-sounding formulae of the polemical portions of the third *Essay* to the poet's detailed treatment of examples.

There are, says Wordsworth, epitaphs which 'strike with a gleam of pleasure, when the expression is of that kind which carries conviction to the heart at once that the author was a sincere mourner, and that the Inhabitant of the Grave deserved to be so lamented' (p. 66). His example is a German epitaph:

> Ach! sie haben
> Einen Braven
> Mann begraben –
> Mir war er mehr als viele

('Ah! they have buried a brave man – he was more to me than many'). What is it about this that 'carries conviction to the heart'? Is it, perhaps, just the terseness, the stiff-upper-lip *tone*, and mightn't something like that become (think of the numerous parodies of Hemingway) just one more trope, one more literary trick?

Well, what is it that would make us feel, in another case, that neither sincerity nor perhaps desert were present? Wordsworth's criterion here is not, as it turns out, 'artificiality' construed as literary elaboration *per se*, but literary elaboration *where that manifests an incoherence between what is written and the putative stance from which it is written*. Of a clumsily Metaphysical epitaph cited in the second *Essay*,

> Under this Stone, Reader, inter'd doth lye,
>   Beauty and virtue's true epitomy.
> At her appearance the noone-son
>   Blushed and shrunk in 'cause quite outdon.
> In her concenter'd did all graces dwell:
>   God pluck'd my rose that he might take a smel.
> I'll say no more: but weeping wish I may
>   Soone with thy dear chaste ashes come to lay.
>   Sic efflevit Maritus

Wordsworth says,

Can any thing go beyond this in extravagance? Yet, if the fundamental thoughts be translated into a more natural style, they will be found reasonable and affecting – 'The Woman who lies here interred, was in my eyes a perfect image of beauty and virtue; she was to me a brighter object than the sun in heaven: God took her, who was my delight, from this earth to bring her nearer to himself. Nothing further is worthy to be said than that weeping I wish soon to lie by thy dear chaste ashes – Thus did the Husband pour out his tears. (p. 73)

Wordsworth's thought is that the epitaph presents itself as written by a husband grief-stricken by his wife's death, is written in a euphuistic vein which at first appears inconsistent with that putative stance, but that when we go deeper and expose the thought we see that all is well; despite the extravagance of the expression there is no ultimate discord: the thought, if not the way it is expressed, is consistent with the stance from which it presents itself as being uttered.

These verses are preceded by a brief account of the Lady, in Latin prose; in which the little that is said is the uncorrupted language of affection. But, without this introductory communication, I should myself have had no doubt, after recovering from the first shock of surprize and disapprobation, that this man, notwithstanding his extravagant expressions was a sincere mourner; and that his heart, during the very act of composition, was moved. These fantastic images, though they stain the writing, stained not his soul. – They did not even touch it; but hung like globules of rain suspended above a green leaf along which they may roll and leave no trace that they have passed over it. This simple-hearted Man must have been betrayed by a common notion that what was natural in

prose would be out of place in verse; – that it is not the Muse which puts
on the Garb but the Garb which makes the Muse. And, having adopted
this notion at a time when vicious writings of this kind accorded with the
public taste, it is probable that, in the excess of his modesty, the blankness
of his inexperience, and the intensity of his affection, he thought that the
further he wandered from nature in his language the more would he
honour his departed Consort, who now appeared to him to have sur-
passed humanity in the excellence of her endowments. The quality of his
fault and its very excess are both in favour of this conclusion.

(pp. 73–4)

Wordsworth next turns to an epitaph by Lyttleton upon the death
of his daughter. Here the expression is equally stilted, but now there
is no way of saving a claim to sincerity by retreating to a simpler
expression of the underlying thought; for there is no underlying
thought.

The Reader will perceive at once that nothing in the heart of the Writer
had determined either the choice, the order, or the expression, of the ideas
– that there is no interchange of action from within and without – that the
connections are mechanical and arbitrary, and the lowest kind of these –
Heart and Eyes – petty alliterations, as meek and magnanimous, witty
and wise, combined with oppositions in thoughts where there is no
necessary or natural opposition.

In the case of the bereaved husband, however,

. . . we have a Mourner whose soul is occupied by grief and urged
forward by his admiration. He deems in his simplicity that no hyperbole
can transcend the perfections of her whom he has lost; for the version
which I have given fairly demonstrates that, in spite of his outrageous
expressions, the under current of his thoughts was natural and pure.

(p. 75)

Now we see why 'Ach! sie haben / einen Braven . . .' impresses
Wordsworth as sincere. If its terseness were a trope, a literary device
in a bad sense, that would show as a tension between the requirements of the presumed stance of the text and the requirements of
literary elaboration (cf. the way in which the muscular qualities of
Hemingway's prose can be rendered by such tricks as using the
sonorities of archaic English to render everyday Spanish); a tension
in which the demands of the latter would ultimately overwhelm and
efface those of the former, as they have done in the Lyttleton epitaph.
There is no such tension in the words 'Ach! sie haben . . .'. They are
words which a man who felt what they express might indeed utter.

When Wordsworth speaks of an 'interchange of action from within and without' he is thinking, that is, not of the hermetic Within constituted by language relative to the metaphysically inaccessible Without of another speaker's Cartesian Self, but of a Within and a Without related as, for instance, are the Within of M. Legrandin's explanation together with the deluded self-consciousness it expresses, the false Without of his putative Jacobinism or Epicureanism, and the actual Without of his repressed but unquiet snobbery.

Two connected points are crucial here. The first is that Wordsworth's criterion for the distinction between language functioning as clothing and language as incarnation is a textual one, a criterion internal to the text, that is, and not a logocentric one at all.[28] The second is that the criterion, although internal to the text, gives access to a reality beyond the text. The grief and the literary simplicity of Wordsworth's bereaved husband are real characteristics of a real person, even though we have access to them only through a text. To put it in that way may sound, perhaps, like a covert reinstatement of logocentrism, but is not. The bereaved husband acted, spoke and wrote in the world. His self throughout was not located outside or behind those acts but inhabited them. So it inhabited, as it inhabited his other acts, the epitaph he wrote for his wife.[29] Suppose, someone will object, the epitaph was in fact invented by some cunning literary fellow, as M. Legrandin's words were invented by Proust? Well, then, what we have is an excellent literary representation of just such a person as the bereaved husband. Either way we have something more than a tissue of signs interacting with other signs in a manner wholly internal to language.

Roland Barthes in 'The Death of the Author' argues that the mere act of composing *narrative* disconnects what is written from the writer.

> As soon as a fact is *narrated* no longer with a view to acting directly on reality but intransitively, that is to say, finally outside of any function other than that of the very practice of the symbol itself, this disconnection occurs, the voice loses its origin, the author enters into his own death, writing begins.[30]

Barthes here seems to be drawing back from the idea that the Death of the Author might infect the everyday communications of practical life. Barthes is clearly right. We cannot take letters or instructions on packets as strings of disconnected sentences subject to indefinite reinterpretation by the application of socially sanctioned hermeneutic procedures. Indeed, if we cannot assume the intentional coherence of the acts and utterances of the individual members of a society, the notion of a socially sanctioned hermeneutic principle itself lapses into vacuity. But Barthes thinks that that restraint is lifted as soon as practical considerations give place to literary ones. Here Barthes is just wrong. All narration presupposes a stance from which it is conducted; and that being so, there is no way of preventing questions of the coherence of discourse and stance, of exactly the kind which govern our assessment of the characters and the sincerity of others and ourselves in everyday life, from leaking into the interior of even the most formal and artificial narrative. If we obstinately insist that they are 'merely textual effects' when they crop up in literary contexts, then we shall have in consistency to say that they are also 'merely textual effects' when they crop up in everyday life. And with what are we contrasting such textual effects when we assert that they are *merely* textual? Presumably with the extra-textual reality of 'pure presence', of the Cartesian Self. But even when granted a kind of courtesy status as viable concepts by being placed *sous rature*, presence and the Cartesian Self lack the content they would need to underpin the required contrast between reality and mere appearances. In literature as in practical life, we know others, and for that matter ourselves, by the coherence, or lack of it, obtaining between how we present our acts and utterances and what the content of those acts and utterances actually consists in. That is why Wordsworth can infer from a clumsy piece of metaphysical verse the sincere feelings of a bereaved husband, or Marcel from M. Legrandin's (fictional) account of himself his (real) snobbery; and why Wordsworth has a perfect right to his distinction between language-as-dress and language-as-incarnation; drawn as it is internally to the text and paralleling as it does the operation of a similar, and indispensable, distinction in real life.

VI

If the content of the contrast between sincerity and insincerity can be established internally to the text in this way, what kind of sincerity, what kind of truthfulness, are we to demand of the autobiographer? How is Wordsworth as author of *The Prelude*, say, to respond to his own dictum that 'Words are too awful an instrument for good and evil to be trifled with'? We seem to have before us two ways of conceiving the autobiographer's project. On the one hand one can think of it as the task of explaining one's mind and personality by giving a true causal account of their development over time. This is the project which de Man implicitly ascribes to Wordsworth. It plainly is a necessary precondition of this project that 'The author

declares himself the subject of his own understanding'. Autobiography in this sense involves a host of factual claims, both about
past events and about their effects upon the author, and for the truth
of any of these claims we have indeed only the warrant of the
author's signature; that signature which in post-structuralist writings
shrivels ineluctably from the fullness of offered presence to a mere
mark: another trope. One hardly needs to have read *Limited, Inc.*,
for that matter, to see the force of this point: the whole situation is
too reminiscent of the clergyman who took it upon himself to assure
Hume of the existence of the Deity and, when asked what warrant he
could offer for such assurance, replied, 'Why, my *word*, sir; the word
of a gentleman!'[31]

On the other hand, we can construe the autobiographer's project
in a different way. We can see it, not as an attempt at retrospective
reconstruction of the causal relationships linking past selves to one
another and to the world, but as the attempt to come to terms,
through writing, with one's present self. Can the 'past' which the
autobiographer recounts then be an imaginary past? That depends.
Whether, for instance, the events which occupy the 'spots of time'
in the early books of *The Prelude*, the theft of the boat, and so on,
happened just as Wordsworth affects to remember them, or whether
there has been some, or much, embroidery, seems to me relatively
unimportant in this context. Wordsworth can perfectly easily hide
the real events of his childhood from us if he wishes: we have, for
most of them, no other warrant. What he cannot hide from us is the
coherence, or lack of it, of the self which unfolds itself before us
through many thousand lines of complex and internally reverberating reflection upon itself, its past and life in general. The ultimate test
which such a monumental self-avowal has to pass is not that applied
by asking whether contemporaries of Wordsworth would have been
able to verify, for instance, if asked, the episode of the boy set ashore
with his flute, but the test which Marcel applies to M. Legrandin's
rigmarole: the test which the more direct epitaphs in Wordsworth's
collection pass. To the extent that we consider, if we consider, that
The Prelude passes that test, we are prepared to accept Wordsworth's
assurances about boys with flutes, or if we doubt them, to grant him
freely the need to shape the past a little for the purposes of the poem.
For to pass that test is to have succeeded, provisionally at least (for
there is always more to be said, more poems to write), in Nietzsche's
enterprise of making a self for oneself; of becoming what one is.

If autobiography were the recounting of a causal truth about the
past, then it would be something which, if it could be done at all,
could be done definitively: there can only be one causal truth about

past events. If it is not the attempt to recount the adventures of a self, but the attempt to constitute one through writing, then it must always be to some degree provisional. Wayne Booth argues in *The Rhetoric of Fiction* that the authorial self of a novel cannot be the author's real self because it changes from book to book. Who, he asks, could predict Fielding's authorial self in *Tom Jones* from his authorial self in *Amelia*? The proper answer, it seems to me, is that while one couldn't *predict* that kind of thing either way, one can certainly find enough of the Fielding of *Tom Jones* in the Fielding of *Amelia* to understand the latter as a development of the former. Nietzsche's vision of the self as permanently under construction is a better guide here, in other words, than the Rationalist vision of the self as an unchanging substance from whose essence all of its capacities and potentialities could be predicted.

The provisional character of autobiography construed as an enterprise of self-constitution does something, I think, to explain both Wordsworth's views on poetic language and the actual language of *The Prelude*. De Man, I am inclined to think, altogether misconstrues the nature of Wordsworth's hostility to the 'antithetical' Augustan style, by assuming it to be rooted in Wordsworth's supposed preference for 'a lucid language of repose, tranquillity and serenity'. Such a language would indeed be appropriate to the practitioner of specular autobiography, and fits the well-known tag about 'emotion recollected in tranquillity'. The trouble is that the language of *The Prelude* is manifestly just not like that. It is tentative, exploratory, marked by the kinds of personal and epistemological uncertainty caught by the recurrent 'whether . . . or' construction, and above all it is a language of crisis and partial resolution; a resolution which always involves loss as well as gain. The self of the 1805/6 *Prelude* is that of a man conscious of violent tensions in his outlook and predilections, and of a past as incoherent and rich in disconfirmation as his present.[32] His task is to find some stable footing for his present self; to find a stance which will weld his present and his past together into a stable and coherent system of significances. The notion of the unity of the self is functioning here, as in Nietzsche, as an ideal limit; something to be striven towards, not something achieved and originary which both founds and guarantees the success of the enterprise. Nevertheless the drive towards unity is essential to the Wordsworthian project of sincerity and 'truth to Nature': of incarnating rather than merely clothing oneself in language. What is wrong with the 'antithetical' language of Pope and Dryden is that, implicitly, it refuses this project.

For de Man, Wordsworth's dislike of antithetical language is *prima facie* disingenuous. Wordsworth's superficial moral reasons for disliking it – that it is fit only to represent the state of mind of an evil or depraved man, and so forth – conceal a more fundamental ground of hostility. Wordsworth dislikes antithetical language because it reveals itself too openly *as* language – as *writing* – and thus threatens the logocentric project of a specular language.

If Wordsworth's argument in the *Essays upon Epitaphs* in no way depends upon the project of a specular language (and I cannot myself see any but superficial reasons for supposing that it does), then of course de Man's argument falls to the ground, and we need to look again at the reasons Wordsworth actually gave for not only disliking but reproving the poetry of Dryden and Pope.

> Pope's mind had been employed chiefly in observation upon the vices and follies of men. Now, vice and folly are in contradiction with the moral principle which can never be extinguished in the mind: and, therefore, wanting this controul, are irregular, capricious and inconsistent with themselves. If a man has once said . . . 'Evil be thou my Good!' and has acted accordingly, however strenuous may have been his adherence to this principle, it will be well known to those who have had an opportunity of observing him narrowly that there have been perpetual obliquities in his course; evil passions thwarting each other in various ways; and, now and then, revivals of his better nature, which check him for a short time or lead him to remeasure his steps: – not to speak of the various necessities of counterfeiting virtue which the furtherance of his schemes will impose upon him, and the division which will consequently be introduced into his nature.   (p.80)

For better or for worse the Wordsworthian autobiographer is attempting not to live like that. He is setting out to try to achieve, through reflection and writing, unity within himself, amongst his various selves, his past and (in a broad sense) Nature. Antithetical language, however well it may serve the purposes of satire or social observation, will not serve the purposes of such a project. But to dismiss it for those reasons, because *in that sense* it fails to respect 'the rights and dignity of Nature', is not necessarily to commit oneself *à rebours* to the entirely metaphysical – and indeed incoherent – project of a specular language in which it is perfectly manifest that Wordsworth never for one moment believed.

Is Wordsworth's project an important one? I mean by these words to pose a question of a type which many critics nowadays would consider absurdly old-fashioned and naïve: something along the lines of 'Is *The Prelude* a great work of literature?' Philosophers, to whom far more ingenious forms of scepticism are daily bread, may perhaps be less timid of asking such resounding questions than critics, to whom subjective idealism served up with a gloss of Saussurian linguistics and some sound debunking of bad metaphysics constitutes a potent and unfamiliar brew. It does no harm, at any rate, to ask a straight question of this kind now and then, and in this case the question is susceptible of a straight answer: namely, yes. I think Wordsworth (and for that matter Nietzsche) was right to connect the effort to achieve coherence, both in one's life and feelings and in the account one gives of them, with deep and important kinds of integrity. Our age, by and large, does not believe that words are too awful a power for good and evil to be trifled with. On the contrary we behave as if we believe that any utterance, no matter how flatulent, obscene, cruel or dishonest, will be blown away on the winds tomorrow, never to rise again to haunt the speaker. I think we need to read more, not less Wordsworth, and we need to read him not sociologized or deconstructed or embedded in some transient and (to some minds) comforting archaeology of knowledge, but straight. That is why any criticism, however brilliant and ingenious, which obstructs a clear view of him should be resisted.

Chapter 8
Parable and Transcendence

Nous vénérons tous secrètement cet idéal d'un langage qui, en dernière analyse, nous délivrerait de lui-même en nous livrant aux choses.

Maurice Merleau-Ponty, *La Prose du monde*

I

Parable is a thorn in the side of theology. Parables defy precise doctrinal or moral interpretation; or, more infuriatingly still, admit it only on the level of moral commonplace, escaping all our attempts to articulate the more profound and numinous meanings which we feel to be obscurely present in them. Even the word 'parable' is a shifting sand:

> The word 'mashal' and its synonyms, which underlie the 'parabolē' of the gospels, cover a wide range of utterance, varying from, at the one end, the brief and self-explanatory proverb, through manifold forms of extended metaphor to, at the other end, – and this is most surprising – the riddle or enigma.[1]

You cannot found a state religion, or a practical homiletic, upon a collection of riddles. Hence, perhaps, the long tradition, from Augustine and Origen onwards, of treating parable as allegory. To allegorize a parable is to turn it at one stroke into something altogether easier for our minds to grasp: a cipher; a piece of 'Aesopian' discourse with an esoteric, but none the less perfectly fixed and definite meaning. Thus Augustine, following Origen, interprets the parable of the Good Samaritan (Luke 10:30–5) as darkly adumbrating the central events of divine history. The Samaritan is Christ, the man going down from Jerusalem to Jericho is fallen Adam: 'the

219

inn is the church, the innkeeper St. Paul..., and the two pence the sacraments'.[2] Every element of the parable is associated with a definite designation, with the result that the whole becomes a brief statement of orthodox theological doctrine in code.

It is not easy to see, as Professor C. F. Evans remarks, 'Why there should have been this curious arrangement in which fundamental theological truths had to be secured by being uttered twice and in two such different modes, once explicitly in the doctrinal language fitted for them and then over again in the language of cipher....'[3]

Nor, of course, is this the only reason for dissatisfaction with the allegorical method. To view a parable as allegory generally involves wrenching it from its narrative context. If Augustine's interpretation of the Good Samaritan were correct, for instance, it would make it hard to see how the parable could be read as any sort of reply to the question 'And who is my friend?' to which, according to Luke's narrative, Jesus offers it as an answer.[4]

Again, the grammatical form of its introduction is sufficient in many cases to show that the parable was intended as a *parallel*, or complex simile; and a parallel is not at all the same thing as an allegory. Each of the elements of an allegory has an independent significance: to grasp the significance of the allegory just is to see what each separate motif represents, or stands for. A parallel, or simile, does not work like that: it is only when taken as a whole that it has significance. One common form of parable introduction, it seems, begins with an abbreviation of a lengthy rabbinic formula which runs thus: 'I will relate a parable to you. With what shall the matter be compared? It is the case with it as with....'[5] What is proposed, in short, is a comparison, between the whole matter of debate and the whole content of the parable, not the delivery of a statement of doctrine concealed within an allegorical cipher.

Such considerations gain added force when we learn that a number of scholars, following Adolf Jülicher, have argued, using the methods of form-criticism, that the interpretation of the parable of the Sower offered by Jesus at Mark 4:11–20, an explicit scriptural example of allegorical interpretation, does not in fact represent the original tradition of the words of Jesus, but a fragment of later apostolic teaching.[6]

The present critical orthodoxy concerning the parables, which rests mainly upon two books, C. H. Dodd's *The Parables of the Kingdom* and Joachim Jeremias's *The Parables of Jesus*, avoids the pitfalls of the allegorizing tradition. Its central methodological conviction is that the parables must be taken in their context as arguments or responses given by Jesus in particular circumstances in his ministry, and taken, moreover, as responses which take on their fullest sense only against the background of contemporary life and the contemporary religious situation. We must not wrench parables from their context, as allegorical interpretation requires us to do: we must look instead at the concrete circumstances which situate them in the fabric of the recorded life and ministry of Jesus: at their *Sitz im Leben*. Moreover we must treat parables as complex similes or parallels, not as doctrinal statements in an allegorical code consisting of essentially discrete elements each of which is capable of being allegorically decoded quite separately from the other elements.

Dodd and Jeremias both see the parables as *arguments,* or rather as moves in a polemic. They point out that parables are often replies to a questioner, who may be openly hostile, like the Pharisees of Luke 14:1–3, who question Jesus' association with tax-gatherers and other disreputable elements and receive in reply the parables of the Lost Sheep, the Lost Coin and the Prodigal Son, or smoothly enquiring like the lawyer of Luke 10:29, who asks 'And who is my friend?' and is answered by the parable of the Good Samaritan. But parables are of course not 'arguments' in the sense of sets of propositional premises entailing conclusions which confute opposing *propositions*. What they confute is a certain religious outlook, and they confute it by announcing and adumbrating an eschatology which that outlook in no way prepares its adherents to receive. The eschatological message of the parables is that the Kingdom of God has arrived, either wholly realized in the actions and words of Jesus, according to Dodd, or partly realized in the presence of Jesus and in process of further realization according to Jeremias. On either view the parables speak primarily to Jesus' immediate hearers in the hour of eschatological crisis produced by his presence. The parables announce different aspects of the eschatological crisis, revealing the nature of the Kingdom of God now realized or in process of realizing itself; and they accuse the 'scribes and Pharisees', the religious leaders who are blind to the nature of the crisis, and unwilling to accept the Kingdom now that it is here.

Thus Jeremias, in a passage dealing with a group of parables which he takes to contain the central message of the Gospels, which is not merely that 'the Redeemer has appeared, but also that salvation is sent to the poor, and that Jesus has come as a saviour for sinners', says:

The parables which have as their subject the gospel message in its narrower sense are, apparently without exception, addressed, not to the poor, but to opponents. That is their distinctive note, their *Sitz im Leben*:

their main object is not the presentation of the gospel, but defence and vindication of the gospel; they are controversial weapons against the critics and foes of the gospel who are indignant that Jesus should declare that God cares about sinners, and whose special attack is directed against Jesus' practice of eating with the despised. At the same time, the parables are intended to win over the opponents.[7]

According to Jeremias, the vindication of the gospel in these parables proceeds on three levels. First, the critics' attention is directed to the poor to whom the message of the gospel is being proclaimed. Second, the critics are themselves rebuked:

> In the parables of this group the vindication of the gospel is accompanied by the sternest rebuke. 'You', he says, 'are like the son who promised to obey his father's command, but afterwards neglected to fulfil his promise (Matthew 21:28–31). You are like the husbandmen who refused year after year to render to their Lord his due share of the produce of his land, heaping outrage upon outrage upon him (Mark 12:1–9, par.; Gospel of Thomas 65). You are like the respectable guests who rudely declined the invitation to the banquet – what right have you to pour scorn and derision upon the wretched crowd that sit at my table?'[8]

And, third, the parables in the central group expound the mercy of God for sinners, most clearly in the Prodigal Son (Luke 15:11–32):

> The parable was addressed to men who were like the elder brother, men who were offended at the gospel. An appeal must be addressed to their conscience. To them Jesus says: 'Behold the greatness of God's love for his lost children, and contrast it with your own joyless, loveless, thankless and self-righteous lives. Cease then from your loveless ways and be merciful.'[9]

In Dodd's and Jeremias's analyses, in short, the crucial questions are the questions to whom, to what sort of people, that is, and in what circumstances, the parables were originally addressed. The later use of the parables, for homiletic and hortatory purposes, within communities which were already Christian, is secondary to their original use in defending and justifying Christ's teaching against those who could not understand it or were opposed to it; and the meanings acquired by parables in later, Christian contexts are likewise to be regarded as secondary and to some extent, though of course not entirely, for there are clearly degrees of distortion involved, unjustified.

One merit of this way of looking at parables is that it steers clear of the main alternative to treating them as allegories: the alternative of regarding them as containing moral lessons, or instructions embodied, as if for the edification of children, in simple, naturalistic stories. Jülicher, wishing to cut off at the root the radiating alternative possibilities of allegorical interpretation, opted for 'the broadest possible application' of each parable to common life. The result is to make the interpretation of each parable end in a moral generality such as the one ascribed by Jülicher to the Parable of the Talents (Matthew 25:14–30 / Luke 19:12–27): 'fidelity in all that God has entrusted to us'.[10] Dodd's comment upon such methods is pointed:

> Was all this wealth of loving observation and imaginative rendering of nature and common life used merely to adorn moral generalities? Was the Jesus of the Gospels just an eminently sound and practical teacher, who patiently led simple minds to appreciate the great enduring commonplaces of morals and religion? This is not the impression conveyed by the Gospels as a whole. There is one of His parabolic sayings which runs: 'I have come to set fire to the earth, and how I wish it were already kindled!' . . . It is exactly the phrase we need to describe the volcanic energy of the meteoric career depicted in the Gospels. The teaching of Jesus is not the leisurely and patient exposition of a system by the founder of a school. It is related to a brief and tremendous crisis in which He is the principal figure and which indeed His appearance brought about.[11]

One might add to Dodd's criticism that unless one has critical and theoretical reasons for taking 'the broadest possible application' of a parable to life as identifying the specific moral generalization it was intended to convey, it is not at all obvious what moral generalization is to be drawn from most parables. The moral point of the Great Feast (Matthew 22:1–10 / Luke 14:16–24), for example, might be, and this is particularly plausible if we accept the Matthaean identification of the feast-giver as 'a king', that it is unwise to refuse the invitations of the great, because they have it in their power to make people who do that look foolish.[12] The 'moral' of the Prodigal Son might be taken to be that one should receive errant children with joy no matter what they have done and no matter how much it involves damaging the interests of one's other children, and so on. Of course, this is a problem with all religious narrative. Kierkegaard, in *Fear and Trembling,* has ghoulish fun at the expense of the plain, commonsensical pastor who, having preached one Sunday in glowing terms about the faith of Abraham, is confronted by a parishioner who, in response to voices, has 'sacrificed' his own son.[13] No doubt that was not what was intended: that is not how we are to read such a narrative: but how, then, *are* we to read it?

Dodd, in attacking the allegorical tradition, makes a great deal of the fidelity of the parables to the concrete circumstances of everyday life,[14] his point being that allegory need not be true to nature, because its significance lies not in the terms of the story but in what each element of the story 'stands for', whereas the point of parable, in Dodd's view, is precisely to present the eschatological crisis in terms having all the vivid immediacy of everyday life. But the accuracy of the commonplace setting of the behaviour described in the parables can be contrasted with the fact that the behaviour itself is frequently odd to the point of craziness: a man gives a feast for beggars and any chance travellers his servants can pick up on the highway; an employer pays his servants the same wage for quite different hours of labour; an absentee landlord sends one slave after another to collect his rents, despite the fact that they all get beaten up, and finally sends his son, who predictably enough gets killed. The most natural conclusion to be drawn from these stories is merely, perhaps, the deflating one that their protagonists are mad, with the consequence that no moral conclusions whatsoever, let alone general moral maxims, can be extracted from their peculiar doings.[15]

Here, then, is a second set of reasons why the polemical-eschatological account of parables may come as a relief: it frees us not merely from the need to extract an allegorical significance from the text, but from the need to extract any set of general moral injunctions from it either. Moreover it heals the gap between parable and dogma, considered as two distinct scriptural genres, or modes of scriptural discourse. If Dodd and Jeremias are correct, the parables are polemical comments upon an eschatology and a moral outlook which can be reconstructed from non-parabolic material in the Gospels. Like the allegorical interpretation, Dodd's and Jeremias's account connects parable with the formal, non-parabolically expressed body of Christian doctrine, but it does so without doing violence to the essential nature of parable.

Nevertheless, I find myself dissatisfied with the Dodd-Jeremias reading of the parables. I speak not as a biblical scholar, but as a literary critic writing in some respects from a philosophical standpoint. Moreover, it is not exactly that I think Dodd and Jeremias have *misread* the parables: indeed, what I am about to say, even if it carries conviction, will leave their position virtually intact as a reading of the parables adequate enough within its limits. My dissatisfaction concerns a series of questions upon which the Dodd–Jeremias interpretation is comparatively silent, but which do seem to demand an answer.

The first, oddly enough, concerns the problem of what general moral interpretation, if any, is to be attached to the parables, about which I have just been so scathing. No doubt we misread the parables if we try to reduce them to narrative illustrations of general moral principles. But is there, then, *nothing* 'general' about the parables; nothing which enables them to speak to all ages, and not merely to Jesus' immediate hearers? In tying them so closely to their historical context the Dodd–Jeremias orthodoxy gives us no explanation of why the parables, for all their brevity, should seem to us to have such resonance, such universality. Parable, after all, is a literary form, and one exemplified in writings, by Kafka or Kierkegaard, for example, which do not belong to the scriptural canon of any religion. And if we took the parables of Jesus out of any scriptural setting which might illuminate their eschatological significance, they would still resonate, would still tease the mind and heart, in the way that, say, Kafka's parables[16] do.

Dodd feels the force of this objection, and tries to answer it:

> What then are the parables, if they are not allegories? They are the natural expression of a mind that sees truth in concrete pictures rather than conceives it in abstractions.

> ... The Gospels do not offer us in the first place tales to point a moral. They interpret life to us, by initiating us into a situation in which, as Christians believe, the eternal was uniquely manifested in time, a situation which is both historical and contemporary in the deepest possible sense.[17]

But such talk butters few literary-critical, or for that matter epistemological parsnips. How can a 'picture' express a 'truth', or to put it another way, how can we say, without benefit of an immense amount of more-or-less *ad hoc* interpretative scene-setting, what truth a picture expresses? Is not the very diversity of theories concerning the interpretation of parables itself evidence of their fragility and uncertainty as a means of conveying 'truths'? What is the difference, exactly, between a 'tale to point a moral' and a tale which 'interprets life to us'? We cannot, as Dodd does, answer this question by gesturing, half-apologetically, towards the eschatological content of Christian belief; because one of the main grounds of Christian belief, once we cast aside the rotten staff of rational or 'natural' theology, must be the inherent force or impressiveness of Christ's teaching in the Gospels; and a great deal of that teaching takes the form of parable; so that we are thrown back once again on the question of what it is that gives the parables of Jesus the profundity and numinousness which we obscurely feel them to possess, irrespective of all questions of polemical context or eschatological significance, just as parables.

The problem, indeed, arises at the heart of Jeremias's or Dodd's interpretation, as the question of what it is exactly that gives the parables, so far as they can be understood as contributions to a polemical controversy between Jesus and his opponents, their force *as polemic*. Jeremias and Dodd have no difficulty in showing how the religious leaders rather vaguely characterized as 'scribes and Pharisees' might detect oblique references to themselves in such figures as the son who agrees to do his father's bidding (Matthew 21:28–32), or the servant who buries his talent wrapped in a napkin (Matthew 25:14–30 / Luke 19:12–27), or the guests who refuse the invitation to the Great Feast (Matthew 22:1–10 / Luke 14:16–24). But this, taken just in itself, is polemic at a fairly low level: no more than a kind of figurative jeering. Both Jeremias and Dodd want to say more than this: that the parables in some way justify Christ's message against its detractors. What Dodd, for example, *wants* to say, as I think is clear from the passage I quoted on p. 225, is that the parables confute the detractors and draw in the uncommitted mind because they communicate a vision – a general way of looking at life – against which the offered objections appear thin and insubstantial. But how can a vision sufficiently powerful to bear the historical weight of the Christian tradition be communicated by narrative, especially narrative of the brief and rudimentary kind employed in the parables?

Faced with this question we can reformulate it in a still sharper form. Why does any of Christ's teaching take the form of *narrative* in the first place? If, as the current orthodoxy maintains, the function of the parables is to announce and to describe the broad outlines of an eschatological crisis, and to accuse those who remain blind to the significance of the events in which that crisis is manifesting itself, why does Jesus not express himself directly and explicitly in the languages of accusation and eschatological annunciation which, as many passages in the gospel show, he was perfectly capable of doing when the occasion demanded it? Narrative and metaphor, indeed, seem devices peculiarly weak and ill-suited to the purposes which the conventional orthodoxy supposes the parables to have been designed to serve.[18] Why, then did Jesus use narrative at all? This is the fundamental question to which I shall address myself in what follows.

II

My suggestion is that parabolic narrative has as one of its functions the subversion of the conceptual scheme in terms of which its hearers construe the world and their lives in it.

Put as baldly as this, the suggestion may seem too drily abstract, and too fashionably semiological to carry much weight. For that reason it will be best, I think, to start by explaining what I have in mind through the medium of some textual exegesis. I am not sure that the story I am going to tell will work for everything called 'parable' in the Gospels – as we noticed earlier, the word '*mashal*' is ambiguous, and covers a number of different literary forms – but I think it will work at least for a number of those central parables which fall into the second of Jeremias's eschatological categories, which he labels 'God's Mercy for Sinners'. These are the parables, Jeremias says (*The Parables of Jesus*, p. 124), 'which contain the Good News itself'. I shall concentrate on three of them: the Great Feast (Matthew 22:1–10 / Luke 14:16–24), the Good Employer (Matthew 20:1–16) and the Prodigal Son (Luke 15:11–32).

A narrative is not merely a description that recounts a sequence of events. Scientists often describe very precisely the sequences of events which take place when, say, a cell divides, or a ball-bearing travelling with a certain velocity strikes a tray of moon dust; but such descriptions are not *narratives*: they are simply descriptions with tenses in them. A narrative contains exposition, developments, and denouements, moments of crisis and relaxations of tension, which give it a structure which is more than mere sequence; and this structure is relative to the point of the narrative, in that grasping which parts of the narrative are expository and which constitute a denouement or a relaxation of tension involves grasping the point of the story as a whole, and vice versa. So much is obvious. What is perhaps less obvious is that a narrative cannot determine its own structure, by a purely internal fiat, as it were. The writer of narrative cannot arbitrarily choose that certain events in the narrative shall constitute background to a denouement, that certain other events shall constitute the denouement, and so on, merely in virtue of his so designating them. Such a fiat would be meaningless, like stipulating that the point in cell-division at which the nuclear membrane re-forms around the genetic material in each daughter-cell is to be regarded as the denouement of the narrative of cell-division. What would be the point of such a stipulation? – It would not, after all, have the effect of turning the biological description of cell-division into a narrative: despite the stipulation, it would remain just a description with tenses in it. In short, a narrative is dependent for its point, and hence for the kind of structure which makes it a narrative rather than a tensed description, upon something outside it. The freedom which narrative writers enjoy is the freedom to invent any fictional events they please, but this freedom, if it is to produce *narrative*, rather than tensed description, must be exercised under the constraint of those extra-fictional considerations (a very diverse lot) which give point to narratives. And of course the art of narrative fiction consists precisely, from one point of view, in living successfully with the tensions which spring from that freedom and those constraints.

Jeremias, in discussing the Great Feast, relates it to a story which occurs in Aramaic in the Palestinian Talmud, and which, as other evidence seems to confirm, was evidently known to Jesus. It concerns a rich tax-gatherer, Bar Ma'jan, and a poor scholar. The Palestinian Talmud tells us that Bar Ma'jan died and was given a splendid funeral. At the same time a poor scholar died, but nobody followed his body to the grave, since the whole city was escorting Bar Ma'jan's body. How could the justice of God permit this? The answer given is that Bar Ma'jan, though not a pious man, had done one splendid good deed. He had invited the city councillors to a banquet, and they, to insult him, refused to come. So in a rage he gave orders that the poor should come and eat the food, in order that it not be wasted.

Jeremias comments that the parallel between the Great Feast and the story of Ma'jan gives us a clear explanation of the otherwise inexplicable behaviour of the guests who refuse the invitation to the Feast. Then he says:

> Just as Jesus does not hesitate to illustrate from the behaviour of the deceitful steward the need for decisive action, or from the conduct of the unscrupulous judge, the despised shepherd, and the poor woman, the boundless mercy of God, so he has not the slightest hesitation ... in choosing the behaviour of a tax-gatherer to illustrate both the wrath and the mercy of God. That the man's motive was ... selfish and ignoble ... has not in any way disturbed Jesus, but has rather induced him to choose just these persons as examples.[19]

Jesus' reasons for making the tax-gatherer's ambiguous revenge on his guests emblematic of the wrath and mercy of God are, according to Jeremias, dramatic ones. Jesus' hearers would be likely to smile at the familiar story of the parvenu's revenge upon snobbish insolence, so that the shock of realizing that what is being described is not, after all, a parvenu's mock banquet but the Kingdom of God, and that the hallful of beggars and cripples upon whom the doors finally close are the final inheritors of that Kingdom would be all the greater.

But I think more is at stake here than dramatic emphasis. What gives point to the narrative of Bar Ma'jan is the social gulf between Bar Ma'jan and his guests, taken together with the function of the institution of feast-giving as a device for conferring and confirming honour or social standing. The honour conferred by giving or attending a banquet is reciprocal. The host, if he is a man of sufficient social standing, confers honour on the guests whom he invites to a banquet. But they, of course, if they are persons of social standing, increase his standing by accepting his invitations. Social standing is the aim of both host and guests, but social standing is defined merely by whose parties one attends and who can be got to attend one's parties. The concept of this kind of honour, defined as it is solely by reciprocal social relationships, seems, in a sense, gratuitous and without real foundation, despite the emotional capital invested in it. Proust speaks of the social talents of Mme Verdurin, the dreadful society hostess in À la recherche du temps perdu, as an expertise in 'sculpturing the void'.

None the less this is the conceptual structure which gives a point to the narrative of Bar Ma'jan, which makes no sense unless we see that this is the kind of honour which Bar Ma'jan and his invited guests are interested in: the goal of the race in which host and guests are jockeying for position. Bar Ma'jan wishes to use his 'guests' to enhance his social standing; those invited choose not to be so used. Bar Ma'jan then publicly insults them by inviting beggars, the implication being that beggars are better guests than the invited ones; or that one might as well invite beggars as such beggarly noblemen. But the insult is an impotent one: Bar Ma'jan, the one shot in his locker fired, remains socially excluded: one does not win the social game, after all, by dining with beggars.

The Talmudic story and the synoptic parable use this basic narrative material in different ways, each of which involves changing the context of the narrative in ways which throw its point into doubt. The Talmudic narrative encloses the story in another narrative: the narrative of the funerals of Bar Ma'jan and the poor scholar. The effect is to shift the point of central interest in the narrative from the question whether Bar Ma'jan's revenge was a good way of replying to the insolence of the nobles, to the question of whether it constituted, incidentally, a good deed. At once we encounter the receding ambiguities, the deep water, characteristic of parable in general and religious parable in particular. Bar Ma'jan fed the poor. But that was only to insult the absent guests. But still, the poor *were* fed, and God saw to it that he got a grand funeral as a reward. Ah, but the reward was a *funeral*. . . . Still, it was a *grand* funeral. . . . So you might say Bar Ma'jan's pride was satisfied in the end. . . . (But was God just, to let the poor scholar go without mourners to the grave? Well, the justice of God was certainly manifest in the nature of Bar Ma'jan's reward.)

The synoptic parable does something of the same sort (that is, it effects a change of context for the narrative) but something rather simpler, and I think rather more radical. Jesus tells the Bar Ma'jan narrative more or less straight, but prefaces it (explicitly in Matthew; by implication, given the context, in Luke) with the words 'The Kingdom of Heaven is like this'.

This at once puts the whole point of the story under strain. The point depends upon Bar Ma'jan's being, despite his wealth, the social inferior of his guests. But if the story of the revenge is a description of the Kingdom of Heaven, the giver of the feast is presumably God. What, then, can be the point in inviting the beggars, the crippled, the blind and the lame? In the Bar Ma'jan story the point is to jeer at the nobility by giving the food meant for them to the scourings of the gutter. But such a display of social pique cannot, surely, with any meaning be ascribed to the maker of the universe. Why then does the master of the feast invite the poor? The only answer left is that he wants to give a feast, and that the poor will do as well as guests as the nobility. But this cuts at the whole conception of honour implicit in the Bar Ma'jan story. That story depends for its point, and its structure as a narrative, on the conception of honour as sculptured from the void; a bauble dependent solely upon questions of who knows whom and who dines with whom. But for the narrative to have a point *as a parabolic description of the Kingdom of Heaven*, the honour conferred upon the poor guests at 'the feast in the Kingdom of God' must be an *absolute* honour. That is, their title to be guests at that feast depends not at all upon their social standing, upon any place which they occupy in human society. God, the master of the heavenly feast, is thus seen as a kind of absolute fountain of honour. He has no need to consider the social standing of his guests: they are *made* fit guests for his table by the bare fact that He has invited them, and that they have accepted the invitation.[20]

In short, to read the description of a sequence of events *as a narrative*, with a point and a structure, involves reading it against a background consisting of a set of presuppositions, together with the conceptual scheme in terms of which those presuppositions are formulated. The presuppositions and the underlying conceptual scheme direct the narrative. But the relationship is reciprocal, and hence narrative can be used to influence, to change, the underlying conceptual scheme. The technique is to tell the narrative in such a way that the mind, in order to discover a point and a structure in it, has to shift and rearrange the underlying conceptual structure. The story of Bar Ma'jan is a story about honour, or dignity, in the ordinary sense of social standing. The parable of the Great Feast is about the difference between worthiness for the feast as it is understood among men and as it is understood in Heaven. It succeeds in introducing the idea that the value, the worth, the standing of a man in the eyes of God is not dependent upon his standing in the eyes of other men, but is absolute; that *anyone* is a fitting guest at the great feast (provided he will accept the invitation, whereby hangs a longer but equally parabolic tale), because the mind has to grasp towards such a conception in order to construe the parable as something having the point and structure proper to a narrative. The parable thus compels its hearers to transcend the limits of their ordinary conceptual vocabulary; to grasp a new concept: a new sense in which a man may be said to have dignity or honour.

Something of the same sort happens in the Good Employer (Matthew 20:1–16). The narrative is about an employer who hires labourers for his vine harvest. 'Employer' and 'labour' are terms in the common language, and like 'host' and 'guest' they are defined, as linguists say, 'structurally', that is, in terms of one another, so that it is not possible to explain the meaning of either without at some point explaining the meaning of the other.[21] Of course, you cannot 'define' two words in terms of one another, if the notion of *definition* you have in mind is verbal, or dictionary, definition. But you can do so if your conception of what is involved in giving the meaning of a word has a more Wittgensteinian tinge; if 'giving the meaning of a word' is showing how it fits into a structure of relationships or 'ways of proceeding': for two or more terms can certainly occupy relationships to one another within such a structure of relationships, and it can certainly therefore be the case that we cannot explain the meaning of either word without explaining how it fits into that structure, and thus how it is related to the other word, and thus how *that* word fits into the structure.

This is pretty obviously the case with 'employer' and 'labourer': what defines them is that they label certain points, certain roles, in a single structure of economic relationships. That structure is set up like this. Men trade goods with one another, with the general aim of diversifying, and at the same time maximizing, the advantages that each individually possesses. In the trading game, labour is one kind of commodity that is sold, the point of buying it being that its possession can enable one to utilize potential goods in the shape, for example, of unharvested grapes; while the point of selling it is that one divests oneself of a commodity for which one has no use (because one possesses no potential goods, such as unharvested crops, capable of being realized by labour) in exchange for a commodity, money, which can be converted into commodities for which one does have a use. An 'employer' is, now, simply someone who buys labour; a 'labourer' is simply someone who sells his labour ('selling' and 'buying', of course, being defined, also, merely as marking correlative relationships within the general structure – the 'language-game', or 'form of life' in Wittgenstein's terms – known as 'trading', or 'commodity exchange').

All the parable tells us about the Good Employer is that he is an employer; a landowner. However, he behaves in a way which makes no economic sense, hiring batches of labourers at different times during the day, but paying all of them, at the end of the day, the wages for a full day's work, even though some of them only started work an hour before sunset. When the men who have worked longest complain, he says 'Am I not allowed to do what I choose with what belongs to me? Or do you begrudge my generosity?' (Matthew 20:5). Again the whole narrative is enclosed by the introductory rubric, 'The kingdom of heaven is like this'.

What, then, is the point of the story? It is a story about an employer who hires labour, so we are driven to search for a point in the system of economic relationships which define the correlative relationships of labourer and employer. But the narrative immediately frustrates that search, since it describes the employer as behaving in a way which precisely removes the point, economically speaking, of hiring extra labour. The economic point of hiring extra labour late in the day is presumably to get the last few grapes harvested; but any profit gained in that way will be wiped out with interest if one pays these marginal labourers a full day's wage for an hour's labour. Such behaviour only has a point if the primary interest of the landowner is not in maximizing his profit, and perhaps not even in getting the grapes harvested, but in *the labourers*. His behaviour does make sense if his primary object is to make sure that every out-of-work man gets a full wage in his pocket. If that is his aim, we can see why he goes out scouring the town for fresh groups of unemployed men at different times of day: it is not that he wants to increase the marginal profit on his grape harvest, it is that he wants as many unemployed men as possible in his employ at the end of the day. The point is sharpened if one takes Jeremias's point, that the day's wage is a *subsistence* wage: all the labourers are paid alike what is necessary in order *that they may live*.[22]

The parable is thus, like the Great Feast, about the difference between the value men find in one another and the value God finds in men. The value of labourers for an employer is, given the whole structure of economic relationships and practices within which the terms 'employer' and 'labourer' find their meaning, relative to the profit which their labour can produce: labourers are ranked in relative value according to their relative profitability to the employer.

The value of men for the employer of the parable is absolute: he feels the same concern for one as for another, irrespective of the economic advantage he has derived from the labour of each, and his concern in each case is the same: that the man should receive the wage that guarantees subsistence: that he should receive life, in other words.

The Prodigal Son (Luke 15:11–32) has a similar structure. The younger son asks for and gets his share of the estate, converts it into cash and spends it all on drink and women, until he is reduced to working as a common labourer minding the pigs of a local landlord who starves him. He decides that if he has to spend his life as a common labourer he will at least spend it working for his father, who pays a good wage, so he goes home. The father welcomes him as a lost son, and kills the calf for a feast. The elder son is furious and complains that not even a kid has been killed for him and his friends, though he has always done as his father wished. The father replies, 'Son, you are always with me, and all that is mine is yours ... this your brother was dead, and is alive; he was lost, and is found' (Luke 15:31–2).

Just as the Good Employer's behaviour makes nonsense of economic common sense, so the father's behaviour makes nonsense of common considerations of fairness and justice in the management of family affairs. The younger son has made all the claims on the estate he has a right to make. Indeed, the elder brother could perfectly reasonably claim that the fatted calf killed for the prodigal is really a part of his portion. In terms of the ordinary reciprocal rights and duties of parents and children, and ordinary considerations of justice in the disposition of an estate between different members of a family, the parable is a story of a besotted old fool. But we cannot take this as its point, because the father's reply to his son is clearly supposed to be in some way a telling one; and in any case the parable is offered as illuminating the nature of the Kingdom of Heaven. So we must look again for a point.

The first clue is perhaps that the returned prodigal does not want to be treated as a son, or think he has any right to his father's best robe and a feast of welcome: he simply wants employment as a paid servant. The father does not, then, weakly accede to a request to let bygones be bygones. He goes, in his response, instantly beyond anything the prodigal hoped or could have hoped for. He orders up a feast, and orders the prodigal to be dressed in his best robe, because he thinks that that is the appropriate response to the situation. What, then, does he think it an appropriate response *to*? Certainly not to the prodigal's *deserts*: if the feast were a feast to reward *desert* it would be a feast given for the elder son (one can, indeed, imagine a parable in which the prodigal returns, asks to be taken on as a paid servant and is indeed taken on in that capacity, at which point a feast is given for the elder son: that would not, indeed, be a parable, but a moral fable). But if the feast is not to reward desert, what on earth is it for? The explanation given by the father to the elder son is that it is simply a celebration for 'a happy day'; the sort of feast that one gives when some great good descends upon the family. What is the good? Again, it cannot be anything which the prodigal has done or that he brings with him. Therefore it can only be the prodigal himself. *He* is the thing of great value which the father has regained, and whose recovery he is therefore celebrating. This is why the elder son's objection is peculiarly out of place. And, of course, it is also what he finds so hard to stomach. In the gulf between the father's joy and the reaction of the elder son at being seriously asked to treat his wastrel younger brother as some sort of Pearl of Great Price, an object of immense intrinsic value, for whose restoration to the family a celebratory feast is in order, we see the abyss which separates the everyday morality which we all know well enough how to handle, from the extraordinary outlook which Christ is not only recommending to us but asserting as a condition of our salvation.

III

These three parables each presuppose some system of practices in terms of which a field of moral concepts (using 'moral' in the old, broad sense) are defined relative to one another: the system of formal social contacts in terms of which social standing, snobbery, social ambition and the corresponding kinds of mortification and chagrin are defined; the systems of economic relations which define the corresponding roles and interests of labourer and employer; the structure of a family around a property or οικος which defines the roles and rights of brothers and sons and determines where, for example, it is and is not proper to feel moral outrage at the flouting of those rights.

But the parabolic narrative is in each case set askew to these underlying structures of social practices and their corresponding systems of concepts, so that the mind can find no resting-place in the story: cannot find, in terms of the underlying scheme of practices and associated concepts, a clear point and structure in the story, as it can, for example, in the simple, pre-parabolic story of Bar Ma'jan's revenge. In order to find a point, to see why the vineyard owner's behaviour might not be just economic muddle-headedness, or the father's simply parental affection turned soft and besotted, or the

feast-giver's summons to the cripples and beggars not social mortification expressing itself in savage mockery of the reluctant guests,
the mind must reach beyond the conceptual resources offered by the
commonplace underlying conceptual structures to something which
transcends those structures and constitutes a kind of judgement upon
them.

In each case the behaviour of the central protagonist (father,
landowner, feast-giver) is explicable only if the value he places upon
other protagonists (beggar guests, labourers, son) is not a value
which those protagonists acquire through their position in an underlying system of practices, which defines a set of morally significant
social roles (the good, obedient son, the man of social standing, the
worthy, profitable labourer who has worked long hours to increase
his master's harvest), but an absolute value; a value which inheres in
the person concerned merely *qua* person. Or, to put it another way, it
is the *guests*, and not their social standing, who justify the feast; it is
for *labourers*, or *in order that labourers should not be unemployed*,
that the landowner scours the town, and not for *labour* to increase
the profits of the vine harvest; it is for *the son* that the father gives
the feast of thanksgiving, and not to reward the son's deserts, or for
any ulterior benefit that his return may or may not bring to the
household.

So there *is*, after all, something general which these parables give
us. They give us what, if we want to put a familiar and therefore
reassuring name to it, we can call the concept of the dignity of the
person; and correlatively with that they give us the concept of God's
grace as absolute; as something which transcends all human moral
categories, and thus perhaps as something (there is a chain of sup-
pressed steps here, but not a very long one) which does not depend
upon works. The role of both these concepts in the subsequent
development of Christendom has been sufficiently momentous and
ambiguous to make it I think obvious that (and why) these sayings of
Christ have had a resonance and an influence beyond the immediate
circumstances of their original utterance. John Stuart Mill, in the
essay on *Utilitarianism*, tried to represent Christ's central message as
a form of that doctrine; as a universal benevolence, a concern for the
felicity of mankind in general. One's feeling that this is an altogether
bizarre reading both of the Gospels and of the general content of the
Christian tradition is brought to a head by these three parables. The
outlook which these parables adumbrate is one which involves
infinite concern for single individuals, and which therefore precisely
does not proportion its concern for individuals to the demands of any
arithmetical computation of the common good. One might say that

according to these parables the justice of God, like logic, 'contains no numbers'; or that the God who is seen through them, if he is a mathematician, is one who does not take into account, morally speaking, any numbers between unity and infinity. Whereas, of course, the calculation of a guest's value to his host, or a son's to his family, or a labourer's to his employer, is as much a computation as any other estimation of utilities.

So, I want to say, these parables do offer us something general. They originate a moral outlook. And that is what gives them polemical force as replies to the question 'How can a respectable religious teacher spend his time consorting with tax-gatherers and riff-raff?' They have polemical force because the moral outlook which they communicate goes beyond and undercuts the moral outlook out of which that question springs.

And yet all this is in one way altogether too pat. In putting a name, 'the Concept of the Dignity of the Person', to what is communicated by these parables, have I not fallen victim to the most ancient and profound of linguistic illusions, the illusion that once we can put a name to something we know what it is?

For, suppose I am impressed by this new idea of 'the dignity of the person', and I want to make it the basis of all my relationships with other people. What, exactly, in practical terms, will constitute doing that? What, when it comes down to it, *am I to do*? Am I, for example, with my strength of character, my moral vision and my remarkable powers of love transcending all commonplace moral relationships, to take charge of my weaker fellow men in the manner of Dostoevsky's Grand Inquisitor? Or, more prosaically, should I, if I have servants, treat them 'as one of the family', taking an interest in their lives, helping them in trouble and so on? The parables do not say: notoriously, they do not offer specific moral principles or injunctions, and the moment we try to reduce them to illustrated moral copy-book maxims we trivialize them. And yet it is obvious that in each of these cases, not to mention many others, the attempt to follow 'the teaching' of the parables is fraught with ambiguity. Spiritual guidance becomes spiritual tyranny; help to those in inferior social positions becomes an odious and hypocritical paternalism, unless we are very careful. And how can we know? What can enable us to tell, can make us sensitive to the difference?

Well, what *can* I do, if I want to articulate, to become sensitive to such a difference, to make it concrete enough to apprehend, but tell a story? For example I must tell a story about just such a Grand Inquisitor, or about a servant who was treated in a certain way as one of the family, so as to show how that in the end made him only more of a servant, bound him more helplessly to the service of the family interests, than a more openly economic way of treating him would have done. Of course that story will be as little amenable as the synoptic parables to being reduced to a general moral injunction; of being reduced, that is, to a safe guide in all future moral difficulties. But then, *that* story was not supposed to deal with *future* moral difficulties, let alone with *all* future moral difficulties, but only to make clear the nature of a *present* moral difficulty.

In telling such a story, what we should do is to rely on our readers grasping the point and rationale of some scheme of values, in this case the values of Christian love, concern for others, and so forth, and we should make the narrative demonstrate a new way in which you can take those values, a way in which you can secure yourself against taking them wrongly. The narrative would say, in effect, 'You think it is simple to love your neighbours as yourself, that it is clear what that involves. But, look...' But is that not, in turn, exactly what the synoptic parables do? They say, in effect, 'You think you know what a guest, or a friend is, or what it is to be a just employer, or to exercise well paternal rule over a family. But, look...' And in the space after the invitation to look comes the parable. In each case the concept of fatherhood, of being a good employer, of being a friend or a host, is not dispensed with. It is precisely what it is to be a friend, a host, a father, and so on, that we are talking about (one cannot, that is, construct parables, or narrative in general, at random). But something is added to the concept, or drawn out of it, or revealed in it, by the parable.

The parables are not, therefore, it seems to me, merely illustrations of a Christian moral outlook capable of being fully expressed in non-parabolic terms, and thus they cannot be *merely* eschatological in content, for Christian eschatology is itself defined partly in moral terms (it concerns not just the arrival of a Kingdom of Heaven, but of a Kingdom of Heaven of a certain kind). Jeremias is closer to the mark, it seems to me, when in refusing to translate 'friend' as 'neighbour' he remarks that the parable of the Good Samaritan *constructs*, and does not merely *employ*, the Christian concept of a neighbour. The parables, in short, do – or better, commence – the work of conceptual construction upon which the eschatology of Christianity partly depends. That is why they are connected with eschatology but are not *simply* eschatological in purport.

Let me try, even at the risk of repetition, to be a little less parabolic myself. What is it to grasp a moral concept? It is, presumably, to grasp the form, the structure, which is common to a number of cases. That is why you can introduce a new moral concept by telling stories:

the content of the stories presents your hearers with a number of cases to consider, and the moral structure, the concept, is shown by (or 'shows itself in', to use a Wittgensteinian tag) the point and narrative structure of the story. This is, in effect, what our three parables do. Each one sets up a different tension between the structure of a narrative and a body of underlying conceptual material in terms of which, if at all, the narrative has to be construed *as a narrative*, and the tension reveals a way of structuring the narrative which is the same in each case. But what does the *same* mean here? Well, in each narrative we are driven to postulate a concern for persons as ultimate objects of value as the predominating interest of the central character. But what does this new phrase, this piece of jargon, 'to have a concern for persons as ultimate objects of value', *mean*? How, if we were asked to, could we explain its meaning? We might, of course, try to replace it with some other verbal formula, such as the Kantian 'treat others as ends and not as means' (a verbal formula which also, incidentally, depends upon narrative illustrations, which have also, like the parables, been felt to be notoriously ambiguous, and to fall lamentably short of the respectable clarities of doctrine).[23] But ultimately, I think we should be reduced to pointing at the parables, or rather at a complex structural similarity which recurs in all of them, but which cannot in the end be disentangled or abstracted from their narrative content.

But if 'what the parables have to tell us' cannot be disentangled from their narrative content, how can we be sure that we have understood it correctly? Let us rephrase the question. How can we *show* that we have understood correctly? Wittgenstein says that we show that we have understood the principle of a series by continuing the series. What we have in the parables, or some of the parables, as I have tried to show, is precisely a series of narratives bound to one another by a single principle: a single complex pattern of structural similarity. How could we show our understanding but by continuing, in other narratives or in our own lives, the series of which we have been given, as it were, the first few integers? Of course, as I have already suggested, in the process of doing this we shall at times stop short because we see that what looked from one point of view like a continuation of the series is not so from another: that what can be seen from one point of view as bearing to the other members of the series the same complex structural similarity that they bear to one another can be seen from another point of view as either lacking or incompletely manifesting that similarity. (Thus, if the father in the Prodigal Son took on his younger son as a paid labourer and treated him kindly and correctly as one in that position, that would in a sense be *justice* all right, but not the fullness, the rather baffling perfection of justice that we find in the parable, where the father does indeed do what is 'due' to the son, or 'due' to the occasion of the son's return, but where *that* turns out to be something infinitely more than the son could have considered to be 'in justice' due to him.) And, of course, one can then describe what happens when we are brought up short in this way either by saying that we have, by an act of self-transcendence, changed or transformed the moral concept which forms the principle of the series; or by saying that we have seen more clearly what was already implicitly given in the set of relationships between cases which set the series in motion.

This duality is, I think, the reason for the *riddling* character of parables. For if it is true that parables are given in answer to questions, it is also true that they answer those questions only by asking a further question, and a question, moreover, which can only honestly be answered 'Yes and no'. Was the landowner just to the servants who had worked so long in paying the ones who had worked so short a time the same wage? Yes and no. Was the father unjust to his eldest son? Yes and no. Does the feast-giver, by using the beggar-guests to rebuke the guests who refused, use the beggar-guests as a mere instrument of his wrath? Yes and no. The doubleness here is not the indeterminacy of bafflement or wilful mystification: it is the necessary duality of self-transcendence: the slow climb to successively more adequate levels of vision.

A few paragraphs ago, I said that grasping a moral concept involves grasping a form – a complex structural similarity between cases – and that that is why telling stories is one way of introducing a new moral concept. It now looks as if we can say something stronger than this: that parabolic narrative is not just one way, but the only way of introducing a new moral concept. For on the one hand, whatever verbal label I attach to the moral concepts in question can only ultimately be explicated by appeal to a series of cases, and on the other hand the full significance of the moral outlook demonstrated by associating or dissociating specific cases to form such a series can only be grasped when one sees what further cases, seen from what points of view, turn out to associate themselves to, or to dissociate themselves from, the series of cases as so far formed. Terms of moral categorization: 'honour', 'justice', 'respect for the person' and the rest, are at best only signposts or markers in this process; markers which, admittedly, are not to be dug up and moved about casually at will, but which life, or moral experience, inevitably eventually digs up and moves in spite of us, unless we are very stubborn indeed.

If I am right, then we have an explanation of why so much of the teaching of Jesus consists of narrative. It is because narrative offers, in the end, the only way of talking seriously about the moral life. It is serious because it is content to *show* what all other kinds of moral talk attempt, in the face of our condition as beings in a state of becoming, to *say*.

Our age dislikes riddles, and stories, because it is still in love with a notion promulgated in the seventeenth century by the founders of modern science, and still believed by many to be central to the practice of science despite the rise of relativistic physics: the conception of the Ideal Observer. The Ideal Observer neither affects nor is affected by what he observes. Hence he can speak a language of detached objective description. The description of the world which he is able to give in this language may increase in richness, and indeed will increase in richness, as a result of the steady advance of science. But the *language* does not change: it remains a neutral medium for recording fact. And hence the observer does not change. Indeed the notion of a change in the observer is, on this view of the nature of knowledge, both something conceptually absurd and something obstructing and theoretically scandalous to the view of knowledge in question. The observer *cannot* change, because the observing mind, *qua* observing mind, is not supposed to possess any content, or structure, of its own. It is simply a camera recording reality. What is observable from the viewpoint of the Ideal Observer (this is why he *is* an *Ideal* Observer) is what would be observed by any other observer. There is nothing, in short, to distinguish one observer from another, if the scientific study of nature is properly conducted; for change in the observer would imply differing observation-states, and the possibility of passing from one of these states to another. But on the Ideal Observer view of knowledge there is only one possible viewpoint from which anything deserving the name of knowledge can be apprehended: the viewpoint from which the properly trained observer observes what any other properly trained observer observes: the viewpoint of the Ideal Observer, in short.

We like to think that everything that is true and worth saying can be put into such a language, and one consequence of this hankering is that we want to know, once and for all, what parables, or for that matter poems or novels, *have to say*: what they 'come down to' (the very phrase suggests that we think of the language of poetry and narrative fiction as a sort of pink cloud or afflatus, upon which perfectly solid, down-to-earth objects are floated about, tantalizingly and infuriatingly in mid-air, just out of reach) in the language of an Ideal (or common-sense) Observer. But the hankering itself is an illegitimate one, not because the notion of an Ideal Observer is an absurd or dispensable one, but because it is a notion which we have allowed to get out of its proper place in our conceptual scheme.

The notion of an Ideal Observer is, I think, essentially that of a *properly trained* observer: the man who knows what he is looking for and knows also what sorts of thing could prevent him from noticing it if it is there, or make him think that it is there if it is not. In this sense a competent chemist looking for barium in a sample is an Ideal, because a trained, Observer. Because he knows chemical theory, and has acquired a certain skill in manipulating the techniques of qualitative analysis, he will get, quite independently of other trained observers, the results which they get, thus providing one step in that endless chain of independent corroboration which both confirms the general adequacy of chemical theory, and entitles us to say that his training *is* a training in the accurate observation of reality, and not just in some conventional ritual mumbo-jumbo.

But at the same time, the concept of a trained observer in chemical analysis is defined against the background of chemical theory. And chemical theory is not something which could be 'observed' in nature at all. The notion of training somebody to observe, say, 'the constitution of matter' is, indeed, senseless, except against the background of some specified theory of the constitution of matter, which we must already possess. Theory, in short, is not read off from experience by a process of *observation* at all, and there is no ideal posture of observation in which a scientist can place himself which will guarantee that he will succeed in making an advance in theory. Nor is there any neutral descriptive language, given antecedently to a theoretical advance, into which the specific content of that advance can simply be transcribed. Any language adequate to express the content of a theoretical advance in science must be formulated in the process of making that advance, and this effort of conceptual formulation is commonly the most difficult part of the process of discovery. Whatever else one accepts of the relativist or 'anarchist' philosophies of science put forward by Kühn or Feyerabend,[24] for example, this much is certainly true.

In erecting a theory of knowledge founded upon the concept of an Ideal Observer, what seventeenth- and eighteenth-century empiricism and its modern philosophical descendants have done is to take an essential but secondary part of the practice of scientific enquiry, and treat it as if it were primary and ultimate in that practice. In reality, in science, as elsewhere, there is a level at which an advance in our comprehension of reality can only come by way of a change in us: in our standpoint as observers: a change in the conceptual schemata in terms of which we ultimately order the world and which direct all our observations, and our responses to what we observe.

We are, in short, beings in a continual process of becoming and self-transcendence. And just as the theoretical languages of science both express and engineer this transcendence in our understanding of nature, so narrative and the language of poetry and parable both express and engineer our self-transcendence as moral beings (taking 'moral' once again in the broad sense which it formerly had). There is no other language in which one can express the life that is in parable, because, for reasons which I hope I may have made a little less opaque in this chapter, the life is in the language (that is, what the parable makes us see is already 'put into words' in the only way it can be – by the parable). I do not think that in saying that I have said anything very original; which is not, of course, to say that I do not think that what I have said needs saying. What I want to say was said quite clearly, though parabolically, by Kafka, and his words will serve very well as summary and conclusion:

> Many complain that the words of the wise are always merely parables and of no use in daily life, which is the only life we have. When the sage says: 'Go over', he does not mean that we should cross to some actual place, which we would do anyhow if the labour were worth it; he means some fabulous yonder, something unknown to us, something too that he cannot designate more precisely, and therefore cannot help us here in the very least. All these parables really set out to say merely that the incomprehensible is incomprehensible, and we know that already. But the cares we have to struggle with every day: that is a different matter.
>
> Concerning this a man once said: Why such reluctance? If you only followed the parables you yourself would become parables and with that rid of all your daily cares.
>
> Another said: I bet that is also a parable.
>
> The first said: You have won.
>
> The second said: But unfortunately only in parable.
>
> The first said: No, in reality: in parable you have lost.[25]

Chapter 9
Secrets and Surfaces*

I

'Both art and life', says Nietzsche, directing a 'critical backward glance' at the youthful Schopenhauerianism of *The Birth of Tragedy*, 'depend wholly on the laws of optics, on perspective and illusion; both, to be blunt, depend on the necessity of error.'[1] As often with Nietzsche, it is unclear whether the implications of this thought are joyful or depressing ones. Does it redeem art by showing it to proceed on the same principles as life, or damn life by showing it to be the same kind of painted sham as art? For the late Nietzsche 'life' is too privileged a category for there to be much doubt which way the argument will go: put the same point in the hands of Frank Kermode and doubts, as chilly as they are no doubt salutary, come seeping in.

The main line of argument in *The Genesis of Secrecy* (hereinafter *GS*)[2] is easily grasped. Literary criticism, in so far as its methods involve pursuing, by means of paraphrase and explanatory gloss, the true meaning of the text ('the recovery of the real right original thing', *GS*, p. 125), shares with a long tradition of biblical hermeneutics the idea that texts have both a 'carnal' and a 'spiritual' meaning; the former accessible to any outsider who can read the language in which the text is written, the latter accessible only to insiders, who have through membership of a privileged hermeneutic community acquired knowledge of the secret relationships and correspondences constituting the true and authentic sense lying beneath, or behind, the surface of the text. Kermode has both epistemological

* This essay was written for a conference, 'Forms and Attention: the work of Frank Kermode', organized by the University of Warwick Centre for Research in Philosophy and Literature, which took place in March 1989.

243

and moral objections to this way of construing the enterprise of interpretation. The epistemological ones I shall get to in a moment. The moral ones often, I suspect, get passed over by readers of the book, and are worth more than a passing glance. In ascending order of seriousness they are, first, that the pursuit of spiritual sense comes at times, and perhaps always, perilously close to the kind of divination that proceeds by sticking a pin into a copy of Virgil or the Bible. Second, and more seriously, the effect if not always the conscious aim of making the distinction between the carnal and the spiritual central to the practice of interpretation is to establish 'the superiority of latent over manifest sense' (GS, p. 2): to exclude outsiders and to reserve to an authoritative institution the practice of hermeneutical divination. Third, and more seriously still, the hermeneutic privilege thus established 'may determine matters of life and death' (GS, p. 20). Thus Matthew's fiction that 'the Jews, after Pilate washed his hands, voluntarily took upon themselves the blood-guilt of the Crucifixion' (loc. cit.) helped to determine the subsequent course of European anti-Semitism.

Fourthly, finally and most seriously of all, there is the forgetfulness of the distinction between truth and meaning which is central to the hermeneutics of secrecy, and which is the chief source of the recurrent tendency of hermeneutics to breed nightmares. The moral centre of Kermode's lectures seems to me to lie here, in their espousal (GS, p. 119) of Spinoza's dictum that in exegesis 'we are at work not on the truth of passages but on their meaning'. This is something most of us would pay lip-service to. Whatever biblical exegesis may yield, most of us would be happy to concede, it cannot yield us knowledge of the Jews' having accepted the blood-guilt of the Crucifixion. But at the same time most of us continue to hope, or to talk as if we continued to hope, that the authors we most admire have 'something to say to us': some insight, some truth or other about 'life' to communicate, which a proper, a just reading would excavate and put on show. Kermode wants to rid us of these last vestiges of the notion that exegesis has anything to do with truth. At the same time he is conscious of the loss that this involves. 'All modern interpretation that is not merely an attempt at "re-cognition" involves some attempt to divorce meaning and truth' (GS, p. 122). But to the extent that it succeeds in this aim structuralist and post-structuralist criticism takes on the aspect of the doorkeeper in Kafka's parable of the Law which recurs as a leitmotiv of *The Genesis of Secrecy*. The door closes, shutting out the radiance beyond; and to prevent or delay its closing it is all too likely that we shall abandon the painful attempt to separate questions of truth from questions of meaning and 'slip back into the old comfortable fictions of transparency, the single sense, the truth' (*GS*, p. 123).

I have dwelt at some length on the moral aspects of Kermode's argument partly as a way of measuring the distance we have travelled from the seemingly febrile Zarathustrian cheerfulness with which Nietzsche, in a late phase, greeted the thought that transparency and the single sense are unattainable, that all is 'perspective and illusion'. *The Genesis of Secrecy* is not a cheerful book. But it is a serious one, and its un-Nietzschian preference for truth over illusion is not one that can easily be laughed off. Nevertheless, I think the gloom can be mitigated a little. I want to suggest that it is possible to preserve something of what Kermode calls the 'radiance' of the text while also preserving a decent respect for Spinoza's dictum that in exegesis what is at stake is meaning, not truth. I want to suggest that it is possible to remain wholly upon the surface of the text, making no attempt to penetrate by judicious paraphrase to a hidden meaning beneath or behind that surface, but yet find on that surface more than an enigmatic shimmer of words and rhetorical devices.

II

Kermode's thesis is that the hermeneutics of secrecy is founded upon an illusion, or rather upon a whole string of them, and pursues a non-existent goal. Texts have no secrets, at least of the kind that interpretation strives to unlock (studies which confine themselves to questions of 'meaning', such as philology, linguistics or structural analysis, being, of course, another matter). Kermode's arguments for this thesis seem to me to fall into three groups:

(1) Arguments which endeavour to show that any text admits of an irreducible plurality of interpretations;

(2) Arguments which endeavour to show that the elaboration of narrative is responsive to purely formal (or 'internal' or 'literary') considerations rather than to the faithful representation of reality;

(3) Arguments which endeavour to show that latent or spiritual sense is a product of interpretation.

Taken separately as types of argument against the hermeneutics of secrecy, (1)–(3) do not all seem to have the same degree of force. Arguments of type (1) seem particularly weak. It is hard to see why any determined champion of the hermeneutics of secrecy should be much disturbed by the thought that latent sense may be irreducibly plural. Texts are produced by persons, and persons, being themselves irreducibly plural, often do mean more by what they say than they appear to mean, and often more than they take themselves to have said or meant. Arguments of type (2) seem a bit stronger, but not all that strong. Much depends here on what one might have in mind by speaking of a text as 'transparent' (something we shall come back to in a moment). If a transparent narrative is one which faithfully records an occurrence, then obviously its transparency is threatened the moment it begins to be subject to processes of literary elaboration designed to make it a more interesting story, or a more telling one from the point of view of some set of moral or institutional demands external to that of mere fidelity to the events recounted. Kermode deploys this point persuasively in Lecture V ('What Precisely are the Facts?') when he observes that Mark is 'not a simple chronicle, such as, in the days when its priority was first established, people hoped it might be, but a history with a literary structure'. But although the point sustains Kermode's immediately following comment, 'To speak so is to speak as one does of a fiction' (*GS*, p. 116), it does not altogether sustain the conclusion which that comment seems to invite, that the presence of any trace of literary elaboration in a text is sufficient to write off its claim to historicity, or more generally to transparency, *in any sense whatsoever of those terms*. There might, that is, be weaker senses of 'transparency' which allow a text to be in very large measure a literary construction while yet allowing it some bearing upon extra-textual reality.

This is precisely what is excluded by arguments of type (3), which I shall call arguments for textual solipsism. These arguments seem to me much stronger than those of types (1) and (2). Not only are they sufficient in themselves, if they can be made to stick, to demonstrate the futility and delusiveness of the hermeneutics of secrecy; they also add greatly to the force of Kermode's other two types of argument. The thesis of textual solipsism is that all latent, 'spiritual' meaning is the product of interpretation. The project of the hermeneutics of secrecy is thus rendered futile because interpretation *per se* is futile, its pretended discoveries no more than the gross, alien-seeming shadows cast by its own processes, and by the patterns of institutional expectation and assumption which motivate and direct those processes, upon the passive and inscrutable surface of words which is all that a text ultimately offers to our excited and self-deluded scrutiny. Both the argument for the irreducible plurality of latent sense and the argument from literary elaboration are probably best seen, therefore, as ways of elaborating and filling out the argument for textual solipsism. 'No doubt', says Kermode of the parable of the Good Samaritan, 'the parable has a carnal sense which does not vary materially; its spiritual sense is not so constant' (*GS*, p. 36). But his account of the diversity of spiritual senses which Augustine and the Fathers drew from it is meant, I take it, precisely to bring into question whether this diversity is really being *discovered* in what is, after all, no more than 'a simple exemplary tale' (*GS*, p. 35), or distilled out of the very processes of interpretation, with their accompanying and directing institutional imperatives and assumptions, to which Augustine *et al.* subject it. As we read Kermode at this point, our cheerful willingness to grasp the nettle of semantic plurality in the manner I suggested a moment ago subsides within us. Similarly, the argument from literary elaboration gains in force if we take Kermode's point (p. 101: 'texts are from the beginning and sometimes indeterminately studded with interpretations'; p. 20: 'spiritual senses . . . may in their turn be treated as if they were carnal'; and *passim*) that the literary elaboration of texts passes with no clear methodological break into their interpretation and vice versa.

Kermode offers in addition to these detailed studies of hermeneutic practice a quite general and knock-down argument for textual solipsism, which is that it follows as a simple consequence of the latitude texts necessarily leave to interpreters. We may not be able to make just any interpretation square with a text (an important *caveat*, to which I shall return), but we can make enough square with it to make the choice between them depend upon supplementary principles of interpretation which are themselves determined, often below the level of consciousness, by history and cultural situation. Our 'acts of divination . . . *determine* undetected latent sense' (*GS*, p. 4, my italics). They exercise this determining role because divinatory paraphrase is in essence the art of connecting up parts and aspects of the text to reveal an occult pattern of coherence. And 'All such operations require the interpreter to practise a grandiose neglect of portions of the text' (*GS*, p. 20); so that 'every time you read *À la recherche du temps perdu* it can be a new novel, says Roland Barthes, because you skip different parts each time' (*GS*, p. 54). The movement of possible senses must be brought to a halt, Kermode suggests, because bringing it to a halt (this, I shall argue, is questionable) 'is our only means of reading until revolutionary new concepts of writing prevail' (*GS*, p. 71). But the only thing that can bring it to a halt is the constraint of some fore-understanding (Kermode's way of rendering into English the German *Vorverständnis*) which will of necessity be 'ideological and institutional' in character.

It is Kermode's awareness of the solipsistic implications of the thesis that latent sense is the product of interpretation, I think, which gives *The Genesis of Secrecy* its pervasive atmosphere of sadness, defeat and loss. For if we accept Kermode's argument, after all, all those insights and glimpses of insight which make reading narrative fiction exciting to us become merely glimpses of our own interpretative practices and fore-understandings. The window which narrative fiction appears to open upon a world of wonders which is also our world becomes a blank sheet of opaque glass offering back nothing but a distorted image of the observer's own eye. Metaphors of screens and opaque glasses have long been familiar to us, of course, as part of the standard rhetoric of philosophical idealism. (Do you really take me, demands Philonous of Hylas, to be defending principles 'that lead us to think all the visible beauties of the creation a false imaginary glare?'[3] – and one senses that the anxiety which reverberates in the extraordinary energy of the concluding phrase, triply buttressed as it is with predicates of sensory and cognitive obstruction, is not only that of Hylas.) So one would expect to find such images cropping up in *The Genesis of Secrecy*. And on p. 125 we duly find Kermode speaking of 'our readiness to submit the show of things to the desires of our minds; of the structures of explanation which come between us and the facts like some wall of wavy glass'. The same metaphor recurs in Kermode's distinction between 'transparent' and 'opaque' texts; and in the door which, in Kafka's parable of the Law, becomes not a means of access to an Elsewhere, of escape from the airless room of the self and its obscurely conditioned fore-understandings, but one more wall closing off the – in any case fictive – radiance beyond.

We have in fact to deal in this book with two Kermodes. There is the sceptical, Lockeian Kermode, out to teach us the plain and unexceptionable truth that a story is a story, and not a message in code; and to debunk the Baconianism, the obsession with ciphers, occult meanings, covert identities such as those of the man in the macintosh in *Ulysses* or the young man in the *sindon* in Mark, Dark Ladies of all kinds, which feeds off the contrary view. And then there is the Kermode who has discovered, like Locke's philosophical heirs, that an empiricism begun in mirth and gladness all too easily ends first in idealism and then in solipsism; but who like them sees no honest way of repudiating these further steps. In the remainder of this essay I shall do my best to set an obstacle or two in the path of this literary version of the familiar philosophical slide from robust empiricism (where that involves among other things respect for the distinction between asking what 'p' means and asking whether 'p' is true) to blank misgivings about the possibility of egress from the closed world of the self.

III

Setting opacity aside for a moment, what would the transparency of a fully transparent text consist in? Kermode defines the terms 'transparent' and 'opaque' only contextually, no doubt because he does not think them particularly problematic; but the contextual clues are sufficient to yield an answer. Lecture V opens with the sentence,

> If so many causes act in concert to ensure that texts are from the beginning and sometimes indeterminately studded with interpretations; and if the texts in their very nature demand further interpretation and yet resist it, what should we expect when the document in question denies its opacity by claiming to be a transparent account of the recognizable world?   (*GS*, p. 101)

Transparency, it seems, consists in what philosophical discussions of the nature of truth call correspondence: a match, in other words, between a true sentence and a fact; in this case between a true narrative sentence and what it asserts to have taken place. The trouble with transparency in this sense is that, as anti-foundationalist philosophers, such as W. V. Quine, or Paul Feyerabend, or Thomas Kühn, or Richard Rorty, have fairly plausibly argued (Kermode employs some related arguments himself), it is simply not available for any discourse sufficiently elaborated to be interesting. Observation is always and irremediably theory-laden. What we recognize and record as a fact is always relative to the current state of scientific and common-sense construal of how things *in general* stand in the world: is already saturated, as Kermode would have it, with fore-understandings. Taking this anti-foundationalist line, however, only commits one to denying guaranteed correctness or finality, in the sense of incorrigibility, to any of our descriptions of Reality. Anti-foundationalism, that is, while it no doubt is incompatible with some forms of philosophical Realism, certainly does not, and cannot, commit us to the view that reality is a 'linguistic construction' in the sense of being made *in principle inaccessible* by the theory-ladenness of our concepts and descriptive schemes – 'shut off from us behind an opaque screen of words', or something of the sort – because to assert *that* would be precisely to assert that whatever concepts or styles of description we happen to dispose of at any given moment, say the present one, are in principle incorrigible: to assert, that is, exactly what anti-foundationalism denies. To hold that all our descriptions are theory-laden is to hold that no scheme of descriptive concepts occupies a place in our language guaranteed by its simply corresponding to reality. But the assertion of the existence of a gap of that kind between reality and our ways of describing it would be vacuous unless there were a real possibility of the displacement of such a scheme coming about because of the discovery of relevant natural possibilities exceeding the capacity of that scheme to handle, or to handle fruitfully or naturally. The answer to someone who says, 'But couldn't we have a pair of competing conceptual schemes of equivalent capacity to handle all observable differences in a given area, so that choosing between them would be a matter of purely social or institutional agreement?' is Wittgenstein's: 'In such a case, since *ex hypothesi* there could be no difference in use, and so no detectable difference in meaning, between the two sets of terms, what would be the force of the hypothesis that we dispose of *two* sets of terms belonging to *two* different conceptual schemes?'

Anti-foundationalism, plausibly and consistently construed, then, presupposes some more or less Popperian picture of disconfirmation as constituting the interface between Reality and our never finally adequate attempts to describe it. The thought which I now wish to pursue is that that picture may have some bearing on the problems which Kermode raises concerning the interpretation of narrative fiction.

The obvious objection which such a proposal invites, of course, is that encounters with narrative fictions cannot reveal defects in our fore-understandings of how things stand in the world, in the way that, say, encounters with awkward experimental data can, because narrative fictions are (no prizes for guessing) fictions. But this objection is not as strong as it looks. The web of fore-understandings from within which each of us confronts the world is not just made up of beliefs, which only experiment or observation could reveal to be mistaken, about specific, discrete matters of fact. Much more importantly it is made up of preconceptions about the limits of natural possibility. Such fore-understandings tell us that Reality divides up into contrasted types of fact which conjointly, as we confidently suppose, exhaust the possibilities of nature or human life. Let us call these *structural fore-understandings*. Such fore-understandings can, certainly, come under pressure from direct experience, as when we come across an apparently undeniable case of Lamarckian inheritance, or meet a man whose acts and personality cannot be satisfactorily classified according to any of the short list of stereotypes we customarily apply to persons of his class, nation or race. But structural fore-understandings can also find themselves under threat from an argument, from a mathematical model; or for that matter from a fiction. For all that need be shown, to put such a preconception under stress, is that commonplace facts about nature or human life can be reordered or transformed, by appeal to principles which we already know to operate in relevant cases, in such a way as to generate a possibility incapable of being brought easily under any of the alternative descriptive rubrics which the structural fore-understanding in question asserts to be conjointly exhaustive of natural possibility.

It is, in fact, because mere fictions can pose substantial challenges to our structural fore-understandings that scandal has always been a main motive of interpretation. Kermode notes this principle in operation:

> An unfamiliar foreign expression, or the interpretation of a difficult part of the Law, or a story which, in the course of time, had come to seem ambiguous or even indecent, such as Sarah's sojourn in the harem of the Pharaoh, might prompt midrash ... how did it happen that Joseph married the daughter of Potiphar, an Egyptian? An Alexandrian romance maintains that the daughter was first converted; a rabbinical explanation has it that she was really the daughter of Dinah, reared by the wife of Pharaoh, but a born Jew. Thus discrepancies, or indecencies, are elim-inated by the invention of romantic narrative.   (GS, p. 82)

The issues raised here, it seems to me, go deeper. Our structural fore-understandings make us what we are: Marxists or Methodists, for instance, mechanists or vitalists. We cannot surrender them without undergoing the pains of insecurity, loss and amputation, that personal change entails. We want knowledge, of course, since knowledge not only satisfies curiosity but is, in both the engineer's and the Foucaultian's senses, power. But we hope very much that our knowledge, as it advances, will compose itself submissively into an orderly array of facts of the types sanctioned by our most cherished structural fore-understandings, not only posing no threat to their integrity but showing how well chosen they were in the first place, and that no mockers or hecklers will intervene to force upon our attention facts, or possible facts, of which we can gain nothing by taking cognizance.

Much serious narrative fiction has, I would suggest, as one of the more important of its many functions, that of thwarting this modest and entirely understandable hope. It adds insult to injury, in a way, that not one of the torrent of sentences of which it consists expresses a single factual, empirical truth. It makes no attempt to sweeten the bitter pill of its contumacy with any admixture of useful knowledge. It confines itself, as Aristotle taught us, to sketching possibilities;[4] but possibilities which, while they may seem sometimes merely fantastic, are even in those cases often too fully and sharply realized, too much in accordance with what we know very well to be the case when we come, or are forced, to think about it, to be easily kept from threatening our structural fore-understandings. Hence the venom which great narrative fictions often attract before interpretation has revealed ways of allowing them modest and discreet entrance into the canon whose gates they rudely assault. And hence also the rage to interpret itself. We interpret often enough, as Kermode suggests, because we *are* scandalized. But that in itself must mean: because we are very far from taking fictional narratives to be mere stories, pipe-dreams without power to challenge our sense of how life itself is organized into structures of possibilities. Being scandalized we trust we have misheard or misread: that, to use one of Kermode's most telling examples, when Jesus says that the true sense of parables is concealed fron the wicked *in order that* (*hina*) they might not turn and be saved he must mean not *hina* but *hoti* ('because'). Being conscious of the presence of a power to disturb we wish to appro-priate that power to the support of the very fore-understandings it appears to challenge, by equipping the text with some wholly benign sense. We hope, to use Kermode's chillingly felicitous phrase (*GS*, p. 54) to 'process the text into coherence'. Thus hoping, we become Insiders.

I agree with Kermode, for his reasons among others, that the Insider's enterprise is doomed to failure. My concern is with what ways of reading remain for the rest of us, for Those Outside to whom *The Genesis of Secrecy* is after all dedicated. Certainly we should accept Spinoza's principle that in exegesis 'we are at work not on the truth of passages but on their meaning'. But should we also accept the two further premises which Kermode in effect adds to Spinoza's principle; namely, (1) that to 'work on the meaning of a text' in any sense other than a purely structural or philological one is necessarily to attempt to make it cohere in the interests of some paraphrase, and (2) that many paraphrases, at best distinct from one another and at worst in conflict, can be grounded in any text? Premises (1) and (2), taken together with Spinoza's principle, yield textual solipsism: the thesis that undiscovered latent sense is the product of interpretation; or, to spell it out more dismally still, that no cognitive gains may be expected to accrue from reading narrative fiction save those of disillusion with such reading; that while the theoretical reflections which break the spell of reading may have some bearing upon real life, nothing that we do or think while under that spell can have. If we accept Spinoza's principle plus (1) and (2) then, it seems, we must choose between the rather drab options which Kermode offers

us. We must embrace disappointment as our lot, allowing the door
to close finally upon the fictive radiance of the text, and betake
ourselves either to structuralist hermeneutics of the type practised
by Jean Starobinski, which Kermode admires in Lecture IV for
its austere taking to heart of Spinoza's dictum, combining it, perhaps, with some form of reductive criticism of the Marxist or the
Foucaultian variety; or else to the celebration of incoherence and
fortuitousness, as offering a release from slavery to 'codes implanted
in our minds by the arbitrary fiat of a culture or an institution', which
Kermode fastidiously refrains from endorsing on p. 54 ('There are
current at present much bolder opinions than this one . . .').

Is there no other option? I think there is one.[5] The instructed
Outsider should reject what I have called Kermode's second premiss,
for the excellent reason that it is false. The meaning of a text need not
be sought by endeavouring to 'process it into coherence' with some
explanatory paraphrase or other. On the contrary it may equally well
be sought by investigating the points at which, and attempting to
understand the reasons why, a text resists specific attempts at paraphrase. Textual solipsists will want to argue, of course, that 'the
meaning of a text' cannot be sought in this way either. Their position
is that the whole notion of 'the meaning of a text' is defective, and
should be discarded, because meaning, or latent sense, is a product
of interpretation. But Kermode's arguments for textual solipsism,
because they work by raising doubts about whether constraints
internal to the text can determine a unique paraphrase, can only
work against an opponent who is committed to the Insider's strategy
of trying to discover a latent sense capable of being expressed as a
paraphrase or 'reading'. They can have no force, that is, against an
Outsider who has discarded what I have called Kermode's second
premiss. In order to block *that* move the textual solipsist needs to
shift his ground and argue for a far stronger and hence less plausible
claim. He needs to argue that the Outsider's project of investigating
the points at which texts resist specific attempts at explanatory
paraphrase is as inevitably doomed to failure as the Insider's, although for different reasons, because there just are no such points:
that *all* the constraints upon interpretation emanate from sources
'external to the text' in the sense of being freely variable from
interpreter to interpreter; from 'culturally-imposed codes', 'institutional requirements', 'fore-understandings' and the like.

Kermode appears at times to flirt with a position as radical as this.
It is certainly strongly hinted at by his suggestion (p. 143) that we
'know' (my inverted commas) that we cannot read the Gospel of
Mark 'as a work of irony or a confidence trick' only because 'We

have acquired fore-understandings which exclude such readings'. And it seems overt in his later remark (p. 145) that narratives 'may be narratives only because of our impudent intervention, and susceptible of interpretation only by our hermeneutic tricks'. But elsewhere in the text the externality of the constraints upon interpretation is not so strongly insisted upon. Thus on p. 13 we find Kermode making room for what I suppose is the basic hunch I am defending here, by granting that 'texts interpret, or deceive, their interpreters, who should know they do and make allowances for it'. And on p. 36, dealing with what Augustine and the Fathers made of the parable of the Samaritan, we find, 'No doubt the parable has a carnal sense which does not vary materially; its spiritual sense is not so constant.' To admit that carnal senses do not vary materially is to admit that there are some constraints upon interpretation which are not variable from interpreter to interpreter; constraints to which an interpreter does not force the text to submit at the behest of a 'hermeneutic community' or his own 'fore-understandings', but rather constraints to which he himself must submit, in common with every other would-be interpreter, as the price of finding himself confronted with *a text*, rather than a string of enigmatic marks. Of course these constraints too are founded in *social conventions*, and recent critics do sometimes write as if they thought that the mere fact that natural languages are *conventional* systems of communication were sufficient in itself to establish the textual solipsist's contention that all constraints upon interpretation are external to the text in the sense of being freely variable from interpreter to interpreter. However, a moment's thought is sufficient to show that this cannot be right. A system of constraints upon interpretation (however conventional in character) which was not, at some level, invariant from interpreter to interpreter would simply not serve to constitute a natural language (there would be no way of ensuring that any sentence of the language would express the same proposition to different speakers, for instance). All talk of 'language', or 'texts', or 'interpretation' in such a context, indeed, would be nugatory, because it would be vacuous.

Kermode is clearly right, therefore, to grant the community and the invariance of the carnal: the contrary view is incoherent. The question is, though, at what level, exactly, does the carnal end and the spiritual begin? Is it just *the meaning of the* (English or Greek) *words* that is carnal, that defeats all attempts by pious Insiders to meddle with them (as Kermode thinks is the case with all attempts to change *hina* to *hoti* at Mark 4:11–12). Or does the autonomy of the text, its power to send our impertinent suggestions packing, extend to higher levels of textual organization than that? The answer, I think, is pretty clearly going to be a matter of degree and of arguing out the pros and cons for particular cases and levels of discourse. My own feeling is that while emblem, metonymy, symbol, upon which quite a lot of Kermode's argument in Lectures I and III focuses and depends, shade off into the spiritual, the structure of narrative and things like the relationship between plot, action and character (despite the very interesting and telling things which Kermode has to say about this, which would open up another chapter of argument) remain rather solidly carnal. But if anything at all in narrative is impervious to our 'hermeneutic tricks' then it remains permanently possible that our hermeneutic endeavours and the fore-understandings which motivate and direct them may find themselves running into a brick wall. Such an experience, while painful and in one way negative, may not, as Karl Popper has argued in other contexts, be entirely devoid of cognitive gains. My suggestion, in short, is that in literature as in science we escape from the limpid darkness of solipsism not at the point at which the triumphal chariots of theory rumble to final victory over the phenomena or the text, but rather precisely at the point of failure, of confusion, of silence and falling short.

IV

By way of conclusion I shall offer a necessarily brief and sketchy example of how a resolutely Outsiderish approach to reading narrative might develop in an actual case. The text I shall choose is a notoriously scandalous one, *The Taming of the Shrew*. The *Shrew* is nowadays considered a difficult play to come to grips with, because on the face of it it tramples upon our century's new-found moral belief in the equality of the sexes. Katherine's final speech in particular, in which as we tend to see it she knuckles under, strikes many people as profoundly shocking. It would be nice, therefore, if we could simply dismiss the play as propaganda for an outmoded and wrong conception of relationships between the sexes; if we could get it out of our minds and finish with it by exposing the power relations it serves and propagates. Unfortunately the play will not altogether play ball with this vision of what it is about. For a start Petruchio does not take the obvious step of simply beating Katherine into silence and submission. Instead he chooses to behave like a lunatic: in effect to outmatch her at her own game of revolt against the ordered structures of society which she sees, rightly, as demanding (at least the appearance of) silence and submission of her. Certainly his strategy disorients her, removing from life the least scrap of rational structure and

Renaissance decorum which she might use as a basis for a revolt of her own, but beyond making her hungry, tired, uncomfortable and infuriated he does not physically harm her. Secondly, the obedience in which he schools her serves her ends as well as his. Petruchio's yoke is easy: all he demands of her is that she fall in trustingly and unquestioningly with his nonsense. Having finally paid that modest price she finds herself delivered from the oppression of her family, presiding at a feast instead of kept in confinement as something approaching a madwoman, and herself beating her superior sister Bianca at Bianca's own chosen social game of being the good, socially acceptable daughter. She has, it might almost seem, been led by Petruchio (whom we are beginning to be tempted to see as the practitioner of a crazy kind of therapy) back into life, from a fatally self-destructive strategy of living to one in which she has a real chance of formulating and achieving some goals of her own.

A perfectly possible reaction to this, of course, would be to say: All right, *The Taming of the Shrew* is a *cunning and subtle* defence of a Renaissance view of male supremacy. But even if one admits its subtlety it is still *false to life*: in real life a fortune-hunter of the kind Petruchio advertises himself to be, having got hold of Katherine's dowry, *would* simply have beaten her into submission, and the story would have ended much sooner. So saying we take a stand precisely upon the question of what options exhaust the possibilities of 'real life': either a strict equality between the sexes, as our theory-laden self-image, not our ambiguous and constantly shifting practice, defines that, or else male domination founded upon brutality. The whole trouble is that the play persuasively elaborates a further possibility which questions and undermines the putative exhaustiveness of those very options, which is why we dislike the play, feel uncomfortable with it, and fear it.

All this is very summary, no doubt. But suppose an exceptionally generous opponent were to find it persuasive, and were to say by way of conceding: All right; I grant that *The Taming of the Shrew* is not merely a subtle but a convincing defence of a Renaissance conception of how relationships between the sexes should be ordered. Would this be any truer? Wouldn't, that is, any imaginable defender of anything one could plausibly represent as 'a Renaissance conception of' the proper subordination of wives to husbands, see just as much scandal in the play, see in it just as much of an attempt to question self-evident proprieties and decencies, as feminists do today?[6] The 'good daughter', the model of Renaissance feminine propriety, is surely Bianca. But equally surely the message of the sub-plot and the wager scene is the familiar comic one that the conventional proprieties she represents are hollow: Bianca is obedient neither to her father nor to her husband. Then again Petruchio is a poor paradigm of that Adamic paternal authority which according to Filmer invests the King and should reign also in the household. He does not behave with the distance, the sure and authoritative wielding of a divinely and legally constituted right, which that conception of paternal authority entails. Instead he enters into a duel of riot and misrule with Katherine: a duel conducted on her ground, played out according to strategies she has determined, his frenzies following and matching hers fit for fit. As he says, this is how a falconer tames a hawk; but as we know from T. H. White's personal account of that process, it is a painful one for the falconer as well as for the falcon. He must sit up all night if need be with his bird, for if he sleeps he has lost her. There is love and self-denial in it as well as mastery: it is as if the magistrate, instead of merely sitting in judgement upon the criminal and sentencing him to a whipping or the wheel, were to go alone into his cell and wrestle with him.

Finally, what emerges from the duel between them is less like the humility and submission proper to the wife of *bien-pensant* Renaissance theory than a collusive and unholy alliance of one enemy of conventional decorum with another. Katherine's ringing defence of meekness and submissiveness in woman is not faltering enough by half, is altogether too flamboyant, in fact, for its senti-ments not to give rise to some suspicion of conscious parody; especially when one remembers that the thicker she lays it on the more she triumphs over a sister at whose hands she has doubtless endured much, and even more so when one recalls the immediate grounds she has for appropriating these conventional sentiments as a convenient means of expressing self-approval of a type wholly foreign to their overt content: after all, as a direct result of her new-found willingness to engage in parodically operatic flights of submission the Katherine–Petruchio gang has just taken the table, as it were, for twenty crowns and Bianca's reputation, not to mention the further twenty thousand which has just been added to the original wager by the marvelling Baptista. Has Katherine seen the light she preaches, or has she just decided that Petruchio's apparent nonsense and clowning, daft and excessive as it may seem to more conventional souls, may be trusted in general to conceal some sound calculation which will not leave her own interests out of account? And how far does that thought itself have the seeds of love and trust as well as calculation in it? Are they not, after all, two of a kind? In any event the magical zone from within which Katherine and Petruchio confront their dumbfounded fellow feasters does seem to have something that one might want to call radiance about it: the radiance of an Elsewhere very remote from those conventional moral pieties about submission and paternal rule in whose breakdown into recrimination, loss and disorder the other characters stand at this point enmeshed.

The possibilities which the play explores, that is, can equally well be seen as undermining a paternalist conception of how the world divides up exhaustively into possibilities – either the copy-book proprieties of paternal rule or else shrewish incivility and domestic disorder – which complements and confronts the feminist construal of the possible options I mentioned earlier. Of course the second half of what I have just said about the play might be taken as a way of 'recuperating' it, as people say, for feminism, just as the first half might be taken as a way of recuperating it for paternalism. The point is, though, that a feminism or a paternalism capable of accepting these as recuperations would have had to have moved a little from earlier and cruder stances.

My thought is, in effect, that the text – the carnal text – stays where it is, unmoving, while readers turn it about, or turn about it, each trying to subdue it to his or her way of looking at things, and each finding in it a meaning which is 'new', and specific to that particular reader, only in the sense that it expresses the commerce of the unmoving carnal text with the special set of fore-understandings which he or she has addressed to it. This, as Gabriel Josipovici pointed out to me, is rather reminiscent of a verse in the *Pirkhe Avot (Sayings of the Fathers)* 5:25: 'Turn it and turn it again, for everything is in it.' But this again suggests a different understanding from Kermode's of the point of Midrash in general: not to impose closure on the text in the interests of the particular type of coherence required by some set of institutional requirements, but to leave it, precisely, stonily and carnally open in order to leave it its power to astonish and confute: to see what it will illuminate next. I have a suspicion that some deep division between Jewish and (at least some kinds of) Christian religious sensibility may lie at the root of these two ways of looking at the business of interpretation.[7]

This brings me to my conclusion, and for one last time to Nietzsche's enthusiasm for 'perspective and illusion'. In my role as self-appointed Outsider I have been content to remain brooding upon the surface of Shakespeare's text. In accordance with Keats's excellent advice to avoid irritable grasping after fact and certainty I have foregone any attempt to grope beneath that surface for a paraphrasable 'meaning' or 'message'. All I have done is to examine in some detail (though for reasons of space not all that much) some of the obstacles which the text, as it presents itself on the most superficial level to any callow Outsider with a seat in the pit but without a hermeneutic key to bless himself with, sets in the path of attempts to equip it with a 'message', either a paternalist or a feminist one. And I have tried to show that such a purely negative, purely on-the-surface enterprise, besides giving the play, and ourselves, room to breathe, permits us to enter into a relationship with the play which allows it to criticize us, to elicit from us some saving modesty before it; some sense that the fore-understandings in terms of which we endeavour to shape it to our liking might themselves come to appear defective under a light – a radiance if you like – which it has power to shed upon them. Such knowledge as narrative fictions can grant us, knowledge of the incapacity of our fore-understandings to exhaust, as they claim to do, the possibilities of things, may not as I said earlier feel much like knowledge, but is knowledge all the same.

Now for a parting glance at Nietzsche. Half the time Nietzsche talks as if he has dispensed with the notion of truth; it is a 'mobile army of metaphors', and so on. The other half he displays a touching faith in the continued availability of the familiar concept of truth as correspondence between what is asserted and what is the case. The reason, I think, is this. Nietzsche wants to say that no human theory, or vision of how things stand in general, comes with a transcendent guarantee. The cheerfulness, in such contrast to Kermode's pre-vailing mood of disappointment, with which Nietzsche embraces 'the necessity of error' comes of course from that thought: no transcendent reality constrains us; we are free, we can create. But Nietzsche also wants to say that the construction of any habitable human order involves *work*, and work of a more than merely practical and physical kind: that the exercise of the Will to Power is not *effortless* because arbitrary, in the way it would be if the choice of a set of values and social arrangements were simply insulated in principle from all contact with reality. There is a kind of sadness, from which the eighteenth century suffered a good deal, which comes from too strong a conviction that the world is transparent to reduc-tive reason; that nothing can stop the spade of theory from exposing the roots of both human and natural reality. And there is another, contrary kind, which comes from the suspicion, nourished by phil-osophical scepticism and relativism, that we can make *just anything we like* of reality, that as creators of the human order we operate in a vacuum. One of the enduring merits of Nietzsche, as in related ways of Keats and Blake, is that he offers, patchily but on the whole effectively, defences against both these ways of depressing art and ourselves. One of the worrying things about a good deal of current critical theory is that it seems at times anxious to reanimate both of them at once. But then, one of the things that gives such philosophical bugbears their perennial power is that they can easily appear to be entailed by very much more interesting and substantial lines of thought from which, in fact, they do not necessarily follow at all.

Chapter 10
The Truth about Metaphor

Gottlob Frege introduced into philosophy two doctrines whose subsequent influence, on analytic philosophers at least, has been momentous. One is the doctrine that to understand a sentence is to know how to set about establishing the truth-value of an assertion couched in those words. The other is the doctrine that a word has meaning only in the context of a sentence.

These doctrines make it hard to understand metaphor. They create difficulties, especially, for any theory of metaphor which assumes the intelligibility of talk about two *kinds* of *meaning*, literal and metaphorical. Frege's doctrines allow only one kind of meaning: one connected essentially with the issue of truth and falsity. But it is only when we take them literally that metaphorical sentences acquire a truth value: usually false.

Two obvious suggestions offer ways of getting around this. The first is the suggestion that metaphors are condensed or disguised *similes*: true or (sometimes) false statements about similarity. The second is the suggestion that a term used in a metaphorical context just has a different *literal* meaning from the one it has in a sentence intended to be taken literally.

Neither is very plausible. The first reduces a metaphorical comparison, 'Man is a wolf', to a literal statement of similarity, 'Men are like wolves'. But what similarity, exactly, is the statement supposed to be asserting? Perhaps that men prey upon one another, as wolves are supposed to do. But then 'prey' can only be meant metaphorically, at which point the puzzle revives. As Goodman says of the attempt to find a simile in the metaphorical assertion that a picture is sad, 'What the simile says in effect is that person and picture are alike in being sad, the one literally and the other metaphorically. Instead of

261

metaphor reducing to simile, simile reduces to metaphor; or rather, the difference between simile and metaphor is negligible.'[1]

An equally fatal objection to the second suggestion is that it is only if we take the terms which compose a metaphor in their plain everyday senses that they compose a metaphor. As R. M. J. Dammann puts it, 'If God is a rock in a different sense from that in which Gibraltar is one, then both are really, literally, rocks, just as what one buys in a sweetshop is rock, though a dissatisfied customer might call it such metaphorically.'[2] It cannot, in other words, be *literally* true that the process of understanding a metaphor involves changing the sense of its constituent expressions, otherwise metaphor would evaporate in the reader's grasp into literality.

What this suggests is that what makes a sentence metaphorical is not any change in the meaning of its constituent expressions, but the way in which those expressions, with their plain everyday meanings, are combined in the sentence. What we need, perhaps, if we are to begin to understand metaphor, is not a theory of metaphorical *meaning*, but an account of what it is to *assert* metaphorically: an account, that is, which would operate at the level of the sentence rather than at that of the word. But this returns us to Frege's two doctrines. If the meaning of a word is to be *wholly* identified with the contribution it makes to the determination of a truth-value for each sentence in which it occurs, then it is difficult to see how the constituents of a sentence could determine anything other than a plain, literal meaning for the sentence as a whole.

What I shall try to show in this essay is that this difficulty can be overcome: that we can give a satisfactory account of the semantic mechanisms of metaphor without giving up either of Frege's doctrines. As Frege thought, understanding a sentence *is* knowing how to set about establishing the truth or falsity of assertions couched in those words. But to say what, exactly, someone knows in knowing that demands, I shall argue, a more complicated story than Fregeans have supposed.

I

First, though, I want to consider a more radical strategy than mine for squaring Frege's doctrines with our experience of metaphor, proposed by Donald Davidson.[3] Davidson holds with Frege that the notion of meaning is wholly explicable in terms of the notion of truth, but draws from this premiss the conclusion that metaphor has nothing to do with meaning. 'The concept of metaphor as primarily a vehicle for conveying ideas, even if unusual ones, seems to me as wrong as the parent idea that a metaphor has a special meaning' (p. 32).

Locke would have agreed with this, because Locke thought the functions of metaphor were decorative, forensic, or emotive – never cognitive. Davidson, however, is not here of one mind with Locke. Metaphors do yield cognitions of a sort, 'prompt insights': so much can be conceded to 'interactionist' theories of metaphor of the sort advanced by Max Black. It is just that the kind of cognition involved is in no way related to meaning. Metaphor is related to 'what it makes us see' rather as a physical event is related to 'what it makes us see'. 'Joke or dream or metaphor can, like a picture or a bump on the head, make us appreciate some fact – but not by standing for; or expressing, the fact' (p. 46). It follows, plausibly, that what a metaphor makes us see is not determinate in extent and may not all be formulable in words. 'How many facts or propositions are conveyed by a photograph? None, an infinity, or one great unstateable fact? Bad question. A picture is not worth a thousand words, or any other number. Words are the wrong currency to exchange for a picture' (p. 47).

Less plausibly, it follows that metaphor is not, strictly speaking, a form of communication between writer and reader: metaphors do not '*convey* ideas' [my italics].

> The central error about metaphor is most easily attacked when it takes the form of a theory of metaphorical meaning, but behind that theory, and statable independently, is the thesis that associated with a metaphor is a definite cognitive content that its author wishes to convey and that the interpreter must grasp if he is to get the message. This theory is false as a full account of metaphor, whether or not we call the purported content a meaning. (p. 46)

There is something not quite right about this. What is fishy is not what the passage asserts, which is unexceptionable, but what it presupposes. Nobody – or not many – would seriously want to contend that a metaphor conveys a 'cognitive content', if by that is meant a paraphrasable 'message' of some sort. But aren't there kinds of verbal communication which, while intimately dependent on meaning, do not involve the transmission of a 'cognitive content' in that sense?

Take jokes. Jokes *have a point*. The notion of a joke's having a point invokes a corresponding notion of relevance. We see the point of a joke only if we see what is relevant to its point and why. Not all of what gets said in telling a joke is relevant to its point. Some of it is mere scene-setting, and one way of being tedious is to resist all attempts to explain the point of a joke by fixing on some bit of incidental scene-setting and demanding, impossibly, that it be shown how *that* is relevant to the point.

The mere fact, now, that some things are relevant and some not to understanding a joke suffices to give sense to a correlative concept of communication. If I tell a joke badly I fail to *communicate* to you the point of the joke. Notice, however, that this is a sense of 'communicate' which is not susceptible of Derridean deconstruction. Derrideans, unlike Davidsonians, doubt whether communication by means of language ever involves the transmission of 'a cognitive content which the author wishes to convey' and that the 'interpreter must grasp if he is to get the message'. Their claim is that understanding neither does nor can pass beyond the text itself to a reconstruction of the intentions or cognitive states of its author, and that any theory which claims otherwise must 'deconstruct' itself because in order to get itself formulated it must itself use language in ways which conflict with the thesis it is attempting to formulate. Jokes conform to the Derridean model in this sense, that the point of a joke is not something that the teller of the joke can intend, or fail to intend, to communicate. The point is inherent in the text of the joke, and the interpreter, in grasping the point, never has to refer beyond the text to the intentions or cognitive states of the teller. The whole transaction remains on the plane of 'textuality'. For all that, however, it makes perfect sense, for the reasons offered above, to speak of communicating or failing to communicate, the point of a joke. And, equally clearly, grasping the point of a joke depends upon first grasping the meanings of the words employed in telling it.

What about the other components of Davidson's string of putatively analogous cases: dreams, photographs, and bumps on the head? Here, where Davidson needs analogies, there are important disanalogies.

We can indeed be led by a bump on the head to 'appreciate some fact', but the fact in question will vary with the context and the head, and can be anything you please; whereas what we 'see' in the case of a joke is its point, which cannot be just anything you please, but is the same for everyone who understands the joke.

Dreams, according to Freudians and Jungians, have a point; but the point is in each case matter of dispute. Some of us may find one or another interpretation of a dream convincing, but none of us ever finds it uncontroversially evident, in the way that the point of a joke is, more often than not, uncontroversially evident.

Again, to say that a photograph has a point is just to say that it has a purpose. To know what that is one has to refer beyond the photograph itself, to a text which it illustrates, a bit of personal experience which it records or a scientific enquiry which it subserves. The point of a joke, on the other hand, is an effect of language; as Derrida would say, an effect of *différance*: to grasp it we have no need to look beyond the text of the joke as told to the intentions or purposes of the teller.

We have, then, a substantial set of disanalogies between jokes on the one hand and dreams, photographs, and bumps on the head on the other. It terms of these disanalogies metaphors pretty clearly belong with jokes. Metaphors have point in the way that jokes do. Not everything counts as relevant to the point of a metaphor. Reading the opening lines of Sonnet LXXIII,

> That time of year thou mayst in me behold
> When yellow leaves, or none, or few, do hang
> Upon those boughs which shake against the cold,
> Bare ruin'd choirs where late the sweet birds sang . . .

might 'prompt the insight' that fan vaulting and deciduous trees resemble one another in the way their structure distributes stress. But this has nothing at all to do with the point of the metaphor, which is to forge connections, of what kind I shall discuss in a moment, between maturity and old age, summer and winter, poetry and the drought of poetry.

Again, to see that this *is* the point of the metaphor, we do not need to know that that is what Shakespeare intended the point to be, any more than to see the point of a joke we need to entertain hypotheses about the teller's intentions in telling it. The point of the metaphor, like that of the joke, is in some sense which we have yet to unravel 'there in the text'. And there is a sense in which the point is the same for every reader, that sense being that whatever Derridean 'supplement' of meaning a reader may draw from the potentialities of the text, there remains a distinction between developing the potentialities which the text offers to interpretation and simply reading into the text the content of some arbitrary private brainwave, such as the 'insight' about stress in fan vaulting and deciduous trees.

What then about the relationship between metaphor and meaning? Davidson's suggestion goes something like this: a metaphorical statement expresses a factual assertion, usually false. But the assertion in question, though false, has the interesting property of suggesting all sorts of thoughts and insights, even though none of these are actually *meant* (expressed) by the metaphorical sentence.

If what we have said is correct, this makes the connection between metaphor and meaning altogether too tenuous. The point of a metaphor is not just any thought which it may suggest to an individual reader: it is 'there to be seen', as the point of a joke is 'there to be seen' by any reader or hearer.

In either case, therefore, someone who sees the point must be applying to the joke or the metaphor some more or less standard procedure of interpretation (what Derrida would call an 'organon of iterability')[4] which supplies the necessary constraints on relevance, and which must at some point engage with the meanings of the words in which the joke or metaphor is framed, because there is simply nothing else on which interpretation could go to work.

I conclude that Davidson is wrong about the relationship of metaphor to meaning, and that it is also a mistake to think that nothing is communicated by a metaphorical sentence. What is communicated is its point.

On the other hand I agree with Davidson that what is communicated is not a 'cognitive content', if by that is meant something which could be given complete expression in a proposition. And I agree with him on a more fundamental matter: his remark that 'as much of metaphor as can be explained in terms of meaning may, and indeed must, be explained by appeal to the literal meanings of words' (p. 41).

This, though, brings us back once more to Frege, who thought that the literal meaning of words consisted wholly in their power to direct the determination of the truth-values of sentences. If Frege was right, and words have meaning *solely* in relation to the determination of truth and falsity, then, it seems, *meaning* could not be the source, or even one source, of the constraints on relevance which, seemingly, have to be supposed to govern the interpretation of metaphor. For in the interpretation of metaphor truth and falsity are not at issue. That is why Davidson's account of metaphor, which simply takes it for granted that no such constraints operate, is so penetrating and so seductive.

Nevertheless, as I said earlier, I think that a way can be found to concede Frege's doctrine without conceding the more counter-intuitive parts of Davidson's. I will now try to say what that way is, and in the process to sketch the sentence-level, rather than word-level, account of the semantic mechanisms of metaphor promised earlier.

II

Frege held that to understand a sentence is to be in a position to determine its truth-value, or to be precise, the truth-value of the corresponding assertion. Many more recent writers who take themselves to be saying the same thing put it this way: to know the meaning of a sentence is to know its truth-conditions.

I want to suggest that this is not just a piece of harmless shorthand, but one which involves a serious misrepresentation of the content of Frege's insight. The trouble is that the term 'truth-condition' can mean either of two quite different kinds of thing, but is almost invariably taken to mean only one of the two.

The ambiguity is not difficult to see, if we consider what is actually involved in knowing how to determine the truth-value of an assertion. Take, for example, 'There is a ruin', asserted of some object or other, call it O.

To assess whether 'There is a ruin' is truly or falsely asserted of O, I shall need, certainly, to be able to *recognize* whether O possesses the *characteristic features* of a ruin. And it seems clear that I could be taught to do this simply by being shown some ruins and taught to discriminate them from other superficially similar sorts of thing. I might, for instance, learn to discriminate the grassy mound which remains of a deserted croft from cairns and other kinds of stone heap by looking for a roughly rectangular shape and the foundations of the chimney.

But now, suppose I am quite ignorant of the English language (and perhaps a little stupid). What is to stop me from thinking that 'ruin' is just a word (perhaps a Gaelic one) for a particular kind of stone heap? Notice that the realization that the kind of heap in question originates in a house would not necessarily prevent me from thinking this. For I might think that 'ruin' is the name for a particular configuration of stones left by that kind of house, as 'dolmen' is the name for the most durable portion (the main burial chamber, consisting of capstone and uprights) of a passage grave, which also possesses certain easily recognizable characteristic features.

Thinking that, I am in the following position. I can assess the truth or falsity of some kinds of assertion made by means of the sentence 'This is a ruin'. To put it another way, I know some of the truth-conditions of 'This is a ruin' where 'truth-condition' is taken to mean something like 'criterion of recognition'. But I do not yet grasp the *meaning* that attaches to 'ruin' in English. If a fellow foreigner (whose English may be better than mine) says of Fountains Abbey 'There is a ruin', then, because the ruins of Fountains Abbey do not exhibit the characteristic features of the kind of object I have been taught to count as a ruin, I shall have no choice but to take him either to be speaking falsely or to be talking nonsense.

What do I need to be taught, if I am to acquire the capacity to extend the application of 'ruin' from the remains of eighteenth-century crofts to the other kinds of object to which the term applies in everyday English?

It might look as if what I need is simply to be taught the characteristic features of those other kinds of ruin. But this suggestion will not do, for two connected reasons. The first is that there is no clear limit to the forms that ruins can take, and thus no clear limit to the sets of characteristic features which may come to be taken as warranting the assertion 'There is a ruin'.

The second is that if my grasp of the meaning of 'ruin' rests simply on a finite list of sets of characteristic features, then I shall not be able to extend the application of the term beyond the limits of that list, *except* by dint of linguistic stipulation. But clearly not every extension of the application of a term by competent speakers rests on linguistic stipulation. As Putnam[5] and others have insisted, there can be discoveries about the applications of terms. Thus, for instance, the archaeologists who first discovered the relationship of dolmens to intact passage graves *discovered thereby* that dolmens are a kind of ruin. The discovery of the relationship of dolmens to passage graves brought about, in other words, an extension of the list of sets of characteristic features warranting the assertion 'There is a ruin'. The characteristic features of dolmens now had to be added to the list. But no new linguistic stipulation was necessary to bring this about. It was a simple consequence of the discovery that dolmens are the remains of passage graves, though admittedly not a causal, but a linguistic consequence.

What I need to enable me to make comparable extensions of the application of terms (ones which will automatically match those made by other competent speakers, that is) is, then, not just more *criteria of recognition*: more sets of characteristic features of things, as it were, worthy-to-be-called-ruins. What I need is rather some principle regulating the admission of sets of characteristic features to the status of assertion-warranting considerations for the assertion 'There is a ruin'. Put another way, what I need is a principle which will tell me what is and is not relevant to the issue of whether or not something is a ruin. I need a *criterion of relevance*.[6]

Once we see that this is what is needed, it is not difficult to see what form it must take. I shall have hold of a suitable criterion of relevance as soon as I grasp that a ruin is the remains of a structure dilapidated beyond the point at which it can still be used to serve the purposes of the original structure. Call this CR.

At first CR might seem to be no more than a statement of some more properties of ruins, differing only in scope or generality from the statement that ruined crofts are roughly rectangular grass-covered heaps of stones with the foundations of a chimney at one end. And of course CR does state some properties of ruins. Where it differs from the statement about the characteristics of ruined crofts is in the way it functions with respect to the procedures of determining truth-values for assertions made by means of the sentence 'There is a ruin'. The statement about ruined crofts gives some criteria by which ruined crofts can be recognized (states a criterion of recognition). CR by contrast does not say how any kind of ruin is to be *recognized*. It says what a ruin *is*. It does that by offering a criterion of relevance by appeal to which we can establish, for instance, the relevance to the issue of ruinhood of the features mentioned in the statement about ruined crofts. They are relevant because they are causally connected with properties characteristic of intact crofts, and because such features do not, in fact, come into being by any means other than the dilapidation across time of such a structure.

Once I know that ruins are structures so dilapidated as to be no longer usable for their original purposes, I can see why Fountains Abbey and a dolmen are just as properly called 'ruins' as the remains of crofts on which I first cut this particular linguistic tooth. I have a principle which enables me to extend the application of the term, without benefit of new linguistic stipulation, in ways which match, unsurprisingly, the extensions made by other competent speakers armed with the same principle of relevance.

No doubt, as Frege said, understanding the meaning of a sentence is knowing how to determine its truth-value. But the process by which we pass from a sentence to a truth-value turns out to be more complex than is customarily supposed, requiring access to criteria of two quite different kinds: criteria of recognition and criteria of relevance.

Should we, then, conclude that knowledge of meaning requires knowledge of both kinds of criteria? The answer is no, for the following reasons. Any account of what is learned in learning a language must meet the following conditions of adequacy: (1) What is represented as learned must be in principle finite. (2) What is represented as learned must be stipulative in character. I shall offer no argument for these conditions here, except to observe that they are commonplaces of theoretical linguistics.

It is to be noted, now, that criteria of recognition meet neither condition. On the one hand the list of features which can serve as diagnostic of a ruin is not in principle finite (for example, something as recondite as a crop mark seen from a helicopter can on occasion serve to warrant the assertion 'There is a ruin'). And on the other hand the issue of what is and what is not a characteristic feature of ruins is not, in principle, the kind of issue that can be settled by linguistic stipulation. It happens to be the case that the characteristic features of dolmens are characteristic features of a type of ruin. But that this is so is not a consequence of the existence of a linguistic stipulation to that effect, but a consequence of its happening to be the case, as a contingent matter of fact, that dolmens are the remains of passage graves.

On the other hand, criteria of relevance meet both conditions. Firstly, such a criterion is in principle finite. To know that ruins are the remains of structures dilapidated beyond the possibility of serving their original purposes is to know all there is to know, linguistically speaking, about what a ruin is. Armed with that knowledge, a speaker is in a position to set about finding out for himself what the characteristic features of ruins happen, empirically speaking, to be. The class of criteria of recognition which he will arrive at in that way need not be, in principle, a finite class. But that fact has no tendency to make the criterion by which he determines membership of that class any the less a finite criterion.

Secondly, the content of a criterion of relevance is clearly going to depend entirely on linguistic stipulation. If English speakers were to begin using the term 'ruin' to pick out, say, a structure to any degree dilapidated, then the relevance criterion governing the use of the term would have changed, and changed by mere stipulation.

I conclude that, since meanings are presumably part of what is learned in learning a language, knowledge of meanings amounts simply to knowledge of criteria of relevance.

This implies that we can distinguish a speaker's linguistic knowledge from the general body of empirical knowledge in his possession and so is at odds with Quine's thesis that the two are in principle inextricable. The inextricability thesis, however, depends via Quine's notion of an 'analytical hypothesis' on the assumption that we can only set about disentangling linguistic from empirical knowledge if we have already managed somehow to make sense of the notion of analyticity, considered as a species of necessary truth.[7]

It is thus sufficient to evade Quine's strictures about inextricability to remark that the way of disentangling linguistic from general knowledge proposed here does not in any way require us to make sense of the notion of analyticity. A criterion of relevance, such as the statement that a ruin is a structure dilapidated beyond the possibility of serving its original purpose, is not an analytic truth, because it is not a necessary truth. It simply records the entirely contingent and empirical fact that speakers of English use a certain criterion for determining what is and what is not relevant to the application of a certain term.

Back now to Frege. Frege held that a term has both a reference (*Bedeutung*) and a sense (*Sinn*), and that the sense is what picks out the reference, or to put it another way, determines the extension of the class of things to which the term applies.

Philosophers since Russell have taken it for granted that a Fregean sense is a description. But, lacking access to the distinction between the sort of description which serves as a criterion of recognition and the sort which serves as a criterion of relevance, they have assumed that the description in question is one which states the criteria by which we are to *recognize* something as falling within the extension of the term. Thus, the Fregean sense of 'ruins' would be some set of instructions for recognizing ruins.

Now plainly, if that is what a meaning (a sense) is, then to understand the meaning of words is simply to possess a great deal of homespun knowledge about what things – real, commonplace things – are like. On such a view, meaning is Gradgrind's province, not the poet's: a sort of plain man's Encyclopaedia of the Obvious. It is easy to see what, on such a view, the connection is between meaning, so conceived, and the literalities of Lockeian plain speech, but hard indeed to see what bearing meaning could have on metaphor.

The above arguments suggest that a Fregean sense is better regarded as a criterion of relevance. I am not of course suggesting that there is the slightest textual warrant for such an interpretation in Frege. What I am saying is that if 'sense' is regarded, in accordance with Frege's use of the word, as what picks out the extension of a name or the truth-value of an assertion, then a sense cannot be a criterion of recognition. It has to be a criterion of relevance.

This makes the determination of truth and falsity in principle a two-stage process. First there is the application of the criterion of relevance to select a criterion of recognition appropriate to a particular context, then there is the application of the criterion of recognition to assess the truth or falsity of a given assertion with respect to that context. Only the first stage involves the application of linguistic knowledge – knowledge 'of the language': of *meaning*.

Now, suppose there is no question of determining the truth or falsity of an assertion because, taken literally, it is either evidently false or evidently absurd. In that case there is no point in proceeding to the second stage of truth-determination. If meanings were just recognitional capacities, then to withdraw from stage two truth-determination would be to set aside any interest in meaning *per se*, since there would be no other purpose which a grasp of meaning could be made to serve. But meanings are not just recognitional capacities, so withdrawal from stage two truth-determination still leaves us with the principles of relevance (the only principles deserving the title of *meanings*, in fact) which direct stage one.

In most cases a criterion of relevance will possess internal complexity: it will exhibit a schematic structure of some sort. There thus exists the possibility of interpreting a piece of text in a way which does not raise the issue of truth or falsity, by systematically mapping the subject-matter of the text on to the structural framework provided by one or more of the criteria of relevance associated with the words of the text.

Not all, but much, of what we think of as metaphor involves the operation of this kind of semantic mechanism. I shall try to show in the next section how it works in a specific case. But if this is, or is often, what is involved in interpreting metaphor, then we shall have fulfilled two promises made earlier. We shall have shown metaphor to be a phenomenon which operates not at word-level, but at the level of the interpretation of whole utterances, including sentences, and one which does not involve any change in the meanings of individual words. And since, if the account is correct, one and the same set of criteria direct *both* the determination of literal truth and falsity *and* the interpretation of metaphor, we shall also have managed to preserve Davidson's plausible demand that, to the extent that metaphor is explicable in terms of meanings, it must be explicable in terms of the plain, literal meanings of words.

III

Let us return to lines 1−4 of Sonnet LXXIII. 'Ruin'd' is the key word of line 4, and the nub of the metaphor contained in the line. It refers back to the boughs of line 3, which it characterizes as 'bare ruin'd choirs'. What are we to make of the invitation to think of bare trees as ruins? Nothing, evidently, if we take the invitation literally. It is simply false that bare trees are or could be ruins. There is an older sense of 'ruin'd', accessible to Shakespeare and still active in Milton, to whose latinizing tendencies it was congenial, in which 'ruin'd' means 'fallen'. But that gets us no further: the boughs are bare, but hardly fallen, ones.

As long as we look in the lines for a true assertion, then, interpretation is blocked. But suppose we put the issue of truth and falsity on one side. We are still left with the meanings of the words, in the sense of the criteria of relevance governing their application.

We can represent the criterion of relevance which governs the application of 'ruin' roughly as follows:

construction — process	structure designed to satisfy some purpose P	dilapidation — process	residue no longer capable of satisfying P

'ruin'

Since the text balks any attempt to apply this schema to the determination of a truth-value, we move to another level of interpretation: we ask whether there is any way in which the subject-matter of the lines can be ordered analogically by reference to the schema.

To begin with, if the bare boughs of lines 3–4 are to be seen, in the terms offered by the above schema, as structurally analogous to ruins, there must be something which the reader can take as analogous to the process of dilapidation which produces the 'ruin'd' state (bareness) of the boughs. Such a process is ready to hand in the fall of the leaves, which is also invoked in line 4 by the older sense of the term 'ruin' mentioned earlier, in which it is an intransitive verb meaning 'fall'.

But introducing the fall of the leaves in this way locates it, not as a mere natural process of change, but as something which subverts and renders houseless some purposive order, which like the order of a household depends for its existence on the continued integrity of some physical fabric.

The word 'choirs', which carries the second metaphor of line 4, makes clear the nature of the purposive order in question. It is the order of sung offices which constitute the life of a cathedral or abbey, and are the purpose for which the building was erected. So we are to see the order of life in the summer words (the order which has been unhoused and rendered homeless by the falling of the leaves: the 'ruining' of the boughs) as analogous to the life of a religious building: the order of sung offices. Finally, on to this elaborate but quite determinate structure of analogies the poem maps the stages of a man's life, from prime (summer, the woods in full leaf, the order and ceremony of nature, conceived as analogous to the Christian ceremonial order, in full swing) to failing strength and approaching age, or perhaps loss of powers[8] (autumn, the leaves fallen, the birds fled, the choristers gone from a deserted and decayed church).

So much for the semantic machinery governing the interpretation of the lines as metaphor. However, the point of the lines, I take it, is not merely to give the reader the opportunity to solve this little hermeneutical puzzle. Their point is to restructure the reader's feelings by opening, between commonplace words, channels of analogy through which feelings attached to one set of words and what they mean may flow and embrace other words, and what *they* mean. The effect of the whole nest of interlocking analogies is to open a passage for a certain way of feeling about ageing or loss of powers.

One powerful tradition of feeling sees the prime of life as an essentially flawed and sin-ridden mode of existence of which we are well rid in death, provided we have lived a Christian life. Sonnet LXXIII works against this. By presenting age and failing powers in terms of the analogy between bare boughs and deserted choirs it confers in retrospect upon the prime of human life and upon the natural order of the summer woods something of the spiritual authority associated with the Christian ceremonial order. It invites us to feel about the prime of life somewhat as we feel about the order of a cathedral: to feel towards it as towards something having that kind of richness, strength, and seriousness. The poem, ostensibly about death, is also about life.

Notice that there is in all this no question of the terms 'bare', 'boughs', or 'ruin'd' taking on new, 'metaphorical' senses distinct from the common everyday ones. On the contrary, it is precisely the reader's understanding of those commonplace senses which sustain his understanding of the metaphor.

At the same time something, a certain response to ageing and failure of powers, is communicated by the poem. So in a sense we can speak of the process of coming to understand the poem as having a cognitive aspect. The outcome of it is that we become acquainted with a certain structure of feeling; and acquaintance is surely a cognitive relationship. On the other hand, the process of becoming acquainted with that structure of feeling is not a matter of assimilating a propositional content. It just *is* the process of analogical restructuring, with the accompanying redirection of emotional responses, which we have just described. The nature of that process can, in a phrase of Davidson's, be 'brought out by using further words' – we have just done so – but the style of criticism which that enterprise yields is a purely explicatory, inherently non-reductive one. The 'further words' in question function not as a paraphrase, but in a way analogous to an explanation of the point of a joke. No words other than the actual words of the poem could paraphrase the poem, could express 'what it is the poem makes us see', because the process of analogical restructuring involved in 'seeing' that depends essentially upon access to the criteria of relevance which attach to just those words, and on relating them to one another in an order determined by the precise order in which those words stand on the page.

IV

Hugh Bredin has recently proposed the following way of drawing the distinction between metaphor and metonymy:

> A metaphor is understood by virtue of its own semantic structure; if it asserts a similarity between things . . . this is something that may strike us for the first time, but which is none the less intelligible for that. But if I use the metonymic 'crown' or 'sceptre' for the institution of monarchy, the auditor must *already know* of the close connection between those objects and the institution. If he does not, he will fail to understand. Metaphor *creates* a knowledge of the relation between its objects; metonymy *presupposes* that knowledge.[9]

It is important to notice that the distinction drawn in this way is not a distinction between two senses of the notion *understanding a text*, or between two textual devices. Metonymy so defined is not a *textual* device at all, since our understanding of a metonym does not originate in the text, but in a piece of adventitious extra-textual knowledge.

At paragraph 4.026 of the *Tractatus Logico-Philosophicus* Wittgenstein remarks, 'The meanings of simple signs (words) must be explained to us if we are to understand them. With propositions, however, we make ourselves understood.' A profound point is at stake here, not just about the recursive character of the relationship between understanding a sentence and understanding its constituents, but about what it is to find oneself addressing a written text and *reading* what is written there. The point is that we are not *reading* if the purport of what is written has to be explained to us if we are to understand it. Nor, in such a case, does the writing in question constitute a *text*; for *ex hypothesi* there is no way in which an understanding of its meaning can be derived from the meanings of its constituent signs. That being so, we are free to ascribe to it any meaning we choose, as in the case of an invented word (a new 'simple sign'); but a string of marks which we are free to interpret in any way we choose is not a *text*, but only a string of marks.

If *reading*, engagement with a *text*, is to occur at any level of interest to literary criticism, then it seems that there must be some rhetorical devices for which understanding depends merely upon the reader's knowledge of the language in which the text is written, and

not upon knowledge of adventitious associations of which he may or
may not happen to be aware. It would be nice if we could show that
metaphor is such a device; and that is, roughly speaking, the task I
have set myself in this essay.

Max Black's interesting and influential theory of metaphor fails,
in my opinion, to engage with this aspect of the problem.[10] I
agree with Black, and for that matter Goodman, that metaphor
involves the perception of structural analogy. But Black identifies
the analogically interacting structures as 'the systems of commonplaces' associated with metaphorically active terms. An 'associated
commonplace' is just that: a bit of general knowledge which is
associated with the word, either because of a relationship of natural
causality or because of an habitual pattern of usage (like the habitual
use of the phrase 'the Crown' to refer to the institution of monarchy),
but which is in no way essential to the meaning of the term. The
patterns of *incompatibility* set up between such 'systems of commonplaces' can, as Black suggests, lead us to focus on some subset of one
or other set of connotations, but what we focus on in such a case
cannot, in the nature of things, ever be something we didn't *know
already*. The difference between metaphor and metonymy remains
unaccounted for; and it comes as no surprise to find not merely
Black's critic Paul Ricoeur, but Black himself, locating this as a
difficulty for the theory. As Ricoeur puts it, 'The major difficulty
(which, by the way, Black himself recognizes . . .) is that to return to
a system of associated commonplaces is to address oneself to connotations that are already established. In one stroke, the explication
is limited to trivial metaphors.'[11]

My object in this chapter has been to remove this difficulty. If the
structures which metaphor analogically reinterprets are not structures *of associations*, then what is revealed by reinterpreting them
will not necessarily be a 'commonplace': something already known
to us. On my account grasping the meaning of a term is not a matter
of knowing its familiar associations, but of grasping a rule for
determining what is and what is not relevant to its application. So
when we analogically reinterpret the internal structure of such a rule,
as we do in reading Sonnet LXXIII, what we get is something new: a
set of entirely *un*familiar associations between one set of things and
another. Coleridge is vindicated: there *is* a difference between the
mechanical operations of 'fancy', which receives 'all its materials
ready made from the law of association', and the workings of the
imagination, which 'dissolves . . . in order to re-create' (*Biographia
Literaria*, ch. 13).

Those who defend Coleridge, it is often supposed, must turn their backs on Derrida. On the contrary, it seems to me, one could hardly find a better instance of Derridean *dissémination* than the operation of the word 'ruin'd' in Sonnet LXXIII, or for that matter, in Owen Barfield's study of the history of the word in *Poetic Diction*.[12] Who would have thought the word 'ruin'd' had it in it? What could show better the power of a purely textual device to lead the mind away from all the customary associations of a word, into a new structure of contrast and collusion, of *différance*? English-speaking 'deconstructionist' literary critics often seem inclined to take Derrida not as proclaiming the priority of the text over what Husserl called the 'living present of consciousness', but as proclaiming the unlimited power of interpretation over the text. Thus Paul de Man takes the contrast between metaphor and metonymy (rightly) to be a contrast between necessity and chance, and comes down on the side of metonymy and chance, arguing that what we take to be metaphor is (often? always?) merely disguised metonymy.[13]

The difficulty with this is the one we have just been exploring. To the extent that a putative interpretation attaches to the text merely through the operations of chance, it is not, after all, an *interpretation*. No denial of this is to be found in Derrida, not merely because his thesis in no way requires such a denial, but because such a denial would be strictly incompatible with his position. Derrida's most fundamental claim is that meaning resides not in consciousness but in the text. His central argument for that claim is that any text is *itérable*: readable in the absence, or after the death, of its author. To maintain that argument he needs to be able to deploy the notions of *text* and of *reading* in ways which would be fatally undercut, in the way suggested earlier, by the claim that interpretation is not governed by what Derrida calls an *organon of iterability*,[14] but is a subjective, or private, or arbitrary process.

Notes

Introduction

1. F. R. Leavis, *The Great Tradition* (New York, 1954), p. 156.
2. Thomas Nagel defends a closely related position in his essay 'What Is It Like to be a Bat?', in *Mortal Questions* (London and New York, 1979).
3. I am thinking here primarily of the way in which the thought that what we can know of the world is a function of our language, that being in turn a function of our existential situation, is developed, in quite different ways, in the work of Heidegger, or Merleau-Ponty, or the later Wittgenstein. But instances are legion. An interesting case of a philosopher finally driven, against the bent of his own mind, one would have said, to grant an irreducible multiplicity of cognitive perspectives (the thought in this case is that intentional descriptions of human actions are essentially irreducible to functional descriptions of brain-states) has been provided, for instance, by Hilary Putnam in his recent book *Representation and Reality* (Cambridge, Mass. and London, 1988); see esp. his ch. 7.
4. Nelson Goodman: *Ways of Worldmaking* (Hassocks, 1978); *Languages of Art* (Hassocks, 1981).
5. Paul Ricoeur: *Temps et Récit* (Paris, 1983–5); 'The Function of Fiction in Shaping Reality', *Man and World* 12, 123–41.
6. Peter J. McCormick, *Fictions, Philosophies and the Problems of Poetics* (Ithaca and London, 1988).
7. This seems to me to be roughly the position towards which Peter McCormick's highly complex and allusive argument in *Fictions, Philosophies and the Problems of Poetics* (n. 6) is moving.
8. Richard Rorty, *Consequences of Pragmatism* (Brighton, 1982), p. 153.
9. Rorty, 'Philosophy as a Kind of Writing', ibid., p. 109.
10. Rorty, 'Idealism and Textualism', ibid., p. 153.
11. Cf. Ludwig Wittgenstein, *On Certainty* (Oxford, 1969), p. 204; 'Giving grounds, however, justifying the evidence, comes to an end; – but the end is not certain propositions' striking us immediately as true, i.e. it is not a kind of seeing on our part; it is our acting, which lies at the bottom of the language-game.'
12. Stanley Cavell, *The Claim of Reason* (Oxford and New York, 1979), p. 177.

13.   Stanley Cavell, *Must We Mean What We Say?* (Cambridge, London and New York, 1969), p. 338.
14.   Ibid., p. 343.
15.   Martha Nussbaum, 'Fictions of the Soul', *Philosophy and Literature* 7 (1983), 156.
16.   Cavell, *Must We Mean . . .* , p. 257.
17.   Wendell V. Harris, critical discussion of Howard Felperin *et al.*, *Philosophy and Literature* 11, no. 2 (Oct 1987), 318.

Chapter 1: How to Reconcile Humanism and Deconstruction

1.   A. D. Nuttall, *A New Mimesis: Shakespeare and the Representation of Reality* (London and New York, 1983), p. 73.
2.   W. K. Wimsatt, 'The Concrete Universal', in W. K. Wimsatt and Monroe C. Beardsley, *The Verbal Icon: Studies in the Meaning of Poetry* (Lexington, Ky., 1954).
3.   This will seem less surprising if one reflects on the parallel between Wimsatt's thesis, if not his arguments for it, and Merleau-Ponty's reflections in *La Prose du monde* on the 'constitutive' role of language, entirely consistent as the latter turn out to be with what Derrida has to say about the dissemination of meanings within the text.
4.   Wimsatt, *Verbal Icon*, p. 77.
5.   Ibid., p. 83.
6.   Philip Thody, *Roland Barthes: A Conservative Estimate* (London and Chicago, 1977), p. 114.
7.   Gérard Genette, *Narrative Discourse*, tr. Jane E. Lewin (Oxford, 1980), p. 163.
8.   For an argument for the existence of links between the thought of Derrida, Quine and Davidson, see Samuel S. Wheeler III: 'The Extension of Deconstruction', *Monist* 69, 1, and 'Indeterminacy of French Interpretation: Derrida and Davidson', in *Truth and Interpretation: Perspectives on the Philosophy of Donald Davidson*, ed. Ernest Lepore (Oxford, 1986), pp. 477–94; Rorty, *Consequences of Pragmatism* (Introd., n. 8). For an excellent discussion of the relationship between Derrida's thought and that of Wittgenstein, see Henry Staten, *Wittgenstein and Derrida* (Lincoln, Nebr., 1984).
9.   Peter Steiner, *Russian Formalism: A Metapoetics* (Ithaca and London, 1984).
10.   This point was suggested to me in conversation by A. D. Nuttall. See also his 'Solvents and Fixatives: Critical Theory in Transition', *Modern Language Review* 82 (Apr 1987), 273–85.
11.   Cited in Steiner, *Russian Formalism*, p. 49.
12.   Frank Kermode, *The Sense of an Ending: Studies in the Theory of Fiction* (London, Oxford and New York, 1966), pp. 127–52.
13.   Ibid., pp. 128, 130, 134–5.
14.   Paul de Man, *The Resistance to Theory* (Manchester, 1986), p. 11.
15.   Paul de Man, 'Semiology and Rhetoric', in *Textual Strategies: Perspectives in Post-Structural Criticism.*, ed. Josué Harari (Ithaca, 1979), p. 131.
16.   Ferdinand de Saussure, *Cours de Linguistique Générale* (Paris, 1972), p. 100.
17.   Ibid., p. 110.
18.   Loc. cit.
19.   Jacques Derrida, 'Différance', in *La Voix et le phénomène* (Paris, 1967), tr. David B. Allison as *Speech and Phenomena, and other essays on Husserl's Theory of Signs* (Evanston, Ill., 1973), p. 139.

20.   Saussure, *Cours de Linguistique Générale*, pp. 163, 166.
21.   Derrida, 'Différance' (n. 19), p. 140.
22.   Saussure, *Cours*, p. 159.
23.   Ibid., p. 160.
24.   Ibid., pp. 160–1.
25.   A Saussure read according to the Strong Interpretation is a Saussure whose work supports radical philosophical relativism of the type propounded, for example, by Nelson Goodman in *Ways of Worldmaking* (Introd., n. 4). Though limitations of space and a decent respect for the patience of the reader make it impossible to argue the issue here, it seems to me that the weak linguistic perspectivism espoused in this book, which is consistent with the Weak Interpretation of Saussure, does not support radical relativism; but does have much in common with the 'Robust Relativism' proposed by Joseph Margolis in *Pragmatism Without Foundations* (Oxford, 1986). Robust Relativism, while allowing some cognitive claims to be assessed in terms of weaker truth-like predicates, allows room for truth in the full-blooded sense to be predicated on occasion of statements which purport to describe a world accessible in common to all speakers.
26.   Cf. J. Young, 'Rabbits', *Philosophical Studies* (1972), 170–85.
27.   Maurice Merleau-Ponty, *La Prose du monde* (Paris, 1969), tr. as *The Prose of the World* by Claude Lefort and John O'Neill (London, 1969), p. 115.
28.   Ibid., p. 14.
29.   Derrida, *La Voix et le phénomène*, p. 115.
30.   See also the discussion of what I call 'reconstitutive irony' in Chapter 3 of my *Fielding's* Tom Jones: *The Novelist as Moral Philosopher* (London, 1975).
31.   Lennard J, Davis, *Resisting Novels: Ideology and Fiction* (New York and London, 1987), p. 11.
32.   Ibid., pp. 20–1.
33.   De Man, *Resistance to Theory*, p. 11.
34.   Howard Felperin, *Beyond Deconstruction: The Uses and Abuses of Literary Theory* (Oxford, 1985), ch. 2 and *passim*.
35.   Cf. Davis, *Resisting Novels*, p. 38 *et seq.*
36.   Iris Murdoch offers a perceptive characterization of this type of voluntarism, which has its exemplars in both existentialist and analytic moral philosophy, in her *The Sovereignty of Good* (Cambridge and London, 1967).
37.   Genette, *Narrative Discourse*, p. 236.
38.   An edited text of Professor Butler's lecture, from which this extract is taken, appeared in *The Times* (London) for Wednesday, 11 Nov 1987.

Chapter 2: The Defence of Wit: Sterne, Locke and the Particular

1.   John Traugott, *Tristram Shandy's World* (New York, 1954), p. 7.
2.   Ibid.; Henri Fluchère, *Laurence Sterne: de l'homme à l'œuvre* (Paris, 1961), p. 503.
3.   Quoted by Traugott, *Tristram Shandy's World*, p. 9.
4.   A. D. Nuttall, *A Common Sky* (London, 1974), p. 83.
5.   Ibid., pp. 71–2.
6.   References to *Tristram Shandy* in the text are to the Penguin Classics edn., ed. Graham Petrie (London, 1967), by volume, chapter and page number.
7.   Nuttall, *A Common Sky*, pp. 87–8.
8.   James A. Swearingen, *Reflexivity in* Tristram Shandy (New York, 1977).
9.   Christopher Ricks, Introd., Penguin Classics *Tristram Shandy*, p. 14.

10. Nuttall, *A Common Sky*, p. 54.
11. A reader questioned whether this move does not emasculate deconstruction, since deferral, etc., is generally thought to survive contextualization. In one sense this must be right: contextualization of a text cannot affect its status as *text*. In another sense it must be wrong, since the processes of *différance, dissémination*, etc., are by their nature processes *of contextualization*. For subjects to appear to us, as Derrida says they do, as *effets de différance*, therefore, it must be possible for us to perceive such effects. The subjects we encounter in Sterne, like those we encounter in real life, no doubt *are* just *effets de différance* – only I doubt whether the implications of this thought are quite as radically and disturbingly sceptical as many have supposed. See, on this, my essay 'Deconstructing Derrida' (now Chapter 4 of the present book), pp. 123–43.
12. Derrida, *La Voix et le phénomène* (ch. 1, n. 29), p. 115.

Chapter 3: Forster and Moore

1. Leonard Woolf, *Beginning Again: An Autobiography of the Years 1911–1918* (London, 1972), p. 24.
2. P. N. Furbank, *E. M. Forster: A Life* (London, 1977), I. 49.
3. Woolf, *Beginning Again*, p. 24.
4. S. P. Rosenbaum, '*The Longest Journey*: E. M. Forster's Refutation of Idealism', in *E. M. Forster: A Human Exploration*, ed. G. K. Das and John Beers (London, 1979), pp. 32–54.
5. E. M. Forster, Introduction to the World's Classics edn. of *The Longest Journey*, cited in Rosenbaum, p. 34.
6. Rosenbaum, '*The Longest Journey*', p. 41.
7. P. N. Furbank, 'The Philosophy of E. M. Forster', in *E. M. Forster, Centenary Revaluations*, ed. Judith Scherer Herz and Robert K. Martin (London, 1982), p. 46.
8. Ibid., p. 47.
9. E. M. Forster, 'How I Lost My Faith', *The Humanist* 78, no. 9 (Sept 1963), 263.
10. J. M. Keynes, 'My Early Beliefs', in *Two Memoirs* (London, 1949), p. 81; subsequent page references in the text are to this edn.
11. Thomas Nagel, 'What It Is Like To Be a Bat', *Philosophical Review* 83 (1974), 435–51.
12. See R. M. Hare, *Moral Thinking* (Oxford, 1981), pp. 25–43, for a clear and trenchant defence of this aspect of utilitarianism. Chapter 5 of John Stuart Mill's essay 'Utilitarianism' is one *locus classicus* for the view.
13. G. E. Moore, *Principia Ethica*, chap. VI, §113.
14. Page references are to the Penguin edn.: E. M. Forster, *Where Angels Fear to Tread* (London, 1959).
15. Norman Kelvin, *E. M. Forster* (Carbondale, Ill., 1967), p. 43.
16. Ibid., p. 48.
17. Furbank, 'Philosophy of Forster', p. 39.
18. Ibid., p. 43.

Chapter 4: Deconstructing Derrida

1. I am grateful to Dr John Llewelyn of the University of Edinburgh, for drawing this and several other passages to my attention, and for allowing me to read the manuscript of his forthcoming (1985) book on Derrida. The paper originated in, and also owes a good deal to, prolonged discussions with A. D. Nuttall, over his *A New Mimesis*.

2. Derrida, in 'La Structure, le signe et le jeu dans le discours des sciences humaines', *L'Écriture et la différence* (Paris, 1967).

3. Christopher Norris, *Deconstruction: Theory and Practice* (London and New York, 1982), pp. 28–30.

4. Rorty, *Consequences of Pragmatism* (Int., n. 8), p. 152.

5. Christopher Norris, 'Derrida at Yale: The Deconstructive Moment in Modernist Poetics', *Philosophy and Literature* 3–4 (1979–80), 243.

6. Jacques Derrida, *Positions* (Paris, 1972), p. 13; tr. and annotated Alan Bass (London, 1980), p. 4.

7. Derrida, *L'Écriture et la différence*, p. 413 (my translation).

8. Derrida, *Positions*, p. 72; English edn., p. 53.

9. M. H. Abrams, 'How to Do Things with Texts', *Partisan Review* 46 (1979), 572.

10. Jacques Derrida, *Éperons, les styles de Nietzsche* (Paris, 1978), p. 108; tr. Barbara Harlow (Chicago and London, 1979), p. 128. I have preferred my own translation here.

11. Jacques Derrida, *Marges de la Philosophie* (Paris, 1972), p. 375; tr. as 'Signature Event Context', *Glyph* 1 (Baltimore, 1977), 180.

12. Derrida, *Positions*, p. 39; English edn., pp. 27–8.

13. M. H. Abrams pursues just this line of criticism in 'How to Do Things with Texts', cited above, n. 9.

14. Jacques Derrida, *De la grammatologie* (Paris, 1967), p. 125; tr. Gayatri Chakravorty Spivak as *Of Grammatology* (Baltimore and London, 1976), p. 84.

15. Merleau-Ponty, *La Prose du monde* (ch. 1, n. 27), p. 19; English edn., p. 12.

16. Derrida, *L'Écriture et la différence*, p. 22; tr. Alan Bass as *Writing and Difference* (Chicago, 1978), p. 11.

17. Nuttall, *A New Mimesis* (ch. 1, n. 1), p. 30.

18. Rorty, *Consequences of Pragmatism*, pp. 90–109 *passim*.

19. Terence Hawkes, *Structuralism and Semiotics* (London, 1977), pp. 145–6; Nuttall, *A New Mimesis*, pp. 30, 29; Rorty, *Consequences of Pragmatism*, p. 139.

20. Saussure, *Cours de Linguistique Générale* (ch. 1. n. 16), p. 99. 'Nous proposons de conserver le mot *signe* pour designer le total, et de remplacer *concept* et *image acoustique* respectivement par *signifié* et *signifiant*.'

21. Derrida, *Positions*, p. 40; English edn., p. 28.

22. Abrams, 'How to Do Things with Texts', p. 571.

23. Laurence Sterne, *Tristram Shandy*, ed. Melvyn and Joan New (Gainesville, Fla., 1978), p. 82.

24. Ibid., p. 85.

25. Norris, 'Derrida at Yale', p. 243.

26. Max Beerbohm, *A Christmas Garland* (London, 1912), p. 13.

27. Derrida, *Positions*, pp. 63–4; English edn., pp. 46–7.

28. In this connection see Gabriel Josipovici on trust between reader and writer, in the fourth of his Northcliffe lectures, *Writing and the Body* (Brighton, 1982).

Chapter 5: Muriel Spark and Jane Austen

1. F. R. Leavis, *The Great Tradition*, Penguin edn. (Harmondsworth, 1972), p. 20.

2. Page references are to the Penguin edn.: Muriel Spark, *The Ballad of Peckham Rye* (Harmondsworth, 1960).

3. Muriel Spark, *The Mandelbaum Gate*, Penguin edn. (Harmondsworth, 1962), p. 245.

4. This aspect of Chesterton's work is discussed by Stephen Medcalf in his

admirable essay, 'The Achievement of G. K. Chesterton', in *G. K. Chesterton, A Centenary Appraisal*, ed. John Sullivan (London, 1974).

5.   Doubts are most often expressed about the coherence of *Mansfield Park*, but I am inclined to discount them as resting on too ready an assimilation of Jane Austen's authorial moral outlook to the moral outlooks of Edmund and 'My Fanny'. The book is not a celebration of humourless and priggish passivity but a study of vanity, ambition and parental feebleness. That Jane Austen is aware of Fanny's deficiencies as a heroine is evident from, *inter alia*, the contrast with Susan, but Fanny is needed as she is to serve as a foil to the Crawfords; to show that wit and gaiety are neither necessary accompaniments nor sufficient conditions of goodness and moral intelligence.

6.   'One of the things which interested me particularly about the Church was its acceptance of matter. So much of our world rejects it. We're not happy with things.' – Muriel Spark, 'My Conversion', *Twentieth Century* 170, no 1011 (Autumn 1961).

7.   E. M. Forster, *A Passage to India* (Harmondsworth, 1961), p. 316.

8.   References are to the Penguin edn. (see n. 3).

9.   'What I like about Max Beerbohm is his attitude of not caring a damn about any of it, but under this he had a real style, a real humility. He didn't worry too much about what's not worth it' (Spark, 'My Conversion', p. 63).

10.   References are to the Penguin edn.: Muriel Spark, *The Prime of Miss Jean Brodie* (Harmondsworth, 1961).

11.   A reader remarked here: 'It could easily turn into a sort of attack on God, couldn't it?' From seeing this it is a very short step to seeing why it doesn't, and to seeing why Mrs Spark, despite her opaque laughter and her regular scourging of the orthodox, really is, after all, a Catholic novelist.

12.   Muriel Spark, *The Girls of Slender Means*, Penguin edn. (Harmondsworth, 1965), p. 69.

Chapter 6: The Text as Interrogator: Muriel Spark and Job

1.   Page references in the text to *The Only Problem* are to the British edition (London, 1984). Extracts from the Book of Job follow the text of the Authorized Version.

2.   What is going on in the text here, it seems to me, bears some analogy to Wittgenstein's way of attacking a philosophical problem: by examining, that is, the nature of the puzzlement and its relationship to our lives rather than by attempting, through the provision of a 'philosophical theory', to answer the question in its own terms.

Chapter 7: Rhetoric and the Self

1.   Wittgenstein's account of solipsism in the *Tractatus* combines two anti-Cartesian doctrines: that the self is not an object in, but a limit of, the world; and that any statement we can make about the world is, if true, contingently true (*Tractatus* 5.631–5.634). There are no doubt-immune statements concerning either the self or its states, that is.

2.   Gabriel Josipovici, *The World and the Book* (London, 1979). p. 309.

3.   Roland Barthes, 'The Death of the Author', in *Image Music Text/Roland Barthes*, essays sel. and tr. Stephen Heath (New York, 1977), p. 144.

4.   Michel Foucault, 'What is an Author?', tr. Josué V. Harari, in *Textual Strategies*, ed. Harari (ch. 1, n. 15), pp. 142–3.

5.   Paul de Man, 'Autobiography as De-Facement', in *The Rhetoric of Romanticism* (New York, 1984), p. 69. The implication of the second half of this passage, that the project of autobiography, because it creates the writer's *acts*, must necessarily result in a correct representation of him, ought, I would have thought, to be unwelcome to de Man.

6.   'I question not but thou hast been told, among other stories of me, that thou wast to travel with a very scurrilous fellow; but whoever told thee so, did me an injury. No man detests and despises scurrility more than myself; nor hath any man more reason; for none hath ever been treated with more: and what is a very severe fate, I have had some of the abusive writings of those very men fathered upon me, who, in other of their works, have abused me themselves with the utmost virulence.

'All these works, however, I am well convinced, will be dead long before this page shall offer itself to thy perusal; for however short the period may be of my own performances, they will most probably outlive their own infirm Author, and the weakly productions of his abusive contemporaries.' (*Tom Jones*, Bk. XVIII) One has a rather sharp sense here, it seems to me, that the claim for the Derridean *itérabilité* of his own writing which Fielding himself is advancing is not, in fact, functioning to divide us from him.

7.   Cf. Proust, *À la recherche du temps perdu*, Pléiade edn. (Paris, 1954), p. 5: 'Mais il suffisait que, dans mon lit même, mon sommeil fût profond et détendît entièrement mon esprit; alors celui-ci lâchait le plan du lieu où je m'étais endormi, et, quand je m'éveillais au milieu de la nuit, comme j'ignorais où je me trouvais, je ne savais même pas au premier instant qui j'étais; j'avais seulement dans sa simplicité première le sentiment de l'existence comme il peut frémir au fond d'un animal; j'étais plus dénué que l'homme des cavernes; mais alors le souvenir – non encore du lieu où j'étais, mais de quelques-uns de ceux que j'avais habités et où j'aurais pu être – venait à moi comme un secours d'en haut pour me tirer du néant d'où je n'aurais pu sortir tout seul; je passais en une seconde par-dessus des siècles de civilisation, et l'image confusément entrevue de lampes à pétrole, puis de chemises à col rabattu, recomposaient peu à peu les traits originaux de mon moi.'

8.   Alexander Nehamas, *Nietzsche: Life as Literature* (Cambridge, Mass. and London, 1985).

9.   Friedrich Nietzsche, *The Will to Power*, ed. Walter Kaufman, tr. W. Kaufman and R. J. Hollingdale (New York, 1968), p. 28

10.   Nehamas, pp. 187, 185.

11.   Ibid., p. 181.

12.   Amelie Oksenberg Rorty, in 'Self-Deception, Akrasia and Irrationality', *Social Science Information* 19 (1980), 905, proposes a Nietzsche-like account of the self as resembling not so much a centralized modern city, but 'the older mediaeval Paris of relatively autonomous neighbourhoods, linked by small lanes that change their names halfway across their paths, a city that is a loose confederation of neighbour-hoods of quite different kinds, each with its distinctive internal organization, and distinctive procedures for foreign relations, even different conditions for entry to the federation. A city of guilds, the courts of grand families, religious orders, and old small towns.' Sissela Bok, in her immediately following discussion, makes the shrewd point that this move effectively solves the problem of how the self can deceive itself by dividing the self into several selves, for each of which the same problem arises, threatening an infinite regress. Put in terms of Rorty's analogy, the problem is to know what makes the Paris she describes *one city*, and this is effectively Nietzsche's problem also. The issue is obscured in her example by the red herring of spatial contiguity, which performs a role here analogous to that performed by Nehamas's appeal to the physiological organization of the body.

13. Which does not, of course, entail thinking of the self as *un*conscious. When I reach out to pick up a cup I am, necessarily after all, conscious of the cup. It is because I see it that it occurs to me to pick it up. Philosophy, as Wittgenstein wisely observed, has to stop somewhere.

14. Robert Nozick, in *Philosophical Explanations* (Cambridgé, Mass., 1981), also tries to make sense of the Nietzschean notion of the self as self-synthesizing, and also bases his analysis on a move from thinking of the self as a *congeries* of states to thinking of it as agent of its acts. Where the present view differs from Nozick's, however, is that Nozick treats the intentional act as the basis for a further process of synthesis. My view, on the other hand, is that once we have a self capable of performing intentional acts we no longer need a synthesis *at that level*, having effectively left behind the traditional problem of 'the unity of the self' as that presented itself to, say, Descartes or Hume. Jay F. Rosenberg, in *The Thinking Self* (Philadelphia, 1986), ch. VI, offers what he calls 'A Logical Phenomenology of Space and Time'. Essentially Rosenberg, like Nozick and myself, is concerned to understand how a self-consciousness which is aware of itself as extending across time can be got, metaphysically speaking, off the ground. Rosenberg's route, following Hume and Kant, is to take memory as fundamental, and then to offer an analysis of memory in terms of second-order awarenesses of acts of awareness, a move which, I am inclined to suspect, begs the question. My view, on the contrary, is that memory is not a primary element in temporal self-awareness, but is derivative from knowledge of *what I am about*; from a kind of knowledge, that is, which is precisely not to be understood as knowledge of any category of 'inner states', states of awareness included. I am grateful to Pat Hanna for drawing my attention to this chapter of Rosenberg's very interesting book.

15. Further discussion of this and other examples of similar tendency can be found in ch. 2 of my *Fielding's* Tom Jones: *the Novelist as Moral Philosopher* (ch. 1, n. 30).

16. Marcel Proust, *Swann's Way*, tr. C. K. Scott Moncrieff (London, 1957), pp. 173–4.

17. Proust, *À la recherche du temps perdu*, p. 129 (my translation.)

18. De Man, *Rhetoric of Romanticism*, pp. 67–81.

19. Ibid., p. 70.

20. William Wordsworth, *The Prelude*, ed, Ernest de Selincourt, 2nd edn., corrected by Stephen Gill (London, Oxford, New York, 1970).

21. A role which Wordsworth rejects even more emphatically at Book II, ll. 203–27:

>   But who shall parcel out
>   His intellect with geometric rules . . .
>   Who that shall point as with a wand and say
>   'This portion of the river of my mind
>   Came from yon fountain.'

22. Page references in the text to Wordsworth's *Essays upon Epitaphs* I-III are to *The Prose Works of William Wordsworth*, ed. W. J. B. Owen and Jane Worthington Smyser (Oxford, 1972), II. 49–96.

23. De Man, *Rhetoric*, p. 79.

24. Ibid., p. 80.

25. Ibid., pp. 78, 80.

26. Ibid.

27. Virgil Aldrich, among analytic philosophers, has consistently and interestingly explored the connections between incarnation and the concept of a person. See his *The Body of a Person* (Lanham, Md., New York, London, 1988).

28. That this is indeed Wordsworth's intention is made blindingly clear on p. 86

(*Prose Works* II): 'Unquestionably, as the Father in the latter speaks in his own Person, the situation is much more Pathetic; but, making due allowance for this advantage, who does not here feel a superior truth and sanctity, which is not dependent upon this circumstance, *but merely the result of the expression and the connection of the thoughts?*' (my italics).

29.   I am obliged to Henry Staten for pointing out the desirability of this amplification at this point.

30.   Barthes, in *Image Music Text*, p. 142.

31.   I am obliged to Fred Hagen for drawing my attention to this anecdote.

32.   Cf. Stephen Prickett, *Coleridge and Wordsworth: The Poetry of Growth* (London, 1970), *passim*.

Chapter 8: Parable and Transcendence

1.   C. F. Evans, *Parable and Dogma* (London, 1977), p. 5.

2.   Ibid., p. 4. Augustine's interpretation is in *Quaestiones Evangeliorum*, II. 19.

3.   Evans, *Parable and Dogma*, p. 4.

4.   'The import of the story is obscured if *plesion* (=*reá*) in Luke 10:29 is translated "neighbour". The Christian concept of the "neighbour" is not the starting-point of the story, but that which the story was intended to create' (J. Jeremias. *The Parables of Jesus*, tr. S. H. Hooke [1954], 3rd rev. edn. [London, 1972], p. 202, n. 53). The last clause of Jeremias's remark cuts close, I believe, to the heart of the matter.

5.   Jeremias, *Parables of Jesus*, pp. 100–2.

6.   C. H. Dodd, *The Parables of the Kingdom* (1935), rev. edn. (London, 1961), p. 3.

7.   Jeremias, *Parables of Jesus*, p. 124.

8.   Ibid., pp. 127–8.

9.   Ibid., p. 131.

10.   A. Jülicher, *Gleichnisreden Jesu*, II. 481, quoted in Dodd, *Parables of the Kingdom*, p. 12.

11.   Dodd, *Parables of the Kingdom*, p. 13.

12.   The moral codes of primitive peoples, as reflected in, for example, the Norse Eddas, contain many injunctions of this kind, and it is only obvious to us that they are not 'moral' injunctions.

13.   S. Kierkegaard, *Fear and Trembling*, tr. R. Payne (Oxford, 1939), pp. 31–4.

14.   'I have shown elsewhere what a singularly complete and convincing picture the parables give of life in a small provincial town – probably a more complete picture of *petit-bourgeois* and peasant life than we possess for any other province of the Roman Empire except Egypt, where papyri come to our aid' (Dodd, *Parables of the Kingdom*, p. 10).

15.   For a view attacking the notion of realism in the parables, and arguing for an allegorical interpretation, see J. Drury, 'The Sower, the Vineyard and the Place of Allegory in the Interpretation of Mark's Parables', *Journal of Theological Studies*, Oct 1973, 367–79.

16.   F. Kafka, *Parables* (New York, 1947).

17.   Dodd, *Parables of the Kingdom*, pp. 5, ix.

18.   Evans, *Parable and Dogma*, p. 12, puts essentially the same point in the form of a doubt about the propriety of the term *Sitz im Leben* as used by Dodd and Jeremias: 'A more general, and possibly far-reaching criticism could be made that in this reconstruction the term *Sitz im Leben* is being used in a significantly different sense from that which it originally has in form-criticism, where it refers to the situation which best accounts not for the content of a passage but for the particular form of

utterance the passage takes, whether that form be regarded from an aesthetic or a sociological point of view. For, whatever the subsequent use made of parable in the tradition, it is not obvious, nor perhaps likely, that it elects itself as a form of utterance for proclaiming an eschatological message or for defending it.'

19. Jeremias, *Parables of Jesus*, p. 179.

20. This interpretation is inconsistent with the episode of the guest without a wedding garment in the Matthaean version of the parable (Matthew 22: 11–13). But there is good ground for regarding the episode as belonging to a quite independent parable; see Jeremias, *Parables of Jesus*, p. 65.

21. The most pithy and informative definition known to me of the terms 'structural' and 'structuralism' is given by J. Lyons, *Semantics*, vol. I (Cambridge, 1977), pp. 231–2.

22. Jeremias, *Parables of Jesus*, p. 37.

23. See B. Harrison, 'Kant and the Sincere Fanatic', in *Philosophers of the Eighteenth Century: Royal Institute of Philosophy Lectures 1977–78*, ed. S. Brown (Brighton, 1979).

24. See T. Kühn, *The Structure of Scientific Revolutions* (Chicago, 1962); P. Feyerabend, *Against Method* (London, 1975).

25. Kafka, *Parables* (tr. Willa and Edwin Muir), p. 11.

Chapter 9: Secrets and Surfaces

1. Friedrich Nietzsche, *The Birth of Tragedy*, tr. Francis Golffing (New York, 1956), p. 10.

2. Frank Kermode, *The Genesis of Secrecy* (Cambridge, Mass. and London, 1979); subsequent references appear in the text as *GS*.

3. George Berkeley, *Three Dialogues between Hylas and Philonous*, in *A New Theory of Vision, and other writings*, Everyman edn. (London, 1910), p. 244.

4. Here my argument parallels that of A. D. Nuttall in his *A New Mimesis* (ch. 1. n. 1), p. 55 *et seq.*

5. I think, for that matter, that there is another way of reading Kafka's parable (as there more or less has to be on Kermode's principles). In my midrash the doorkeeper's authority represents the authority of our structural fore-understandings. When he says, 'This door was meant for you, and now I am closing it for ever', what he means is, 'This door was meant for you, and you might have passed through it had you not, by clinging to your fore-understandings, raised up doorkeepers to bar the way.'

6. Katherine Belsey explores this possibility in 'Disrupting Sexual Difference: Meaning and Gender in the Comedies', in *Alternative Shakespeare*, ed. John Drakakis (London, 1985).

7. I find myself confirmed in this thought by an article by Rabbi Dr Jonathan Sacks, Principal of Jews College, London ('A Challenge to Jewish Secularism', *Jewish Quarterly*, July 1989, 1–2): 'Rabbinic Judaism is a protest against privileged hierarchies of knowledge. It had no place for the prophet's revelation that silences argument by its self-authentication.... The culture of argument had to defend itself against a succession of over-authoritarian establishments. One religious head of the community, Rabban Gamliel, was deposed for his refusal to let a contrary opinion be heard.... A leading theme of rabbinic thought is that Torah is acquired only through dialogue between teacher and pupil and between colleagues. "It is impossible for there to be a house of study without new discoveries". Through dialogue Judaism is renewed.' Kermode himself, in a fascinating study of the interplay of hermeneutics and dogma ('The Plain Sense of Things', in *An Appetite for Poetry:*

Essays in Literary Interpretation [London, 1989], p. 185), observes that 'the Jewish tradition has accommodated change and adaptation without sacrificing the original deposit'. One could in certain respects, of course, take the views advanced in this book as an application to the relationship between readers and texts in general of Dr Sacks's account of the relation between Torah and the rabbinic tradition.

Chapter 10: The Truth about Metaphor

1.   Nelson Goodman, *Languages of Art* (New York, 1968), pp. 77–8.
2.   R. M. J. Dammann, 'Metaphors and Other Things', *Proceedings of the Aristotelian Society* 78 (1977 / 78), 128–9.
3.   Donald Davidson, 'What Metaphors Mean', *Critical Inquiry* (1978), 31–47; subsequent page references in the text refer to this article.
4.   Derrida. 'Signature Event Context' (ch. 4, n. 11), p. 180.
5.   Hilary Putnam, 'The Meaning of "Meaning"', in *Mind, Language and Reality* (Cambridge, 1975).
6.   For the further development of this argument, see my 'Meaning, Truth and Negation', *Proceedings of the Aristotelian Society*, Supplementary Vol. 57 (1983), 179–204.
7.   W. V. Quine, *Word and Object* (New York, 1960), ch. 2. The phrase 'inextricability thesis' is borrowed from Michael Dummett, 'The Significance of Quine's Indeterminacy Thesis', *Synthèse* 27 (1974), 351–97.
8.   I owe this suggestion to A. D. Nuttall, in conversation.
9.   Hugh Bredin, 'Roman Jakobsen on Metaphor and Metonymy', *Philosophy and Literature* 8 (1984), 101.
10.   Max Black, 'Metaphor', in *Models and Metaphors* (Ithaca, 1962).
11.   Paul Ricoeur, *The Rule of Metaphor*, tr. Robert Czerny (Toronto, 1977), p. 88.
12.   Owen Barfield, *Poetic Diction* (London, 1928).
13.   Paul de Man, *Allegories of Reading: Figural Language in Rousseau, Rilke, Nietzsche, and Proust* (New Haven, 1979), pp. 14–15.
14.   Derrida, 'Signature Event Context'.

Index